39041

370.9 RM

COLLEGE OF RIPON AND YORK ST. JOHN
RIPON CAMPUS

LIBRARY

EDUCATION IN THE WEST OF ENGLAND, 1066–1548

EDUCATION IN THE WEST OF ENGLAND
1066 – 1548

Cornwall Devon Dorset
Gloucestershire
Somerset Wiltshire

NICHOLAS ORME

UNIVERSITY OF EXETER
1976

First published 1976 by the University of Exeter

© 1976 Nicholas Orme

ISBN 0 85989 041 4

The University of Exeter gratefully acknowledges a grant by the Marc Fitch Fund towards the cost of publishing this book

Set in Monotype Bembo 270, 11 on 12 point
Printed in Great Britain by James Townsend and Sons Limited

FOR A. B. EMDEN

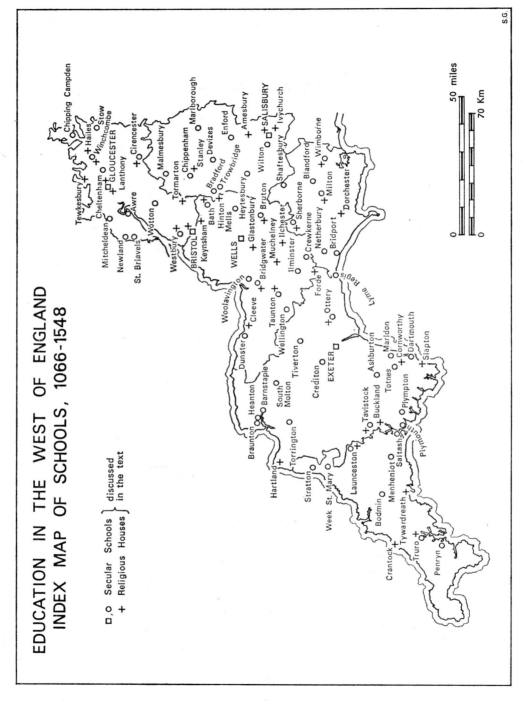

Contents

	Page
List of Maps and Text Figures	ix
Preface	xi
List of Abbreviations	xiii

INTRODUCTION

Medieval Schools	1
Distribution and Continuity	4
Institutions and Endowments	12
Masters, Pupils and their Work	18
Higher Education	23
The Reformation	26
Conclusion	32

1	FIVE CITIES AND THEIR SCHOOLS	35
2	TOWNS AND VILLAGES WITH SCHOOLS, BUT NOT ENDOWED	93
3	ENDOWED SCHOOLS AND CHANTRY SCHOOLS	111
4	EDUCATION IN RELIGIOUS HOUSES	201
	Bibliography	217
	Index	229

List of Maps and Text Figures

MAPS

	Page
Index Map of Schools, 1066–1548	vi
Schools in the West of England, 1200–1300	5
Religious Houses Involved with Education	9
Endowed Grammar Schools, 1330–1548	17
Schools in the West of England, 1500–1548	27
Movement in Education, 1500–1548	33
The Lands of Robert Greyndour	155

GENEALOGIES

Hungerford of Heytesbury	145
Greyndour of Clearwell	157
Berkeley of Beverstone	195

Preface

This book is a study of education in the six counties of the west of England between the Conquest and the Reformation. It centres upon the histories of all the schools, 120 in number, which are known to have existed in the area during that period. The account of each school is concerned to reproduce the whole available evidence for its history. It attempts, as far as possible, to describe the origin of the school, its subsequent continuity, the details of its constitution, and the lives of its benefactors, masters and pupils. The result, it is hoped, will be of value in two respects. In the first place, a large body of evidence has been collected which is applicable to the general history of education in England. A local study of this kind, more fully than a national one, throws light on the number and distribution of schools at different times and their continuity from one period to another. Many significant details emerge about their organisation and curricula which help in understanding these matters at a national level. The other major application of the book is in the field of local history. Schools are not only institutions in their own right; they are closely involved with the localities in which they lie. They exist to serve the community by educating its children, and their patrons, benefactors and schoolmasters play other roles in local affairs. The history of a school supplies much information of general local interest, and the history of local communities is incomplete without a study of their schools.

The work begins with an introduction explaining the general features of English school education in the middle ages and drawing attention to those of particular interest in the west of England. The remaining pages are devoted to histories of the individual schools. The schools are arranged for this purpose in four groups according to their type, rather than in alphabetical or geographical order (which may be quickly ascertained by means of the maps and the index). This arrangement allows the schools to be easily compared and their features more readily distinguished. The first group includes the schools of the five principal cities of the region: Bristol, Exeter, Gloucester, Salisbury and Wells. The second consists of the fee-paying schools, public and private, of the remaining towns and villages. The third contains the endowed schools and chantry schools which began to be founded in the fourteenth century for the support of a master teaching wholly or partly without fees. In the fourth appear the educational institutions of the religious houses of monks, canons, friars and nuns. These include both almonry and song schools for secular boys, and cloister schools of grammar and theology for the religious themselves.

Like all my work on medieval schools, this book owes much to the guidance of the late Mr K. B. McFarlane and of Dr J. R. L. Highfield. Its composition over the years has been immeasurably eased by the courteous assistance of the west-of-England archivists and

PREFACE

librarians, and by the staff of the Bodleian Library. Many other considerate people have put me in their debt. They include Mr L. S. Colchester who facilitated my access to the records of Wells Cathedral, and Lady Vestey who provided memorable hospitality on the occasion of my visit to Stowell Park. Mr D. Thomson has generously communicated his researches on the study of medieval grammar, as has Mr P. L. Hull on the school at Week St Mary. Dr P. Chaplais, Mrs A. M. Erskine, Dom A. Watkin and Mr R. J. Whiting have all drawn my attention to points I would otherwise have missed. The production of the book is largely due to Mrs M. Dale, who has patiently typed and retyped the manuscript, to Dr J. B. Harley, the editor appointed by the Exeter University Publications Committee, and to their secretary Mr R. A. Erskine, whose constant help has been invaluable. The maps were drawn by Mr S. Goddard. The publication itself in these difficult times has only been rendered possible by the generosity of the University of Exeter and of the trustees of the Marc Fitch Fund. Last of all, I am conscious how much I have gained from the great registers and the kindly encouragement of the author of *BRUO*. To him, in gratitude, the book is dedicated.

N. I. ORME
CROSSMEAD
EXETER

November 1975

List of Abbreviations

BCL	Bachelor of Civil Law
B Can L	Bachelor of Canon Law
BRUC	A. B. Emden, *A Biographical Register of the University of Cambridge to 1500* (Cambridge, 1963)
BRUO, i–iii	A. B. Emden, *A Biographical Register of the University of Oxford to 1500*, 3 vols (Oxford, 1957–9)
BRUO, iv	A. B. Emden, *A Biographical Register of the University of Oxford, 1501–1540* (Oxford, 1974)
CCR	*Calendar of Close Rolls*
CFR	*Calendar of Fine Rolls*
CPR	*Calendar of Patent Rolls*
DNB	*Dictionary of National Biography*, ed. L. Stephen and S. Lee, 63 vols (London, 1885–1900)
ESMA	N. I. Orme, *English Schools in the Middle Ages* (London, 1973)
ESR	A. F. Leach, *English Schools at the Reformation, 1546–8* (Westminster, 1896)
Hist. MSS Comm.	Historical Manuscripts Commission, Reports and Calendars
HWRO	Hereford and Worcester Record Office, St Helen's Church, Fish Street, Worcester
LPFD	*Calendar of Letters and Papers, Foreign and Domestic, Henry VIII*, ed. J. S. Brewer and others, 21 vols and Addenda (London, 1864–1932)
Mag.	*Magister*, the title originally used to denote university graduates but by at least the fifteenth century applied indiscriminately
M Gram	Master of Grammar, a university 'degree'
PRO	Public Record Office, London
Reg.	Register[1]
SME	A. F. Leach, *The Schools of Medieval England*, 2nd edition (London, 1916)
STB	Bachelor of Theology
STP	Doctor of Theology
TBGAS	*Transactions of the Bristol and Gloucestershire Archaeological Society*
VCH	*The Victoria History of the Counties of England*

1 As usual, the practice is followed of noting bishops' registers with the name of the bishop first, then that of the diocese. Thus *Reg. Bekynton, Wells* should be read *The Register of [Thomas] Bekynton, Bishop of [Bath and] Wells*.

Introduction

MEDIEVAL SCHOOLS

Ever since the twelfth century the principal source of English education has been provided by secular schools open to the public. A secular school is one where both master and scholars are secular priests, clerks in minor orders or laymen, rather than members of a religious order like monks or friars. The scholars, though doubtless having some future in mind for themselves, are not committed through attending the school to following any particular career afterwards. The largest and most prominent of the secular schools in the middle ages were those which served the general public. They were not restricted to any particular group or class of people, but stood open to anyone whom the master accepted and could pay the fees he charged. At first all the secular masters charged fees, but by the end of the fourteenth century wealthy benefactors were beginning to endow schools with property so that the master might receive the income and teach for nothing. Endowed schools of this kind became known as 'free schools', the word 'free' indicating the absence of fees. While it is hazardous to trace the history of particular foundations down the centuries, secular schools in general have been in existence throughout the later middle ages and in modern times. Indeed the twelfth century may be said to have begun a new era in English education, being the first century to possess numerous schools exhibiting major features in common with those of today.

There were also private secular schools in the middle ages. Many of the great monasteries maintained small numbers of secular boys who were not under monastic vows in their almonries or attached to their Lady chapels. These boys were often instructed by a secular master, though never, it seems, by one of the monks themselves. The households of the great magnates, both clerics and laymen, sometimes included a secular master to teach the magnate's children and the other boys—wards or protégés—whom he was bringing up. Some schoolmasters preferred to teach a few private pupils rather than a public school, and members of the parish clergy occasionally tutored boys as well. The education provided in these private schools may have been as good as or better than that available to the public, but the numbers of scholars involved were much smaller, usually less than twenty or a dozen. Finally, there existed a third category of schools—those of the religious orders. During the thirteenth century monks and friars evolved systems for educating their members in a variety of subjects from grammar to advanced theology. Their 'cloister schools', as they are sometimes termed, were small, private and principally intended for the members of the religious order concerned. The masters were usually (but not always) monks or friars as well, and the scholars, being also committed to the order, were trained more specifically for the type of life it involved. On the whole the religious orders on the one hand and the secular clergy and laity on the other kept to their own schools, and there was little mingling.

There were three principal stages in the medieval school curriculum, all involving the study of Latin. Children began by mastering the alphabet, then practised how to read Latin words and pronounce them. Using the liturgical texts of the Church, they learnt how to chant the words according to the rules of plainsong. This taught good pronunciation as well as helping to train the scholar for the clerical life to which it was likely he would one day be called. Reading and 'song', meaning plainsong, formed the first stage of the curriculum. Next came the study of grammar. Its students learnt how words were inflected and tried to memorise their meanings. They practised prose and verse composition and were taught how to speak the language boldly and fluently. They studied literary texts and were introduced to the principles of literary criticism. Those who had mastered Latin thoroughly were able, if they wished and could afford it, to go into higher studies: the arts course, medicine, civil and canon law, and theology. These subjects, all of which were taught and studied in Latin, constituted the third and highest grade of medieval education.

This range of studies was a wide one, and it was obviously impossible for one man to be interested or able to teach them all. Medieval schools were nevertheless one-man enterprises. They were taught by a single master, assisted at most by an usher, and the question therefore arises, which schools concerned themselves with which parts of the curriculum? It is a question of fundamental importance, but it is not an easy one to answer. A. F. Leach, the first to investigate the matter, postulated a general division in medieval times between song schools, concerned with reading and song, and schools of grammar. There is some evidence to support this view. We hear of separate schools of song and grammar as early as the twelfth century in the cathedral cities and in one or two other important places. They also appear side by side in a few other towns during the thirteenth and fourteenth centuries, notably Bury St Edmunds, Northallerton and Warwick. At Warwick in about 1315 a demarcation was agreed between what was to be taught in the two schools of song and grammar.[1] At the same time, it is hard to believe that a rigid division of the curriculum between song and grammar schools was observed in England as a whole. There is little or no sign of its presence in the South West. The only places in the region where separate song schools and grammar schools appear before the fifteenth century are the three cathedral cities—Exeter, Salisbury and Wells. There is no definite proof, however, that the song schools concerned were public institutions, and they may have been confined to the boys and clerks of the cathedral choirs. In all the other towns (excepting Bristol, a special case[2]) a single public school and schoolmaster appear during the middle ages. Up to 1300 they are simply described, without any distinction, as 'the school' or 'the schoolmaster' of Bridgwater, Cirencester, Marlborough, or wherever it may be. Even the grammar schools of the cathedral cities are generally referred to as 'the school',

---

1 On these schools see *ESMA*, pp 69–70.
2 See below, pp 35, 37.

as if they were the only ones. After about 1300 the term 'grammar school' gradually comes into use, but it is still uncommon to find grammar schools existing alongside public song schools; indeed the west of England supplies no such example until the sixteenth century.

It seems reasonable to conclude from all this that reading and song did not at first merit public schools of their own. Sometimes they may have been taught informally by the clergy or by other literate people, but in most cases they were probably studied along with grammar in the one school of the town. The failure to categorise schools before 1300 would therefore reflect the absence of specialisation, and even the use of the term 'grammar school' after 1300 would denote the principal subject of study, rather than the only one. We know that song and grammar were often studied in the same school during the fifteenth and sixteenth centuries because of the survival of school statutes to this effect. Newland (1445) and Heytesbury (1474) are two examples from our region, as are Ewelme (1437), Rolleston (1524) and Manchester (1525) from elsewhere.[1] Elementary schools probably became common only toward the end of the middle ages. In the fifteenth century we begin to hear of choir schools in some of the larger churches, where boys learnt to read and sing to help perform polyphonic settings of the liturgy.[2] The statutes of Winchester (1400) and Eton (1447) seem to suggest the existence of elementary schools since they require the scholars to arrive already instructed in reading, song and elementary grammar.[3] In 1520 Bruton became the first school in our region, as far as we know, to exclude the elementary subjects. Its statutes specifically forbade the master to teach the alphabet, reading or song, so that he could concentrate the better upon grammar. Clearly these subjects were available elsewhere in Bruton. The chantry certificates of 1548 reveal the existence of elementary schools at Enford, St Briavels and Truro, as well as at Launceston and Penryn where there were separate schools of reading and grammar, or at any rate separate masters. In Tudor times, it seems, the teaching of reading or song and that of grammar were beginning to diverge, but even at this date the divergence was by no means complete.

There was also a lack of demarcation at a higher level, where the study of grammar at school merged with that of the arts course at university. In the twelfth century, universities as such had not developed and it is possible that several local schoolmasters, especially those of the cathedral cities, taught logic as well as grammar, and even ventured beyond the trivium of the arts course into the quadrivium. As late as 1274 the school of Wells was called 'the school of liberal arts'. Even after 1300, when the universities established a monopoly over the arts course, the distinction between their studies and those of the schools was not absolute. Boys studied grammar before going to university, but in so doing they were introduced to some of the principles of logic which was properly a university subject. On the other hand you could also study grammar at Oxford from scratch, and the university arts course included a certain amount of grammar of an advanced kind. The demarcation between school and university was thus obscured, and this had its verbal equivalent since

---

1 On these schools see *ESMA*, pp 69–70.
2 E.g. Ashburton, Bristol, Cirencester and Trowbridge.
3 T. F. Kirby, *Annals of Winchester College* (1892), p 457; *The Ancient Laws of King's College, Cambridge and Eton College*, ed. J. Heywood & T. Wright (1850), p 479.

the universities were generally known as 'the schools' in medieval times, and their undergraduates as 'scholars'. You 'went to school' at Oxford and attended the 'schools' or lecture rooms of the masters there. It is all very confusing for the unwary.

The question of what was taught in the schools of the South West will therefore be answered in the following way. In most places there was a single, organised public school, if there was one at all. This school was basically a grammar school, presided over by a master who was appointed primarily because he was a grammarian. Until at least 1400, and in many cases until after the Reformation, he taught reading and song as well, sometimes assigning his usher or a senior scholar to do so in his stead. Before 1300, particularly in the cathedral cities, he may also have encroached upon the arts course and taught some advanced grammar and logic. The public schools which occur in the following pages are therefore to be understood as grammar schools teaching some reading, song and possibly logic. We shall also encounter schools which do not fit into this pattern: elementary schools pure and simple, schools of advanced grammar in the monasteries, and schools of theology in the cathedral cities. These, however, have all left evidence of their specialities, and can be recognised accordingly.

DISTRIBUTION AND CONTINUITY

Secular schools open to the public are known in at least thirty places in England during the twelfth century, mainly in important centres such as the cathedral cities and county towns. The South West contained five or six places of particular eminence where schools might be expected to have operated by this date: Bath (later superseded by Wells), Bristol, Exeter, Gloucester and Salisbury. Four of them certainly possessed schools: Salisbury after 1091, Gloucester by 1112, Bath soon afterwards, and Wells by about 1140. Bristol and Exeter probably had them too. Exeter was a resort of scholars by 1160, perhaps as early as 1133, and although they may have been students of theology, an advanced subject of this kind can hardly have been taught without preparatory facilities for learning grammar. Similarly at Bristol, though the existence of a school shortly before 1183 depends on the testimony of a sixteenth-century antiquary, the evidence is both credible and supported by our general knowledge of the town. All five of these major centres are therefore likely to have possessed a school in the twelfth century, for at least part of the time.

Schools begin to appear in the smaller towns of the region during the thirteenth century, a development which is also true of England as a whole. It is hard to be sure whether this represents a real expansion of education or is simply the result of more plentiful source material. Schools or schoolmasters are first mentioned at Marlborough in 1232, Shaftesbury in 1234, Wilton in 1238, Bridport in 1240, Cirencester in 1242, Plympton in 1263, Malmesbury at about the same time, Taunton in 1286, Wotton-under-Edge in 1291–2, and Bridgwater in 1298. The fourteenth century provides further references at Crediton, Launceston, Ottery, Wellington and probably Dunster, and in later times there are many more. Schools in villages on the other hand are rare during the middle ages. Awre appears to have possessed one in about 1287 and Woolavington may have done so in the

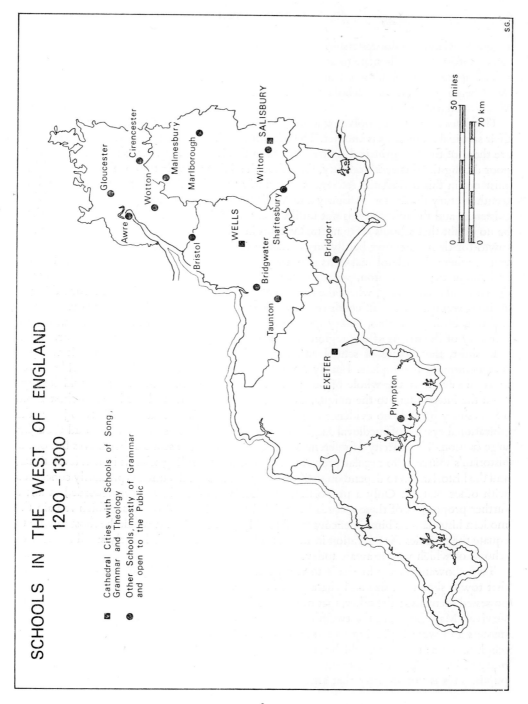

1380s. Newland in Gloucestershire was the fortunate recipient of an endowed school in 1445. But we should hesitate to assume that country schools were common on the basis of this evidence. In general it is not until the early Tudor period that the villages of the South West begin to boast their schools: places like Braunton, Enford, Mells, Netherbury and Week St Mary.

The dates at which schools first appear in particular kinds of settlements is one matter; their survival afterwards is another. The schools which offer the best evidence of continuity are those of the five principal centres, but even this is not clear as we should like. It is still poor during the thirteenth century, for although all five provide two or three signs of their existence in this period, the references are widely spaced in time. Not until the early fourteenth century do Exeter, Salisbury and Wells furnish frequent and regular proofs of their existence, and the other towns not until the end of the century. Only after 1400 can there be no doubt that schools were normally open in all five places. The schools of the smaller towns for their part offer hardly any evidence of continuity. What can we say of Bridgwater, where the school makes its appearance only once between the reigns of Edward I and Elizabeth; or Taunton, where nothing survives between the 1280s and the 1520s; or Bath and Shaftesbury, where the first appearances are also the last? There is something of an improvement in the fifteenth century when schools began to be endowed with lands, ensuring both greater continuity and more frequent appearances in records. But only a minority of the towns of our region possessed endowed schools even by the Reformation.

In short, the picture of school education in medieval England as we see it today is disappointingly incomplete. Hardly a single school can provide satisfactory evidence for its continuity over the whole of our period. Most furnish us with references which range from the intermittent to the unique, and one or two important places like Dorchester and Tewkesbury provide no evidence of schools at all. Yet if our first reaction is to judge the educational system of medieval England as poor, limited and spasmodic, second thoughts urge caution. The scarcity of references is not the fault of the schools themselves but of the historian's sources. No regular procedures existed for recording schools in medieval times, and the historian has to depend on their casual appearance in documents primarily concerned with other matters. Only a proportion of schools can ever have been recorded at all; a further proportion of these records have failed to survive, and of those which remain the modern historian has himself encountered merely a proportion. It would be most unwise to equate the facilities for education in medieval England with the relatively small number of schools of which we are aware today.

Two allowances may be made to compensate for the deficiency of the sources. One is that towns similar in size and character to those where schools existed are likely to have possessed them also; the other, that medieval schools once established had a good chance of survival. Many, even in the twelfth century, possessed patrons responsible for appointing masters and were beginning to attract benefactions: buildings, books and exhibitions for scholars. These resources, which we shall consider presently, must have assisted the continuity of schools by making them more attractive to successive generations of masters and pupils. This is not to deny that schools were sometimes subject to interruptions in their work. Ottery school was said to have been vacant for over a year in 1380. The quarrel between rival schools in Gloucester was alleged in 1400 to have made useless the coming of scholars to the town. Even Salisbury grammar school lacked a master for short periods during the fifteenth century. The dissolutions of monasteries and chantries were later to disturb the schools of several other places. But occasional lapses of this kind are very different from a normal state of affairs and do not prevent the reinterpretation of our evidence in accordance with the allowances we have proposed. When this is done we shall probably agree that there were more public secular schools in the South West than the evidence suggests. The five major centres must have normally possessed a school from the twelfth century onwards. Many of the lesser towns had one after the middle of the thirteenth century, and although in some places they may have been short-lived, in others they were probably open for long periods. The scarcity of village schools on the other hand still forbids us to assume that they became common as settled institutions until just before the Reformation.

The public schools of the cities and towns were the chief source of education in medieval England, but not the only one. There were also private schools and private tutors, dealing individually with small numbers of children but equal in the total facilities they provided to several of the public institutions. Throughout the middle ages a vast reservoir of potential tutors existed among the secular clergy—rectors, vicars, chaplains and chantry priests—scattered as they were over town and country alike, and qualified (as they should have been) in the knowledge of reading, song and grammar. The early importance of the secular clergy as tutors is established by several writers of the twelfth century, notably Ordericus Vitalis, who tells us how in 1080, when he was five, his father put him into the charge of Siward, a priest of Shrewsbury, to be taught his letters.[1] It is also possible that a good deal of informal teaching was done by the clergy of the South West, though the examples forthcoming from this region alone are naturally fewer than those from England as a whole, and are mostly rather late. The earliest instance is that of the eminent scholar, John of Salisbury. He learnt the psalter from a priest in the 1120s, apparently in the neighbourhood of Old Sarum where he was born.[2] In the early fourteenth century Bishop Droxford of Wells and Bishop Stapledon of Exeter arranged for poorly educated priests, newly instituted to benefices, to be tutored by neighbouring incumbents with better qualifications, and the same was done by Droxford's successor, Bishop Beckington, in the fifteenth century.[3] The next instance, after John of Salisbury, of a boy being tutored by a priest is that of John Hody at Woolavington in the 1380s, if the account is true; otherwise, the examples belong to the fifteenth and sixteenth centuries. The chaplain of Godshouse, Exeter, was charged with teaching half a dozen children in the alphabet and psalter in 1436, and the curate of

---

1 *The Ecclesiastical History of Ordericus Vitalis*, ed. Marjorie Chibnall, vol ii (Oxford, 1969), p xiii.
2 John of Salisbury, *Policraticus*, ed. C. C. I. Webb (2 vols., Oxford, 1909), i, 164.
3 *Reg. Drokensford, Wells*, ed. E. Hobhouse (Somerset Record Soc., i, 1887), p 119; *Reg. Stapeldon, Exeter*, ed. F. C. Hingeston-Randolph (1892), pp 242, 268; *Reg. Bekynton, Wells*, ed. H. C. Maxwell-Lyte (Somerset Record Soc., xlix-l, 1934-5), i, 372-3, ii, 540.

Bridgwater tutored a boy in reading and song in the 1460s.[1] Two of the leading Devonians of Elizabeth's reign also got part of their education in this way. John Jewel, bishop of Salisbury, was tutored by his uncle the rector of Heanton Punchardon in about 1529, and John Hooker, the historian of Exeter, by the vicar of Menheniot in the 1530s. By this time clerical tuition was officially approved by the English Church authorities, and the convocation of Canterbury advised all the secular clergy in 1529 to teach boys to read English, when they were not involved with other duties.[2]

Another source of private education with considerable importance was provided by the religious orders—friars, monks and regular canons. It was a general practice among the friars from at least the thirteenth century to take in boys and educate them, in the hope that they would join the order when they reached maturity. Sometimes perhaps this intention was not fulfilled, so that from time to time recruits passed out into the world again having been schooled at the friars' expense.[3] The orders of monks and regular canons did not accept recruits below the age of twenty, but the greater houses usually maintained a small number of children who were boarded apart from the brethren and tutored by a secular schoolmaster. These 'almonry boys' were particularly common in the later middle ages, being associated with liturgical developments among the monks and canons during this period. Some acted as clerks to those of the brethren who had been ordained as priests and consequently needed to celebrate a private mass each day. Others were employed as choristers to sing elaborate polyphonic masses and anthems to the honour of the Virgin in the Lady Chapel. Sometimes the same boys may have doubled both roles. The maintenance of almonry boys appears to have been at its height in England in the fourteenth century, and in 1377 the monks of Glastonbury, the largest house in our region, were supporting and educating as many as 39—the size of a public school. Later on such numbers declined, and in the fifteenth century a dozen or so became normal in the larger Benedictine and Augustinian houses. Tewkesbury had sixteen in the early sixteenth century and Gloucester thirteen. Almonry boys were usually taught grammar and at least three houses, Gloucester, Ivychurch and the Cistercian abbey of Forde, retained special masters to teach them. The choristers may have joined the almonry boys at their lessons, but their curriculum was principally a musical one, involving the assimilation of plainsong, polyphony and organ playing under a special choirmaster or 'master of the boys'. They were a small, select company: three, four or six boys being commonly found in the larger houses of early Tudor England. Among the Benedictines Glastonbury, Gloucester, Muchelney, Tavistock and Winchcombe all maintained them at this time, as did the Augustinian houses of Bristol Cirencester, Lanthony and Taunton. There is little evidence about the Cistercians, but at least one of their houses—Buckland, Devon, in 1522—retained an organist to teach music to four boys and to those of the monks who also wished to learn.

1 Compare also what may have been an educational relationship between Richard White, priest of the chantry of Robert Godmanston in the church of St Thomas, Salisbury, and William his 'boy and servant' to whom he bequeathed a breviary in his will, 14 November 1474 (Salisbury Dean & Chapter, Reg. Machon p 241).
2 D. Wilkins, *Concilia Magnae Britanniae et Hiberniae, 446–1717* (1737), iii, 722–3.
3 On this question see *ESMA*, pp 232–3.

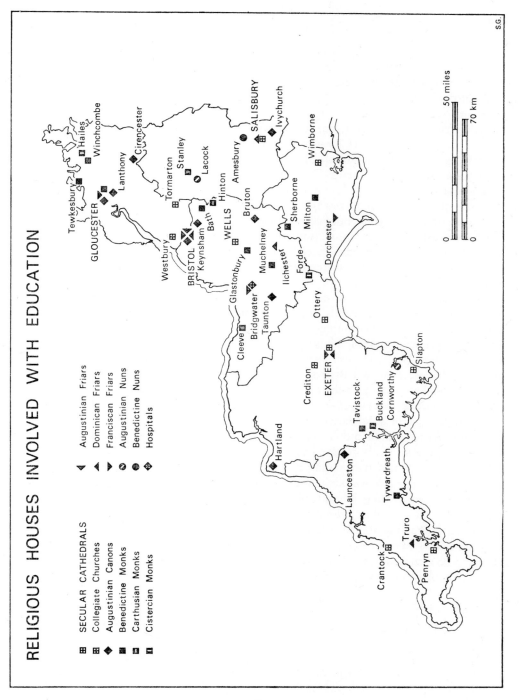

The examples of monastic schools for secular boys, like those of the cities and towns, are only random ones and there are many houses of which we know nothing. If we relate our examples to a list of monasteries based on wealth, we shall find that eight of the eleven with incomes of over £500 a year in 1535 were supporting and educating boys in the early sixteenth century. Presumably the other three did so too.¹ Of about 27 other houses worth between £100 and £500, at least four had almonry or song schools in this period, two of them, Ivychurch and Tywardreath, lying at the bottom of the list with about £120 each.² Certainly some, if not all, the others in this group must have had boys too. The impression—it can be no more—is that over 200 scholars were receiving their education in the monasteries of our six counties under the early Tudors.³ This is very different from the old image of the monks as the principal schoolmasters of medieval England, yet at the same time their contribution ought not simply to be measured in numbers. With smaller classes, better libraries and (sometimes) graduate masters, the quality of the education they provided may often have exceeded that of the public schools. The addition of board and lodging provided what were effectively scholarships and exhibitions for all the boys whom they benefited.

The education of boy choristers also developed among the secular clergy during the later middle ages. The cathedrals, of course, maintained them as early as the twelfth century. After 1300 a fashion set in among wealthy clerics and lay magnates for founding colleges of chantry priests to sing the divine office and celebrate masses, often with elaborate polyphonic settings. Boys and clerks with mature voices then became necessary, as they did in the Lady chapels of the monasteries, to help sing the parts. Four clerks and sundry choristers are mentioned at Glasney College in 1276; four of each at Crediton in 1334; and two and three at Crantock in 1352. The statutes of Ottery St Mary in 1338 provided for eight choristers and eight secondaries; Westbury-on-Trym maintained twelve boys in 1474, and there were four at Slapton in 1536. The clerks and boys were full-time members of the establishment and usually received their board and lodging. At Crediton and Ottery the statutes prescribed that they should be taught to sing, and the same must have been true elsewhere. It is fair to conclude that most of the chantry colleges of the later middle ages maintained a small song school for their members, and possibly even provided some grammar when no public grammar school was available nearby. After 1400 the passion for choral polyphony spread into the larger parish churches, although here the boys (as they are today) were amateurs, not in receipt of board and lodging. The earliest parochial choirs to be recorded in the South West are those of Bristol, where they are found in the churches of All Saints (1407), St Mary Redcliffe (1417) and St Nicholas (1481). Elsewhere

---

1 The houses in descending order of wealth were *Glastonbury (£3,311), *Tewkesbury (£1,598), *Gloucester (£1,430), *Cirencester (£1,051), Plympton (£912), *Tavistock (£902), Malmesbury (£803), *Winchcombe (£759), *Bristol (£670), *Lanthony (£648), and Bath (£617). Those starred had schools or scholars. For the relevant statistics see D. Knowles & R. N. Hadcock, *Medieval Religious Houses: England & Wales* (2nd ed., 1971).
2 The others were Muchelney and Taunton.
3 This postulates an average of ten boys in the eleven larger houses and four in the 27 smaller ones.

they are mentioned at Ashburton in 1481, Trowbridge in 1484, Cirencester in 1518, and Lyme Regis in 1548. Many other churches of similar wealth and importance must have maintained them. The number of boys in each place was small, four or six being common, but the same educational considerations seem to apply as they do in the colleges. The boys are often referred to as 'scholars' and they probably learnt reading and plainsong under the parish clerk or rector of the choir in order to qualify them for polyphonic work. There is also some reason to think that the clerks of Bristol may have taught other boys. The teaching, however, is likely to have been of an elementary nature, and there is no evidence that it reached as high as grammar.

All the institutions mentioned hitherto have been local ones. It should also be noted that a minority of boys travelled out of the region to receive their education. The foremost English grammar schools until the early sixteenth century were those of Oxford, and they probably attracted many boys from all over England who wanted and could afford a better education than the local schools provided. Two other institutions were founded in England during the later middle ages which recruited on a national rather than a local scale: Winchester (1382) and Eton (1440). Both offered seventy scholarships with preference to the sons of college tenants and other boys from the areas where their lands were to be found. Both held possessions in the South West, chiefly around Somerset and Wiltshire, and took scholars from this region. Over 500 boys are recorded as having proceeded to Winchester from our six counties between 1393 and 1530. Wiltshire provided about 200 of these, chiefly from Salisbury, Devizes, Marlborough and the college livings of Downton and Colerne. Another 150 came from Somerset, especially Taunton, Wells and the villages of Beckington, Rode and North Curry. Gloucestershire sent about 70, mainly from Bristol, and a similar number came from Dorset, principally Dorchester and Shaftesbury. The other two counties were sparsely represented.[1] Eton besides being a later foundation was less of a magnet, and only about 70 scholars are recorded going there from our region between 1441 and 1530. Here too most of them came from Gloucestershire, Somerset and Wiltshire.[2] Even together the two colleges accounted for only a tiny proportion of those in need of schooling—some two or three boys each year—but the quality of those they educated surpassed the numbers. Five became bishops and one an archbishop, while in Thomas Chandler and John Doggett the region produced two prominent scholars and university leaders.[3]

It should now be clear that a wide variety of educational sources grew up in the South West during the later middle ages, as indeed in England as a whole. The public schools which begin to appear in the twelfth century were joined in the fourteenth by private schools in the chantry colleges and in the almonries of the greater monasteries. After 1400

---

[1] T. F. Kirby, *Winchester Scholars* (1888), passim.
[2] Sir W. Sterry, *The Eton College Register 1441–1698* (Eton, 1943). This records 8 names from Devon and Cornwall, 9 from Dorset, 15 from Gloucestershire, 17 from Wiltshire and 20 from Somerset.
[3] The Wykehamist bishops were Thomas Beckington and William Knight (Bath & Wells), Thomas Jane (Norwich), John Kingscote (Carlisle), and the archbishop Hugh Ing (Dublin). Edward Fox (Hereford) was an Etonian. For their biographies see *BRUC* and *BRUO*.

the range was further extended by the appearance of choir schools in parish churches, teaching by the secular clergy, and by the scholarships offered at Winchester and Eton. Many great magnates were also retaining schoolmasters by this period to instruct their children and the other wards and dependents in their care.[1] It can hardly be stated too often that the records of education which survive are merely examples, preserved by accident, and that a complete list of schools can never be made. The only matter of certainty is that more existed than are known today. In every century of the later middle ages signs may be found that schools were not rare or uncommon institutions, but widespread and familiar ones. There is the insistence of the bishops in the thirteenth century that scholars shall serve as clerks in the churches near to the schools of the cathedral cities and of the other walled towns of the dioceses.[2] Does this not presuppose the existence of schools in towns like Bath and Devizes, Barnstaple and Launceston, no traces of which have yet been found? There are the ordination ceremonies of the fourteenth century, at which hundreds of men were admitted to holy orders from all over the west of England, with at least a perfunctory test of literacy. When Bishop Stapledon first entered his diocese in 1308, he ordained an army of over 1,000 clerks on one occasion, half of them from Cornwall where no school is known at that date.[3] If anyone wishes to argue that no education was available in the county, 500 Cornishmen will know the reason why. There is the requirement in the fifteenth century that the scholars of Winchester and Eton shall arrive already competent in reading, song and elementary grammar.[4] Where then did Thomas Beckington, the weaver's son of Beckington, and the other Wykehamists who came from country villages, pick up this information? Finally there is the remarkable boyhood of Bishop Jewel in the early sixteenth century. Born in the village of Berrynarbor in North Devon in 1522, he went to three local schoolmasters, at Heanton Punchardon, Braunton and South Molton, all of whom are otherwise unknown, before he reached Barnstaple, the principal school of the area. Clearly, to underestimate the educational facilities of medieval England from the scanty knowledge which we now possess is an assumption far more dangerous than those which we have agreed to adopt ourselves.

INSTITUTIONS AND ENDOWMENTS

The early secular schools must have been primitive bodies, little more than gatherings of pupils around a master who lived off the fees they brought him. Their constitutional history during the middle ages is largely the story of how they developed institutions and resources to assist their work. Some institutions, like the classroom traditions which all schools

---

1 On these schools in general see *ESMA*, pp 219–20. Little is known of them in any single region, but John Scolemaystre appears in the household of the Luttrells of Dunster in 1424 (see below, pp 99-100) and Tyndale the Reformer was hired to teach the children of Sir John Walsh of Old Sodbury in 1522 (see his biography in the *DNB*).
2 See below, p 14.
3 *Reg. Stapeldon, Exeter*, ed. F. C. Hingeston-Randolph, pp 446–56.
4 See above, p 3.

acquire, doubtless grew up spontaneously. Resources on the other hand, such as buildings, books and scholarships, had to be largely supplied from outside, since the schools themselves generated insufficient capital for the purpose. Well-disposed people throughout the middle ages responded to this need by making benefactions, and although at first their gifts were small, the quantity and value gradually increased during the fourteenth and fifteenth centuries into the flood of educational endowments which characterised Tudor and Stuart England. The importance of these benefactions was very great. They helped the schools to acquire stability and maintain continuity, offering a powerful argument against the intermittent evidence of the record sources. They also provide the best surviving guide to the relations between the schools and society. Our ignorance of medieval schoolboys and their subsequent careers prevents us from knowing exactly how schools served the communities around them, but benefactions suggest something of the regard which medieval people had for schools and how they valued their work.

One of the earliest institutions acquired by medieval schools was a patron. No sooner had schools begun to spring up in the towns of twelfth-century England than authorities appeared to claim jurisdiction over them. The motive for this interference probably varied. Sometimes it was a creditable wish to regulate and organise the school in the best interests of its masters and pupils. At other times it may have been a venal desire to share the master's profits by charging him for permission to teach. The venal were eventually routed by a canon of the third Lateran Council of 1179, repeated in England at the council of London in 1200.[1] This tacitly permitted authorities to claim the right to license or appoint schoolmasters in particular places, but forbade them to take fees for doing so. After this reform the patrons of schools, as these authorities may be called, exerted a beneficial effect upon their charges. When the schoolmaster died or retired, they were at hand to fill the vacancy and had the opportunity, if they so desired, of appointing a good candidate rather than a bad one. They could also prohibit other masters from teaching in the area under their jurisdiction, a measure which was usually necessary in the early days to assure the authorised master of enough boys to pay his fees.

The majority of patrons in medieval England exercised jurisdiction over a single town, and in only a few areas, notably Lincolnshire and Nottinghamshire, did any authority manage to establish control over an area as large as a county. The earliest example of patronage in the South West comes from Gloucester where it had been given by 1112 to the free chapel of St Oswald in the city. Subsequently the effective right passed to Lanthony Priory, a local house of Augustinian canons. The canons of this order were often entrusted with the patronage of schools in the twelfth century and Bristol may have been subject at this time to a similar control from Keynsham Abbey. Examples of patronage by the secular clergy include Salisbury and Wells, where it was exercised by the cathedral chancellor, and Exeter where the right belonged to the local archdeacon. Crediton seems to have been under the control of its collegiate church. Most of the early patrons of schools were clerics, but Plympton belonged to the earl of Devon in 1263 and it is highly probable that Wotton-

1 *ESMA*, p 144.

under-Edge came under the oversight of the Berkeley family. Whether patronage was effective in every English town throughout the middle ages is doubtful. In some places it may never have been claimed, let alone exercised, and Bristol in particular suggests a lack of control after the twelfth century, leading to the appearance of more than one school. In Exeter and Gloucester on the other hand, the patrons were still trying to enforce their rights in the early sixteenth century.

Next in importance was the facility of a suitable building. Sometimes this was provided by the patron, as at Gloucester where the canons of Lanthony let the schoolhouse in Smith Street to the master at an annual rent of 24s. In other places the building was contributed by a benefactor. Roger of Chewton, canon of Wells, in about 1235 presented the chancellor with houses for the use of the school in return for a small rent from the master and daily prayers from the pupils for himself and his parents. At Exeter it was the dean, Richard Brayleigh, who gave the schoolhouse and master's lodging in 1344 at an annual rent of 24s., part of which paid for an annual obit or commemoration of the dean in the cathedral. The magnificent schoolhouse at Taunton, costing £226, was built in 1524 by Richard Fox, bishop of Winchester, the lord of the borough and a wellknown friend of education. Smaller benefactions of the same kind occur in Elizabeth Toll's gift of £10 to repair the schoolhouse of Cirencester in 1534, and the remittance by Bristol corporation of the rent of a chamber over the Frome Gate during the 1530s, when it was in use as a grammar school.

The relief of poor scholars, who often attended schools away from home, was another early object of benefactors. An immeasurable quantity of educational charity must have been given privately and personally throughout our period, but by the thirteenth century scholarships and exhibitions of an institutional kind were also becoming available. The Church itself set an example by seeking to provide poor scholars with posts as holy-water clerks in parish churches, and bishops of all four dioceses in our region during the thirteenth century ordered that this should be done.[1] The clerk assisted in the parish services on Sundays and festivals, received a share of the alms and offerings, and attended a local school during the week. It was a suitable post for an aspirant to holy orders, since he could acquire a familiarity with the liturgy while he was learning his grammar. Hence the medieval proverb that 'the parish priest forgetteth he was ever clerk'.[2] After the end of the fourteenth century little or nothing is said about scholars as clerks, which may mean that the charity had fallen into disuse. By Tudor times the modern kind of clerk had become prominent: an educated lay parishioner, holding his office for a long period and often for life.

There were also scholarships in particular places. The largest concentrations were to be found at the cathedrals. where boys were recruited to serve the choir and older youths to perform other choral or liturgical tasks about the church as altarists or secondaries. There were six choristers at Wells in the later middle ages, and fourteen at Exeter and Salisbury. Wells also maintained six altarists and Salisbury between seven and ten, while Exeter had

---

[1] *Councils & Synods: II, 1205–1313*, ed. F. M. Powicke & C. R. Cheney (1964), i, 174, 309, 514, 606; ii, 1026–7.
[2] *Oxford Dictionary of English Proverbs*, ed. F. P. Wilson (3rd ed., 1970), p 609.

twelve secondaries with comparable functions. The emoluments varied from time to time and place to place, but generally included board, lodging, schooling and a small stipend. Clerks and boys of this kind are usually considered from the liturgical point of view and they were, of course, maintained partly for the sake of their voices. At the same time the institutions had an educational value, as they had in the monasteries and chantry colleges. By supporting boys and youths and seeing that they went to school, the cathedrals provided the equivalent of exhibitions for scholars, and it is likely that many of the poor and deserving were able by this means to complete their education and to qualify for holy orders. Exeter and Salisbury also offered additional opportunities of this kind. At Salisbury, De Vaux College, founded by Bishop Bridport in 1262, supported about ten poor scholars studying arts and theology, who were therefore older youths or young adults. At Exeter Bishop Stapledon's benefaction, completed in 1332, established twelve more scholarships for boys in the hospital of St John, the beneficiaries being allowed board and lodging for up to five years while they studied in the city grammar school. In this way we can reckon twelve places available for scholars at Wells, over thirty at Salisbury, and thirty-nine at Exeter, to say nothing of other boys who appear intermittently in bishops' chapels, canons' houses, and the halls of the vicars choral.[1]

The other towns of our region were not so fortunate in this respect, but at least a few enjoyed facilities at one time or another for supporting the poor boys who attended their schools. The hospital of St Mark, Bristol, founded in 1230, originally provided for twelve scholars to receive board and lodging, though it is not certain whether the provision was ever effective. At Bridgwater in 1298 the brethren of St John's Hospital undertook to maintain thirteen poor scholars of grammar and to feed seven others every day from their kitchen. Similar meals were ordered to be given to poor scholars by the canons of Launceston in 1342. At Wotton-under-Edge the endowed school founded in 1384 included full maintenance for two of the pupils, while Newland by the late fifteenth century had one endowed scholarship and a small exhibition fund. Finally there is Sherborne, where in 1535 the monks were paying £3. 18s. to three boys in the local grammar school. Adding these examples to the benefits provided by the parishes, cathedrals, collegiate churches and monastic almonries, it becomes clear that a substantial number of facilities existed throughout the middle ages for subsidising the education of the poor. By concentrating on relieving the costs of board and lodging, they doubtless reflected a situation in which many scholars were lodging away from home in a neighbouring town or a distant city, at a cost which has always far exceeded that of tuition alone.[2]

A major development took place in educational charity during the fourteenth century with the appearance of endowments to pay schoolmasters to teach for nothing or at reduced rates. The subsidised element now became the tuition fees rather than the expenses of board

---

[1] For boys of the bishop's chapel at Exeter see J. F. Chanter, *The Bishop's Palace, Exeter* (London, 1932), pp 43–4, and for boys of the hall of the vicars choral at Salisbury, below p 69 n 5.
[2] We hear of scholars boarding away from home at Exeter, Ilminster, Week St Mary, and probably Bruton (below, pp 50–1, 100, 123, 178).

and lodging, and so many endowments of this nature were eventually made that the term 'endowed schools' has generally come to be used in this sense. Two types of endowed schools ultimately developed, associated respectively with collegiate churches and chantries. The origins of both kinds of endowments are hard to uncover, since the early examples differ widely and it is difficult to arrange them in a sequence. There had been college schools, however, as early as the twelfth century in the sense of masters associated with the secular cathedrals and with other large churches staffed by secular canons, such as Beverley and Hastings. The masters received a small stipend for teaching the choristers but otherwise lived from teaching the public for fees. Ottery St Mary in our region founded in 1338 was of this type, but Winchester College (1382) provided its masters with full salaries to teach for nothing, and this eventually became the common system. Two endowed schools attached to colleges and offering free education to outsiders made their appearance in the west of England between then and the Reformation: Westbury-on-Trym (1463) and Glasney (by 1548). In addition Crediton and Ottery may have come to do so by the time they were dissolved as colleges in the 1540s.

The origin and early diffusion of chantry schools is also a mystery. The first to be founded in our region, Wotton-under-Edge, seems also to have been the earliest of all. It was established by Lady Katherine Berkeley in 1384 after an abortive attempt in 1349, but who originally conceived the idea is doubtful. The schoolmaster of Wotton operated as a single entity, dividing his time between singing the divine office, celebrating masses for the soul of the foundress, and teaching grammar freely to all who sought his services. These basic features were common to most later chantry schools, but whether they were copied from Wotton or evolved independently are matters of uncertainty. It was not until the 1440s that the foundation of chantry schools became popular in England as a whole, and this is also true of the South West. The reign of Henry VI gives us Chipping Campden (*c.* 1441), Newland (1445) and Cirencester (*c.* 1457), together with the abortive foundations at Gloucester (1447) and Heytesbury (*c.* 1449). A pause ensues until the appearance under the early Tudors of Crewkerne (1499), Week St Mary (1506), Wimborne Minster (1511) and Bradford-on-Avon (1524). The last chantry school to be projected in our region was the Crypt school, Gloucester, in 1528, but by this time the association of education and the mass was coming to an end. Schools were beginning to be founded for their own sake, so that the master could spend the whole of his time in teaching and be a layman, as well as a priest. Institutions of this kind in the South West include Bruton (1520), Milton Abbas and Winchcombe (both 1521), and the Crypt school as finally established in 1540. They set the pattern for educational foundations after the Reformation.

There remains a further group of about a dozen chantry schools, the existence of which only becomes clear at the moment of their dissolution in 1548. Ashburton, Bodmin, Cheltenham, Launceston and Netherbury are all examples of this type. As endowed chantries they had been founded at various times during the later middle ages, but none of them, it seems safe to say, had originally set out to provide education. The addition of teaching to the priest's duties was a later development, which frequently took place as late as the 1530s and 40s. This was a time when not only was public interest in education

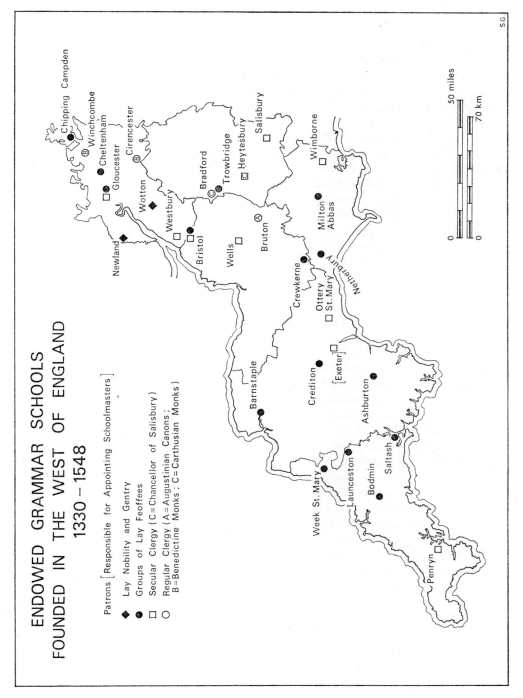

increasing, but hostility to chantries as such was beginning to manifest itself among prominent statesmen and ecclesiastics. The churchwardens and feoffees who in most cases controlled the chantries and appointed priests responded to this situation by requiring the incumbents to teach as well as to say mass. In this way they made an educational contribution as significant in its effects as the actions of wealthier benefactors who founded schools outright.

The list of those who benefited schools in our region is a varied one. There are bishops like Stapledon and Grandisson of Exeter, Carpenter of Worcester, Chedworth of Lincoln and FitzJames of London. From the lay nobility there are Lady Katherine Berkeley, Walter Lord Hungerford and his daughter-in-law, and Henry VII's mother Lady Margaret Beaufort. The gentry provide Joan Greyndour, the wife of a wealthy esquire; two royal clerks with landed possessions, John Ferriby and Thomas Gloucester; and a chief justice, Sir John FitzJames. The lesser clergy are represented by a dean, Richard Brayleigh of Exeter; three prebendaries, Roger of Wells, John Combe of Exeter and John Edmunds of London; and a country rector, John Loder. The Benedictines are not absent, and the schools of Milton and Winchcombe owed much to the interest and support of local monasteries. The merchant class contributes Thomasine Percival from London, Thomas Horton from Bradford-on-Avon, John and Joan Cook from Gloucester, and Roger Hill from Taunton. Beneath them the burgesses of the towns and the yeomanry of the countryside deserve to be honourably mentioned for the educational direction they gave to the chantries under their government. It would be foolish to try to divide the honours proportionately among these groups of people, but one thing is clear: the increasing involvement of the laity in educational matters. In the twelfth and thirteenth centuries, though there are examples of lay benefactions to schools, most of the progress in English education was due to the clergy. It was largely they who appointed schoolmasters and provided for the support of their pupils. In the fourteenth century a new note is struck with the endowment of Wotton school, an original kind of foundation, by a lay family, the Berkeleys. By Lancastrian times the involvement of the laity was manifestly growing, and although the clergy continued to play an important part in the development of education, the balance of forces was very different under the Tudors from what it had been in earlier times. The patronage of thirty-one schools in the west of England is known or may be hazarded during the early sixteenth century. Thirteen were still under clerical control, but eighteen were governed by laymen, while Gloucester changed to lay supervision during the period. By 1550 the dissolution of religious houses and the intervention of the crown had caused the balance to shift further towards the laity, though this was readjusted by the requirement of 1556 that all schoolmasters should be licensed by the bishops.

MASTERS, PUPILS AND THEIR WORK

The institutions we have discussed were important, but none more so to a medieval school than its masters and pupils. Good masters, it will be agreed, are worth their weight in endowments, and good scholars as well. About 150 names of schoolmasters alive between

1200 and 1548 appear in the following pages of this book, excluding masters of choristers and clergymen who were not primarily engaged in teaching. Most of them are wholly obscure and offer the would-be biographer nothing beyond a name, a date and a place. What were their qualifications? How did their status compare with that of other ecclesiastics during the middle ages? Even when we assemble all the evidence and consider them as a profession, the questions remain difficult to answer.

The basic requirements in a medieval schoolmaster were simple: sufficient knowledge of grammar and an honest reputation. Founders of schools rarely stipulated anything else. Holy orders were not absolutely necessary; indeed teaching was a traditional resort of clerks whom marital entanglements had barred from the priesthood. In this respect our masters fall into two categories. A minority, about 56, were employed in chantry schools and had to be priests of necessity, since their duties involved the celebration of mass each day. The remaining 94 were either self-employed or held posts in schools where there was no requirement about holy orders. Only 27 of this group are definitely priests; 15 were clerks in minor orders, and the status of the rest is unknown. It is more likely that the latter were clerks or laymen than that they were priests, although only one of them, Thomas Moffat (Bristol, 1513–40) is known to have been married. Among the profession as a whole, the priests may have been slightly more numerous, as they are in this sample: 83 to 67. It is clear, nevertheless, that plenty of openings existed for those who had not yet taken priests' orders, or did not wish to do so. The same was true of university degrees. Very few schools in England required their masters to be graduates, and Week St Mary (1506) is the sole example in our region. In consequence most of our schools appointed graduates and non-graduates indiscriminately. To estimate the proportions involved, our 150 masters can be divided into 80 who lived and worked before 1500, nearly all of them after 1300, and 70 who occur between 1500 and 1548. The first group includes 45 non-graduates, nine graduates and 26 who are merely styled 'master' in the records. Since the title 'master' was applied with increasing freedom during the later middle ages, it is quite unsafe to take the graduate status of its bearers for granted, and it may be sufficient to transfer about ten to the graduate total. This being done, it is clear that the vast majority of schoolmasters in the fourteenth and fifteenth centuries were non-graduates: probably in the ratio of three to one.

A slight change took place after 1500. The 70 masters who taught between then and 1548 include 43 non-graduates, 22 graduates and five 'masters'. Discounting the latter, it appears that the number of graduates has risen from about a quarter to a third. Whether this marks an improvement in their quality is doubtful, since a degree was not essential for proper teaching, any more than it is today. Grammar was only one of the subjects of the university arts course, and few people thought that a knowledge of the others was essential in order to teach. Evidence is not lacking to suggest that schoolmasters whose graduate status is doubtful were qualified grammarians nevertheless. John Chalurys of Bridport and John Borington of Exeter were both authors of tracts on Latin grammar during the fifteenth century. John Littleskill of Wells (1535) had a good collection of books, including volumes in Greek and Latin and several of the early Fathers of the Church.

Finally the chantry certificates of 1548 preserve a number of testimonials in favour of schoolmasters from the communities in which they worked. Eight in our region were praised as being 'well-learned', of whom seven were non-graduates, and the graduate master of Wotton-under-Edge was the only one to be criticised for inefficiency. The country schoolmasters of Tudor England may have been a good deal better than the educational reformers of the time would have us believe.

The status of schoolmasters, 'instructors of rude boys' as Richard Bury playfully calls them, was rather a humble one. The ecclesiastical authorities took little interest in supervising them, and the social satirists paid them no attention. They hardly figure even in the *fabliaux* and humorous songs of the period. So professional a schoolmaster as Robert Londe of Bristol, whose career spanned a large part of the fifteenth century, was only described as a chaplain on his memorial brass. Teaching was often relegated to junior clerks who were making their way in the world, and some important English schools in the fourteenth century—Lincoln, Oxford and York—deliberately limited their schoolmasters to short terms of three or five years. This may also have been true at Wells round about 1500. In the twelfth century Alexander Neckham and John of Salisbury rose after teaching to become distinguished scholars and ecclesiastics, and this began to be the case again in the sixteenth century with men like Wolsey and Cox. During the later middle ages however no ambitious man would have wasted his time in teaching. Fame and preferment lay through law and administration, and no west-of-England schoolmaster of this period, as far as we know, became anything more than a moderately successful parish priest.

In short, a schoolmaster came only halfway up the ecclesiastical ladder. If he taught in an endowed school he could expect a salary of £10 a year with a house or chamber, which was probably meant to equal the wages of a successful fee-earning master. This made him better off than hired curates, chantry priests or vicars-choral, whose earnings in the early sixteenth century were rarely more than £5 or £6. Such men became schoolmasters but seldom the reverse. At the same time the beneficed clergy, rectors and vicars, were usually better off in status and wealth, their stipends before the Reformation commonly ranging between £10 and £20. Many schoolmasters therefore escaped when they could to a cure of souls, 29 of the 83 who were priests being known to have held a parish at one time or another. Others soldiered on in their schools because they were married or had no 'pull' in the scramble for benefices. One or two of the more austere may even have liked their work. Long terms of service were achieved by masters such as Thomas Moffat of Bristol (more than 23), William Furbner of Bradford-on-Avon (at least 24), and John Paradise of Wotton (29). Robert Coldwell of Wotton broke the record with over 40.

The masters' obscurity is matched by that of their pupils. We can guess, of course, the ages at which they went to school. Boys probably started to learn song at about seven or eight, proceeding after a year or two to elementary grammar. The grammar course proper seems to have begun at about the ages of ten to twelve and to have lasted for five or six years. The oldest boys at school were eighteen or nineteen, although a few late starters or pupils engaged in advanced work may have stayed until their early twenties. A great many of their names have also been preserved. The lists of tonsured clerks in bishops' registers are probably lists of schoolboys, since boys were tonsured when they went to school, until at least the fourteenth century. Bequests to scholars in wills preserve the names of other boys who were to be educated, and reveal the identity of their parents and friends. Two large collections can be made of the names of those who attended particular schools: 500 scholars of Winchester from the west of England and nearly 400 secondaries of Exeter Cathedral, most of whom studied at Exeter High School.[1] Smaller lists survive of 50 of the choristers of Salisbury, a similar number from Exeter, 39 scholars of Glastonbury in 1337 and 34 of Wells in the same year. Faced with mere names, however, which are often very common ones and not easily to be traced in other records, the historian's task is a daunting one. Who went to school, from what families, with what motives and with what results, are questions which cannot yet be answered in a general way. Only a handful of people, chiefly in the sixteenth century, have put on record when and where they were educated and what they did afterwards. The best of these is the list of fifteen pupils at Wotton-under-Edge in the latter years of Henry VIII. One of them was later a gentleman, two each were parish clerks, broad-weavers and yeomen, and one was a chapman. One day we may succeed in tracing when the schools began to train the laity in this way.

We must picture the boys in a single large schoolroom furnished with benches, the master presiding from a desk or chair. In most schools, even those of the cities, only a single functionary is mentioned, but Gloucester had an undermaster in 1400 and by the early sixteenth century references begin to be made to ushers. Exeter, Taunton, Week St Mary, Wells and Wimborne each possessed one at this time. Perhaps we do not hear of ushers before because they were hired privately by the master; in the city schools where classes were large assistants must have been required at an early date. The 34 scholars of Wells in 1377 were only the boys of fourteen or more and the whole school may have been double the size. Figures given for school attendance in the chantry certificates of 1548 include Chipping Campden with 60–80 and Crewkerne and Taunton with 120–140 each. In the smaller towns, on the other hand, the schools must also have been smaller. Wotton-under-Edge, if we can trust the old boys of 1616, numbered only 20 to 30 pupils in the 1530s and 40s. The school day was a long one, for an age which saw children as small adults expected them to work similar hours to their parents. It began in the early sixteenth century at six or seven o'clock in the morning and ended at five or six in the afternoon, with intermissions for breakfast and dinner. There were however holidays. Most masters probably stopped teaching during the summer vacation in August, but there may have been different ways of organising holidays during the rest of the year. Some schools appear to have been open on most weekdays, shutting only for festivals or when the master gave special holidays, or 'remedies' as they were called. Others may have followed Wotton and Newland in teaching continuously for a term (except Sundays) and then stopping for a week or two in the fashion of today. The holidays at these two schools—two weeks at Christmas and Easter, one at Whitsun and six in the summer—bear a striking resemblance to modern ones.

The medieval school curriculum is imperfectly illustrated from the South West alone

---

[1] It is hoped to publish a list of the secondaries of Exeter in the near future.

and has to be reconstructed with evidence from all over the country. Its main features were probably as follows. After learning the alphabet and having throughly practised the reading and pronunciation of Latin words from liturgical works like the primer and psalter, a boy was ready to begin his grammar. The standard elementary Latin textbook was the *Ars Minor* of Donatus which, originating in the fourth century, was revised and improved during the course of the middle ages and eventually translated into English. This explained the eight parts of speech by means of questions and answers, set out the commonest inflexions of nouns and verbs, and imparted the elementary rules of syntax. More detailed and comprehensive treatments of grammar were to be found in the *Doctrinale* of Alexander de Villa Dei and the *Grecismus* of Evrard of Bethune, French scholars of the early thirteenth century. These works were in Latin verse, of which the pupils doubtless memorised large sections by heart. Word lists and dictionaries were also available. The most popular elementary ones were the *Synonyma* and *Equivoca* attributed to the English grammarian, John of Garland. These were collections of synonyms and homonyms respectively, arranged like the *Doctrinale* and the *Grecismus* in verse hexameters. Latin dictionaries of a kind we would recognise included the *Elementarium* of Papias, the *Derivationes* of Hugutio and the *Catholicon* of John of Genoa. They gave alphabetical lists of words, inflexions and meanings, all in Latin. A copy of Hugutio was given to Wellington school in 1371, and there was another at Bridport by 1476. A *Catholicon* was bequeathed to the schoolmaster of Wells in 1498. By the middle of the fifteenth century dictionaries had also been produced with English use in mind. The *Medulla Grammatice* gave a list of Latin words with English meanings, while the *Promptorium Parvulorum* offered the reverse: English to Latin.

With these and other volumes masters and pupils set to work. It is well known that teaching was carried out in French until the middle of the fourteenth century and in English afterwards, but this probably applied only to the younger boys. Older scholars, like their undergraduate seniors, seem to have studied and conversed in Latin. Besides learning to become fluent with their tongues, pupils practised how to write and compose. They translated English sentences, or 'vulgars' as they were called, into Latin, a process known as 'making latins'. They learnt *dictamen,* the art of composing letters, and laboured to turn out verse in hexameters. A few such verses from the school at Bath in 1113 have been preserved. Finally they were introduced to good literature, which during the fourteenth and fifteenth centuries meant Latin poetry with a strongly moral and religious tone. The works most commonly read in schools before the Renaissance included the *Distichs of Cato* and the *Liber Parabolarum* of Alain de Lille, both sets of precepts and proverbs. The *Liber Penitencialis* treated of confession and penance and the *Cartula* of the vanity of human wishes. The *Eclogue of Theodulus* debated the relative merits of pagan mythology and Christian history. Other widely read poems were concerned with good manners and etiquette, the most popular being *Stans Puer ad Mensam,* which dealt with table manners, and the *Facetus* which expounded self-discipline and social behaviour. A scholar who had been well taught should have emerged from his grammar school able to read, write and speak Latin with ease and elegance. He had been introduced to the principles of literary criticism and should have possessed a better than average understanding of Christian ideas and ethics.

INTRODUCTION 23

HIGHER EDUCATION

A grounding of this kind should have enabled any cleric to perform the principal task of his life, the recitation of the liturgy, which friars, monks and the secular clergy alike repeated every day in their churches. Yet this to the idealists of the medieval Church was not enough. The parish clergy and the friars also had pastoral duties: preaching, religious teaching and hearing confessions. Even in the monasteries study was valued as a means of nourishing prayer. It was therefore the ideal of reformers by the thirteenth century that all clerics, whatever their rule, should be able to study theology, the better to understand, practise and expound the ideas and ethics of the Christian religion. The universities offered good facilities for the study of theology at an academic level, but since only a minority of clergy had the time, the money and the abilities to attend them, there was also a need for local institutions to teach the subject in a more elementary way. For this reason all three orders of clergy evolved systems of higher education in theology as a complement to the grammar-school training of the rank and file of their members.

Local centres of higher education for the secular clergy were provided by the cathedrals. Theology was being taught at Exeter as early as the twelfth century. Robert Pullen may have lectured there before he moved to Oxford in 1133, and a master named John was certainly doing so by about 1200. Lectures in civil and canon law were also given towards the end of the twelfth century. The earliest evidence about Salisbury comes from 1220 when one of the canons, Henry of Bishopston, was holding forth, apparently on canon law. Four years later the precentor, Roger of Salisbury, is mentioned as reader in theology. Up to this time the provision of lectures appears to have been informal and executed by any suitable person who was available. Later, as the thirteenth century wore on, the teaching of higher studies was put on a regular basis and assigned to the care of a particular dignitary. In the three cathedrals of the South West the duty was given to the chancellor. This took place at Salisbury in 1240 and in 1283 at Exeter. In each case the chancellor's income was increased by the appropriation of a benefice, and he became bound to lecture in theology at regular times, either in person or through a qualified deputy. The arrangements at Wells probably date from the thirteenth century too, but they remained customary rather than statutory, and it was not until 1348 that the custom was made binding upon the chancellor by force of a papal decree.

Lecturing continued at all three cathedrals during the first half of the fourteenth century. We find the chancellors of Exeter requesting the bishop to suspend the lectures for short periods, or when they wished to lecture by deputy. At Salisbury and Wells the bishop and the chapter intervened on several occasions to make the chancellors discharge their duty. The later history of the institution is obscure, but lectures are recorded at Salisbury and Wells in the fifteenth century and at Salisbury in 1535. At Exeter the memory of the tradition at least remained until the Reformation. Furthermore in Worcester diocese Bishop Carpenter made a determined attempt to improve higher education in 1464. Choosing two moribund institutions, the Carnary chapel at Worcester and the guild of Kalendars at Bristol, he arranged that each should maintain a secular priest who had studied theology at a university, with a salary of £10. Their task was to deliver a lecture once a week and to care for a library of volumes given by the bishop, both library and lectures being open to the public. This meant effectively the local clergy. The institution at Bristol does not seem to have made much impact and may have petered out by the early sixteenth century but at Worcester both library and lectures continued to function until the Reformation.[1] As a result the secular clergy of the South West had opportunities for studying theology at three or four local centres during the middle ages, besides going to university. This does not mean that the opportunities were widely taken. The higher education of the parish clergy must often have remained an ideal rather than a reality. Preferring as they did the liturgy to the sermon and scattered as they were among hundreds of parishes, who was to wander the highways and byways compelling them to come in?

The friars on the other hand took higher education more seriously. Their work of preaching and hearing confessions had to be rooted in the study of theology in order to be effective. The strong organisations which they developed facilitated the evolution of systems of education for their members. All four orders of friars were to be found in our area. The Dominicans and Franciscans were the most important with seven and eight houses respectively, while the Augustinians and Carmelites had one and four. Both of the larger orders took in young recruits and educated them in grammar. Each developed a system during the thirteenth century by which promising students could be trained in arts, philosophy and theology to university standard, while the less able pursued theology at a more elementary level sufficient for ordinary pastoral work. Most friaries probably offered some instruction in higher education. We hear specifically of lecturers or students in the Dominican houses at Bristol, Ilchester, Salisbury and Truro, and in those of the Franciscans at Bristol, Dorchester, Exeter and Gloucester. No house necessarily offered the whole range of studies, and student friars moved at appropriate stages of their education to the places where suitable lecturers were available. These movements were not confined to England, for the organisation of the friars was an international one and some English friars went abroad to study, just as foreign friars came to England for the same purpose. Lists of friars ordained from English convents include a proportion of foreign names, particularly those of Germans, and this is also true of the South West. The Dominican houses of Bristol, Exeter, Ilchester and Salisbury contained foreign students during the fourteenth and fifteenth centuries, as did those of the Franciscans at Bristol, Gloucester and probably elsewhere. A west-country friary should therefore be seen not merely as a local house of clergy but as a centre of higher education forming part of a well-organised, international system of learning. That the friary schools were open to the secular clergy, though suggested has never been proved, but the four orders appear to have cooperated among themselves. The Warwickshire antiquary John Rous wrote in about 1486 that 'wherever there are two, and still more three or four houses of friars, scholars are exercised in disputations each week, now in one house and now in another.'[2] Bristol, Exeter,

---

1 On these institutions see *ESMA*, pp 84–5.
2 John Rous, *Historia Regum Angliae,* ed. T. Hearne (Oxford, 1716), p 73.

Gloucester, Plymouth and Salisbury were the five towns in our region with more than one convent of friars.

The monastic orders also developed systems of higher education during the thirteenth and fourteenth centuries. Tentative moves in this direction were made by the Cistercians in 1245 and by the Benedictines soon afterwards, the process being completed with legislation promulgated by Pope Benedict XII in the 1330s. Broadly speaking the educational arrangements of the three major orders—Benedictines, Cistercians and Augustinian canons—developed in the following way. Novices were recruited at about the age of twenty, having already undertaken the basic study of grammar at a secular school or as boys of the almonry. They were then instructed by a schoolmaster, either a monk or a secular priest from outside, in advanced grammar, logic and philosophy. The best students were dispatched to study theology at the universities at an academic level. Some of the greater monasteries also provided theology lectures of a more elementary kind for their own members, and in the case of the Benedictines and Augustinians, on canon law as well. The students who had gone to university were sometimes used for this purpose.[1]

Traces of this system can be found in the monasteries of our region, though the surviving records come mainly from the hundred years before the Reformation. Monks or canons are recorded as schoolmasters at Glastonbury in 1456, Bristol in 1491 and Bath in 1532. These all appear to have been senior brethren, but elsewhere in England the post was also given to juniors who had just come down from university. The monk or canon was permitted to receive a salary for his extra work, £1. 6s. 8d. being allocated for this purpose at Bristol and £4 at Bath. When no suitable monk was available, the house was obliged to hire the services of a teacher from elsewhere. Gloucester in 1515, Stanley in 1526 and Forde in 1537 appointed secular masters on a regular basis with salaries of £6, £4 and £3. 6s. 8d. respectively, as well as board and lodging. At Bristol the vicar of a neighbouring church gave instruction in grammar in 1491. We hear little or nothing of the study of theology until the early sixteenth century when Richard Kidderminster instituted daily lectures at Winchcombe on the Old and New Testaments. He himself expounded the *Sentences* of Peter Lombard, the great medieval textbook of theology, twice every week. In 1535 Thomas Cromwell ordered all religious houses to provide a lesson of one hour a day on holy scripture, and there are examples of this being done at Forde, Gloucester, Hailes and Winchcombe.

The late Dr W. A. Pantin gave a salutary warning against supposing lack of evidence for education in the medieval monasteries to mean that none was available.[2] Yet it cannot be denied that individual houses sometimes failed to maintain the facilities required of them by the canon law. Schoolmasters were lacking for the brethren at Tewkesbury in 1378, Tavistock in 1388, Bruton in 1452, Tywardreath in 1526 and allegedly at Glastonbury in 1538. No doubt this was partly due to the intermittent supply of recruits, which led to a need for special facilities at irregular intervals. The study of theology ought not to have been

---

1 On this subject in general see *ESMA*, pp 224–51.
2 W. A. Pantin, 'Abbot Kidderminster and Monastic Studies', *Downside Review*, xlvii (1929), p 203.

affected in this way, but frequent complaints that monasteries were not sending students to Oxford invite the question whether they all had much interest in higher education. In the absence of graduate monks the supply of lecturers would have been uncertain. The Benedictine and Augustinian orders also faced the same educational problems as the secular clergy. How was a nominal system of higher education to be successfully imposed on a large number of autonomous communities with only their rule in common? The larger houses seem on the whole to have observed the law with regard to the teaching of grammar, but their concern with theology, like that of the smaller houses with education in general, is something that has still to be established.

THE REFORMATION

During the first half of the sixteenth century English school education underwent important changes, more so than at any time during the previous four hundred years. The New Learning, with its revival of interest in the literature of Greece and Rome, caused a revolution in the school curriculum. The study of grammar began to be dominated again by the great classical authors: Horace, Livy, Terence and Virgil. They displaced the grammarians of the middle ages as arbiters of usage and models of style. They drove out the twelfth- and thirteenth-century moralists from the canon of authors read in schools. Between about 1480 and 1520 the curriculum changed into that of the Renaissance, and Alexander and Evrard, Theodulus and Alain de Lille, dropped out of use. These purely curricular changes were accompanied by rising public interest in schools and their work. From the king and the aristocracy downwards, parents were giving more attention to the literary education of their children. Those who taught found themselves taken more seriously. Teaching became once more a passage to fame and wealth which might even take a man, as it took Wolsey, to high office in Church or civil government. The rate of educational benefactions also accelerated. In the South West alone seven grammar schools were fully endowed between 1499 and 1524, a greater number than had been achieved during the whole of the fifteenth century.

These changes were enough in themselves to open a new era in English education. They were seconded in this respect by the Reformation. The religious revival and its conflicts had considerable effects upon the schools. Public interest in education increased still further as Catholics and Protestants alike discovered the importance of schooling as a means of increasing religious fervour and enforcing orthodoxy. The crown itself through assuming control of the Church was obliged to concern itself with education. In 1540 Henry VIII imposed a uniform Latin grammar on all masters and pupils, and he and his successors founded or refounded a large number of schools during the 1540s and 50s as a consequence of the dissolution of monasteries and chantries. State control of education was strengthened in 1556 with the introduction of a system for the licensing and supervision of schoolmasters by the bishops. This royal interest in schools was something new, and even the concern of the ecclesiastical authorities increased from what it had been in the later middle ages. At the same time the English Reformation involved the destruction

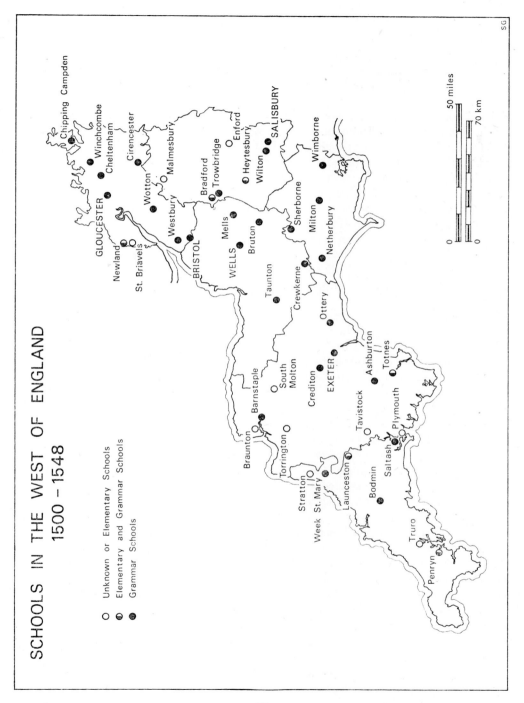

of ecclesiastical institutions thought to be harmful or superfluous. Monasteries, collegiate churches and chantries were dissolved in turn, and a large number of schools associated with them modified or destroyed in consequence. The appearance of new forces in education was thus accompanied by the disappearance of old ones, and by 1560 the English schools differed both in organisation, work and public importance from when the century began.

The first stage of the dissolution of religious foundations, the closure of the monasteries and friaries, lasted from 1535 until 1540. This naturally involved the disappearance of all the educational facilities which the houses had provided within their walls: the cloister schools of grammar, logic and theology for the brethren, together with the schools of song and grammar for the choristers and the almonry boys. The masters who had taught in these schools, if monks or seculars (but not friars), were eligible for personal compensation, and were awarded pensions if they proved their rights in the court of Augmentations. In our own region pensions were given to the grammar masters of Bath, Forde and Stanley, to the choirmasters of Cirencester, Glastonbury, Lanthony, Taunton and Tavistock, and perhaps to others as well.[1] The benevolence of the crown to individuals, however, should not allow us to forget that an important section of English education had been removed almost at a stroke. Through the scholars and ecclesiastics whom they trained, the cloister schools had contributed to English learning in general, and by maintaining choristers and almonry boys the religious houses had subsidised the education of many children who might otherwise have fared badly. The losses, as far as the South West was concerned, were only offset by the conversion of St Augustine's, Bristol and St Peter's, Gloucester into secular cathedrals in 1541–2. The new foundations included a free grammar school open to the public and assisted places for eight choristers. These facilities did a little to compensate for the loss of the almonries.

Besides their own internal schools, a few monasteries had been involved with public education, acting as the trustees of endowments, appointing schoolmasters, and paying them salaries. There were four major examples of this relationship in the South West before the Reformation. The Augustinians of Bruton paid and appointed the master of Bruton grammar school; the Benedictines of Winchcombe did so at Winchcombe and Cirencester; and the Carthusians of Hinton appointed the master at Bradford-on-Avon. Henry VIII's regime, which included many supporters of education, was not in principle averse to sparing institutions of this kind which catered for the public, but no general arrangements were made for extricating them from the ruin of the monasteries. As a result they each suffered to some extent, except for Bradford where the mastership did not fall vacant during the period of disturbance. Winchcombe school experienced difficulties after 1539, though it may have continued to operate, and four years elapsed before its future was finally assured in 1543. Bruton school was disordered for eleven years after 1539. Teaching ceased to be free and the school was apparently suspended for a period until it was refounded in 1550. Cirencester also fared badly. The school was extinguished in about 1540, and was only

---

[1] The decree and order books of the court of Augmentations do not appear to include a complete record of all the pensions granted to schoolmasters.

revived some five years later when the local inhabitants converted a chantry under their government to replace it. An endowed school thereafter continued, but with an endowment of £3 less than the £10 it had enjoyed before the Reformation. All four schools therefore survived in the long term, but three of them experienced temporary dislocation during the course of the 1540s.

The next houses to be dissolved were the secular colleges. Between 1540 and his death in 1547, Henry VIII encouraged them to surrender themselves into his hands, although the process was still uncompleted when he died and remained to be finished under his successor. The internal schools maintained by the colleges for their clerks and choristers were allowed to perish in exactly the same way as the almonry foundations of the monasteries, but public schools, where they existed, were treated more favourably. Three colleges in our region dissolved under Henry VIII had probably maintained public schools: Crediton, Ottery and Westbury-on-Trym. Ottery school was immediately refounded without apparently closing, and Crediton was re-established after a lapse of two years in 1547. Only Westbury school was allowed to die, no doubt because of the proximity of the king's new cathedral school three miles away at Bristol. In England as a whole the schools of the colleges escaped the consequences of the dissolutions more easily than those of the monasteries had done.

Shortly before he died Henry VIII made plans to reform another group of ecclesiastical institutions, the chantries. A statute of 1545 gave him power during his lifetime to appoint commissioners in each county to make a survey of the foundations. The survey was carried out in 1546 but had scarcely been completed when the statute lapsed as a result of the king's death in January 1547. It remained for the government of Edward VI to dissolve the chantries, together with the religious guilds and the remaining colleges by means of a second statute, the Chantry Act of December 1547.[1] This authorised it to appoint new commissioners, to make a fresh survey of chantries, to dissolve the foundations and to seize their possessions. At the same time a promise was made to spare all grammar schools maintained by the condemned foundations which had been in existence since Michaelmas 1547. Hopes were even held out that new schools might be endowed with some of the confiscated properties. The Edwardian commissioners went to work in the spring of 1548, collecting evidence about the chantries and their schools. This was remitted to two officers in London, Sir Walter Mildmay and Robert Kellway, who authorised the dissolution of chantries, allocated pensions to their incumbents, and ordered the grammar schools associated with them to be continued. The dissolution of the chantries therefore belongs to the spring and summer of 1548.

The commissioners both of Henry VIII and Edward VI collected valuable information about the chantries then extant in the form of records now known as the 'chantry certificates'. The method followed in 1546 and probably also two years later was to send a questionnaire to each parish asking the clergy and churchwardens to certify the origins, purposes and endowments of the local chantries and the names of their incumbents. Since

---

1 For the text of the Chantry Act see *Statutes of the Realm* (1810–24), iv, part i, 24–33.

the certificates originated in the parishes, opportunities arose for the concealment of information from the commissioners. Some foundations were never reported at all while others, like the schools at Chipping Campden, Crewkerne and Wotton-under-Edge, which had probably originated as chantries, were not admitted to have been so. The chantry commissioners checked this information when they could, but they were not always successful in discovering frauds and modern historians who use the certificates must remember their apologetic nature, to say nothing of their frequent inaccuracy over details. Neither the Henrican nor the Edwardian chantry certificates survive for all our counties. Those of 1546 exist for Cornwall, Devon and Gloucestershire; those of 1548 include every county but Dorset. A third set of certificates also remains from 1548 with notes for awarding pensions and continuing schools. These survive for every county except Somerset, and give us our only information about Dorset. Finally the warrants for the continuance of grammar schools issued on 20 July 1548 survive for Cornwall, Dorset, Somerset and Wiltshire.[1]

The Chantry Act of 1548 promised that grammar schools attached to chantries would be spared, and this was conscientiously observed by Mildmay and Kellway. Seven grammar schools in our region founded or probably founded in association with chantries before the 1540s therefore survived: Bradford-on-Avon, Chipping Campden, Crewkerne, Newland, Week St Mary, Wimborne Minster, and Wotton-under-Edge. So did nine grammar schools which although not originally part of chantry foundations had come to be maintained by them in recent years: Ashburton, Barnstaple, Bodmin, Cheltenham, Cirencester, Netherbury, Saltash, Trowbridge and the college school at Penryn. Only one chantry grammar school was treated differently. This was Launceston, where the local inhabitants asked for the grammar school of Week St Mary to be transferred to their town. Launceston's own grammar-master appears to have been allowed to go on teaching there for a few years, but after 1560 Launceston possessed only the Week foundation, and its own disappeared.

There remain four other chantry schools at Enford, Malmesbury, St Briavels and Truro, which failed to secure an order for their continuance. None of the four was described in the certificates as a grammar school, and it is most likely that the chantry priests concerned had been teaching reading or song. Elementary schools did not qualify to be spared under the Chantry Act, since it was assumed that education at this level was easily available from other sources. The two undoubtedly elementary schools which figure in the certificates at Launceston and Penryn were dissolved for the same reason. The commissioners also encountered two doubtful cases of chantries said by the local inhabitants to have maintained schools: Blandford Forum and Marldon. Neither of them was thought worth saving and the historian, in so far as he can check the evidence presented to the commissioners, is inclined to agree with their decision. In short, the peculiar circumstances of Launceston notwithstanding, the chantry commissioners appear faithfully to have carried out the instructions of the Chantry Act. In the light of the information transmitted to them they preserved all the grammar schools which came within their jurisdiction.

1 Most of the relevant documents are printed in *ESR*, part ii, but with one or two minor omissions.

That the chantry grammar schools survived the dissolution of the chantries themselves in 1548 is not in doubt; their survival in the longer term is more of a problem. The Chantry Act of 1547 undertook to provide them with endowments of land, but in the summer of 1548 the government decided instead to appropriate the lands they already held and to pay the masters stipends at the rate they had previously received until such time as lands could be spared to endow them. Only four schools in our region managed to keep their lands—Chipping Campden, Crewkerne, Netherbury and Wotton-under-Edge—and this only because they had not been proved to be chantries. The other twelve went on receiving their stipends during Edward VI's reign, but after Mary's accession confusion developed. In 1555 the crown transferred the payment of all ecclesiastical pensions to the Church and although the chantry schoolmasters were stipendiaries not pensioners, some of the local receivers of crown lands responsible for paying their stipends refused to go on doing so. This happened in Cornwall and Gloucester but not in Dorset where the stipend of Wimborne school was duly paid throughout the reign. When Elizabeth succeeded in 1558 twelve schools remained entitled to the payment of stipends. Some then sued for their rights in the court of the Exchequer and won recognition, the payments being carried out faithfully during Elizabeth's reign. Newland, however, may have gone defunct for a period between 1555 and 1576, and Bradford and Trowbridge were robbed of their stipends in 1569 at the instance of the citizens of Salisbury.

The Chantry Act of 1547 also promised to endow new schools out of the confiscated chantry lands in the areas where they were needed. During the survey of the following year suitable places for such schools were noted by the commissioners or suggested by the local inhabitants. In Cornwall Liskeard and Penryn were recommended; in Gloucestershire Cheltenham, Cirencester, Newent and Tewkesbury; in Somerset Bridgwater and Taunton; and in Wiltshire Marlborough, Salisbury and Warminster. In the end however only two new schools were endowed in our region during Edward VI's reign—Bath and Sherborne, while the endowments seized from Bruton school in 1539 were restored in 1550. No others were founded by Mary, and although under Elizabeth the crown often assisted the foundation of schools by private benefactors, its actions were not directly related to the promises of 1547.

Whether the effects of the Reformation upon English education were beneficial or harmful has been the subject of much debate. The view traditionally held until the end of the nineteenth century was favourable to the Reformation, being based on the assumption that since there were few English schools in the middle ages, the foundations of Henry VIII and Edward VI must be considered a positive improvement. In 1896 on the other hand, A. F. Leach in his book *English Schools at the Reformation* demonstrated the existence of a considerable number of medieval English schools. He emphasised the disorganisation of education under Edward VI, with the closure of elementary schools and the conversion of grammar school lands into fixed stipends which failed to keep their value at a time of inflating prices. The truth probably lies halfway between the two judgments. No one can doubt that the Reformation caused a good deal of temporary inconvenience to local education during the 1540s and 50s. Several of the endowed schools of our region lost their revenues for part of this period and a few even closed altogether, but in the long run gains and losses tend to cancel one another out. It is possible to compile a balance sheet for the counties of the South West which is not untypical of the situation in England as a whole. The greatest permanent losses to local education were the schools of the religious orders with their teaching places and facilities for board and lodging. One free public grammar school disappeared at Westbury-on-Trym, another at Week St Mary (but by local request), and perhaps a third at Newland. Cirencester lost endowments worth £3 and Winchcombe its schoolhouse. Five elementary schools also ceased to exist. So much for the debit account. On the credit side the Reformation produced four new endowed schools offering free instruction in grammar at Bath, Bristol, Gloucester and Sherborne. The foundations also included sixteen places for choristers. Two other schools at Crediton and Ottery were endowed by the crown on an improved scale. Leach's point about the conversion of land revenues into fixed stipends can be modified by observing that some of the schools concerned had also taken fees, and were still able to do so. In any case the endowed schools affected by the Reformation were only a part of the educational facilities generally available. Many fee-paying schools continued to exist throughout the century, and so did several schools endowed by private benefactors which had no connection with religious foundations. Looking beyond the years between 1540 and 1560 over the history of Tudor education as a whole, it is difficult to ascribe either a significant expansion or recession of schooling to the Reformation alone.

CONCLUSION

It remains to summarise the impact of the west-of-England schools upon the region where they lay. From the twelfth century onwards, the main centres of school education were situated in the towns. Schools were as characteristic a feature of urban life in the middle ages as guildhalls, friaries and hospitals, at any rate in the larger towns. Like other urban institutions such as the fair and the market, they provided an amenity for the surrounding countryside. They stimulated movement in society. Many schoolmasters came to the place of their work from elsewhere. Some, it is true, were local men of local education, but others had been away to university and a few were strangers from well outside the South West. Their pupils too were travellers from other towns and villages as well as local residents. Schools like those of the cathedral cities probably drew their entry from a wide surrounding area. For many of these pupils the journeys they made to school continued after they left, taking them to offices and benefices away from home and sometimes as far as university. In short, schooling added to the ceaseless coming and going within the region, as well as between the region and the nation as a whole.

The schools affected local life in several ways. They had a modest economic impact. The master gained a living from his fees while his neighbours profited from lodging and feeding his pupils. More significantly, the schools enriched the mental life of the community. They added a schoolmaster and ultimately some of his pupils to the local élite of learned men. The graduate masters brought with them the experience of university life and at least a smattering of European learning in general. They diffused the ideas and methods

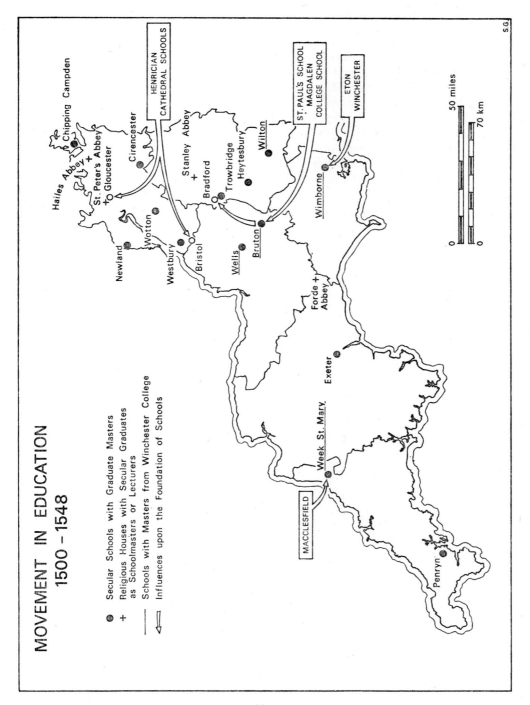

of the leading grammar masters of the day. The works of John Leland, the Oxford grammarian, were brought to Bristol and Bridport in the fifteenth century, and the curricula of Eton and Winchester reached other places in the sixteenth. Finally, the schools had a wide social impact. They provided the region with clergy and administrators, and later also with literate gentlemen, merchants and yeomen. The exact history of this process remains to be established. Their work was received by and large with approval. We hear little or nothing of anticlericalism in relation to the west-of-England schools. What ordinary people thought about them is not indeed recorded, but there can be no doubt of the goodwill they aroused among the great and wealthy. It bore fruit in the stream of benefactions: buildings, books, doles, exhibitions and finally landed endowments. The steady flow of gifts to schools from the twelfth to the sixteenth century is as fine a testimony as any to their popularity.

I
Five Cities and their Schools

BRISTOL
Gloucestershire

With Bristol we come at once to the largest and wealthiest of the towns and cities of the west of England. If in the twelfth century contemporaries might have attached more importance to Exeter or Gloucester, by the fourteenth Bristol had undoubtedly overtaken them both in size and resources. With a list of 6,345 taxpayers in 1377 and over 6,000 church communicants estimated in 1548, its population, including children, must have numbered between nine and ten thousand during the later middle ages. This made it not only the largest town in the South West but one of the three or four largest outside London.[1] Its economic importance was reflected in its religious institutions: eighteen parish churches, a large Augustinian abbey, four friaries, and half a dozen lesser priories and hospitals, supporting between 150 and 200 clergy in all. Its status, as far as the Church was concerned, was rather unusual. It had until 1542 no bishop or cathedral, being by far the biggest town in England without them, and it straddled the boundaries of two dioceses. The city proper lay in that of Worcester and its southern suburbs in that of Bath and Wells. The combination of a large town with a weak ecclesiastical jurisdiction seems to have left its traces on the development of education. It probably explains why medieval Bristol came to possess several schools with little or no official status, unlike most of the other large English towns where a single school with official recognition held a virtual monopoly of education.

Despite the size and importance of Bristol, references to its schools are few and far between until the fifteenth century, and need to be handled carefully. A town of its rank may be expected to have possessed a school as early as the twelfth century, but the evidence for this is mostly poor and late. Henry II studied letters and good manners at Bristol during the 1140s when he was under the tutelage of his uncle, Robert of Gloucester. One of his tutors was a man named Matthew and another may have been Adelard of Bath, who later became a distinguished scholar, but there is nothing to show that either one did any public teaching.[2] Next we have the testimony of an inquisition carried out in about 1318 into

---

1 J. C. Russell, *British Medieval Population* (1948), p 142; Sir John Maclean, 'Chantry Certificates: Gloucestershire', *TBGAS*, viii (1883–4), pp 232–51.
2 *The Historical Works of Gervase of Canterbury,* ed. W. Stubbs, vol i (Rolls Series, 1879), p 125; C. H. Haskins, 'Adelard of Bath and Henry Plantagenet', *English Historical Review*, xxviii (1913), pp 515–16.

the history and privileges of the guild of Kalendars, a brotherhood of priests and laymen attached to the town church of All Saints. This states that between 1154 and 1171 Robert Fitzharding, the ancestor of the Berkeley family, established 'the schools of Bristol for the education of the Jews and for the teaching of other children' under the government of the guild of Kalendars.[1] The statement is not very convincing. It makes Robert of Gloucester a party to the arrangement although he died in 1147, and its reference to 'schools for the Jews' appears to be a misunderstanding of the Latin *scola Judeorum* which means in fact a synagogue. It is just possible that Robert Fitzharding put the ordinary school of Bristol under the control of the Kalendars, but even this is doubtful. Instances of guilds controlling schools in this period are rare or nonexistent.[2]

Third, there is the evidence of the sixteenth-century antiquary, John Leland. He repeats the story of the 'school for the Jews' and the guild of Kalendars, but goes on to say that William, earl of Gloucester, the founder of Keynsham Abbey, 'gave the prefecture and mastership of the school in Bristol to Keynsham and took it from the Kalendars'.[3] This would have to be dated between the foundation of the abbey in about 1166 and the earl's death in 1183. Late though it is, this seems by far the most credible piece of information about the early school of Bristol.[4] The canons of Keynsham were members of the Victorine branch of the Augustinian order, an order which was often involved with the government of schools in the twelfth century. Bedford, Derby, Gloucester, and Huntingdon were other contemporary towns where control of the school was given by charter into the hands of the local house of Augustinian canons. The canons did not teach in the schools themselves; they were merely responsible for appointing the masters who did. Leland's evidence receives support from the location of the school in the thirteenth century opposite the church of St Peter which belonged to Keynsham, in a district where other abbey tenements were to be found. But we never hear of Keynsham exercising jurisdiction over education in Bristol in later times, and this may indicate that the right eventually lapsed. The six miles of distance involved and the comparatively large size of the town would have made it difficult to supervise and control the teaching that went on there.

From the thirteenth century come two further pieces of information: the site of the early school, and an attempt at benefiting its scholars. In 1243 John Hose confirmed the grant by his sister Iseuda to Simon the Clerk of a large stone house 'called the school' near St Peter's church.[5] It is not clear whether the house was actually in use for teaching at this time, but it had certainly fallen into disuse by the end of the century, for an inquisition of 1285 mentions Adam Buckton as holding the tenement of the 'old' school opposite the church, and an undated rental of the same period shows Roger Pert paying 12d. on

1 *The Little Red Book of Bristol*, ed. F. B. Bickley (1900), i, 206.
2 The nearest in time and character seems to be one in Bury St Edmunds in the thirteenth century (*VCH Suffolk*, ii, 309–10).
3 John Leland, *Itinerary*, ed. Lucy Toulmin Smith (5 vols, 1907–10), v, 92.
4 At least one cartulary of Keynsham Abbey was circulating until the seventeenth century (G. R. C. Davies, *Medieval Cartularies of Great Britain* (1958), p 58).
5 F. B. Bickley, *A Calendar of Bristol Deeds* (1899), no 4.

behalf of Walter, rector of St Philip's, for the same 'old school'.[1] Meanwhile in 1230 Robert de Gournay had founded the hospital of St Mark in the north-western suburbs of the town. Its ordinances, confirmed by the bishop of Worcester in 1259, provided for the maintenance of a master, brethren, almsmen, and twelve scholars admitted by the master. The scholars were apparently to receive board and lodging in return for assisting in the choir of the hospital, one of them being chosen to discipline and teach the others.[2] On the analogy of similar foundations made elsewhere at this time, the scholars were probably chosen from those who attended the town school and continued to receive most of their education there. The teaching in the hospital seems merely to have been related to their singing in the choir. There is again no mention of the scholars of St Mark's in later times, and the statutes in this instance may never have been put into effect. The chief value of the reference is to suggest the presence of scholars in general in Bristol in 1259.

By the end of the fourteenth century it is evident that Bristol no longer possessed a single authorised school under a definite jurisdiction. On the contrary, there were several schools and they were largely free of supervision or control. In 1379 two schoolmasters are mentioned in different parts of the town, contributing to the clerical poll tax. Only their Christian names are given. One, Robert, is listed under the church or parish of St Peter, where he paid 4d. as a clerk in minor orders. The other, Hugh, occurs among the chaplains of St Nicholas, and was evidently a priest for he was charged at the full rate of 2s.[3] The evidence of the fifteenth and sixteenth centuries confirms that schools continued to function in more than one area. We shall shortly encounter a schoolmaster teaching above the New Gate, another in the suburbs south of the bridge, and a third who lived in Christmas Street and carried on his work above the Frome Gate. The wills of John Somerville in 1407 and John Shipward in 1473 suggest further locations. They each bequeathed a tenement called 'the schoolhouse', the one in St Nicholas Street and the other near the tower at the end of the Quay.[4] The situation is analogous to London, an even larger centre of population and literacy, which also needed several schools. Unlike London however, which possessed both public and private institutions, those of Bristol all seem to have been private and ephemeral rather than public and continuous. No single school appears to have survived throughout the middle ages.

The question of what was taught in these schools also presents problems. As in most towns the early references merely mention 'schools' or 'schoolmasters' without further qualification. Not until the early fifteenth century can we identify grammar schools as such, although doubtless the school or schools of earlier times provided teaching in grammar. The facilities for elementary education are even more elusive. Whether specialised petty schools existed to teach reading, or whether this was taught in the grammar schools, remains, as in England generally, a matter of speculation. But it seems clear that some Bristol

---

1 *The Great Red Book of Bristol,* ed. E. W. W. Veale, vol i (Bristol Record Soc., iv, 1933), pp 75, 76, 100.
2 *The Cartulary of St Mark's Hospital, Bristol,* ed. C. D. Ross (ibid., xxi, 1959), especially pp 1, 7.
3 PRO, Exch. KR. Clerical Subsidy Rolls, E 179/58/5.
4 *The Great Orphan Book of Wills,* ed. T. P. Wadley (1886), pp 82, 161.

boys of the fifteenth and early sixteenth centuries learnt to read and sing in the larger city churches. This was the case at All Saints, which maintained a choir of boys as early as 1407. In 1438 there was a room attached to the church called the schoolhouse, where one assumes they were trained.[1] The choir survived into the sixteenth century, and when in 1524 the parish clerk, William Bridgeman, left a valuable collection of music to the church, he stipulated that it should not be used for teaching children.[2] This meant that it was not to be thumbed over by young children, who customarily practised reading from liturgical service books. At least two other churches supported boy choristers and seem to have provided for their teaching. The will of Belinus Nansmoen mentions scholar boys serving in the church of St Mary Redcliffe in 1417[3]. Furthermore at St Nicholas, a series of rules for the conduct of the parish clerk drawn up in 1481 includes one which forbids him to take books out of the choir for children to learn from, without licence of the churchwardens.[4] Like All Saints, St Nicholas possessed a 'schoolhouse', from which in 1549 the wardens arranged for the carrying away of forms, boards and images.[5] The strength of these parochial choirs was probably limited to half a dozen boys apiece, but it is not unlikely that the clerks or cantors who trained them made a little extra money by teaching other children as well.

We come now to the fifteenth-century grammar masters and their schools. The earliest whose name we know was a man of distinction about whom, by medieval standards, a good deal can be learnt. His name was Robert Londe and he first appears as a secular chaplain in the parish of St Peter at the confluence of the years 1419 and 1420.[6] This would put his birth back to at least the mid 1390s. In the following June he was instituted as warden of St Michael's, or Bradeston's, chantry in the church of Winterbourne, six miles north of Bristol. This was a large chantry founded seventy years previously for a warden and two chaplains. Londe exchanged it in 1425 for the rectory of Ditteridge, a poor upland church near Box in Wiltshire which none of its recent incumbents had held for long.[7] The exchange was probably never completed, for although the rector was instituted to the chantry, Londe himself seems not to have secured Ditteridge. For whatever reasons, his career as a beneficed priest came to an end, and he turned instead to schoolmastering.

Londe was already established as a schoolmaster in Bristol by September 1426 when the

1 Bristol Record Office, All Saints Church Book, pp 438, 480.
2 Ibid., All Saints Church, Halleway Chantry Accounts, 1522/3 fo 5. For Bridgeman and his bequest see F. Ll. Harrison, 'The Repertory of an English Parish Church in the Early Sixteenth Century', *Renaissance-Muziek, 1400–1600: Donum Natalicium Rene Bernard Lenaerts* (Leuven, 1969), pp 143–7.
3 *The Great Orphan Book,* ed. Wadley, p 96.
4 J. R. Bramble, 'Records of St Nicholas Church, Bristol', *Clifton Antiquarian Club Proceedings,* vol i (Bristol, 1884–8), p 148.
5 E. G. C. Atchley, 'The Medieval Parish Registers of St Nicholas, Bristol', *Transactions of the St Paul's Ecclesiological Soc.,* vi (1906), p 63.
6 PRO, E 179/58/10. This is undated, but its terms agree with the clerical subsidy granted on 20 November 1419 (*Reg. Chichele, Canterbury,* ed. E. F. Jacob, iii, 58).
7 Londe was instituted to Bradeston's chantry on 20 June 1420 and exchanged it for Ditteridge on 15 January 1425 (HWRO, Reg. Morgan, Worcester, i, fo 13v; ii, fo 29).

merchant Thomas Bewflour made him a small bequest in his will.[1] The site of his school, according to the antiquary William Worcester who may have been one of his pupils, was the Newgate on the edge of St Peter's parish, which other evidence confirms as the chamber over the gate itself.[2] Unlike most medieval schoolmasters of whom we know at best that they merely lived and taught, we can gain a rare insight into Londe and his work from a manuscript which was almost certainly compiled by the master himself or for his use at the school. This is a miscellaneous volume, now at Lincoln College, Oxford, containing about twenty short Latin tracts on the study of grammar, together with odd verses, letters, and recipes, some 244 pages in all.[3] Of the various treatises and extracts which have been copied into the manuscript, several are signed by the scribe, a certain Thomas Short, and two of them are dated. The first, a tract on grammatical rules, was copied by him 'at Bristol, above the New Gate' on 8 May 1427; the second, on the gender of nouns by John Leland, the famous Oxford grammarian, was 'written at Bristol' on 20 May 1428. Since Londe was already a schoolmaster in Bristol by 1426, and since we know that he taught at some time or another above the Newgate, it is hard to resist the conclusion that Short's transcriptions coincided with Londe's tenure of the Newgate school and reproduce his teaching material.

The most interesting part of the manuscript for a modern reader is the set of *vulgaria*, English sentences with Latin translations, intended to illustrate different points of grammar and syntax. They are many years ahead of the similar and better-known *vulgaria* collections of the English Renaissance schoolmasters like John Stanbridge, and not only in years. They are also an early anticipation of the characteristic Tudor attempt to capture the interest of the class by allusions to topical events and everyday life—so different from the stilted subjects preferred by modern textbooks. Some of the *vulgaria* in Londe's collection are current proverbs, others are specimens of schoolboy wit, and yet others refer to local life:

> Sum gay squyere of Davynschere schal wed my dowghter, the weche go to schole ap on the new yate.
>
> To Brystow, the wyche ys an havyn towne, comyth moo strangerys than to Covyntre, the wych is no havyn towne, notwithstondyng that bothe bethe lyche good.
>
> Y had as lefe be servyd with a cawlestokke as with heryng in [a] flesche day.
>
> Owre parson schal schreyve me in lent, holyist of tymys, and not a fryre nother non other relygyusmon.

---

1 *The Great Orphan Book*, ed. Wadley, p 116. Other possible references to Londe occur in the will of Thomas Devenish, 1426 (PRO, Prob 11/3 (PCC 2 Luffenam)), and in *CPR 1429–36*, p 64. On Londe in general see C. E. Boucher, 'The Lond or Loud Brass in St Peter's Church, Bristol', *TBGAS*, xxx (1907), pp 265–72, and 'St Peter's Church, Bristol', ibid, xxxii (1909), pp 274–5.

2 *Itineraria Simonis Simeonis et Willelmi de Worcestre*, ed. J. Nasmith (1776), p 178. Worcester enigmatically describes Londe as 'principal schoolmaster with John Leland'. Did he mean that Londe once worked with Leland in Oxford, or that they were the two leading schoolmasters of the day?

3 Oxford, Lincoln College, MS lat. 129. I am greatly indebted to Dr R. W. Hunt who first brought the volume to my notice.

> There buth mony lolerdys ytake in dyverse scheris of this contrey as y hyrd say now late of trewmen.
>
> Y kan ryde to Bathe in a day and als far beyond for nede.

The English was probably dictated to the pupils, who then produced Latin translations which the master compared with his own. The orthography of the Latin, it should be said, is far superior to that of the English where no rules applied. Towards the end of the *vulgaria* there are two sections headed by the words 'Wotton' and 'Chyppnam'. These would appear to indicate material that had been borrowed from the contemporary grammar school at Wotton-under-Edge and from a similar institution which presumably existed at Chippenham in Wiltshire. The manuscript certainly draws on the work of other schools for, besides the tract by the Oxford master John Leland, it contains another on heteroclite nouns 'following the use of London'.

Londe's name appears from time to time during the following years in lists of clergy and other documents, and it is to be noticed that while he is always described as *dominus* until 1446, the title given to all priests, he is designated *magister* after 1449.[1] This may simply reflect his growing status as a school*master,* or it may indicate that he had taken the university degree of 'master of grammar', one of the lesser honours at Oxford and Cambridge for which practising schoolmasters sometimes supplicated. He may also have dabbled in canon law, for an inventory of books belonging to the church of St John the Baptist in 1469 includes a volume on this subject 'given by Master Robert, sometime schoolmaster of this town'.[2] Londe died on 23 February 1462 and was buried in his parish church, St Peter's, where his memorial brass survived until the last war. It showed him dressed as a priest in mass vestments, holding the chalice and host, and called him 'Master Robert Lond, chaplain', without noticing the schoolmastering for which he must have been best known. The omission is a good testimony to the modesty of the English schoolmasters before the Renaissance.[3]

We do not know if Londe's school was a private venture or whether it survived his death. The school had gone from Newgate by 1480 when Worcester noted its disappearance. The next grammar master appears in the south suburbs of Bristol which lay in the diocese of Bath and Wells. On 16 August 1463 Bishop Beckington licensed John Faukeys, clerk, to keep a grammar school in Bristol during the bishop's pleasure and take fees from all who came to him for instruction.[4] Beckington was an enthusiast for education, but there is no reason to show why he felt it necessary to grant a licence on this occasion. Episcopal intervention in medieval teaching was uncommon. Eight years later we encounter another

---

[1] The first reference I have found to Londe as *magister* (1449) is in Reg. Carpenter, Worcester, i, fo 79v.
[2] Bristol Record Office, St John the Baptist, Churchwardens' Accounts, fo 5.
[3] The brass is illustrated and described by C. E. Boucher in *TBGAS*, xxx (1907), pp 265–72, the inscription being in Latin. The date does not agree with that noted by William Worcester (*Itineraria*, ed. Nasmith, p 222) as being 23 February 1469/70, but I have found no reference to Londe alive after 1462. The brass itself disappeared after the bombing of St Peter's church in 1940.
[4] *Reg. Bekynton, Wells*, i, 393. He is perhaps the same man as in *BRUO*, ii, 671.

schoolmaster in the Master Bulkeley whom the merchant John Gaywood requested to attend his funeral in 1471 along with his scholars, 'that they may be present in the church of St Thomas and say each one of them the Paternoster, Ave Mary, and the Creed'. In recompense the testator bequeathed them 8d., so that they might afterwards refresh themselves with wine.[1] A third schoolmaster of this period was the Thomas Fosse who sent a petition to the chancellor of England at some point between 1480 and 1483. The petition alleged that John Peers, a leading Bristol merchant, agreed that Fosse should teach his son Thomas in grammar, promising him in due course a suitable reward. The boy duly attended the master, but when Fosse sent in his bill, Peers refused to pay and counterclaimed that Fosse had beaten and ill-treated his son to the damage of £40. The case came into the Tolsey Court at Bristol but Peers, being 'one of the chief rulers of the town', was so influential that Fosse feared he would not get justice. He therefore petitioned the chancellor to allow the case to be brought before him in the court of chancery. The outcome of it all remains unknown.[2]

Thirty years now pass before in February 1513 we find Thomas Moffat, schoolmaster, occupying a new house which the merchant David Leyson had recently built next to the churchyard of St Lawrence in Christmas Street.[3] He was still living in this or an adjoining house in 1533 but a rental of two years later shows that he had left the area. His grammar school was held nearby over the Frome Gate and enjoyed a measure of public recognition since the corporation of Bristol, who owned the premises, permitted him to occupy them rent free. The Frome Gate school first appears in the mayor's audit book of 1532; it is mentioned in succeeding audit books up to 1536 but by 1540 the tenement, 'sometime the schoolhouse', had been let out to a collier.[4] Moffat was a layman and a friend of Robert Thorne, the famous merchant adventurer, who bequeathed him £25 in his will of 1532 as well as £10 to Moffat's son Robert.[5] Thomas himself retired from teaching, and the Frome Gate school came to an end, at some time between 1536 and 1540, and by 1542 the corporation, who evidently valued his services highly, were paying him an annual pension of two marks. The last payment of the pension at Midsummer 1522 was probably followed by the old schoolmaster's death.[6]

Moffat's retirement coincided with the foundation of new grammar schools in Bristol. The earliest of these, the modern Bristol Grammar School, was planned by the Bristol

1 *The Great Orphan Book,* ed. Wadley, p 145.
2 PRO, Early Chancery Proceedings, C 1/61/390. A Thomas Fosse owed money to Cannings' chantry in St Mary Redcliffe in 1490 (Edith E. Williams, *The Chantries of William Canynges* (Bristol, 1950), p 115).
3 Bristol Record Office, E. M. Thompson's MS Calendar of Fox Deeds, no. 97. In the 1523 subsidy Moffat's goods were assessed at £4 in value (PRO, Exch. KR, Lay Subsidy Rolls, E 179/113/92).
4 Bristol Record Office, Mayor's Audit Books, 1532 p 15; 1533 p 141; 1535 p 13; 1536 p 85; 1540 p 169. Moffat's house is clearly that held by Ellis Reed, pointmaker in 1535.
5 *The Great Red Book of Bristol,* ed. E. W. W. Veale, vol iii (Bristol Record Soc., xvi, 1950), p 126.
6 See for example the Mayors' Audit Books, 1542 p 107, and entries from then until 1552 pp 47, 55, 57 (last reference), and 67.

merchant Robert Thorne who died in 1532 and established by his executors during the following years.[1] The second, now the Cathedral School, was attached by Henry VIII to the cathedral which he created in the former abbey of St Augustine in 1542.[2] These new schools differed from their predecessors. They were stable foundations with endowments and governors, offering free education unlike the earlier schools which could only subsist on fees. Both schools have survived into modern times. Consequently the 1530s and 40s can be said to conclude the medieval period and to begin a new era in the history of education in Bristol.

EXETER
Devon

The history of medieval Exeter is that of a 'modest provincial town' which grew at the end of the middle ages into a city of national importance.[3] Its pre-eminence in local government was very ancient. As the administrative centre of the third largest county and diocese in England, it was always a place of resort for clerks and litigants from the rest of Devon and Cornwall. Like other towns it served the surrounding countryside with necessary trades and crafts. As a trading port, however, its size at first was modest, and so was its population. In 1377 the inhabitants are thought to have numbered between 2,500 and 3,000. This made Exeter the largest town between the Mendips and Land's End, but left it well behind Bristol, Gloucester and Salisbury within the west of England as a whole, and only twenty-third in the national league. The change in its fortunes came at the end of the fifteenth century, when a flourishing cloth industry grew up in Devon generally and at Exeter in particular. The rise of the guild of weavers and tuckers testifies to this development. The demand for cloth abroad was a stimulus to shipping, and the city soon became the centre of a valuable trade with France and Spain, in which cloth and tin changed hands for wine, linen, iron and other commodities. The growing prosperity of the early Tudor period led to a rise of population. By the 1520s it had reached about 8,000, more than doubling the figure of 1377 and causing the relative position of Exeter to jump from twenty-third to sixth. On the eve of the Reformation it was greater than Gloucester, equal with Salisbury and second only to Bristol as far as its nearest rivals were concerned.

Just as trade and local government drew people into Exeter, so too did education. Many of the boys who went to the grammar school or 'high school' of the medieval city were probably members of the local community, but others, as will appear, were drawn from all over Devon and Cornwall. There were thus two kinds of scholars, natives and immigrants, but their relative numbers were not necessarily constant. During the twelfth and thirteenth centuries when the city was small, the immigrants may have predominated, especially if there was a shortage of schools in the outlying towns. By early Tudor times

---

1 *The Great Orphan Book,* ed. Wadley, p 180. For the history of this school see C. P. Hill, *Bristol Grammar School* (London, 1951).
2 *VCH Gloucs.,* ii, 379.
3 E. M. Carus-Wilson, *The Expansion of Exeter at the Close of the Middle Ages* (Exeter, 1963), pp 1–35.

when the city was larger and local schools were plentiful, the majority may have been natives. If such a shift occurred, it would explain why the Exeter schools do not appear to have changed very much in organisation or character during the fourteenth, fifteenth and even the sixteenth centuries, despite the changes in the city itself. Speculations of this kind are tempting, but they are also dangerous. More has survived about the early history of education in Exeter than almost anywhere else outside London and the university towns, but the evidence remains limited. The exact relationship between medieval cities and their schools is still a mystery.

Within the city, education was a matter of interest to both the clergy and the laity. The latter were involved with scholars in as much as they sold the food and lodgings required by those who came from a distance. Perhaps they also distributed a little by way of alms to those who were poor. Formally however the Exeter schools were the concern of the clergy, particularly those of the cathedral chapter. Each level of local education came under the care of one of its dignitaries. The study of theology was the responsibility of the chancellor, the grammar school was supervised by the archdeacon of Exeter, and the precentor and succentor had the oversight of the song school. The cathedral also supported education in an economic sense. Since it maintained and educated a number of boys and youths in its choir, it provided what were effectively scholarships for students with good voices. Individual canons and dignitaries also left money in their wills for poor scholars to be educated.[1] Finally two important clerics were responsible for major benefactions. It was a dean who provided the grammar school with new buildings in 1344, and a bishop who endowed the scholarships at St John's in 1332. Both these facilities endured throughout the following two centuries, until the Reformation.[2]

Like most of the other English secular foundations, Exeter Cathedral maintained and educated two groups of boys and youths during the middle ages: the choristers and the secondaries. The choristers, who were fourteen in number by 1236, came under the nominal direction of the precentor, who admitted and supervised them.[3] In practice however the precentor had already relinquished their day to day supervision to his deputy, the succentor, by the end of the thirteenth century. In 1276 the dean and chapter, with the precentor's approval, granted the song schoolhouse and the office of succentor for life to Elias of Cirencester, one of the vicars choral. He promised in return to build a new house at his own expense for the use of the succentor, the choristers and the song school.[4] At this time the succentor appears to have been both the supervisor of the choristers and their trainer, but later on he followed the precentor's example and transmitted these duties to inferior officers. By 1528 the choristers were being trained by the clerk of the Lady Chapel, and in 1544 one of the vicars choral was appointed to be their supervisor and 'provider of their needs'.[5]

1 See for example the wills in *Reg. Stafford, Exeter,* ed. F. C. Hingeston-Randolph, pp 379–423.
2 See below, pp 47–9.
3 On the choristers in general see Exeter Dean & Chapter 600; statutes of 1268 in British Museum, MS Harley 1027 fo 11; Bodleian Library, MS Rawl. statutes 38 fos 2v–3, MS Wood empt. 9 fo 4v.
4 *Reg. Bronescombe, Exeter,* ed. F. C. Hingeston-Randolph (1889), pp 77–8.
5 Dean & Chapter 3551 fo 52v; 3552 fo 37.

We must therefore picture the choristers living together in a special house with an adult cleric to look after them. In 1554 the song school was a building next to the deanery, immediately opposite the south-west corner of the cathedral nave, and it may be that this represents the ancient site.[1] The choristers presumably occupied a room adjacent to the school. They had no kitchen of their own, since they depended for food upon the charity of the canons in residence. This involved them calling at the canons' houses to receive the left-overs. A document of 1547 describes with some disapproval how, when the canons were absent, the choristers had no certainty of provisions, how they often took their dinners and suppers at undue times, became distempered through eating unwholesome meat, and fell into the danger of corruption from the canons' serving men.[2] The boys also received a small sum of money from the dean and chapter for their other expenses. In 1234 Bishop Brewer assigned them 6s. 8d. each out of the church of Alternun in Cornwall, and this sum was gradually augmented by other donations. At the middle of the sixteenth century it reached a total of 26s. 8d.[3]

The choristers' duties were twofold. They joined the canons and vicars in the choral services proper, and they also took part in the worship of the Virgin which was organised separately. This involved them in at least some attendance at the Lady chapel, where the mass and hours of the Virgin were said each day, and in the singing of antiphons in her praise every night at the north door of the church.[4] The importance of these devotions provides the likely reason why the succentor's responsibility for training the boys eventually passed to the clerk of the Lady chapel. Unlike their successors today, the choristers only joined the canons and vicars on Sundays and festivals during term, because of their work in school. During the holidays, on the other hand, they came to the high mass and the whole of the daily office, in further contrast with the modern custom. This tells us something about medieval attitudes to leisure. It was not considered desirable for boys to be given an absolute vacation, and they changed rather than rested, from choir to school and back again. Their lessons must have centred upon the study of song in the school adjacent to their own dwelling, but it can hardly be doubted that they also learnt grammar. Grammar was studied by the choristers of most of the medieval secular cathedrals, and this was certainly so at Exeter after the Reformation. As we do not hear of a special grammar master of the choristers, it is likely that they attended the city grammar school for the purpose, as was the case at Salisbury.

Above the choristers came the twelve secondaries, who sat on the second form in the choir below the stalls of the canons and vicars. The secondaries were adolescents and young men: sometimes choristers who had been promoted after the breaking of their voices, sometimes subdeacons and deacons who were not yet old enough to be ordained priests. As a result their ages probably ranged from fifteen to twenty-five. They were appointed

1 Ethel Lega-Weekes, *Some Studies in the Topography of the Cathedral Close, Exeter* (1915), pp 74–6.
2 Dean & Chapter 3674 p 56.
3 Ibid., 600; statutes of 1544 in MS Rawl. statutes 38 p 41; Devon Record Office, Reg. Veysey, Exeter, ii, fo 103.
4 *Ordinale Exon*, ed. J. M. Dalton, vol i (Henry Bradshaw Soc., xxxvii, 1909), pp 5–7.

by the dean, who was ordered to choose candidates who could sing well and were adequately lettered. Their surnames, and what can be gathered of their biographies, suggest that they came not only from Exeter but from various parts of Devon and also from Cornwall. They did not live in a community of their own, like the choristers, but seem to have lodged individually with the twelve senior canons, who gave them their meals and no doubt supervised and patronised them informally. They each received an annual payment of 40s. from the chapter, in return for which they had to assist in the choral services and the cult of the Virgin. They learnt song in the song school, and grammar in the high school of the city where they were expected to pay the master's fees out of their own stipends.[1] Their time on the second form varied from a few months to four or five years, though a handful stayed on for longer, probably as the holders of other minor offices in the cathedral. Their later careers also varied widely. About half are known to have been ordained priests in the early fifteenth century. Some of these were given posts at the cathedral as vicars-choral and chantry priests; others became rectors, vicars and chaplains elsewhere in Devon. The rest, whose ordination is not recorded, may have failed to proceed to holy orders and have taken up secular employment. A handful went on to Oxford. In general, the secondaries seem to have been of modest wealth and status, and none of them is known to have achieved great fame or to have held high office.[2]

Let us now turn to the schools themselves. The earliest references come from the twelfth century, but as is common at that period the word 'school' is used without further qualification, making it difficult at first to be sure what was taught. By the thirteenth century however it becomes possible to distinguish three different schools representing the three principal grades of medieval education: song, grammar, and the higher studies of theology and canon law. The song school is first mentioned in about 1175, in connection with a miracle of St Thomas Becket who had been martyred five years earlier. Bartholomew, bishop of Exeter, was lying sick, when the saint appeared to one of the clerks of the cathedral, named Master Raymund, who taught the boys of the song school. He told the master to make all his scholars sing the psalter on the bishop's behalf, because God had promised to hear them. The little boys who had not yet learnt the psalter completely were to say the Lord's Prayer instead. The work was done, and the bishop recovered.[3] It is not clear what office Master Raymund held in the cathedral, but as we have seen, in 1276 the

1 Dean & Chapter 3551 fos 55v, 62.
2 The names of nearly 400 of the secondaries survive among the Dean and Chapter records; it is hoped to publish the list, with notes, in a forthcoming volume of the *Transactions of the Devonshire Association*. The other principal references are as follows: ordinance of 1236 (Dean & Chapter 600); statutes of 1268 (MS Harl. 1027 fos 11, 17v; MS Rawl. statutes 38 fos 2v–3, MS Wood empt. 9 fo 4v); of 1337 (*Ordinale Exon*, i, 2, 6); visitation of 1337 (*Reg. Grandisson, Exeter,* ed. F. C. Hingeston-Randolph, ii, 857, 859); statutes of 1511 (Devon Record Office, Reg. Oldham, Exeter, fo 145v); ordinance about meals, 1534 (Dean & Chapter 3551 fo 88v); and statutes of 1544 (MS Rawl. statutes 38 p 41; Reg. Veysey, Exeter, vol ii fos 102v–103).
3 The miracle was reported by the clergy of Exeter Cathedral to the prior of Canterbury between 1171 and 1175 (*Materials for the History of Thomas Becket,* ed. J. C. Robertson, vol i (Rolls Series, 1875), p 407).

song school came under the succentor's supervision. This was still the case in 1337, but by the early sixteenth century the clerk of the Lady chapel had become responsible for teaching the choristers, and he presumably directed the song school at this time.[1]

Who attended the song school in the middle ages, and for whom it catered are matters of some difficulty. It may have been the one authorised elementary school of the city, where reading and plainsong were taught to children as a preparation for the study of Latin in the grammar school. This was the case at Lincoln and York, the precentors of which established a monopoly of control over the teaching of song and kept diligent watch for local priests and clerks who attempted to do such teaching in private.[2] At the other extreme the song school may have been merely the place where the choristers and secondaries were taught, with little or no entry from outside. The truth, perhaps, lies in between. We do not hear in Exeter of the precentor or succentor taking action against rival teachers of song as happened at York and Lincoln. There were indeed at least one or two other elementary schools in the city at different times. When William Wynard established his charitable foundation, Godshouse (now known as Wynard's Almshouses) in 1436, he ordered that the chaplain of the foundation, to occupy his time, should teach the alphabet, reading, and the psalter to a number of boys, not less than three nor more than nine, at the cost and expense of their parents and friends.[3] Ninety years later the school which Thomas Bennet, the Protestant heretic, taught in the Butcher Row between 1525 and 1530 may also have included elementary teaching, for he is said previously to have taught *young* children in Torrington.[4] It was generally recognised too that a priest could teach one boy to read and sing in order to wait upon him at mass, and there was a similar custom that parish clerks could train the choristers needed in their churches. It therefore looks unlikely that the Exeter song school enjoyed a complete monopoly of elementary education. At the same time the absence of much other information about elementary teaching and the distinction drawn by the document of 1276 between the choristers and the song school suggest, albeit very faintly, that the song school was open to a wider audience than the junior members of the cathedral alone.

We come next to the grammar school. There can be little doubt that it already existed by the second half of the twelfth century, partly by analogy with the other secular cathedral cities and partly because of the undoubted study of theology at Exeter during that period. Clerks who studied theology must first have become proficient in grammar. It was at any rate a settled institution by about 1225, the approximate date when the office of chancellor

---

1 MS Rawl. statutes 38 p 41; Reg. Veysey, Exeter, vol ii, fo 103. Nicholas Toker was appointed clerk of the chapel on 10 November 1535 (Dean & Chapter 3551 fo 95). He occurs as 'chorustagogus' or instructor of the choristers at Magdalen College, Oxford, in 1532 (J. R. Bloxam, *A Register of Magdalen College, Oxford,* vol iii (1863), p 20).
2 *ESMA*, pp 64–6.
3 Exeter, East Devon Record Office, ED/WA/2; G. Oliver, *Monasticon Dioecesis Exoniensis* (1846), p 406.
4 John Foxe, *Acts and Monuments,* ed. J. Pratt (London, 1870), v, 18–26. The information about Bennet was supplied by John Hooker, who further records that he was a Cambridge MA and a married man (Synopsis Corographicall in Exeter, East Devon Record Office, p 109).

was established in the cathedral. In every one of the other eight secular cathedral foundations it was the chancellor who appointed the grammar schoolmaster. At Exeter alone this duty belonged to the archdeacon, which implies that a system of appointing masters was already well established by the 1220s. For the rest of the middle ages, in fact until 1547, the masters of the grammar school were appointed by the archdeacons of Exeter or, if the archdeaconry were vacant, by the bishop.[1] The master had a monopoly of teaching grammar in the city and by 1384 this extended for seven miles into the country round.[2] He received no stipend and lived wholly from the fees of his pupils, a rate of 6d. a term being apparently charged until 1529 when it was raised to one shilling.[3] By 1537, if not before, he had an usher to assist him.[4] But he had little or no connection with the cathedral itself. He had neither stall nor duties in the choir; his school lay outside the cathedral close; and it was invariably referred to as 'the high school' or 'the grammar school of the city', not 'of the cathedral'.

The site of the high school in the thirteenth century lay in Smythen Street, the middle section of the way which led from South Street parallel with Fore Street, towards the West Gate.[5] This was not far from Preston Street where the parish clergy lived before the city was divided into parishes in 1222. An entry in the mayor's court rolls records how on 23 March 1288 as the clerks of the grammar school were making their way homewards, one of them, named Nyweton, spied Henna the Jewess in South Street and threw stones at her, drawing blood and causing her to raise the hue and cry.[6] It is easy to imagine the clerks coming out of Smythen Street into South Street, and it is possible that the school remained in this area until the middle of the fourteenth century when it was provided with new accommodation by Richard Brayleigh, the dean of Exeter. Brayleigh was a protégé of Walter Stapledon, the great local benefactor of education, and seems to have shared his patron's interests.[7] His own contribution to the subject was to pay for a new schoolroom and a dwelling house for the schoolmaster on the north side of the High Street towards the East Gate, next to an alley called Christchurch Lane which has since disappeared.[8] On 26 January 1344 when the buildings, it seems, had just been completed, the schoolmaster,

1 As in 1515 (Dean & Chapter 2477).
2 British Museum, MS Harley 3300 p 166, a reference kindly brought to my notice by Mrs A. M. Erskine.
3 Dean & Chapter 3551 fo 55v. But see also fo 62.
4 *LPFD*, xii, part i, no 30. The usher, a young man of a romantic temper, went off with an Oxford scholar to Cardiff, allegedly to learn Welsh, and thence to Ross-on-Wye where he hoped to open a school.
5 A rent in Smythen Street 'where the school used to be' was given to St John's Hospital by Denise Blund, probably in the early thirteenth century (Exeter, East Devon Record Office, St John's Hospital Cartulary, fo 36 col 2). 'Used' is in relation to the much later date of the cartulary.
6 Exeter, East Devon Record Office, Mayor's Court Rolls 16/17 Edward I m 25d, a reference kindly communicated by Mr A. Jackson.
7 Richard Brayleigh held various parishes in Devon and Cornwall before being appointed sub-dean of Exeter by Bishop Stapledon in 1318 (*Reg. Stapeldon, Exeter,* ed. F. C. Hingeston-Randolph, pp 256, 217–18, 252, 236, 247, 212–13, 216–17). He was elected dean of Exeter on 6 September 1335 and died on 13 August 1352 (*Reg. Grandisson, Exeter,* ii, 798; Dean and Chapter 3625 fo ivb).
8 Later called Musgrave's Alley, about halfway between Lloyds Bank and Messrs. Marks & Spencer.

Walter Exbourne, promised on behalf of himself and his successors to pay an annual rent of 24s. while they occupied the premises.[1] In a second document of 25 February 1345 the dean specified that this sum, together with a rent of 26s. 8d. from the cellars underneath the buildings, should be employed to celebrate an annual obit for the repose of his soul. The residue was to be used to help maintain the fabric of the cathedral.[2]

Richard Brayleigh's contribution of new school buildings coincided with an even more important benefaction to learning in Exeter—the foundation of the grammar scholarships in the hospital of St John. These scholarships were in origin the idea of Walter Stapledon, who as bishop of Exeter and treasurer of England had already rendered an important service to English education by his foundation of Exeter College, Oxford in 1314.[3] Exeter College was intended for thirteen scholars of the west of England: eight from Devon, four from Cornwall, and a chaplain chosen by the dean and chapter of Exeter. The scholars when admitted had to be undergraduates of two years standing, and their scholarships were then available to support them for up to thirteen years while they studied the arts course and proceeded to the degree of MA.[4] The establishment of the college had been pretty well completed by about 1324, and Stapledon was then able to turn his attention to further schemes. According to John Grandisson who succeeded him as bishop of Exeter, he decided to follow his university benefaction with another for the study of grammar, and for this purpose he acquired three acres of glebe land in the village of Yarnscombe in north Devon together with the advowson of the church. On 10 April 1326 he was licensed by Edward II to appropriate the church and glebe to the master and brethren of the hospital of St John for purposes which Grandisson later declared to have been the increase of divine worship, the support of boys studying grammar, and the maintenance of prayers for his soul and that of his predecessor Thomas Bitton.[5]

Stapledon did not live to see his plans bear fruit. On 15 October following he was murdered by a London mob during the disturbances which followed the overthrow of Edward II's government by Queen Isabella. It was his successor Grandisson who finally put the scheme into effect, partly at the instance of Stapledon's executors and partly from his own conviction, for Grandisson took a notable interest in school education throughout his life. On 18 November 1332 he therefore carried through the appropriation of Yarnscombe to the hospital of St John and drew up a set of statutes.[6] The revenues of the church, after the deduction of a stipend for the vicar of Yarnscombe, were to support between ten and twelve poor scholars of grammar in the hospital. Up to eight were to be chosen by the master of the high school—two each from the archdeaconries of Barnstaple and Exeter, and one or two each from those of Cornwall and Totnes. Three more were to be selected

[1] Dean and Chapter 2477; 3625 fos 176v–7.
[2] Ibid. 2228.
[3] There are accounts of Stapledon's career in *Reg. Stapeldon, Exeter,* pp viii–xxxiv; *DNB* article by F. C. Hingeston-Randolph; and *BRUO*, iii, 1764–5.
[4] For the organization of Exeter College, Oxford see *VCH Oxon.*, iii, 107–9.
[5] *CPR 1324–7*, p 257.
[6] *Reg. Grandisson, Exeter,* ii, 666–9.

by the dean and precentor of Exeter from among the choristers whose voices had broken, and one was to be nominated by Sir Philip and Lady Eleanor Columbers, lord and lady of the manor of Yarnscombe, and their heirs. The scholars were to have a tutor in grammar, chosen by the master of the hospital, who was to be a priest if possible. His duties were to supervise the scholars both in the hospital and at school, but although he may have helped them with their grammar, he was not their only schoolmaster, for the statutes make it plain that the scholars were to attend the high school. What they received in the hospital was a suitable lodging with straw for making their beds, a daily mess of pottage like that of the brethren themselves, and 5d. apiece per week to buy bread, meat and fish, which the hospital servants were then to cook for them. The tutor received an additional 26s. 8d. per annum. The scholars had to assist in the hospital services on Sundays and festivals, and presumably attended school during the week. They could hold their scholarships for five years, but after this they were expected to go on to higher studies or to receive ordination.

Stapledon thus conceived and Grandisson completed two parallel foundations of thirteen members at Exeter and Oxford. In some respects they anticipated the great double foundations of later times—Winchester and New College, Eton and King's—and Stapledon might be claimed as the first of the long line of philanthropists who founded a school benefaction and a university college. At the same time his originality should not be overemphasised. Whereas most later benefactions of this kind established a link between the school and the college by means of closed scholarships, there was no connection between Stapledon's two foundations. The college had no relations with the hospital, and the education which they both provided was not even contiguous. A scholar who left the hospital to study at Oxford would have had to support himself there for two years before he became eligible to join the college. It remained for William Wykeham in the 1370s to devise an educational endowment in which school and college fitted neatly and harmoniously together.[1] Nevertheless the scholarships in the hospital appear to have been reasonably successful. Their existence permitted up to 38 youths, including the choristers and secondaries, to receive an assisted education in Exeter. Only one or two of the names of the scholars are known, but a succession of Exeter clerics during the fifteenth century left doles of money to support them, which certainly suggests an esteem for the foundation in local circles.[2] There are still nine boys in the hospital in 1535, 'studying grammar and being educated in manners', by which time their allowance had risen to 8d. a week.[3] But the hospital was dissolved in 1540 and the rectory of Yarnscombe granted away by the crown three years later.[4] The scholarships must have come to an end at the same time.

1 Unless one reckons The King's Hall, Cambridge, founded by Edward II in 1317 for boys from the Chapel Royal (A. B. Cobban, *The King's Hall within the University of Cambridge in the Later Middle Ages* (1969)).
2 E.g. *Reg. Stafford, Exeter*, pp 381, 395, 414–15, 418, 421; *Reg. Lacy, Exeter*, ed. G. R. Dunstan, vol iv (Canterbury & York Soc., cxxxvii, (1971), pp 25, 32, 38). John Rowe occurs as a 'poor clerk' of the hospital in 1406 (*Reg. Stafford, Exeter*, pp 394–5), and John Smith is mentioned later in the fifteenth century (below, p 51 n 3).
3 *Valor Ecclesiasticus*, ii, 314.
4 *LPFD*, xv, no 613 (44); xix part i, p 648.

The masters of the high school, as has been mentioned, were appointed by the archdeacons of Exeter, and it is much to be regretted that the records of the medieval archdeacons have not survived. For the masters' names we are dependent on stray references in the bishops' registers and on the fortunate survival of the cathedral fabric rolls. The rent of the school buildings, it will be remembered, had been applied by Dean Brayleigh to the fabric fund, and from 1423 to 1508 the fabric rolls record not only the rent but the names of the masters to whom the school was let. Seventeen masters in all have left traces of their existence between 1329 and the Reformation, and although some of them survive only in name, the total evidence is enough to suggest the type of man who usually presided over the school during this period.[1] The average Exeter schoolmaster before the Reformation was a man of local origin: at least nine of the seventeen were probably born and bred in the west of England. He was either a priest or a clerk in minor orders, but in no instance is he known to have been married. People usually addressed him as 'master', without meaning that he was necessarily a university graduate. Only four or five holders of the office can be certainly identified as graduates, all of them from Oxford. In general they were men of modest status, working away unobtrusively in their school as they expounded their well-worn art to generation after generation. In the early sixteenth century they performed the additional duty of helping to examine the candidates for ordination, when this ceremony was held in Exeter.[2] The only one of them to have left any record of his work is John Borington (1433–48), two of whose tracts on grammar survive in fifteenth-century manuscripts.[3] Borington himself held office for at least fifteen years, and one of his successors, Richard Low, taught intermittently for over thirty, but the average length of service was much shorter. Half a dozen years seem to have been common, after which the occupants managed to escape into more lucrative and less demanding employment. Several gained parochial benefices and ended their lives as rectors or vicars, but of none can it be said that he achieved any great distinction in later life. In this respect they were typical of the profession to which they belonged.

The high school itself included a wide range of pupils, diverse in ages, origins and wealth. The secondaries, as we have seen, were probably drawn from various places in Devon and Cornwall. The scholars of the hospital also represented each of the four archdeaconries. It is likely that many others travelled to Exeter from a distance, either for lack of schools in their own localities or because the high school had a better reputation. Some of them must have been modest in their means. Poor clerks of Devonshire at school in Exeter are mentioned specifically in 1415 when Thomas Barton, one of the cathedral canons, left money in his will to support them.[4] Others were well off. Peter Carew, who went to the high school in the 1520s, was the son of Sir William Carew of Mohun's Ottery near Honiton, and later became well-known as a courtier and soldier. He lodged in

1 For the list of names, and further references, see below, pp 56–7.
2 Devon Record Office, Reg. Oldham, Exeter, fos 82v–95v; Reg. Veysey, Exeter, vol i, ordination lists.
3 See below, p 51.
4 *Reg. Stafford, Exeter,* p 414.

a manner appropriate to his rank, with Thomas Hunt, a leading draper and alderman.[1] There was also a greater diversity of ages than any modern schoolmaster would encounter. Boys in medieval England sometimes began learning grammar at seven or eight, although the youngest pupils of the high school whose ages we know were somewhat older. John Belde and Richard Duellard, who were both at school in 1280, are said to have been twelve, and the same age is given for Richard Farewell in 1510 and Peter Carew in 1526.[2] The upper end of the school, on the other hand, must have included young adults in their early twenties. Several of the secondaries held their offices until they took priest's orders at the age of twenty-five, and it is likely that the younger vicars-choral (as at Salisbury) were also encouraged to attend the school. How the Exeter masters coped with this breadth of age and experience is as uncertain as it is in England as a whole. The system of six organised forms does not appear in English education until the early sixteenth century, and the medieval organisation may have been more informal and *ad hoc*.

Three manuscripts survive which reflect the teaching of grammar at Exeter in the mid-fifteenth century.[3] There does not seem to have been a formally organised curriculum, and each manuscript has a different selection of texts. Some of these texts are clearly local compositions,[4] and most of them were reworked by the scribes to suit their own particular needs. The contents of the manuscripts do, however, show a pattern similar to that of other fifteenth-century schoolbooks. Elementary Latin grammar is taught in simple prose treatises, such as the English *Accedence* and *Informacio* by John Leland, which deal with the parts of speech and constructions, and the Latin *Dominus, que pars?* which is in question and answer form. John Borington's own treatises cover this ground, but are written in Latin with a more advanced format and frame of reference. These elementary texts were supplemented by short Latin works on individual topics—concord, the formation of preterites and supines, or the declension of heteroclite nouns—and by such popular treatises in verse on vocabulary as the *Bursa Latini* and *Os facies mentum*.[5] In addition, the manuscripts contain

1 [John Hooker,] *The Life and Times of Sir Peter Carew, Knight*, ed. J. Maclean (London, 1857), pp 3–5.
2 PRO, Coram Rege Rolls, KB 27/176 rot. 1d, Easter 32 Edward I (kindly communicated by Dr P. Chaplais); John Hooker, *The Description of the City of Excester*, ed. W. J. Harte and others, part ii (Devon & Cornwall Record Soc., 1919), p 20; J. Maclean, op.cit., pp 3–5.
3 The following paragraph and its footnotes were generously contributed by Mr D. Thomson of Keble College, Oxford, who is currently preparing a thesis on 'Middle English Treatises on Grammar Written before 1479'. The three manuscripts are: Cambridge, Gonville & Caius College, MS 417/447, written c. 1450–70 by William Berdon (tonsured 1447, acolyte 1453 (*Reg. Lacy, Exeter*, iv, 211, 248)) and John Smith, who lived 'in domo Sancti Iohanis', i.e. St John's Hospital; British Museum, MS Add. 19046, written in the mid-fifteenth century by John Jon or Jonys and witnessed by [Peter] Carter, both *custores* of Exeter Cathedral (*Reg. Lacy, Exeter*, ii, 210; iv, 14, 33, 36, 40); and Oxford, Bodleian Library, MS Rawlinson D 328, written between 1444 and 1483 by Walter Pollard of Plymouth, whose family were cloth merchants and landowners in Plymouth and Exeter.
4 As well as John Borington's *De Regimine Casibus* (MS Caius fos 24v–46v, and compare MS Add. 19046 fos 75v–81) and *Liber Communis* (MS Caius fos 65v–81), note the *latinitates* of MS Rawlinson fos 120, 121–2; the Latin paragraphs in MS Caius fos 17–24v; and the treatise on differences in grammar in ibid., fos 99v–130; all of which include references to Exeter.
5 Edited by T. Wright, *A Volume of Vocabularies* (Liverpool, 1857), i, 177–82, 183–4 respectively.

several sets of *latinitates*—model Latin sentences which show the theory followed in practical composition. Alongside the grammar we find moral treatises such as the *Distichs of Cato*,[1] and religious matter—the breviary hymns, ten commandments, and an alphabetical Bible epitome—mixed with a variety of scribbled additions which include schoolboy anecdotes, letters and specimen documents. In essence the collections, like the education they reflect, are personal and pragmatic.

Apart from its schools of song and grammar, medieval Exeter, like the other secular cathedral cities, offered facilities for older students to study theology and canon law at a higher level. In the twelfth century, before such studies had become centralised at Oxford and Cambridge, there was a flourishing school of theology at Exeter.[2] Robert Pullen may have taught there before 1133 when he went to Oxford, where we know that he gave lectures.[3] In 1160 a grant of land by the canons of Exeter to the nuns of Polsloe was witnessed by ten scholars, including Nicholas of Flanders and Gilbert of Ireland, who would not have come to Exeter, one feels, merely in order to study grammar.[4] Thomas of Marlborough, who became a monk of Evesham in the late 1190s, is said to have brought with him the books of canon and civil law with which he had ruled the schools of Exeter, while at much the same time (in about 1200) Alexander, prior of Canon's Ashby, mentions Master John of Exeter among the theologians of his time who taught without a fee.[5] This suggests that there was already some kind of arrangement by which the cathedral supported a theological lecturer to teach for nothing.

During the thirteenth century the role of the cathedrals in higher education gradually diminished as the universities came into being. The academic study of theology and canon law became concentrated at Oxford and Cambridge where books and teachers were more plentiful and where degree courses could be followed. Both subjects continued to be taught in the secular cathedral cities, but, it seems, at a more elementary level for the benefit of the local clergy who could not afford the time and expense of going to university. At Exeter, for example, Hugh of Wilton, who was archdeacon of Taunton in 1236, gave three volumes of the New Testament to the cathedral 'for the use of poor scholars', which remained in the library until the early seventeenth century.[6] Finally in 1283 Bishop Quinel established the teaching of theology in Exeter on a firm footing and chose a particular person to look after it. On 20 April of that year he annexed the revenues of the rectory of

1 Edited by M. Boas & H. J. Botschuyer, *Disticha Catonis* (Amsterdam, 1952).
2 The following paragraph is based on Dr Kathleen Edwards, *The English Secular Cathedrals in the Middle Ages* (2nd ed., 1967), pp 186–7.
3 R. L. Poole, 'The Early Lives of Robert Pullen and Nicholas Breakspear', *Essays in Medieval History Presented to T. F. Tout,* ed. A. G. Little & F. M. Powicke (London, 1925), pp 61–3.
4 *Hist. MSS Commission, Report on Various Collections,* vol iv (1907), p 49.
5 *Chronicon Abbatiae de Evesham,* ed. W. D. Macray (Rolls Series, 1863), p 267; R. W. Hunt, 'English Learning in the late Twelfth Century', *Transactions of the Royal Historical Soc.,* 4th series xix (1936), p 20.
6 The volumes are now in the Bodleian Library: MS Bodl. 494, MSS Auct. D.1.7, 12 (*A Summary Catalogue of Western MSS in the Bodleian Library,* ed. F. Madan & H. H. E. Craster, vol ii part i (1922), nos 2108, 2133, 2629).

Newlyn in Cornwall to the office of chancellor in the cathedral and laid down that all future chancellors should lecture in Exeter on theology or canon law. No one was to be appointed chancellor unless he were able to discharge this duty, but if the incumbent of the office were prevented by illness, he could, with the bishop's permission, appoint a suitable graduate in theology or canon law to lecture on his behalf.[1]

For at least the next fifty years the chancellor's lectures appear to have been given in a regular fashion. In 1283 two local clergymen, the vicar of South Tawton and the rector of Sydenham Damerel, were licensed to reside away from their benefices in order to study theology at Exeter.[2] Under the two great patrons of education, Stapledon and Grandisson, chancellors who wished to lecture by deputy had to seek formal permission to do so. A dispensation from lecturing between April and October 1310 was given to Roger Ottery, but only because he had just become chancellor and was not in receipt of emoluments. He had to negotiate a second licence shortly afterwards when he wished to appoint a deputy to teach for a year.[3] There was another suspension of lectures from October 1322 until the following Michaelmas, but again it involved a new chancellor, Henry Newton, and the interim, during which he was allowed to attend university, may well have allowed him to prepare his course.[4] In 1334 Bishop Grandisson permitted Walter Meriet to lecture by deputy, in recognition of his 'knowledge, honesty of morals, and distinction of birth', and although Meriet was really a rogue with whom Grandisson was soon to cross swords over non-residence and other villainies, we never hear, despite all the other charges that were made against him, that the duty of lecturing was not being done.[5]

After the middle of the fourteenth century the history of the lectures becomes obscure, at Exeter as at most of the other secular cathedrals, and the question arises whether they did indeed continue. Two things suggest that they did, in the absence of evidence to the contrary. First, of the seventeen chancellors who ruled between 1246 and the Reformation, all but two had degrees in theology or canon law and would have been able to discharge their educational duties.[6] One of them, John Orum (1429–36), is known to have given lectures at Wells before he became chancellor.[7] Second, the memory of the institution survived into the era of the Reformation. As we shall see, Bishop Veysey's synopsis of the cathedral statutes, Dean Heynes's proposals for their reform, and the royal visitation of 1547, all take it for granted that there is, or should be, a personage—either the chancellor or his deputy— with the duty of lecturing to an audience on theology at due and customary times.

1 Dean and Chapter 2109; *Report on Various Collections,* iv, 71–2.
2 *Regg. Bronescombe and Quivel, Exeter,* p 375.
3 *Reg. Stapeldon, Exeter,* p 152.
4 Ibid.
5 *Reg. Grandisson, Exeter,* ii, 757–8, and cf. pp 851–2, 910–11.
6 For the list of chancellors see J. Le Neve, *Fasti Ecclesiae Anglicanae, 1300–1541,* vol ix, ed. Joyce M. Horn (1964), pp 8–10.
7 *BRUO,* ii, 1406.

When the Reformation began in the 1530s the schools of Exeter were very much as they had been in Grandisson's time. A grammar master appointed by the archdeacon still taught for fees in Brayleigh's schoolhouse and Stapledon's scholars were still being maintained in St John's Hospital. At the cathedral a synopsis of the statutes made by Bishop Veysey in 1544 reveals that the chancellor was still bound to lecture and that the precentor had still to provide for the maintenance of the choristers. There were still fourteen choristers, and twelve secondaries appointed by the dean.[1] But by 1544 there was beginning to be pressure for change. The king was converting the old monastic cathedrals into new secular foundations, their schools were becoming free, and their schoolmasters more closely integrated with the cathedral chapters. The situation at Exeter, where the school was not free, was becoming an anomaly, especially after the disappearance of the Stapledon scholarships in 1540. The dean of Exeter, Simon Heynes, was a strong supporter of reform who subsequently became an active Protestant, and at about this time he submitted a series of proposals for remodelling the cathedral to Henry VIII.[2] The foundation, he suggested, should be reorganised on apostolic lines with a 'pastor' (the former dean) and eleven preachers instead of prebendaries. The chancellor's lectures in theology should continue to be read by a 'learned man in holy scripture' with a salary of £26. 13s. 4d. Two free schools were to be established at the cathedral, one for song and one for grammar. The song school would include a master and forty children receiving food and clothing. He was to teach them to read—not only in Latin but in Greek and Hebrew—and also to write, sing, and play upon instruments. The grammar school would be staffed by a master and usher, with salaries of £20 and £10 each, and a house. They were apparently to teach all comers freely and sixty of their poor scholars were to receive exhibitions of a shilling a week so that they might buy their food in the city. For those who had mastered the study of grammar, there ought to be twelve scholarships to Oxford and twelve to Cambridge, the whole expenses being borne by the cathedral.

Heynes's proposals bear some resemblance to the schemes which the king and his advisers were currently instituting in the remodelled monastic cathedrals, but they were also more expensive, and in any case Henry never got around to reforming the old secular foundations. It was not until after his death in January 1547 that the situation became more favourable for cathedral reform, with the establishment of an openly Protestant regime under Protector Somerset. In the autumn of 1547 a royal visitation of the whole clergy of England was set in motion, and new injunctions were drawn up for the cathedrals in particular. The most important of these from the educational point of view provided that each cathedral still lacking a free grammar school should maintain one out of its own revenues, paying £13. 6s. 8d. to a schoolmaster and half as much to an usher, with accommodation.[3] Four royal commissioners, including Heynes, accordingly visited Exeter Cathedral in October 1547 but, not content with administering the king's general

---

1 Reg. Veysey, Exeter, ii, fos 100v–105v; G. Oliver, *Lives of the Bishops of Exeter* (1861), pp 471–6.
2 Ibid., pp 477–83. They must date from between 1537 and 1547.
3 W. H. Frere, *Visitation Articles and Injunctions of the Period of the Reformation* (Alcuin Club, xiv–xvi, 1910), ii, 139; Dean and Chapter, 3674 pp 28–35.

injunctions, they proceeded to order other changes in its constitution, with particular emphasis on its role in education.[1] The choristers, who had hitherto begged their victuals from the canons' houses, were to be fed at a common table in the hall of the vicars choral. The secondaries were to be abolished and replaced by twelve scholars of grammar chosen by preference from among the choristers whose voices had broken. They were still to be nominated by the dean, to receive £3. 6s. 8d. a year, and to attend the choir on Sundays and festivals. The high school was not only to become free, but the nomination of the master and usher was to be taken away from the archdeacon of Exeter and given to the dean and chapter. Finally the chancellor's lectures in theology were to be given in English, instead of the traditional Latin, and all the cathedral clergy were to attend them if possible: the prebendaries by preference and the vicars under compulsion.

These measures were less revolutionary than those which Heynes himself had proposed but their effect, nonetheless, was short-lived. The dean and chapter appear to have paid the schoolmasters while Edward lived, but under Mary and Elizabeth there was a gradual reversion to the old state of affairs. The high school remained in the High Street and failed to become a cathedral school; in 1559 even the queen's injunctions called it the school of the town.[2] The archdeacon recovered his right of appointment, and in 1569 the school ceased to be free, the dean and chapter exacting a promise from the schoolmaster that he would not ask for his salary.[3] In short, the Reformers' intentions were largely frustrated, and the school survived the religious upheavals firmly stamped with its medieval character. Although one or two other masters were licensed to teach in Exeter under Elizabeth and James, it was not until the reign of Charles I that the high school ceased to be the main source of education in the city. There is something to be said for fixing the end of the medieval period as late as 1631, when the cathedral and the corporation agreed to open a new free school, the present Exeter School. In the acquisition of two grammar schools, to say nothing of free education, Exeter lagged behind Bristol, Gloucester and Salisbury by two or three generations. As for the high school, it lingered into the eighteenth century, still operating for fees in Richard Brayleigh's premises, until it came to a final end in 1750.[4]

1 Ibid., pp 55–6, 59.
2 W. H. Frere, op. cit., iii, 43.
3 Dean and Chapter 2477.
4 H. Ll. Parry, *The Founding of Exeter School* (1913), pp 15–58, 80–3.

MASTERS OF EXETER HIGH SCHOOL

1	John Sevenaysshe, MA	occurs 1329
2	Walter Exbourne, *Mag.*	occurs 1344
3	John Lucas, *Mag.*	instituted 1384, still in 1388
4	John Spenser	instituted 1389
5	Richard Maister	occurs 1423–31
6	John Borington, *Mag.*	occurs 1433–48
7	John Hanley, *Mag.*	occurs 1451–2
8	Laurence Bodington, *Mag.*	occurs 1452–7
9	John Major, M Gram	occurs 1460
10	Richard Low, *Mag.*	occurs 1461–5 and 1486–94
11	Henry Oakwith, *Mag.*	occurs 1479–80
12	William Every	occurs 1505
13	William Andrew	occurs 1505–6
14	John Calwoodleigh	occurs 1507–8
15	Thomas David, MA	instituted 1515, probably till 1521
16	Philip Fryer, M Gram, BCL	probably instituted 1521, still in 1526
17	Walter Hart, *Mag.*	dismissed 1555

1 *Reg. Grandisson, Exeter*, i, 240. For his life see *BRUO*, iii, 1672.
2 Exeter Dean & Chapter 2477, 3625. One of this name was coadjutor to the rector of Lifton, Devon, till 9 March 1329 (*Reg. Grandisson, Exeter*, i, 216–17, 473), and another was rector of Zeal Monachorum, Devon, instituted 14 November 1349 (ibid., iii, 1401).
3 British Museum, MS Harley 3300, p 166; Dean & Chapter 2648. Although undated, the Harley reference is evidently contemporary with Archbishop Courtenay's visitation of Exeter in 1384. It describes Lucas as a clerk.
4 Dean & Chapter 3550 fo 47.
5 Ibid., 2678–83. He was a secondary of Exeter Cathedral, 1409–19 (ibid., 2594/3–2595/5) and was ordained acolyte on 24 September 1418 (Reg. Stafford, Exeter, fo 295). Rector of St Pancras, Exeter, in 1421, till death. Died by July 1454 (*Reg. Lacy, Exeter* vol i, ed. F. C. Hingeston-Randolph, pp 15, 384).
6 Dean & Chapter 2685–93. His first appearance is as a secondary of the cathedral, 1425–8 (ibid., 2595/9–12). He was ordained acolyte in 1437, deacon 8 March 1438, priest 28 February 1439 (*Reg. Lacy, Exeter*, ed. G. R. Dunstan, ii, 42; iv, 166, 171). Rector of St Mary Major, Exeter, (patrons, Dean and Chapter), instituted 30 April 1437, till death (ibid., vol i, ed. F. C. Hingeston-Randolph, pp 220, 339). Licensed to study at Oxford for two years, 24 March 1438 (ibid., ii, 79). Died by June 1449.
7 Dean & Chapter 2696.
8 Ibid., 2697–2701. He was born in Salisbury diocese, but was living in Exeter diocese by 1449 when ordained acolyte (*Reg. Lacy, Exeter*, iv, 224). He occurs as a secondary of the cathedral, 1456–7, and was dead by 31 January 1458, having bequeathed ten marks to the college of vicars choral (ibid., 3675 fo 66v).
9 Ibid., 2702. He was admitted M Gram at Oxford in 1452 (*The Register of Congregation, 1448–63*, ed. W. A. Pantin & W. T. Mitchell (Oxford Historical Soc., new series xxii, 1972), pp 127–8.) He was in priest's orders by 1454 and was rector of St Mary Steps, Exeter, collated 3 June 1454,

vacated by October 1465 (*Reg. Lacy, Exeter,* vol i, ed. F. C. Hingeston-Randolph (1909), p 384; Devon Record Office, Reg. Bothe, Exeter, fo 3).
10 Dean & Chapter 2703/1–2, 2704/3–4. He is perhaps the same as the fellow of Exeter College in *BRUO,* ii, 1169.
11 Dean & Chapter 2704/2.
12 Reg. Oldham, Exeter, fo 82v. *Dominus.* Was he the same as the next?
13 Dean & Chapter 2704/5. *Dominus.* He is probably the same as Sir William Andrew, usher of Magdalen College School, Oxford, in 1497 (*BRUO,* i, 36).
14 Dean & Chapter 2704/6.
15 Ibid., 2477. His career was probably as follows: fellow of Exeter College, Oxford, 1507–13; MA 1509 (*BRUO,* iv, 164); master of Exeter School, 1515–21, since an examining chaplain at Exeter 1520–1 (Reg. Veysey, Exeter, i, ordination lists); vicar of Salcombe Regis, Devon (patrons, Dean & Chapter), resigned 1533 (ibid., i, fo 70v); chantry priest of Exeter Cathedral but with other duties, 1541–4 (Dean & Chapter 3552, fos 18v, 23v, 33).
16 Philip Fryer was usher of Magdalen College School, Oxford, 1518–21, not till 1523 as in J. R. Bloxam, *Register of the Members of Magdalen College, Oxford* (Oxford, 1853–85), iii, 80. Master Philip Fryer was an examining chaplain at Exeter, December 1521–34 (Reg. Veysey, Exeter, i, ordination lists). Finally a master named 'Freer' is mentioned as teaching Peter Carew at Exeter school *c.* 1526 (John Hooker, *The Life and Times of Sir Peter Carew, Kt.,* ed. J. Maclean (London, 1857), p 4). For the rest of Fryer's career see *BRUO,* iv, 221.
17 Dean & Chapter 3552 fo 65. He was a secondary of the cathedral until he resigned in 1534 (ibid., 3551 fo 90).

GLOUCESTER

Gloucester was one of the leading English towns throughout the middle ages.[1] Its importance came from its position beside the lowest bridge across the Severn which made it the gateway to Wales, the focus of many roads, and a port with a not inconsiderable traffic both up and down the river. Its strategic value was recognised by the Conqueror who wore his crown there once a year, and until at least the middle of the thirteenth century the English kings came regularly to stay in their palace at Kingsholme. It still had enough political standing under Richard II and the Lancastrians to be chosen as the venue of parliament in 1378, 1407, and 1420. Ecclesiastically it was well provided with its great Benedictine abbey, two Augustinian priories, three houses of friars, and ten parish churches. As the county town it was always a place of much resort, and in the fourteenth and fifteenth centuries it flourished on the cloth trade and the iron manufactures for which it was famous. With 2,239 tax-payers in 1377 and over 3,000 estimated communicants in 1548, its population must have numbered three and a half thousand during the later middle ages. In short it enjoyed favourable conditions for the growth of a flourishing school.

The earliest allusion to the school comes from the beginning of the twelfth century. According to an undated charter of Henry I, 'the schools of all Gloucester' were granted by Samson, bishop of Worcester 1096–1112, to the royal free chapel of St Oswald in the town. Henry's charter was a confirmation of this grant.[2] The charter itself only exists in a

1 For a sketch of its medieval history see M. D. Lobel & J. Tann, 'Gloucester', *Historic Towns,* ed. M. D. Lobel, vol i (1969), pp 1–11.
2 *CPR 1385–9,* p 525.

later confirmation by Richard II in 1388 at a time when St Oswald's, as we shall see, was very anxious to establish its rights to control the schools of Gloucester. Yet although the phrase '*all* Gloucester' is a little suspicious, being uncommon in grants of this kind, there is no reason to doubt the rest of the charter. Gloucester is the sort of town where we should expect to find early signs of a school, and if Samson were looking about for some stable authority to control it, St Oswald's was the obvious candidate. It was staffed by six secular canons having a perpetual corporate existence, yet not prevented by religious vows from attending to a worldly matter like public education.[1] The monks of St Peter's Abbey, the only other religious community then existing in Gloucester, were undeniably less suitable in this respect, and in any case Samson appears to have disliked monks—hence the choice of St Oswald's.

There is no further notice of St Oswald's in connection with local education for over 150 years. We next hear of Gloucester school in quite a different quarter. In 1136 a third religious house was founded in the town, or rather in its southern suburbs—the priory of Lanthony, of the order of Augustinian canons. This order, as we have seen at Bristol, often became involved in supervising schools in the twelfth century, and the involvement of Lanthony was due to Henry II. At some time after 1154 he granted the canons the chapel in the castle of Gloucester and 'one school' (*unam scolam*) in the town. The charter itself does not survive, but it was confirmed by Richard I in 1198 and by John in the following year.[2] Meanwhile three of the bishops of Worcester, Roger (1163–79) and his two successors Baldwin and William of Northall, had added their own confirmations, so that we can put back Lanthony's acquisition of a school to at least 1179[3]. The grant was to cause much trouble in the future. We do not know why it was made. St Oswald's appears to have had a continuous existence as a royal free chapel until about 1153 when it too was made into a priory of Augustinian canons. It is suggestive that all the early charters of Lanthony mention 'one school', a term unique in twelfth-century school grants, which makes it appear as if Lanthony was being given only partial rights. Perhaps at one stage there were two schools, each under the control of one of the two Augustinian houses, but this cannot have been for long. All the indications suggest that by the late twelfth century St Oswald's had ceased to be actively concerned with education in Gloucester

---

1 The best history of St Oswald's is A. Hamilton Thompson, 'The Jurisdiction of the Archbishops of York in Gloucestershire', *TBGAS*, xliii (1921), pp 85–180, which supersedes the account in *VCH Gloucs.*, ii, 84–7.
2 Lanthony Cartulary (PRO, Chancery Masters' Exhibits, C 115), vol A 2; *Rotuli Chartarum, 1199–1216*, ed. T. D. Hardy (Record Commission, 1837), p 7. The Lanthony Cartulary (some of the volumes are actually registers) comprises 14 volumes numbered A1–A14, but that numbered A13 should perhaps be A10. Another A13 is in the possession of Lord Vestey of Stowell Park, Northleach, and is here cited by that number. Lady Vestey kindly gave me access to the MS in 1964. The cartulary was extensively used by Richard Furney, the eighteenth-century historian, in his MS history of Gloucester (Bodleian Library, MS Top. Glouc. c. 4–5). Since Furney's extracts are always found to be accurate when they can be checked against the cartulary, I have cited him on occasions when it has been difficult or impossible to find the original reference.
3 Cartulary, A1, A2, A4 fo clxxxi–ii.

and that Lanthony's 'one school' became the general school of the town. We hear of two schools in Gloucester only on the two or three later occasions when St Oswald's tried to reassert its ancient rights.

Little is known of the early school of Gloucester. It was almost certainly a grammar school and may have taught song as well. The canons of Lanthony would have appointed a series of secular priests, clerks, or laymen as schoolmasters. One, Master Roger, 'rector of the school of Gloucester', occurs in 1203.[1] By 1396 the canons also owned the schoolhouse on the corner of Bull Lane and Smith Street, which they rented out to the master.[2] He would have taught for fees, and considering the size and importance of Gloucester he probably made a deal of money. The schoolmastership was as good as a benefice, worth possessing and worth having in your gift. It may have been envy at this, together with the memory of Samson's grant, which led the canons of St Oswald's to challenge Lanthony in 1286 by opening or patronising a rival school. The animosity which this caused in Lanthony is a good indication of the long-standing monopoly which its schoolmasters had enjoyed over local education. Lanthony appealed for support to the bishop of Worcester, Godfrey Giffard. He was all the more ready to give it because St Oswald's had long been a thorn in the side of his diocese. Since before 1100 the site of the priory together with half a dozen parishes to the north of Gloucester had constituted a peculiar jurisdiction under the direct control of the archbishops of York. This territory, the 'jurisdiction of Churchdown', lay like an island in the middle of Worcester diocese, free of control not only by the bishop but by the archbishop of Canterbury himself. So on 21 November 1286 Giffard wrote to the archdeacon of Gloucester reminding him that the schools of Gloucester, where scholars gathered both from the diocese and from elsewhere, had belonged to Lanthony since ancient times. No one was to teach in the town except for the master appointed by Lanthony, and any other schools which existed were to be suspended. The prohibition was to be announced by the parish clergy of Gloucester and its neighbourhood in their churches on three successive Sundays.[3]

It is curious that the bishop's resolute support for Lanthony's claims should have been followed on 31 January 1287 by a more tentative enquiry to his diocesan official as to who had the right of teaching scholars in Gloucester.[4] But since St Oswald's lay outside the bishop's legal jurisdiction his orders could have no effect, and it appears that the aggrieved parties resorted to force against the rival school. On 13 December 1289 John Romeyn, archbishop of York, wrote to Giffard complaining that he had oppressed the convent of St Oswald's by taking from them their rights over the schools of Gloucester which had

1 MS Top. Glouc. c. 4, p 192.
2 See below, p 61.
3 Giffard's ordinance, although confirmed by at least three later bishops, does not appear in an episcopal register until 1513 (HWRO, Reg. Silvestro de Gigli, Worcester, fos 202v–3).
4 *Reg. Giffard, Worcester,* ed. J. W. Willis-Bund, vol ii (Worcs. Historical Soc., 1902), p 305. A. F. Leach (*VCH Gloucs.,* ii, 316) supposed that this command preceded Giffard's ordinance, which he wrongly dated 1287, but both belong to the nineteenth year of the bishop which ran from September 1286 to September 1287. Giffard's ordinance therefore preceded the enquiry to his official.

been in their gift from ancient times. He asked the bishop to revoke the penalties he had laid upon the priory and its schoolmaster and to desist from such actions in future. After receiving an answer from Giffard, Romeyn sent a second letter repeating his request and expressing the hope that thereby mutual peace might grow.[1] The outcome is not certain, but it is most likely that Lanthony emerged victorious and that St Oswald's school eventually came to nothing. The larger quarrel between the bishop and the archbishop over their respective jurisdictions continued fiercely for a good deal longer, without any alteration to the *status quo*.

For almost a century there is little record of education in Gloucester[2], but we may assume that Lanthony continued to manage the general school. The charter of John which had confirmed Henry II's original grant was inspected and again confirmed by both Edward II and his son.[3] Walter Sigrith and Edward Cleche are mentioned as schoolmasters in the reign of Richard II and both seem to have local surnames.[4] St Oswald's on the other hand was distracted by a rapid succession of priors in the fourteenth century, and it suffered badly from the great plagues. In 1356 Archbishop Thoresby warned that ruin would overwhelm the house unless some remedy were found quickly.[5] These difficulties may have left little opportunity for a new challenge to Lanthony, but greater stability seems to have returned with the priorship of Thomas Duke during the last quarter of the century. It was in his reign that a fresh attempt was made to dispute the appointment of schoolmasters.

St Oswald's seems to have re-opened a grammar school in about 1380. Once again Lanthony prepared to resist the encroachment, and the documents which marked the successive stages of the battle were carefully recorded in its registers. The opening sallies, like those of the thirteenth century, consisted of the hurling of censures by the episcopal supporters of Lanthony. On 10 April 1380 the bishop of Worcester, Henry Wakefield, confirmed Giffard's ordinance and commanded it to be published again by the beneficed clergy in the town.[6] Next on 28 April 1382 John Nelme, clerk, of Gloucester was ordered to appear in the consistory court at Worcester Cathedral to show why he was publicly teaching boys in grammar to the prejudice of the general school in the town which belonged to Lanthony.[7] Finally in 1384 Archbishop Courtenay made his metropolitical visitation of Worcester diocese and the canons of Lanthony took the opportunity to enlist his support. This took the form of a command, dated 4 November, that the archdeacon and clergy of Gloucestershire should warn all who disturbed or encroached upon the liberties of Lanthony

---

1 *Reg. Romeyn, York,* ed. W. Brown, vol ii (Surtees Soc., cxxviii, 1916), pp 64–6.
2 For an early fourteenth-century reference see *Reg. Trillek, Hereford,* ed. J. H. Parry (Canterbury & York Soc., viii, 1912), p 56.
3 In 1309 and 1340 (*Cal. Charter Rolls,* iii, 128; iv, 470).
4 MS Top. Glouc. c. 4, p 191.
5 *TBGAS,* xliii (1921), p 166.
6 Cartulary, A4 fo clxxx (verso); A6 fo B xliv–v (modern foliation 72–3); A 7 fo 160; Reg. Silvestro de Gigli, fos 202v–3.
7 A13 fo 58. For a contemporary John Nelme see *CPR 1385–9,* p 472.

to appear before him or his commissary and show cause why they so acted.[1] None of the episcopal interventions produced any effect on St Oswald's whatever.

The battle now shifted from the ecclesiastical sphere to that of the crown. The initiative for this came from St Oswald's, which on 17 November 1388 secured a royal inspection and confirmation of its charters, including the original grant of the schools of all Gloucester from Henry I.[2] Its canons were then able to procure the issue of a royal writ on 20 October 1392 against John Hamelin, the master appointed by Lanthony. This ordered him to allow St Oswald's to enjoy its rights over the schools and not to obstruct or annoy them in any way.[3] No effect of the writ is known, and its only result appears to have been to persuade Lanthony also to seek justice from the crown. The canons prepared for this by making a formal grant of the schoolmastership of Gloucester on 1 March 1396, to their master John Hamelin. This was apparently to legalise his title, since he had already been teaching for at least three and a half years. In a formal indenture the canons granted to him their schoolhouse in Smith Street, with a careful description of its boundaries, for a term of forty years if he should live so long, at an annual rent of 24s. payable on the usual quarter days. Hamelin was to keep the tenement and curtilage of the schoolhouse in good repair at his own expense and hand it back in as good a state as he had received it. He might not convey it to anyone else or let it to farm, and should he die, or if he were more than a month behind with his rent, the canons could resume the mastership and the schoolhouse, and dispose of them as they pleased. If Hamelin became ill and could not teach, or if the canons allowed him to study for a year in a university, another suitable person, competent in grammar, might be admitted to deputise for him.[4]

Lanthony and its schoolmaster now took the initiative. On 3 May 1396 they elicited a new confirmation of Giffard's ordinance from Bishop Tideman who had recently succeeded Wakefield.[5] More significantly they secured a royal writ ordering Thomas Duke, the prior of St Oswald's, and Thomas More, formerly schoolmaster in Hereford and now teaching the rival school, to appear at Westminster before the justices of the Common Pleas to explain why they had recently erected a school to the damage of John Hamelin, the lawful schoolmaster, reckoned at £40. A second writ forbade More to infringe the charters of Lanthony and ordered him to allow the house to enjoy its school without impediment.[6] The defendants did not at first comply, for on 9 May 1397 the sheriff was ordered to seize the prior's goods and arrest More to ensure their appearance before the justices in Trinity term.[7] More then came into court and gave sureties for his appearance, after which the

1 MS Top. Glouc. c 5, p 622. This does not appear in Courtenay's own register, but on 3 November he had made his archiepiscopal visitation of Lanthony (Lambeth Palace Library, Reg. Courtenay, fo 127).
2 *CPR 1385–9*, p 525.
3 A7 fo 186; A13 fo 58.
4 A7 fo 187.
5 Ibid. fo 185v; A6 fo B xliv–v (modern folios 72–3).
6 A7 fo 189, A13 fo 57, dated 20 Richard II, probably the second half of 1396.
7 A7 fo 190, A 13 fo 57v.

previous order was cancelled by a writ of *supersedeas*.¹ Meanwhile he was bringing a counter-plea against his opponents, and a writ of the same summer (probably July) ordered the taking of John Hamelin and his safe keeping to appear in Michaelmas term to answer about the grammar school which he had allegedly erected in prejudice to the rights of St Oswald's, at a damage assessed by More at £30.²

We have no record of what happened in the court of Common Pleas but since both sides emerged unscathed it is evident that the court could give no judgment. Recourse to the king was no more successful that it had been to the bishop. The truth was that neither of the rivals could dislodge the other by any legal process since both could justify their claims with charters. The priories were therefore obliged to make their own compromise. On 30 April 1398 two brethren of Lanthony, John Lymnour and Richard Awre, were appointed proctors to negotiate with St Oswald's about the schools.³ But it took two years before an agreement was signed, and in the meantime Hamelin became involved in more trouble. On 30 October 1398 a king's serjeant was ordered to arrest him and two others, and bring them before the king and council. They were said to have extorted large sums of money under colour of a grant of the office of 'searcher' or water-bailiff of the Severn from Thomas, duke of Gloucester, who had been murdered in the previous autumn and whose affairs were now being wound up.⁴

The two houses of Austin canons finally made peace on 7 July 1400 for the sake, or so they said, of the scholars who had been coming uselessly to Gloucester, which implies that the struggle had caused some disorganisation of the schools.⁵ By the agreement St Oswald's granted its grammar school to Lanthony for a period of thirty years, after which both parties were to be free to enjoy their rights. In return Lanthony made monetary concessions: an annual sum of 13s. 4d., and fifteen cocks in Lent when schoolmasters traditionally received the spoils of the Shrove Tuesday cockfighting. The Lanthony schoolmaster was to teach without charge eight boys sent from St Oswald's by way of alms and the undermaster was to walk in processions at St Oswald's on Sundays and festivals. Both houses were to choose a boy bishop for the ceremonies of St Nicholas Day, and to divide the offerings collected in school for the bishop. The two parties bound themselves to observe the convention with sums of £5.

St Oswald's seems then to have abandoned Thomas More, but he remained in Gloucester and continued to draw pupils by charging less than the Lanthony schoolmasters. This provoked the final encounters in the long dispute. In 1409 the prior of Lanthony (John Wyche) together with John Hamelin and Richard Darcy, who was now the undermaster, brought a fresh action against More. On 6 October the sheriff was commanded to take pledges for his appearance in the court of Common Pleas.⁶ The prior of Lanthony could

1 A7 fo 190v; PRO, Plea Rolls, CP 40/544 m 112v.
2 A7 fo 191.
3 A7 fo 198.
4 *CPR 1396–9*, p 441.
5 A7 fo 207.
6 A3 fo 10.

now declare that he held the sole right of appointment to the schools of Gloucester, and More was accused of holding his own school in the town for so long that he had damaged the lawful masters to the extent of £40. But even More had not exhausted all his resources, and he was somehow able to call in his turn on the not inconsiderable aid of the duke of York. A letter survives in French, written apparently to St Oswald's, in which the duke related how More had been put out of the government of the grammar school of Gloucester which he had by its grant, and asked that he should be allowed to enjoy his grant in peace, 'so that he can feel that our request has been worth something to him'. It was useful to have backing of this kind in the middle ages.[1]

The case was finally heard in Hilary term 1410 before the justices of the Common Pleas, headed by the chief justice, William Thirning, along with William Hankford and Robert Hill.[2] The plaintiffs had secured William Skrene as their counsel, while More had retained Roger Horton. Skrene maintained the plaintiffs' case with energy, declaring that More had drawn away their scholars to such an extent that whereas they had formerly taken 2s. or 3s. 4d. apiece from the boys every quarter, they could now get scarcely a shilling. But the judges were not sympathetic, and they each made different points to show why they could not enforce the monopoly claimed by the Lanthony schoolmasters. Hankford and Hill considered that the plaintiffs had no estate of their own in the schools of Gloucester, but merely a ministry for the time being. They had based their action on a grant from the prior of Lanthony, and Thirning observed that whether the prior had the right to collate schoolmasters could not concern the court, for the teaching of children was an ecclesiastical matter. Hankford thought that it would be unreasonable to disturb a master from holding school where he pleased, except in the case of universities or (rather vaguely) 'schools founded in ancient times'. Hill even said that for another master to come and teach children was a virtuous and charitable thing and a convenience for the people. And so the opinion of the judges was that the court could do nothing. The plaintiffs had no rights in common law, and the court could not deal with any that they might have under the law of the Church.

Thus the dispute which had begun thirty years earlier ended without giving Lanthony a firm title to control the schools of Gloucester. We hear no more of the rival masters,[3] and whether More triumphantly resumed his career or was bribed to go away, we do not know. But Richard Darcy, the undermaster, prospered sufficiently to be appointed headmaster of Winchester in 1418. He resigned in 1424 after being ill and consequently absent from his duties, for which the authorities unkindly withheld his stipend. Darcy was evidently a competent schoolmaster, and he gave to Winchester copies of two standard grammatical works: the *Grecismus* of Evrard of Béthune and the *Doctrinale* of Alexander de Villa Dei.[4] One of the candidates to fill his place was another Gloucester schoolmaster,

1 Ibid. fo 10v.
2 *Reports del Case en Ley que furent argues en le temps de . . . Henry le IV et Henry le V* (London, 1679), no pagination, *sub* Hilary term 11 Henry IV; PRO, Plea Rolls, CP 40/595 m 484. Leach in *VCH Gloucs.*, ii, 317, mistakenly thought that Hill was the defendant's counsel.
3 On 13 November 1415 however a Master John Hamelyn, clerk, of Worcester diocese, was commissioned to prove the will of John Hasarde, late of Gloucester (PRO, Prob 11/2 (PCC 30 Marche)).
4 *SME*, pp 237–8; *BRUO*, i, 543.

Richard Davy, who rode over to Winchester to be interviewed, but he was not chosen.[1] The convention with St Oswald's was due to end in July 1430, so that when Lanthony appointed another schoolmaster on 20 September the fact was carefully enrolled in its register to be on the safe side. The new master was William Breter, described in his letters of appointment as competently learned in grammar. He was permitted to gather scholars and teach them, taking his stipend from them and their friends, but no other terms of his tenancy are mentioned.[2] Yet it does not seem that St Oswald's was prepared to resume the battle, perhaps because of increased difficulties which now beset the house. Its small size, its inadequate income, and perhaps its remoteness from supervision, brought laxity and abuses. More than one prior was removed from office in the fifteenth century, and in 1486 Archbishop Rotherham found that observance of the rule and the maintenance of divine service were both slack. At last in 1491 a canon of Lanthony was chosen as prior. But even that house had not avoided internal confusion, and in the 1460s there was a fierce struggle between rival priors which led to the withdrawal of the canons for eight months to the protection of the earl of Warwick.[3]

Lanthony continued to appoint schoolmasters during the fifteenth century, but only one other master of this period is known by name—John Goode. He was being sued by the prior in 1441 over a debt of 40s.[4] The schoolhouse in Smith Street figures in the 1455 rental compiled by Robert Cole for the priory.[5] But by the early sixteenth century the canons' control of education was again being challenged. On 26 January 1513 Thomas Hannibal, vicar-general of the bishop of Worcester, having heard that new disputes had arisen over the school, declared that he had cited all the interested parties to appear before him, but that only the prior and convent of Lanthony, through their proctors, had made an appearance. He therefore confirmed once more the original ordinance of Giffard with Wakefield's confirmation.[6] There is nothing to show that St Oswald's was involved on this occasion, that house being still a byword among reformers, so that in the next year Abbot Kidderminster of Winchcombe characterised the prior as a dissolute man who kept no discipline, and recommended his replacement by the cellarer of Lanthony.[7]

But the days of the old school were already numbered. In 1528 John Cook, a wealthy mercer of Gloucester, died leaving money to endow a free grammar school in the town.[8] His plans were pushed forward by several prominent burgesses, and the prior of Lanthony seems also to have given the project his approval. Certainly in October 1529, acting as patron of the church of St Mary Crypt, he sanctioned the conveyance of part of the churchyard for the building of John Cook's new schoolhouse.[9] Lanthony may well have made a

1 *VCH Gloucs.*, ii, 319.
2 A3 fo 210.
3 C. L. Kingsford, *English Historical Literature in the Fifteenth Century* (London, 1913), pp 355–7.
4 *CPR 1436–41,* p 461.
5 *Rental of all the Houses in Gloucester, 1455,* ed. W. H. Stevenson (Gloucester, 1890), pp 22–3.
6 Reg. Silvestro de Gigli, fos 202v–3.
7 *LPFD*, i part ii, no 3195.
8 On the foundation of the Crypt School, see below p 137.
9 See below, p 138.

graceful resignation of its rights over the town school, for there was already a schoolmaster in the parish of St Mary Crypt by 1534, and in the following year the old schoolhouse in Smith Street, 'lately in the holding of Sir William, schoolmaster', lay vacant.[1] This man or another was involved in one of the many scandals reported or invented to blacken the religious orders as their days drew to an end. A letter of 1535 in the state papers recounts unpleasant allegations of sodomy between the prior of Lanthony and some schoolchildren from the town. According to the correspondent, the affair was discovered by a schoolmaster, but the chancellor of Worcester to whom the matter was communicated took no action. The master went twice to rebuke the prior who became so angry that he had the critic set in the stocks for three days and nights, put him in fear of his life, and drove him from the town.[2] With these untrustworthy allegations, the medieval period of education in Gloucester comes to an end. By 1540 the new Crypt School had taken the place of its predecessor.

SALISBURY
Wiltshire

The history of education in Salisbury begins on the hill of Old Sarum, to which the sees of Ramsbury and Sherborne were transferred in 1078.[3] For the next 140 years the cathedral of Salisbury and its schools shared the cramped surroundings of the old hill-fort with the king's castle and a small borough—smaller than the county town of Wilton, but large enough to have a market, a guild merchant, and at least two parish churches.[4] Educational facilities, if not actually coeval with the cathedral, evolved at an early date. They seem to be taken for granted in the *Institution* which St Osmund drew up for the cathedral in 1091. He was the first bishop of Salisbury, and his *Institution* provided the cathedral with its earliest set of statutes. Osmund established four principal dignitaries in his church: dean, cantor or precentor, treasurer, and *archischola*. The duties of the *archischola* were defined as arranging the lessons to be read in church, keeping a rota of the readers, looking after the seal, and composing letters and charters.[5] The identity of this person has been the cause of some conjecture, but Dr Kathleen Edwards argues convincingly that he was the officer who later became known as the chancellor.[6] We do not encounter a chancellor of Salisbury

---

1 See below, p 138; *VCH Gloucs.*, ii, 320.
2 PRO, State Papers, SP 1/100 pp 5–8; *LPFD*, ix, no 1081.
3 This article is largely based on the work of Dr Kathleen Edwards ('Cathedral of Salisbury', *VCH Wilts.*, iii, 156–210; *The English Secular Cathedrals in the Middle Ages* (2nd ed., 1967)); and that of Mrs Dora H. Robertson (listed below, p 70 n 6). The work of Dr Edwards is admirable in its clarity and completeness; that of Mrs Robertson, while it covers most of the ground, includes a number of incorrect dates and misleading references.
4 On Old Sarum see *VCH Wilts.*, vi, 51–65.
5 W. H. Frere, *The Use of Sarum* (Cambridge, 1898), pp 260–1; *Statutes and Customs of the Cathedral Church . . . of Salisbury*, ed. C. Wordsworth & D. Macleane (1915), pp 28–33.
6 *VCH Wilts.*, iii, 157–8; Kathleen Edwards, *The English Secular Cathedrals*, pp 181–3.

in any other document until 1139, but it is known that Guy of Étampes went there as schoolmaster soon after 1107, and later accounts of his life describe him as *scholiarcha* and as *magister scholarum* of Salisbury.[1] In about 1139 King Stephen gave three Hampshire churches—Odiham, Liss and Bentworth—to the *magister scholae* of Salisbury, and these were later part of the chancellor's endowments.[2] Subsequently we cease to hear of the *archischola* or the *magister scholarum*, and a succession of chancellors appear with very similar duties to those which Osmund had assigned to the *archischola*. The conclusion is irresistible that the dignity was the same throughout, and that the only differences lay in the titles employed.

The *Institution* does not include teaching among the *archischola*'s duties. It is nevertheless unlikely that an officer whose name meant 'head of the school' and who was also known as 'schoolmaster' should not have been a teacher himself, or one who appointed teachers and supervised them. It seems reasonable to assume that from 1091 onwards Salisbury possessed a school of grammar and possibly arts, taught by or under the direction of the *archischola*, as well as opportunities for learning song under the precentor. The early teaching arrangements may have been simple and informal, but by the opening of the thirteenth century stable institutions were beginning to evolve. This is apparent from the so-called *Consuetudinary*, or code of customs of the cathedral church, which was drawn up in about 1210; unlike the *Institution* it has several distinct references to the schools and their masters.[3] There were now definite institutions for learning song and grammar. Song came under the general oversight of the precentor and his deputy, the succentor. The precentor was responsible for admitting the choristers and for their instruction and discipline. This does not mean that he gave them tuition himself; for this there existed a song school. The song school was the succentor's responsibility, but since we are told that he ran it 'through his official', his involvement was also supervisory, the actual work being done by a special master. The rest of the teaching came under the care of the chancellor. His duty was to 'rule the schools' as well as discharging the secretarial tasks which Osmund had entrusted to the *archischola*. 'Ruling the schools' may be glossed as 'ruling the grammar school'. This is because the rule of the song school belonged elsewhere, while the teaching of theology did not become the chancellor's responsibility until 1240. Like the other dignitaries in 1210, the chancellor was no longer directly concerned with teaching his school. His abdication from this function may well have accompanied the disuse of the titles of *archischola* and *magister scholarum* in the middle of the twelfth century. Instead there was a deputy schoolmaster in 1210, appointed by the chancellor (on the analogy of later periods) and invested with his old title of *magister scholarum*.[4] For the rest of the middle ages the deputy schoolmaster taught the grammar school and the chancellor merely acted as his supervisor, a development which has its counterpart at nearly all the other secular cathedrals.[5]

---

1 Ibid., p 182.
2 Ibid., p 183; *Regesta Regum Anglo-Normannorum 1066–1154*, vol iii, ed. H. A. Cronne & R. H. C. Davis (Oxford, 1968), p 290.
3 Frere, *The Use of Sarum*, pp 3–4, 7–8.
4 Ibid., p 104.
5 For the case of Wells see below, p 82.

The *Consuetudinary* thus gives us our first glimpses of the choristers, the song school, the grammar school, and their masters. All were evidently created during the years at Old Sarum. Shortly afterwards, however, in 1219 the discomforts of the hill-top finally caused the bishop and the chapter to move to more spacious surroundings beside the River Avon, two miles away. The schools went with them. New Salisbury proved to be a great improvement on its precedessor. Not only was there more room for the cathedral and its precinct, but a larger and more prosperous town began to grow up outside. The schools must also have benefited. At a time when many scholars still came to the cathedral cities from elsewhere, New Salisbury was able to provide more lodgings than before, and better supplies of food. Its attractions, as we shall see, were enough to bring scholars from Oxford in 1238. As it grew in size and prosperity it must also have produced many boys of its own who wished to be educated. Already in the second half of the thirteenth century, New Salisbury was drawing away the trade of its neighbours, Old Sarum and Wilton. There were wool merchants in the city by 1306, and during the fourteenth century a lucrative trade in wool grew up, to be followed by a flourishing cloth industry. Drapers, mercers, grocers and other merchants are found during the later middle ages, and wine, fish, fruit and spices were imported from Southampton for redistribution in the locality. In 1377 there were 3,226 taxpayers, which suggests a total population of about 5,000—larger than any other town in the west of England except for Bristol. By the 1520s the population is estimated to have reached 8,000, making the city second to Bristol, equal to Exeter, and sixth in size in England as a whole.[1]

The expansion of New Salisbury was accompanied by its growth as a centre of education, not merely of song and grammar but of more advanced studies as well. For a short time it may have come near to developing a university in the manner of Oxford and Cambridge. Lectures in advanced studies such as theology and canon law were being given in the new cathedral city from the earliest years of its foundation. In 1220 Master Henry, canon of Bishopston, is described as 'teaching school' in New Salisbury, apparently in canon law, on which he had previously lectured at Oxford.[2] Five years later the precentor, Master Roger of Salisbury, is mentioned as 'reader' in theology.[3] At this time the giving of advanced lectures seems to have been arranged among the chapter informally, but in 1240 the duty was formally laid upon the chancellor, as it was at Exeter, Wells and most of the other secular cathedrals. On 6 November in that year the bishop, Robert Bingham, at the request of the chancellor, Master Adam of Ashby, annexed to his office the prebend of Brixworth on condition that he and his successors should cause solemn lectures in theology to be read in the city of Salisbury. The chancellor was either to read them personally or depute the task to other learned men.[4] The audience probably consisted of the city and cathedral clergy, and others who could get in from the surrounding countryside. The priests of the

1 On the history of New Salisbury see *VCH Wilts.*, vi, 68–105, and K. H. Rogers, 'Salisbury', in *Historic Towns*, vol i, ed. M. D. Lobel (1969), 20 pp.
2 *The Register of St Osmund*, ed. W. H. R. Jones, vol ii (Rolls Series, 1884), p 16.
3 Ibid., p 41.
4 *Sarum Charters and Documents*, ed. W. R. Jones & W. D. Macray (Rolls Series, 1871), pp 259–60.

collegiate church of St Edmund, founded by Bishop Walter de la Wyle in 1269, were specifically ordered to attend them.¹

Lectures in theology did not in themselves go far towards making a university. All the secular cathedral cities had similar facilities, and the core of a university was the study of the liberal arts rather than that of theology. The theory that Salisbury contained an incipient university in the thirteenth century rests upon three other pieces of evidence. The first is the arrival of scholars from Oxford in 1238, after one of the periodic disturbances which shook the premier English university during Henry III's reign. This one began with a brawl between some Oxford students and the papal legate Otho; it ended with the town being placed under interdict, the university suspended, and the scholars fleeing to escape the vengeance of the king.² According to two writers of the late fourteenth century who probably drew on earlier sources, the scholars made their way to Northampton and to Salisbury.³ This raises the possibility that they introduced the study of the liberal arts to Salisbury, or even that they came to the city because the arts were already established there. We do not know how long they stayed, but the study of the arts seems to have continued. In 1262 Bishop Bridport established an academic community in Salisbury between the south wall of the close and Harnham Bridge, dedicated to St Nicholas and subsequently known as De Vaux College. The name was probably derived from that of a college in the university of Paris. De Vaux College, which is two years older than Merton at Oxford, can claim to be the earliest English college for secular scholars. It was planned to support a warden, two chaplains and twenty poor, needy, honourable and teachable scholars engaged in the study of theology and the liberal arts. In the event, the number of scholars at any one time was rather less and nearer ten. Bridport's foundation strongly suggests that the arts, as well as theology, were being studied in Salisbury when it was made. It is hard to believe that he would have chosen a site remote from the study of the arts, where there were no poor students in need of the scholarships he provided.⁴

The third piece of evidence comes from 1279. It is an act of the cathedral chapter defining the rights of the chancellor and the sub-dean, both of whom claimed jurisdiction over the scholars of the city. The compromise provided that the chancellor should exercise jurisdiction over all civil and personal actions between scholars, of whatever faculty, or between scholars and laymen. The mention of laymen suggests the disputes which arose when scholars rented lodgings in the city, or ran up bills with the local tradesmen. The definition of a scholar was to be someone who lived in the city and had the recommendation

---

1 Sir R. C. Hoare, *The History of Modern Wiltshire: Salisbury* (1843), pp 735–6; *VCH Wilts.*, iii, 385–6. Whether St Edmund's was an academic college, as Dr Edwards suggests (*The English Secular Cathedrals*, p 192), seems doubtful. The founder probably had in mind the general education of his priests; compare a similar case at York (*ESMA*, p 82).
2 On the episode see J. H. Rashdall, *The Universities of Europe in the Middle Ages*, ed. F. M. Powicke & A. B. Emden (1936), iii, 87–9.
3 Thomas Walsingham, *Ypodigma Neustriae*, ed. H. T. Riley (Rolls Series, 1876), p 141; *Eulogium Historiarum*, ed. F. S. Haydon, vol iii (Rolls Series, 1863), p 118.
4 On the history of the college see the admirable account by Dr Edwards in *VCH Wilts.*, iii, 369–85.

of a particular teacher whose school he was attending. The sub-dean, who acted as archdeacon of the city, was to retain authority over clerks who were not attending the school of a particular teacher, and over the scholars themselves in cases of fornication and other moral crimes. Finally, the vicars and clerks of the cathedral itself, whether scholars or not, were to fall as before under the jurisdiction of the dean and chapter.[1] As Rashdall long ago observed, this document indicates that Salisbury was still an important centre of studies. There were evidently several teachers, and the scholars in the city belonged to more than one faculty.[2]

The total evidence suggests that an unusual number of scholars resorted to Salisbury between 1238 and 1279, and that they probably studied not only grammar but the liberal arts and theology. Whether such a concentration of scholars and studies amounts to an incipient university is more of a problem. The universities in the thirteenth century had not yet come to monopolise the liberal arts; there were, for example, schools of grammar and logic in Nottinghamshire in 1248, and Wells cathedral school was called 'the school of liberal arts' in 1274.[3] It is likely that the oldest pupils in thirteenth-century schools were in their late teens or early twenties, following part of the arts course and getting involved in the same troubles with local tradesmen as scholars did at Oxford. In short, it is difficult to define a university at this time through the study of arts alone, and if we attempt a constitutional definition, it is clear that Salisbury fails to qualify. The firm subordination of the scholars to the two cathedral dignitaries in 1279, together with the non-appearance of the scholars' masters either as parties or witnesses to the agreement, shows that the academic community had not developed any corporate rights or privileges. Nor is there any sign after 1279 that the community survived; it seems to have withered away. The scholars of De Vaux alone remained, and their position in Salisbury became an anomalous one. Many of the abler ones went off to Oxford, there to study arts and take degrees, and in 1526 it was ruled that they should all go, leaving only the warden and chaplains at home. The college itself was dissolved in 1542.[4]

For the rest of the middle ages, Salisbury possessed the same educational facilities as the other secular cathedral cities. As in the early thirteenth century there were a song school, a grammar school, and a system of lectures in theology. The cathedral chapter and its dignitaries supervised these institutions and appointed the masters who taught them. Scholarships for poor students were effectively provided, as they were at Exeter and Wells, by the maintenance and education of fourteen choristers, a group of older youths called altarists, and possibly other boys as well.[5] The altarists, of whom little is known, can be

1 Rashdall, *The Universities of Europe in the Middle Ages,* iii, 487–8; A. F. Leach, *Educational Charters and Documents, 598–1909* (Cambridge, 1911), pp 168–9; *Statutes of the Cathedral Church of Salisbury,* ed. Wordsworth & Macleane, pp 110–15.
2 Rashdall, op. cit., p 88.   3 *VCH Notts.,* ii, 184; below, p 86.
4 *VCH Wilts.,* iii, 379–82, 384.
5 E.g. in 1468 Robert Cothe, chaplain of the Hungerford chantry, left a grammar book to Thomas Bowyer, clerk of the chantry (Sarum Dean & Chapter, Reg. Machon, p 237); in 1525 Richard Austen was tonsured as a boy of the hall of the vicars choral (Reg. Campeggio, Sarum, fo 55); and Henry Leke similarly in 1529 (ibid., fo 65v).

treated first for convenience.[1] They seem to have numbered between seven and ten in late medieval times: five or six of them being *altaristae intrinseci* and two or four of them *extrinseci*. The former apparently served the altars of the inner choir and the latter those of the outer choir or the nave. Their appointment was claimed by the treasurer, but on 7 January 1388 it was asserted by the chapter that the power belonged to its members as a whole and that preference was customarily given to the choristers whose voices had broken.[2] Like most of their contemporaries elsewhere, the altarists did not enjoy any common facilities or corporate status. If the same was true at Salisbury as it was at Exeter, they may have lived one by one in the canons' houses.[3] Beside whatever food and lodging came their way, they seem to have received money from the endowments of their altars, and in 1399 they *may* have been getting 36s. 4d. *per annum*.[4] Their duties were to look after their altars, serve the priests who celebrated masses there, and attend the city grammar school, though visitation records of the fifteenth century complain that they often played truant.[5] The insistence on their education suggests that, like the Exeter secondaries, they were trainee clerics who were intended to provide the cathedral with vicars-choral and the diocese in general with priests. Their names, however, have not been preserved, and the reconstruction of their careers is therefore impossible.

The early choristers lived under the same disorganised conditions as the altarists.[6] Before 1300 they received little supervision and had no specific endowments; it is even uncertain where they lodged. They were forced to beg for their food at the houses of the canons in residence, 'to the manifest scandal of the church', as it was later asserted. The regulation and improvement of their way of life was due to the first two bishops of the fourteenth century: Simon of Ghent (1297–1315) and Roger Martival (1315–1330). On 6 May 1314 Bishop Ghent received the king's permission to alienate the rents of certain properties in Salisbury for the maintenance of the choristers and a master to instruct them in grammar.[7] He intended to do more, but his death in the following year left his schemes unfinished and the task of completing them fell upon Martival. He was responsible for the other major benefaction: the appropriation of the rectory of Preshute near Marlborough, which he

---

[1] On altarists in general see Kathleen Edwards, *The English Secular Cathedrals*, pp 303–7.
[2] Dean & Chapter, Reg. Dunham, pp 7–8; *Visitation Articles and Injunctions of the Period of the Reformation*, ed. W. H. Frere, iii, 32–3.
[3] See above, p 45.
[4] *Statutes of the Cathedral Church of Salisbury*, ed. Wordsworth & Macleane, p 307.
[5] Dean & Chapter, Reg. Dunham, p 130; Reg. Burgh, p 101; Reg. Newton, p 7; Reg. Machon, p 173. In 1535 four clerks assisted the choristers to sing the mass of Our Lady in the chapel of the Salve, and it is possible that these were altarists (*Valor Ecclesiasticus*, ii, 85).
[6] On the choristers in general see Dora H. Robertson, *Sarum Close . . . the History of the Choristers for 900 years* (London, 1938); 'Notes on some Buildings in the City and Close of Salisbury Connected with the Education and Maintenance of the Cathedral Choristers', *Wilts. Archaeological & Natural History Magazine*, xlviii (1937–9), pp 1–30; and (with C. Wordsworth), 'Salisbury Choristers: their Endowments, Boy-Bishops, Music Teachers and Headmasters', ibid., pp 201–31.
[7] *CPR 1313–17*, p 112.

was licensed to carry out in 1321 and executed in the following year.[1] These two endowments provided the choristers with valuable revenues. In 1535 the net income of their property in Salisbury was £14. 18s. 2d., while that of Preshute was £20. In 1352 they also gained a share of the church of Hanney in Berkshire, and another small annual payment reached them after 1395 from the estate of Bishop Waltham. These sources produced £2. 10s. and 8s. 6d. respectively in 1535. The total revenue of the choristers' endowments in that year, including £1. 15s. 2d. paid from the common fund of the cathedral, was £39. 12s. 1d. gross, and £35. 17s. 8d. net.[2]

As well as providing endowments, Bishop Martival improved the arrangements for the choristers to be supervised and taught. The statutes which he drew up for the cathedral in 1319 include a section on their government, and he made further ordinances in 1322 on completing the appropriation of Preshute.[3] The effect of these measures was to place the choristers under the general supervision of a warden, appointed by the chapter from among the canons in residence. He was to keep an account of their income and expenditure, and render it before the chapter every Michaelmas. The charge of the boys from day to day was deputed to a sub-master appointed by the warden with the chapter's consent. The sub-master was to be an honest man, learned in the art of grammar, and as far as is known, the office was always filled by a vicar choral. He was to live with the choristers in a dwelling house built for the purpose by Bishop Ghent in the north-west of the close, on the site at present occupied by the Hungerford Chantry. This house was vacated in about 1347 for another in Bishop's Walk, now Number 5, The Close, and it was here that the choristers and their master remained for the rest of the middle ages. They ate in the house at a common table, and a cook and manservant were employed to provide for their needs. Clothes and shoes were supplied for their use; a visiting barber cut their tonsures; and a laundress came in to do the washing when necessary.

Martival's statutes left the appointment of the choristers with the precentor, or the succentor in his absence. Boys of the diocese were to be chosen in preference, unless strangers were forthcoming with particular skill in music. Their duties were to assist in chanting the divine office in the choir and after the middle of the thirteenth century they helped to sing the mass of the Virgin in the chapel of the Salve. They were also the chief participants in the ceremonies of Childermas, the feast of the Holy Innocents, when one of their number was chosen to be boy-bishop. The statutes include an attempt to moderate the disorders which often took place on that day. The choristers were originally taught to sing, we presume, by the master of the song school, which adjoined their dwelling in Bishop's Walk. Later, in the fifteenth and sixteenth centuries, the master of the song school became more specifically the 'instructor of the choristers in music', and his appointment passed from the succentor to the chapter as a whole. Two of the contracts of the

1 *CPR 1317–21*, p 568; *Reg. Martival, Sarum*, vol iii, ed. Susan Reynolds (Canterbury & York Soc., lix, 1965), pp 96–7.
2 *Valor Ecclesiasticus*, ii, 85.
3 *Statutes of the Cathedral Church of Salisbury*, ed. Wordsworth & Macleane, pp 262–7; *Reg. Martival, Sarum*, vol ii part ii, ed. C. R. Elrington (Canterbury & York Soc., lviii, 1972), pp 412–16.

pre-Reformation instructors have survived. That of John Kegewyn, dated 1463, stipulates that he shall teach chant 'and other subjects' to the choristers, as well as helping to keep Our Lady's mass. In return he was granted the same emoluments as a vicar choral, 12d. a week from the choristers' funds, and three yards of broad cloth for a gown.[1] The other is that of Thomas Knight in 1538. He was appointed as organist and master of the choristers, with the duty of teaching them plainsong, pricksong (or noted music), faburden and descant. His salary was £6. 11s. 8d. a year, 'after the old laudable custom', and he was also entitled to meat and drink twice a day.[2] As well as learning song from these masters the choristers studied grammar. Martival's statutes provided that the sub-master should teach them manners and letters (meaning Latin grammar), but this need not imply that they were excluded from attending the grammar school of the city. They were certainly going there in 1448, and twenty years later their failure to do so was a matter for disapproval.[3] It may be that they had their formal lessons at the grammar school, and that the sub-master acted as their tutor, conversing with them in Latin when they were not in school or choir.

Unlike the song school, which seems to have been chiefly concerned with the choristers, the grammar school was a more public institution. It stood outside the close, and was usually known as 'the grammar school of the city'—a situation which exactly corresponds to that in Exeter.[4] In 1308 it occupied some tenements on the east side of the old High Street, now Exeter Street, outside and opposite St Anne's Gate; it was still there in 1455.[5] The grammar master was appointed by the chancellor, usually during the latter's pleasure, but at least once, in 1404, for the term of his life.[6] By 1350 he was paid a small sum by the chapter from the common fund and was expected to attend the choir for mattins and prime. At prime it was his duty to supervise the reading of the lessons.[7] In this respect he was more closely connected with the cathedral, like the schoolmaster of Wells, than was the case at Exeter. His chief business, however, was with teaching, and his main source of income came from the fees of his pupils. That his school was not free is shown by the requirement that he should pay a rent of 13s. 4d. *per annum* towards the obit of Ralph the Chancellor. This obligation first appears in 1370, but it was doubtless much older, for although there were several chancellors named Ralph, the latest of them died in 1309.[8] The payment was exacted until 1448 when it was remitted by the chapter in order to make the master's post a more attractive one, the stipulation being added that he should work hard at his teaching.[9] His clientele in the fifteenth century included the choristers, the altarists and the younger vicars choral, the latter being specifically ordered to attend the

1 Reg. Newton, pp 57–8.
2 *Wilts. Archaeological & Natural History Magazine,* xlviii (1937–9), pp 216–18.
3 Reg. Burgh, p 18; Reg. Machon, p 173.
4 See above, p 47.
5 *Hist. MSS Commission, Report on Various Collections,* vol i (1901), p 343; *Wilts. Archaeological & Natural History Magazine,* xlviii (1937–9), pp 13–14; Reg. Burgh, p 124.
6 Dean & Chapter, Reg. Draper, pp 38–9.
7 Dean & Chapter, Reg. Corffe, p 54.
8 Dean & Chapter, Communars' Rolls, 7–46 passim. Mrs Robertson's date of 1318 is incorrect.
9 Reg. Burgh, pp 18, 31; Communar's Roll, 47. Mrs Robertson's date of 1446 is also inaccurate.

grammar school in 1463 after they had mastered the psalter and the hymnal.[1] Boys from the city and the diocese are not mentioned as such, but the evidence about cathedral schools in general leaves little doubt that they were also present. Some of the monetary disputes over which the chancellor claimed jurisdiction must have involved youths who came to the school from elsewhere, and in 1468 the failure of the grammar master to give good service was said to have harmed the city as well as the cathedral.[2]

About a dozen of the masters' names survive from the thirteenth, fourteenth and fifteenth centuries, but little can be gathered of their histories.[3] Most of them seem to have been clerks in minor orders, and none appears to have combined the mastership with another benefice. Seven of them were entitled *magister* but only two, Richard Piere (1404) and John Russell (1448) are known to have been university graduates, and both were only masters of grammar. Two of the men appointed were found to be unsatisfactory. In 1350 Master Henry Nugges was accused of failing to teach the school or fulfil his duties in the choir; two years later the chapter dismissed him.[4] Similar charges were made against the master in 1468.[5] On three other occasions during the fifteenth century—1418, 1440 and 1454—there was no master at all, so that the life of the grammar school during this period was by no means smooth and untroubled.[6] At other times, however, there are signs that the school was better conducted.[7] Richard Maslyn was probably the grammar master in 1424 when he was interviewed for the post of headmaster of Winchester College. In 1448 the chapter invited John Lane, MA and master of the city school in Winchester, to come and teach in Salisbury and though he refused, they secured in his place John Russell, who had hitherto been teaching grammar in Oxford, the leading centre of such studies. Later, in 1469, they appointed the usher of Winchester College, John Hawkbrooke. Appointments and offers of this kind suggest that the teaching, at its best, was comparable with that in other major schools of the day.

For those who mastered their grammar and entered upon a clerical career there was, or should have been, the school of theology under the chancellor's direction. This, however, like the grammar school, was intermittently suspended, owing to the negligence of some of the chancellors about finding and paying a lecturer. On the other hand they never managed to evade their duty altogether, since the bishop and the chapter kept a watch on the school and more than once took steps to safeguard its future. In 1300 for example, Bishop Ghent became aware that Chancellor Ralph of York had allowed the theology school to remain closed for most of the previous year, and ordered him to provide a suitable

1 Reg. Burgh, pp 18, 100–1; Reg. Newton, pp 7, 20; Reg. Machon, p 173.
2 Ibid., p 171.
3 For the list of names and references see below, p 76.
4 Reg. Corffe, pp 54, 87.
5 Reg. Machon, p 171.
6 Dean & Chapter, Reg. Pountney, fo 51v; Reg. Hutchins, p 10; Reg. Burgh, p 100.
7 In addition to the evidence which follows, it may be added that Thomas de la Wile (1254) commissioned an illuminated Bible which survives at the British Museum, while Walter Weryng (1381–9) was chosen in 1389 to keep the cathedral records (Reg. Dunham, p 102).

person to lecture there within a month.¹ In 1349 the chapter took a close interest in the provision of a lecturer by the elderly and inefficient chancellor, Elias of St Albans. Elias proposed to appoint a Dominican friar to lecture, one John Newton, having been asked to do so by the countess of Lancaster. One of the canons, John Whitchurch, thereupon protested that the lectures were customarily given by a university bachelor or doctor of theology, Newton being neither of these. Elias was obliged to compromise, and an agreement was reached that the friar should lecture alternately with the archdeacon of Salisbury, Roger Kington, who held the doctor's degree. In 1350 Kington appears to have taken over the duty completely, Elias agreeing to pay him ten marks for a year's lectures.² The next chancellor, Simon Sudbury, was a non-resident, and in 1357 the chapter complained that the lectures had lapsed. Sudbury explained that he had indeed appointed a doctor to lecture but the man had fallen ill, and he undertook to find a substitute for the following year.³ We know that he carried out his promise, because in 1358 William Forncett, doctor of theology and vicar of Mildenhall in Suffolk, was given a papal licence to reside at Salisbury for two years while he lectured there.⁴ The subsequent history of the institution is less clear, but it continued to function at least intermittently until the Reformation. In 1454 the chapter built a new theology school above the west walk of the cloister and in the same year, after hearing accusations that the lectures were not being given in a regular manner, an order was made that one at least should be read every fortnight.⁵ Later still in 1535 the chancellor, Edward Carne, is recorded paying an annual sum of £4 to his deputy lecturer, and the institution continued in being after the Reformation.⁶

The early sixteenth century is a time of particular obscurity for the history of education in Salisbury, largely through the deficiency of the chapter act-books from which most of the earlier information is to be gathered. The choristers certainly went on living at their house in Bishop's Walk along with their sub-master and instructor in music, and the school of theology also survived, as we have just seen. The history of the grammar school, on the other hand, is quite unknown between 1468, when it was still apparently in Exeter Street, and 1540 when it appears on a new site in Bishop's Walk, not far from the choristers' house. Henceforward it is generally referred to as 'the grammar school in the close'.⁷ Nothing else is known of its constitution or its masters at this time, and the impact of the Reformation upon it can be stated only in general terms. Two principal changes were made to the teaching of grammar during the middle of the sixteenth century. In the first place the school in the close became free and the master was given a salary in lieu of fees.

---

1 *Reg. de Gandavo, Sarum*, ed. C. T. Flower & M. C. B. Dawes, vol i (Canterbury & York Soc., xl, 1934), pp 41–3.
2 Reg. Corffe, pp 38, 40, 49, 62.
3 Ibid., p 128.
4 *Calendar of Papal Letters 1342–62*, p 596. Like Sudbury he was probably an East Anglian.
5 Reg. Burgh, p 115.
6 *Valor Ecclesiasticus*, ii, 73; *Visitation Articles and Injunctions of the Period of the Reformation*, ed. W. H. Frere, iii, 31–2.
7 *Wilts. Archaeological & Natural History Magazine*, xlviii (1937–9), pp 21–2.

This resulted from the Royal Injunctions of 1547 which ordered all cathedrals to maintain a free grammar school, the cost presumably falling upon the dean and chapter.[1] The other development was the foundation of a second free grammar school in the city. This appears to have been partly made necessary by increasing demands for education and partly due to tensions between the city and the cathedral, which may have increased after the medieval grammar school was moved into the close. The city was seeking a school of its own by 1548, when the chantry certificates include a petition that the king might appoint a schoolmaster in Salisbury for the benefit of the city and the adjoining countryside.[2] This should be understood as a request for a second, endowed schoolmaster to supplement the grammar master of the close. The Edwardian regime did not respond to this request, but in 1569 the citizens managed to gain what they wanted from the government of Queen Elizabeth. The method employed to endow the new school was highly immoral. Since 1548 the crown had been obliged to pay annuities to the schools of Bradford-on-Avon and Trowbridge, in lieu of lands confiscated at the dissolution of the chantries. These annuities were now transferred to Salisbury, under the pretext that Bradford and Trowbridge were 'upland towns' without a need for schools. The mayor and corporation were allocated the combined annuities of £26. 1s. 8d. *per annum,* in return for which they promised to build and maintain a suitable schoolhouse.[3] In this way Salisbury acquired two free schools: one at the cathedral, under the jurisdiction of the clergy, and the other in the town under the citizens' control. The same development had already taken place at Bristol and Gloucester in the early 1540s, and was to do so at Exeter in 1631.

1 *Visitation Articles and Injunctions,* ii, 138–9.
2 PRO, Chantry Certificates, E 301/105 p 4; *ESR,* part ii, p 263.
3 *Report of Charity Commissioners* (*House of Commons Papers,* 1833, vol xix), p 366.

MASTERS OF SALISBURY GRAMMAR SCHOOL

1	Thomas de la Wile, *Mag.*	occurs before 1254
2	Henry Nugges, *Mag.*	occurs 1350
		deprived 1352
3	Richard ———, *Mag.*	occurs 1358
4	Richard Dene	occurs 1376
5	Walter Weryng, *Mag.*	occurs 1381–9
6	Richard Piere, M Gram	appointed 1404
7	Robert ———	occurs 1408
8	[perhaps] Richard Maslyn	occurs 1424
9	*John Lane*, MA	offered appointment 1448
10	John Russell, *Mag.*	appointed 1448
11	Unknown	appointed 1455
12	John Russell	re-appointed 1468
13	John Hawkbrooke, *Mag.*	appointed 1469
14	Thomas Wynn	perhaps by 1470; died 1474

1 British Museum, MS Royal 1 B XII fo 431; Sir G. F. Warner & J. P. Gilson, *Catalogue of Western MSS in the Old Royal and King's Collections, British Museum*, vol i (1921), pp 12–3.
2 Salisbury Dean & Chapter, Reg. Corffe, pp 54, 87.
3 *CCR 1354–60*, p 508.
4 Dean & Chapter, Press I, Box 26, Deed of 1376.
5 PRO, Clerical Subsidy Rolls, E 179/277/8; Dean & Chapter, Reg. Dunham, p 102.
6 27 October 1404 (Dean & Chapter, Reg. Draper, pp 38–9).
7 *Dominus*. On 10 November 1408 he was appointed chaplain of Blunsdon's Chantry in the cathedral, and promised to resign as schoolmaster on Christmas Day (Dean & Chapter, Reg. Vyryng, p 26). A Robert Carpenter was a chantry priest of Salisbury cathedral in 1419 (PRO, Clerical Subsidy Rolls, E 179/52/230).
8 He was interviewed, with other schoolmasters, for the post of headmaster of Winchester College (*VCH Hants.*, ii, 284).
9 He was offered the post on 7 September, being then master of the grammar school in the city of Winchester, but evidently did not accept it (Dean & Chapter, Reg. Burgh, p 18). See also *BRUO*, ii, 1091.
10 1 October 1448 (Reg. Burgh, p 31). He is probably the same as John Russell, grammar master at Ing Hall, Oxford, in April 1447 (*BRUO*, iii, 1608).
11 31 May 1455 (Reg. Burgh, p 124).
12 No exact date (Dean & Chapter, Reg. Machon, p 173).
13 6 October 1469 (ibid., p 33). He was born at 'Stoke' in Hereford diocese (there are four such villages) in *c.* 1439 (ibid.) He was appointed usher of Winchester College in September 1468 and resigned on moving to Salisbury (H. Chitty, 'The Second Masters of Winchester College', *The Wykehamist*, no 551 (April, 1916), pp 2–3). For his namesake and probable relative David Hawkbrooke see *BRUO*, ii, 890.
14 *Wilts. Archaeological & Natural History Magazine*, xlviii (1937–9), p 17. It has not been possible to trace the original document from Mrs Robertson's reference. But Wynn certainly existed, and as a 'literate', meaning someone not in holy orders, he witnessed the will of John Godrich, chaplain, in 1470 (Reg. Machon, p 238).

SALISBURY

SUB-MASTERS OF THE CHORISTERS
(All were vicars choral of the cathedral)

1	Peter Fadyr	appointed 1419
2	Robert Driffield	appointed 1428
3	William Malton	appointed 1435
4	John Farle	occurs 1440
5	John Cook	occurs 1460–1
6	Robert Lavington	occurs 1463–6
7	Richard Sussex	occurs 1467–8
8	———— Pevesey, *Mag.*	occurs 1495
9	———— Sway, *Mag.*	occurs 1496
10	Richard Whittock	occurs 1500
		resigned 1511
11	John Burdox	appointed 1511
12	John Fryer	occurs 1517–26
13	Laurence Man	occurs 1529–41
14	Richard Power	occurs 1549

1 6 October. Dean & Chapter, Reg. Harding, fo 7.
2 27 October. Ibid., fo 95.
3 21 April. Ibid., fo 107. He was also succentor.
4 Reg. Hutchins, p 20.
5 Choristers' Accounts, 1460–1.
6 Ibid., 1463–4, 1465–6.
7 Ibid., 1467–8.
8 Ibid., 1495–6.
9 Ibid.
10 Ibid., 1500–1; Harward's Memorials, p 128.
11 19 September. Ibid.
12 Choristers' Accounts, 1517–18 – 1525–6.
13 Ibid., 1529–30, [probably] 1540–1.
14 Reg. Holt & Blacker, p 26.

INSTRUCTORS OF THE CHORISTERS IN MUSIC

1	John Caccherowe	occurs 1460–1
2	John Kegewyn	appointed 1463
		still in 1466
3	John Caccherowe	recurs 1468
4	Alexander Bell	occurs 1495–6
5	John Weaver	occurs 1500–26
6	Thomas Knight	occurs 1529–49

1 Dean & Chapter, Choristers' Accounts, 1460–1.
2 7 May. Reg. Newton, p 57; Choristers' Accounts, 1456–6. He was originally from Hereford diocese and was ordained acolyte 10 March, sub-deacon 31 March, and priest in September 1464 (Reg. Beauchamp, Sarum, i, ordination lists fos 187v, 188–v).
3 Reg. Machon, p 173.
4 Choristers' Accounts, 1495–6. He was chapel clerk and choirmaster of Magdalen College, Oxford, in 1486–7, and proceeded MA at Cambridge in 1507–8 (*BRUO*, i, 160).
5 Choristers' Accounts, 1500–1, 1525–6.

6 Ibid., 1529–30, 1540–1. He was formally appointed on 30 April 1538 (Church Commissioners, Lease Book 25 Henry VIII–4 Elizabeth, no 136777). He was appointed sub-treasurer in 1537 and was prebendary of Ruscombe in 1546 (F. Ll. Harrison, *Music in Medieval Britain* (2nd ed., 1963), pp 178–9, 200, 274, 288, 377–8, 410, where his musical compositions are also described).

WELLS
Somerset

The importance of Wells as the ecclesiastical capital of Somerset dates back to the early tenth century. Ever since the reign of Edward the Elder it has been the seat of a bishop and of a cathedral staffed by secular canons, with the sole exception of the early Norman period. In 1090 Bishop John de Villula removed his seat to Bath, and for the next fifty years the erstwhile cathedral at Wells suffered a period of eclipse. The church and its canons, however, never ceased to exist, and after the middle of the twelfth century their fortunes rose again. In 1140 Bishop Robert reorganised the church on the lines of the cathedrals at Lincoln and Salisbury, in 1176 Pope Alexander III decreed that it should have cathedral status as well as Bath, and the canons also gained joint power to elect the bishop. By the middle of the thirteenth century Wells was once more the sole cathedral for most purposes, and it remained the ecclesiastical centre of the diocese for the rest of the middle ages. There were about 100 resident priests and clerks in the cathedral close when the poll-tax was taken in 1377, and another 22 in the city itself.[1] But Wells was not simply a settlement of ecclesiastics. It had the tradesmen and craftsmen incidental to an important place of resort, and a flourishing cloth trade in particular. Weavers, tuckers and dyers appear frequently in its records during the later middle ages.[2] The 901 lay tax-payers recorded in 1377 made Wells the largest town in Somerset—a little ahead of Bridgwater and almost twice the size of Bath and Taunton.[3] Nearly two centuries later in 1548 the parish of St Cuthbert, which covered the city (except for the close) and part of the country round, was estimated to contain 2,000 communicants.[4] Using these figures as a rough guide we may guess that the whole population of Wells numbered 2,000 during the later middle ages and maintained this level until the Reformation.

The existence of the cathedral determined the structure of education in the city. Here as elsewhere it provided the local schools with supervisors, teachers, and benefactors, besides maintaining a number of boys who needed to be educated. Let us begin with the arrangements which the cathedral made for supporting and educating its own members. As at Exeter and Salisbury we find two groups of teachable boys and youths in the middle ages. The 'Ancient Statutes' of Wells which date from about 1140 mention both choristers and clerks of the second form. The choristers were chosen by the precentor, who was bound

1 PRO, Exch. KR, Clerical subsidy rolls, E 179/4/1 m 1; H. C. Maxwell-Lyte, 'The Clergy of Wells in 1377', *Somerset & Dorset Notes & Queries*, xxi (1935), pp 18–19.
2 E.g. *Wells City Charters*, ed. D. O. Shilton & R. Holworthy (Somerset Record Soc., xlvi, 1932), passim.
3 J. C. Russell, *British Medieval Population* (1948), pp 142–3.
4 *Somerset Chantries*, ed. E. Green (Somerset Record Soc., ii, 1888), p 155.

to provide for their instruction, and the secondary clerks, who were older youths, were admitted by the dean.[1] The numbers in both groups were small. Compared with the twelve secondaries at Exeter and the seven or ten altarists at Salisbury, Wells maintained no more than half a dozen clerks in medieval times: three altarists and three tabellars. The altarists, or keepers of the church, are first mentioned in 1298 when there were three of them, this number being usually maintained until the Reformation. In this period they were appointed by the treasurer, not the dean, and their duty was to be on hand in the church every morning from sunrise until High Mass in order to prepare the altars and serve at the private masses. Their stipends were 4d. a week, or 17s. 4d. a year.[2] The tabellars, who also numbered three, appear to have been assistants to the tabellar properly speaking, a vicar choral who checked that the clergy kept regular attendance in the choir. They are usually mentioned together with the choristers, and it is not improbable that they were choristers or altarists deputed for the purpose, rather than separate personnel.[3] Little is said about the education of these clerks, but it is possible that as at Exeter and Salisbury the posts provided support for a few poor youths while they studied at school.

The choristers were also few in number in the early days. In 1298 there were six, and this number was maintained until at least the early fifteenth century. At first they received only an annual robe and a share in the money distributed at obits, or commemorations of the dead.[4] No doubt they begged for food from the canons, as their fellows did elsewhere. At last in 1349 Bishop Ralph of Shrewsbury took pity on them. He allocated the sum of ten marks a year for their support out of the vicarage of Chew Magna, and he built them a new house on much the same site that they occupied at Exeter: between the south-west corner of the cathedral nave and the market place.[5] From at least 1409 there was a master of the choristers, who probably acted both as their guardian and as their teacher under the general supervision of the precentor.[6] The fifteenth century also saw an increase in the number of boys. There were still only six in 1431,[7] but the choristers' statutes of 1460, which we shall consider presently, appear to envisage well over that number. In 1535 there were definitely thirteen maintained, it was said, 'by ordinance of John Stafford and others'.[8] This makes it likely that the increase was due to Bishop Stafford (1425–43), unless the credit belongs to Bishop Beckington (1443–65), who issued the choristers' statutes. The growth in numbers was matched by a growth of revenues, and in 1535 the choristers' endowments produced over £27 *per annum*.[9]

1 *Dean Cosyn & Wells Cathedral Miscellanea*, ed. A. Watkin (ibid., lvi, 1941), pp 1–2; H. E. Reynolds, *Wells Cathedral* (1881), pp 45, 55.
2 *Miscellanea*, ed. Watkin, pp 16, 24; *Valor Ecclesiasticus*, i, 127–8.
3 *Miscellanea*, pp 16, 22; *Hist. MSS Commission, Calendar of MSS of the Dean & Chapter of Wells*, 2 vols (1907–14), hereafter cited as *HMC*, ii, 68, 94, 95, 208; Wells Cathedral Library, Communars' Rolls, 1430–1.
4 *Miscellanea*, ed. Watkin, p 16.
5 *HMC*, i, 454; H. Wharton, *Anglia Sacra* (London, 1691), i, 569.
6 *HMC*, ii, 47.
7 Communars' Rolls, 1430–1.
8 *Valor Ecclesiasticus*, i, 128. 9 Ibid.

For the musical training of its ministers the cathedral maintained a song school. In the Ancient Statutes of about 1140 the precentor is said to rule the song school through his official, the succentor, who presumably carried out the teaching in the early days.[1] Whether the school was confined to the cathedral staff or open to the public is, as usual, a difficult question to answer. The former is the more likely. We never hear of a public song school in later times, only of a song school for the choristers and tabellars, to which one or two outsiders at most were admitted. Boys in Wells must either have received private tuition in reading and song from clerks or chaplains in the city, or else have learnt these subjects in the grammar school under the general supervision of the grammar master. In this respect it is worthy of note that the grammar school and its master are usually called 'the school' and 'the schoolmaster' in medieval records, suggesting that their range was not limited to grammar.

It is not until the fifteenth century that the song school emerges from its obscurity. By this time it was definitely confined to the choristers and concerned with their training for the choir. Our knowledge of its work in this period comes largely from the statutes which were drawn up for its government under the guidance of Thomas Beckington, the greatest, perhaps, of all the medieval bishops of Bath and Wells. Beckington was a leading spirit in the circle of enthusiasts for education who gathered around Henry VI in the 1440s, with whom the English Renaissance may well be said to have begun. Unlike the king himself and several others of the circle, Beckington never got as far as founding a new grammar school, but he did exert himself greatly on behalf of the choristers of Wells. He enlarged their house in 1459 and also built them a spacious song school in the west range of the cloisters together with a lodging for their master.[2] Finally in February 1460 he issued a careful, detailed and enlightened set of statutes to regulate their life and studies.[3] These statutes, according to their preamble, were said to have been first instituted by Robert Cater, the master of the choristers, but it is unlikely that Cater, of whom we know almost nothing, was solely responsible for drawing them up. Some of the practices they sanction were probably traditional, but the unusual wisdom and humanity with which they are expounded suggest Beckington irresistibly. It seems likely that after making a draft of the statutes, he with his usual care, got the master of the choristers to try them out, and only published them when he was sure they were suitable.

The choristers, in Beckington's statutes, were placed under the rule of a master nominated by the precentor. He was to be a priest, moderate and temperate in his character, knowledgeable in grammar, plainsong, and polyphony. He was empowered to appoint an undermaster to assist him in teaching reading and song. The master was paid 40s. a year out of the choristers' endowments and his deputy 26s. 8d., besides other unspecified emoluments. The boys probably received only their board, lodging, and clothing on the foundation, but they also got fees for attending funerals and obits, as well as two traditional

---

[1] *Miscellanea,* ed. Watkin, p 2; Reynolds, *Wells Cathedral,* p 45.
[2] *Reg. Bekynton, Wells,* ed. Sir H. C. Maxwell-Lyte, vol i (Somerset Record Soc., xlix, 1934), p 318; John Leland, *Itinerary,* i, 291.
[3] *Miscellanea,* ed. Watkin, pp 98–109.

donations of money from the canons on the eves of St Edmund the King and St Nicholas. Each boy's money was placed in a purse with his name on it, and kept in a special chest. Beckington envisaged the choristers as proceeding to university if possible, and the money was to be handed over to them when they set out. The statutes went into careful detail about how the choristers should spend their days. Some were deputed to rise in the night to sing mattins; the others could lie until dawn. After rising they had to cross themselves and repeat certain prayers while they dressed. They were expected to make their beds, tidy their chests, and wash their hands before going down to school. There they began the day by studying plainsong and polyphony until the bells rang for prime, and then they had breakfast. Afterwards some went off to the choir and the others remained in school until eleven when they adjourned to their hall for dinner. In the afternoon they had more lessons, some of them returning to the choir for evensong and the rest remaining in school. After evensong came supper, and after supper those who had to sing next morning's mattins were heard by the master to make sure they were perfect. The others stayed in school as before, apparently until bed-time. It was, as the statutes later admitted, 'a long and heavy day'.

What sets Beckington's statutes apart from similar ordinances is the understanding they display of human nature and the relative moderation of the discipline they impose. The master and his deputy should aim at making their teaching brief and clear, lest their pupils become bored, weary or forgetful. They must remember that stupidity or dullness in boys is often natural rather than deliberate, and deserves pity not anger. Dull boys should be taught with special care, and be allowed to receive help from their more intelligent companions. When they neglect to study, boys are first to be warned kindly, then, if they do not amend, to be rebuked sharply, and only afterwards, if it is still necessary, to be flogged. And lastly, since reason dictates that the cares of study and of the choir should be varied by some pleasure, the boys are to have time for recreation—half an hour or so before supper, after supper as well in summer, and after dinner on festivals. But they are to be kept separate from other men and boys, their amusements must be restrained, and the master is to keep a sharp look-out for brawling, swearing and 'bursts of raucous laughter'. These emollients to discipline may not seem very much today, but for their time they show an unusual patience and understanding.

For the rest of the middle ages the choristers appear to have led this secluded life under their own masters, a few of whose names survive.[1] The statutes are not clear about what or where they were taught, but it looks from their timetable as though they always remained in their own school rather than attending that of the public grammar master. They evidently studied grammar, however, as well as learning plainsong and polyphony for their choral duties. This is established by the requirement that their master should be a grammarian, by the order that they should speak Latin in their hall at meal times, and by the provision for them to proceed to university. Wells, it appears, may be counted as one

---

[1] *HMC*, ii, 47, 104, 205, 208, 231, 236, 248, 701. For a discussion of these masters see F. Ll. Harrison, *Music in Medieval Britain* (2nd ed., 1963), pp 179–80.

of the secular cathedrals like Lichfield and Lincoln where the choristers had their own private grammar school, unlike Exeter and Salisbury where they seem to have gone to the school of the city. This arrangement did not survive the Reformation, and in later times the choristers once more attended the public grammar school.

The grammar school of Wells, like the song school, can be traced back to the Ancient Statutes. They mention a dignitary called the *archischola*. His specified duties included organising the lessons in church, keeping the chapter seal, and writing letters on its behalf—the *archischola* being simply an early name for the chancellor.[1] Nothing is said of his teaching school, but the statutes of Wells were closely modelled on those of Salisbury, and at Salisbury the *archischola* appears to have been identical with the schoolmaster.[2] It is therefore highly probable that the *archischola* was also teaching grammar at Wells by about 1140. The first holder of the office to survive by name is Peter of Winchester, who is described as 'schoolmaster' (*magister scolarum*) in the period between 1174 and 1189.[3] At about this time however the schoolmasters in most of the English secular cathedrals were changing their functions. They were confining themselves to their secretarial work and appointing deputies to do their school-teaching. To mark their greater sense of dignity they took the new title of 'chancellor' and the old one of 'schoolmaster' passed to their deputies. The new title was in use at Wells by about 1200.[4] The chancellor retained a general responsibility for local education, and a phrase in the Wells statutes, perhaps inserted after 1200, says that he had the rule of the schools.[5] But in practice, as we shall see, his own teaching was limited to giving lectures in theology, and he appointed a succession of deputy schoolmasters to teach grammar in his place.

The earliest surviving act book of the cathedral chapter, which dates from 1486 to 1514, shows that the schoolmaster was nominated by the chancellor and admitted to office by the dean. On his admission he took an oath of obedience, was assigned the habit of a vicar and given a stall in the choir, with the customary emoluments of his office. He thus had a closer connection with the cathedral, like the schoolmaster of Salisbury, than was the case at Exeter. Payments to him occur in all the account rolls of the communar which survive from 1328 until the Reformation. He received £1. 10s. 4d. a year from the common fund and a salary of 26s. 8d. out of the manor of Biddisham.[6] This arrangement continued without change until 1547. In 1318 the chapter decreed that he should also receive as much as a vicar when money was divided for funeral services.[7] These emoluments would not have been enough to live on, since he was expected to pay rent for his schoolhouse and to keep it in good repair. His school, however, was definitely open to the public, and the rest of

1 *Miscellanea*, ed. Watkin, p 2; Reynolds, *Wells Cathedral*, p 45.
2 See above, pp 65–6.
3 *HMC*, i, 492.
4 *Wells City Charters*, ed. D. O. Shilton & R. Holworthy, p 3.
5 *Miscellanea*, ed. Watkin, p 2; Reynolds, *Wells Cathedral*, p 45.
6 *HMC*, ii, *passim*.
7 Ibid., i, 176.

his salary came from charging his pupils fees. This was the general custom in the medieval cathedral schools.[1]

For those who had mastered their grammar, the cathedral provided facilities for the study of theology and canon law at a higher level. These were intended for the parish clergy of the diocese who could not afford to study at university. We have seen how at Exeter and Salisbury it became the chancellor's duty in the thirteenth century to provide lectures on these subjects, and it is probable that the institution grew up at Wells at about the same time. It certainly existed by 1335 when Bishop Ralph of Shrewsbury ordered that the chancellor should always lecture in person or by deputy on canon law or theology from 15 October until 7 July. This was after a visitation had disclosed that Thomas Retford, the chancellor since 1316, had neglected to do so, and the sub-dean was ordered to see that he complied.[2] Soon after this the chancellorship began to change hands frequently and the bishop tried to impose the obligation on successive newcomers. Thus on 20 November 1337 John Middleton was appointed to the dignity and swore to read his lectures or else find a reader within a month, but within that month he exchanged the chancellorship with Simon Bristol on 15 December. Bristol in turn swore to hold forth on theology or the papal decrees at such times that lectures were given at Oxford.[3] The duty remained sufficiently in doubt, however, for the bishop, the dean and the chapter to combine in making an appeal to Rome, in which they said that lecturing had been faithfully carried out but asked the pope to confirm the custom, a confirmation duly forthcoming in 1348.[4] It is not certain how long it continued, but Dr John Orum, canon of Wells and Exeter who died in 1436, is known to have lectured in the cathedral on the Apocalypse.[5] Most of the medieval chancellors held higher degrees in law or theology and should have been able to discharge the duty if required.[6]

Wells thus came to possess the same three schools as the other secular cathedral cities in the later middle ages: a song school for the choristers, a public grammar school, and a system of lectures in theology. Our remaining attention will be given to a further study of the grammar school. Far more survives about its history than about those of the song school or the lectures, and this reflects its greater importance. It is possible to trace the sequence of its buildings, the names and careers of several of its masters, and even a few details of its organisation. The history of its site and accommodation begins in about 1235 when Canon Roger, chaplain to the bishop and rector of Chewton Mendip, gave a curtilage containing some houses formerly belonging to Reginald of Waltham, to the chancellor and his successors for the use of the school. The property was to be conferred on the schoolmaster for the time being, on condition that he kept the buildings in repair and commemorated the benefactor's death each year with the help of the scholars. Daily prayers were also to be

1 On the subject of fees in medieval cathedral schools see *ESMA*, p 157.
2 *Reg. Shrewsbury, Wells,* ed. T. S. Holmes, vol i (Somerset Record Soc., ix, 1896), pp 341, 255.
3 *HMC*, i, 239–40, 548, 545.
4 *Cal. Papal Petitions,* i, 134; *Cal. Papal Letters,* iii, 284.
5 *BRUO,* ii, 1406. The lectures are preserved in Bodleian Library, MS Bodl. 286.
6 J. Le Neve, *Fasti Ecclesiae Anglicanae 1300–1541,* vol viii: *Bath & Wells,* ed. B. Jones (1964), pp 7–9.

offered in school for Roger and his parents.¹ Teaching went on in Roger's building throughout the fourteenth century, but by the early fifteenth the chancellor had exchanged the site with the chapter for new premises on the east side of the Torre Gate in Torre Lane. The school did not remain there long, for in 1410 the chancellor, Richard Bruton, returned the Torre Lane house to the chapter and received instead an outhouse, part of the messuage in the Mountroy held by Thomas Frome, one of the senior canons. He was compensated for the intrusion of the school, and the schoolmaster was forbidden to make any doors or windows in the new schoolhouse which might overlook the buildings still occupied by the canon.² The school soon found the accommodation inconvenient and Bishop Beckington, always ready to improve the facilities for education, observed in statutes promulgated between 1451 and 1462 that although there were people at Wells skilled in grammar, they could not benefit the church by teaching because there was no fixed place for the school to be held. He ordered that henceforth grammar should be taught in a house opposite the gate of the college of the Annuellars in the Mountroy, part of or adjacent to the canons' barn and the dwelling of the sub-dean, John Speckington.³ It was perhaps in consequence of this decision that in 1458 the keepers of the cathedral fabric paid 3s. for repairing the schoolhouse roof.⁴ In 1491 the schoolhouse in Mountroy Lane was vacant for the whole year and the accustomed rent of 6s. 8d. was not being paid.⁵ Perhaps the school had been moved again, for we next hear of it at the end of the sixteenth century occupying a site near the west end of the cathedral.⁶

The boys who attended the school probably came both from the city and the diocese as a whole. A few of their names survive. In 1377 the list of Wellensian clerics paying the poll-tax ends with a section headed 'scholars in the city of Wells', comprising 34 persons paying 4d. each, and therefore clerks unbeneficed but over the age of fourteen.⁷ The school at this time is likely to have numbered at least 50 or 60 pupils. Many of the surnames in the list are local to Wells and Somerset, but the bishops' registers of ordinations and admissions to benefices in which their careers might be traced do not survive for this period. Even adults may have come for instruction at times, for Bishop Beckington in 1453, on finding a new rector of Weston-in-Gordano greatly lacking in knowledge, ordered him to study for two years in the school at Wells and offer himself for examination each Easter.⁸ The school was not unnoticed by the dignitaries of the cathedral, one or two of whom gave small benefactions in return for prayers. As well as Roger of Chewton's gift of the schoolhouse, Dean Walter Medford who died in 1423 bequeathed 6s. 8d. to the schoolmaster and 13s. 4d. among the scholars on condition that every day for a month before leaving

1 *HMC*, i, 35, 150, 307.
2 Ibid., p 441.
3 *Miscellanea*, ed. Watkin, p 11.
4 *HMC*, ii, 87.
5 Ibid., p 124.
6 Ibid., p 333.
7 PRO, E 179/4/1 m 1.
8 *Reg. Bekynton, Wells*, i, 203.

school for supper they should say the psalm *De Profundis* with the customary prayers and the oration *Fidelium Deus*.[1] In 1498 John Austell, a canon, left two printed books to the school from his library. One was the *Catholicon*, the standard Latin dictionary of the later middle ages compiled by John of Genoa, and the other a volume called *Liber Gutrumni*. The latter appears to have been a Latin grammar of Spanish origin.[2]

The names of twenty of the grammar masters survive between the end of the thirteenth and the middle of the sixteenth centuries.[3] A few general observations can be made upon their qualifications and careers. Of the half whose territorial origins may be hazarded, four were Somerset men, as no doubt were several of the rest. Others however had come to Wells from elsewhere, and more, it seems, than found their way to Exeter. Roger Winwood (1506) and Richard Edon (1546) originated from Gloucestershire, and William Champernown (1510) from Devon. The provenance of James Greenhalgh (1488), from the diocese of Lichfield, was still more remote and so was that of William Absolon (usher, 1556–7), who came via Oxford from Kent. As for Alexander Barclay (1548), he was probably a Scot but whatever his origins, a widely travelled man. Nine of the masters are known to have attended university and another four entitled 'master' may have done so. Four of the first group were undergraduates, strictly speaking. They had either suspended their studies to earn money (as was permissible) or had quitted the university altogether without a degree. Of the remaining five one was a BA, two were MAs, and two were graduates in theology. The qualifications of the latter were unusually high for schoolteaching and arose from the special circumstances of the Reformation; both were ex-monks. The mastership was not confined to priests. Although at least seven of the occupants held that status, three were certainly in minor orders, as were probably most of the unknown remainder. Their length of tenure can only be computed in the sixteenth century, when they usually held office for short periods of between two and five years. Three of the masters subsequently went on to occupy parochial benefices, three of the younger ones returned to university, and the fate of the rest is unknown. In general they seem to have been young men, as was usual in schools, but a few—William Champernown and the two ex-monks, Richard Edon and Alexander Barclay—came to the work in their maturity. The latter was indeed a septuagenarian.

The list of the known masters begins with Richard Northcurry, who occurs in 1274–5. The preservation of his name has come about through his appointment to deputise for the prior of St John's, Wells, whom the pope had nominated as a judge-delegate to determine a case involving the chancellor of Salisbury, the archdeacon of Winchester,

1 *Reg. Chichele, Canterbury*, ed. E. F. Jacob, vol ii (Canterbury & York Soc., xlii, 1937), pp 250–252.
2 PRO, Prob 11/11 (PCC 29 Horne); *Somerset Medieval Wills*, ed. F. W. Weaver, vol i (Somerset Record Soc., xiv, 1901), p 371. On the *Catholicon* see *ESMA*, p 93. The '*Liber Gutrumni*' is probably the *Opus Grammaticale*, 'excerptum ex Prisciano, Alexandro, etc'. by the Spanish friar Andreas Guterius Ceresianus, who dedicated it to Luis, bishop of Burgos (1456–95). The work was printed at least three times, 1485–91 (L. Hain, *Repertorium Typographicum* (reprinted Milan, 1948), nos 8333–5). Its rarity in England may account for the curious spelling in the registered copy of Austell's will: Gutrumni for Guterii.
3 For the list of names and for references see below, pp 89–90.

and the rector of Bentworth in Hampshire. In the documents relating to the case Northcurry is designated as 'the master of the school of liberal arts in Wells', a most interesting title.[1] It suggests, along with evidence from elsewhere, that the major thirteenth-century schools did not only study grammar but also concerned themselves with other subjects in the arts course, particularly logic.[2] After Northcurry no schoolmaster is mentioned by name until 1352 when William Sutton held office. He was a tenant in the city of Wells and a modest contributor of 20s. towards the building of the new college of vicars-choral.[3] The next known master was Walter Frysmark, who ruled in 1377. It is recorded of him that he left in due course for a parochial benefice and became what contemporaries called a 'chopchurch', exchanging one parish after another in rapid succession, in Sussex, Berkshire, and Wiltshire. Whatever his motives, he never appears to have risen very high among the beneficed clergy. His next recorded successor, William Westerly, is only a name, and it is not until 1409 that another master survives of whom anything can be said. The occupant is not identified but he was evidently unsatisfactory, for he received no commons and only half of his salary, 'because he did not wear his habit in the choir, nor did anything therein'. During the same year John Helcombe, the master of the choristers, was paid 6s. 8d. 'for training boys in grammar', and it is possible that he acted as a substitute on this occasion.[4]

In the period of the first surviving chapter act-book (1486–1514) seven schoolmasters were appointed. Two or three of them stayed for terms of about three years, which looks as if this may have been the custom, as it had formerly been at Lincoln and York.[5] In 1511 on the other hand a prospective schoolmaster was invited to remain for six years.[6] John Smith who came in 1500 and had left by May 1503 was probably the same man who was headmaster of Eton from 1503 to 1507. His successor at Wells, John Draper, was the son of a tenant of Winchester College at Montacute. He became a scholar of the college in 1488 and proceeded to New College, Oxford, four years later. He was a BA and a priest by the time he became schoolmaster, with which office he held the chantry of Corpus Christi in the cathedral. By 1510 he had resigned both to be instituted as rector of Foxcote, but he did not live to enjoy his new benefice for he was dead by November of that year.[7] Another schoolmaster who held a cathedral chantry was William Champernown, appointed in 1510 and instituted in the following year to the chantry of St Calixtus.[8] On 30 October 1511 the

1 Salisbury Dean & Chapter, Press III: Chancellor, Deeds of 1274–5. Northcurry's name is not mentioned in the documents, but it appears on his seal, inscribed 'Sigill[um] Rica[rdi] Nortcuri Cap[ellani] Dei'. The surname Nortcury also appears in *HMC*, i, 124. North Curry belonged to Wells Cathedral.
2 See above, p 3.
3 *HMC*, ii, 618; Reynolds, *Wells Cathedral*, p cxviii.
4 *HMC*, ii, 44, 46, 47.
5 *VCH Lincs.*, ii, 423; A. F. Leach, *Early Yorkshire Schools*, vol i (Yorks. Archaeological Soc., Record Series, xxvii, 1899), p 13.
6 *HMC*, ii, 228.
7 Draper was appointed to the chantry of Corpus Christi on 26 August 1503, resigning by July 1510 (*Regg. King & Hadrian, Wells*, ed. Sir H. C. Maxwell-Lyte (Somerset Record Soc., liv, 1939), pp 84, 143.
8 *HMC*, ii, 222, 226.

office of schoolmaster was promised to John Godard, one of the vicars choral, to be held from the following May and for six years, if he should do well. In consequence Godard, who had been instituted a vicar choral in 1504, was excused attendance at midnight mattins.[1] It is by no means certain that he ever took up the post, and in 1513 a new incumbent arrived in the person of Robert Hill, MA. None of the masters' names survives after this until 1535 when John Littleskill held the office, with which he combined a chantry in the cathedral and lived with the other chantry priests in their college in the Mountroy. His will of 1539, the year of his death, shows that notwithstanding his name, he was actually a man of some attainment. He bequeathed his Latin books to one Oxford scholar, his books of Greek to another, and mentioned five volumes of theology, including works by Ambrose, Chrysostom, Cyprian, Origen and Erasmus. Littleskill does not appear to have been a graduate, but his books and his friends at Oxford suggest strongly that he had studied there. His will gives a salutary lesson against underestimating the interests and acquaintances of non-graduate chaplain-schoolmasters.

The grammar school retained its traditional character until the reign of Edward VI. Up to that time it continued to possess a single master receiving the ancient salary of £2. 17s. and charging his pupils fees.[2] In 1547 however the government of Edward VI ordered that every cathedral chapter should establish a free grammar school where none already existed in the close or had been founded nearby from a private benefaction. The schoolmaster was to receive twenty marks a year (£13. 6s. 8d.) plus a house, and there was also to be an usher with a salary half as great and a free chamber.[3] The master then in office was Richard Edon, who had been appointed in the previous year. Edon, a former Cistercian monk of Hailes in Gloucestershire and an Oxford bachelor of theology, appears to have been a protégé of the bishop, William Knight, whose chaplain he was. He seems to have suffered some personal trouble in 1547, possibly illness,[4] and in consequence it was necessary to appoint another master in his place to satisfy the government's injunctions. The man chosen was Alexander Barclay, of whom it can best be said that he was willing 'to have a go' at anything. In the course of his long life (he was probably in his early seventies) he had been a traveller, secular poet, doctor of divinity, schoolmaster, monk, friar and parish priest at one time or another. He had established a connection with the cathedral in 1546 when the sub-dean presented him to the vicarage of Wookey near Wells, and it is probable that he took up the office of schoolmaster at Michaelmas 1547. Twelve months later he was paid the statutory sum of £13. 6. 8d. for a year's teaching, and an appropriate salary

---

1 Godard was admitted a vicar non-perpetual, stall of Combe VIII, on 30 April 1504, and awarded the thirteenth chamber of the west side of the vicars' close in 1510 (*HMC*, ii, 177, 145). He was promised the schoolmastership in 1511 (ibid., p 228), but was still a vicar choral in 1535 (*Valor Ecclesiasticus*, i, 137).
2 Communars' Books, 1545–6.
3 *Visitation Articles and Injunctions of the Period of the Reformation*, ed. W. H. Frere, ii, 138–9.
4 Mentioned in the will of Bishop Knight, 12 August 1547 (*Somerset Medieval Wills, 1531–8*, ed. F. W. Weaver (Somerset Record Soc., xxi, 1905), p 98.

was also given to his usher, Rowland Mynever.[1] It is to be suspected that the latter did most of the actual work.

Barclay did not stay long at Wells after Michaelmas 1548. By the autumn of the following year Richard Edon was back in office, which he retained until 1551. This suggests that Protestantism made little impact on the school during Edward's reign since Edon, although he may have outwardly conformed to the religious changes, was a Catholic at heart who returned to the monastic life in 1556. Mynever the usher was also conservative enough to be appointed schoolmaster for a time after Mary's accession in 1553. It was in her reign that Wells school, like so many others, became finally involved with the Reformation in a close way. The queen and her bishops were well aware of the crucial importance of schools in re-establishing the Catholic religion. In 1556 a synod of the English Church ordered that each cathedral should maintain a seminary of boys to be trained for the priesthood.[2] No seminary was ever set up at Wells, but in 1556 new schoolmasters were appointed of good quality and approved Catholic principles. The master, William Good, was an Oxford MA and his usher, William Absolon, was studying for the BA. Both were fellows of Corpus Christi College, a strong centre of the old religion. They were both given canonries of the cathedral for their support, and Good was also presented by the crown to the vicarage of Meare.[3] Both appear to have left Wells after Mary's death, and Good eventually made his way to the Netherlands where he entered the Jesuit order. The school on the other hand remained, and has enjoyed a continuous existence until the present day.

1 Communars' Rolls, 1547–8; *HMC*, ii, 267.
2 *ESMA*, pp 286–7.
3 *Reg. Bourne, Wells*, pp 146–7.

MASTERS AND USHERS OF WELLS CATHEDRAL SCHOOL

Masters

1	Richard Northcurry	occurs 1274–5
2	William Sutton	occurs 1352
3	Walter Frysmark	occurs 1377
4	William Westerly	before 1393
5	Richard Cosyn	occurs 1411
6	John Rydeler, *Mag.*	occurs 1418
7	James Greenhalgh, *Mag.*	appointed 1488
8	John Smith, *Mag.*	appointed 1500
9	John Draper, BA	appointed 1503
10	Roger Winwood	appointed 1506
11	William Champernown, *Mag.*	appointed 1510
12	*John Godard*	offered appointment 1512
13	Robert Hill, MA	appointed 1513
14	John Littleskill	occurs 1535
15	John Dakyns	ceased 1546
16	Richard Edon, STB	appointed 1546
17	Alexander Barclay, STP	probably appointed 1547
18	Richard Edon	re-appears 1549
19	John Thorne	probably appointed 1551
20	Rowland Mynever	occurs 1553×4
21	William Good, MA	occurs 1556–8
22	William Lyde	occurs 1559–61

Ushers

23	Rowland Mynever	occurs 1548–52
24	Walter Price	occurs 1553–4
25	William Absolon	occurs 1556–7

1 Salisbury Diocesan Record Office, Dean & Chapter Records, Press III: Chancellor, deeds of 1274–5. Chaplain.
2 *HMC*, ii, 618.
3 PRO, Clerical Subsidy Rolls, E 179/4/1 m 1. Priest. He exchanged the vicarage of Billingshurst, Sussex, for that of North Moreton, Berks., on 10 December 1389 (Reg. Waltham, Sarum, 1389 fo 24); North Moreton for the vicarage of Marden, Wilts., on 14 August 1390 (ibid., 1390 fo 33); and Marden for the rectory of Calstone Wellington, Wilts., on 2 August 1392 (ibid., 1392 fo 55v).
4 *HMC*, ii, 23.
5 When ordained acolyte (*Reg. Bubwith, Wells,* ed. T. S. Holmes, vol ii (Somerset Record Soc., xxx, 1914), p 500).
6 Ibid., p 317.

7 1 October (*HMC*, ii, 113). Originally of Coventry and Lichfield diocese, he was ordained subdeacon on 22 February and priest on 29 March 1494 (Taunton, Somerset Record Office, Reg. Fox, Wells, fos 43–4).

8 3 October (*HMC*, ii, 160). He may well be the same as John Smith, headmaster of Eton College 1503–7 (*BRUO*, iii, 1717).

9 3 May (*HMC*, ii, 171). Priest. For his career see *BRUO*, i, 592.

10 16 January (*HMC*, ii, 190). He came from Worcester diocese, probably Bristol, and was subsequently ordained subdeacon on 18 March, deacon on 8 April and priest on 23 September 1508 to the title of St Mark's Hospital, Bristol (Somerset Record Office, Reg. Hadrian de Castello, fos 146a, 147a, 148a).

11 17 August (*HMC*, ii, 222). He was ordained subdeacon on 31 May 1488 (Somerset Record Office, Reg. Stillington, Wells, fo 228a), deacon on 20 September 1488 (Exeter, Devon Record Office, Reg. Fox, Exeter, fo 152v), and priest on 20 December 1488 (Reg. Stillington, fo 230b), to the title of Totnes Priory. This suggests that he was a member of the well-known Devon family of the same name. He was presented to the chantry of St Calixtus, Wells Cathedral, on 25 January 1511 (*HMC*, ii, 226).

12 *HMC*, ii, 228. It is not clear if he occupied the post.

13 6 July (ibid., p 233).

14 *Valor Ecclesiasticus*, i, 127. For his career see *BRUO*, iv, 370–1. His will, dated 19 May 1539, is calendared in *Somerset Medieval Wills, 1531–8*, ed. F. W. Weaver (Somerset Record Soc., xxi, 1905), p 53.

15 Wells Cathedral Library, Communars' Books, 1545–6. He supplicated for BA at Oxford in February 1546 (*Register of the University of Oxford*, vol i, ed. C. W. Boase (Oxford Historical Soc., i, 1885), p 211). No doubt he was a younger relative of Dr John Dakyns, the chancellor.

16 Communars' Books, 1545–6. He became master in May 1546. For his career see *BRUO*, iv, 277, where he appears under his other name of Hayles.

17 He was probably appointed at Michaelmas 1547, since he was paid a year's salary one year later (Communars' Rolls, 1547–8; *HMC*, ii, 267). Priest. There is a sketch of his complicated career in the *DNB*.

18 Communars' Books, 1549–50 fo 5; 1550–1 fos 5, 9v; 1551–2 fo 29v. He probably resigned at Christmas 1551.

19 Communars' Books, 1551–2 fo 29v; 1553–4 fo 5. He was probably appointed at Christmas 1551 and resigned late in 1553 or 1554.

20 Communars' Books, 1553–4 fo 5. He had previously been usher.

21 *Reg. Bourne, Wells*, pp 146–7; *Somerset Medieval Wills, 1531–8*, p 214. A Somerset man, he was admitted a 'pupil' or scholar of Corpus Christi College, Oxford, on 26 February 1545 and a 'scholar' or probationary fellow on 15 June 1548. He incepted as MA in 1552 (*Register of the University of Oxford*, i, 218). He was presented to the vicarage of Meare, Som., by the crown on 28 August 1556 (*CPR 1555–7*, p 500). After Elizabeth's accession he withdrew to Tournai where he became a Jesuit in 1562. He subsequently worked for his order in Ireland, the Netherlands, Poland and Italy. He died at Naples in 1586 (*DNB*).

22 *HMC*, ii, 287, 289. He supplicated for BA at Oxford in February 1564 (*Register of the University of Oxford*, i, 253).

23 Communars' Rolls, 1547–8; Communars' Books, 1549–50 fo 5; 1550–1 fos 5, 9v; 1551–2 fo 29v. He later became master.

24 Communars' Books, 1553–4 fo 5.

25 *Reg. Bourne, Wells*, p 147; Communars' Books, 1556–7. A Kentishman, he was admitted a 'pupil' or scholar of Corpus Christi College on 9 June 1554 and a 'scholar' or probationary fellow on 2 June 1556. He determined as BA in 1560 and incepted as MA in 1565 (*Register of the University of Oxford*, i, 234).

INSTRUCTORS OF THE CHORISTERS

1	John Helcombe	occurs 1409
2	Robert Cater	occurs 1460
3	Richard Hygons	occurs 1487
		resigned 1507–8
4	Richard Bramston	appointed 1507
		resigned 1531
5	John Clawsey	appointed 1508
6	John Gye	occurs 1512
7	John Gaylard	occurs 1514
8	John Smith, junior	occurs 1538

1 *HMC*, ii, 47.
2 *Miscellanea,* ed. Watkin, pp 98–109. *Dominus.* He occurs as a vicar choral 1467–70 (*HMC,* ii, 684, 688).
3 Ibid., pp 104, 205.
4 Ibid., pp 205, 701. His first appointment may have been temporary; he probably returned during the 1510s. He was admitted a vicar non-perpetual on 23 January 1507, had left Wells by 1510, but was back by 1531 (ibid., pp 200, 219–20, 700–1).
5 Ibid., p 208. He was apparently a vicar choral by 1487 (ibid., pp 693–4), but was admitted a vicar choral non-perpetual on 28 July 1496 and perpetual on 27 July 1497 (ibid., pp 145, 147). He died by 1509 (ibid., p 215).
6 Ibid., pp 231–2. He was admitted a vicar choral non-perpetual on 16 March 1508 and perpetual on 16 March 1509 (ibid., pp 207, 212). He was still one in 1519 (ibid., p 699).
7 Ibid., p 236. He was admitted a vicar choral non-perpetual on 30 September 1512 and perpetual on 30 September 1513 (ibid., pp 231, 235).
8 Ibid., p 248. He was a vicar choral by 1535 (ibid., p 702.)

2
Towns and Villages with Schools, but not Endowed

AWRE
Gloucestershire

In 1310 at the proving of the age of John Bleith, a royal ward of Newnham-on-Severn, one of the witnesses, John le Moul, remembered that on Michaelmas Day 1287 Master John of Awre had taken his son John to the school of Awre, where he stayed for a year.[1] Recollections of this kind, produced for a formal inquiry, need not be taken too seriously as to dates, but it seems unlikely that anyone should have bothered to invent a school in such an odd place. The village of Awre, with its attendant tithings, was then of greater importance than it is now, and its position near the River Severn on cleared land was more significant than its present isolation down winding lanes from a main road. Its rectory, appropriated in 1351, was worth £40 in 1291; Bishop Swinfield of Hereford dated a letter to the king from Awre in 1286; and in 1328 Thomas, Lord Berkeley is said to have built a house there on his manor.[2] Awre was evidently no backwater, but it is an unusual place to find any kind of school so early, and we can only wish for more information on the subject.

BATH
Somerset

There was a public school at Bath early in the twelfth century. The evidence comes from the obit roll of Matilda, daughter of William the Conqueror and abbess of Caen, who died in 1113. A messenger, as was often the custom, carried the news of her death around the religious communities of France and England, taking with him a roll on which their members could inscribe their names, with prayers and sympathetic verses. The twenty-seventh item on the roll is the formal subscription of the cathedral priory of St Peter, Bath;

[1] *Cal. Inquisitions Post Mortem*, v, 167,
[2] *Taxatio Ecclesiastica* (Record Commission, 1802), p 161; John Smyth, *Lives of the Berkeleys*, ed. J. Maclean, i, 308.

the twenty-eighth, 'the voice of the scholars of the same town', consists of twenty elegant rhyming Latin hexameters.[1]

At this period, after the removal of the see of Wells to Bath in 1090, the importance of Wells as a centre of religion and learning was at a low ebb, and in 1113 Bath is more likely to have been the principal haunt of scholars in Somerset. By the middle of the twelfth century, however, the status of Wells began to rise again and its school, first mentioned in about 1140, subsequently replaced that of Bath as the major centre of education in the diocese. Bath probably continued to possess a town school of a more local importance, but at present no details of its history are known until after the Reformation.

BRAUNTON
Devon

Braunton had a school in the early 1530s when Bishop Jewel studied there for a short time under a master named Thomas Stot. Jewel subsequently went on to other schools at South Molton and Barnstaple.[2]

BRIDGWATER
Somerset

There was a grammar school at Bridgwater in 1298 when arrangements were made for the poor boys supported by the hospital of St John the Baptist to study there. Robert Burnell, bishop of Bath and Wells 1275–92 and for eighteen years chancellor of England, had provided for thirteen boys to be maintained by the hospital from the revenues of their rectories of Morwenstow and Wembdon, probably as a condition of allowing the two benefices to be appropriated to the hospital.[3] On 28 July 1298 Geoffrey of Mark, the master of the hospital, bound himself and his house to maintain thirteen poor scholars, fit for instruction in grammar, within their walls. The house itself had no school, so the scholars were excused from taking a full part in its religious services so that they could attend daily at the school in the town. The master of the town school was also allowed to send seven of his poor scholars for daily pittances from the kitchen of St John's.[4] These scholarships and exhibitions, if they endured, must have greatly assisted the continuity of education in medieval Bridgwater.

The next allusion to the town school is in 1379 when an un-named master in priest's orders contributed 2s. to the clerical subsidy of that year.[5] In the fifteenth century it is also

1 L. Delisle, *Rouleaux des Morts du IXe au XVe siècle* (Société de l'histoire de France (Paris, 1866), p 192).
2 Laurence Humfrey, *Joannis Juelli Angli Episcopi Sarisburiensis Vita et Mors* (1573), p 17.
3 *Valor Ecclesiasticus*, i, 208–9.
4 *Reg. Drokensford, Wells*, p 268.
5 The words *magister scolarum* appear third in a list of chaplains in the archdeaconry of Taunton paying the subsidy of 1379 (PRO, Exch. KR, Clerical Subsidy Rolls, E 179/4/4/). Although the list has no heading, it clearly refers to the rural deanery of Bridgwater. The schoolmaster must belong to the town itself, for he occurs in the company of two other known chaplains from there.

recorded that a boy named William Tredwyn was educated in the vicarage, probably in the 1460s, during the long incumbency of John Colswayne, vicar of Bridgwater from 1423 to 1474. In an attestation which he wrote in the early sixteenth century, Tredwyn recalled that at the age of thirteen or fourteen he was

> contynually abidyng yn the vicarage of Briggewater with one Sir John Wheler, parishe prest of the seid towne, to lerne reede and syng with the seid Sir John Wheler at the commaundement of Mr Sir John Colswayne, then ther vyker of the seid towne, and dayly and nyghtly for the more party at borde and bedde withyn the seid vycarage.[1]

The teacher, John Wheeler, first appears as parish chaplain of Bridgwater in 1450, and from 1464 until his death twenty years later he was also chaplain of the chantry of St Mary. His pupil also became a chantry chaplain at North Newton in 1485, remaining there until his death in 1521 after an unsuccessful attempt to secure the rectory of Brushford in 1504.[2] It is most unlikely that the vicarage provided all the schooling needed in Bridgwater at that time, and the parish chaplain's tuition was probably additional to the work of the town school.

In 1535 the hospital was still paying £15. 13s. 4d. to support thirteen boys, but nothing is said about their education.[3] The house itself was dissolved four years later. In 1548 the inhabitants of the town petitioned the chantry commissioners for the establishment of a *free* grammar school, but without success.[4] An endowed school was finally set up in the town in 1561.[5]

BRIDPORT
Dorset

The earliest reference to education in Bridport comes from a deed of 1240 conveying rights of pasturage to the hospital of St John and witnessed, among others, by Vincent, 'then master of the school of Bridport'.[6] There was also a school in the town during the fifteenth century. A grammatical miscellany of this period, now at Lincoln Cathedral, includes a short tract of a single page on prosody, called *Flores Accentus,* with the note that

---

1 Bridgwater Corporation MSS, vol x no 1, document no. 115; *Hist. MSS Commission, Third Report,* p 312.
2 William Tredwyn of Bridgwater was ordained subdeacon on 23 September, deacon 24 December 1480, and priest on 21 April 1481 (Taunton, Somerset Record Office, Reg. Stillington, Wells, fos 205b, 206b, 207a). He was chantry chaplain of North Newton, instituted 16 March 1485, till death (*Regg. Stillington & Fox, Wells,* p 130; *Reg. Wolsey, Wells,* p 18), and temporarily rector of Brushford, instituted 16 January 1504 (*Regg. King & Hadrian,* p 90). He died by October 1521.
3 *Valor Ecclesiasticus,* i, 208–9.
4 *Somerset Chantries,* ed. E. Green, p 57; *ESR,* part ii, p 191.
5 *VCH Som.,* ii, 447.
6 J. Hutchins, *History of Dorset,* ii, 20; *Hist. MSS Commission, Sixth Report,* p 482.

'Master John Chalurys composed this, who dwells at Bridport'.[1] Further evidence of a fifteenth-century grammar school comes from an inventory of books belonging to the parish church of St Mary in 1476. This mentions four volumes which might normally have been used in a grammar school: 'Hugutio', probably that author's etymological Latin dictionary;[2] 'the treatise of Thomas of Hanney', in other words the *Memoriale Juniorum*, a general survey of grammar completed in 1313[3]; 'an alphabet of Latin words', apparently some kind of vocabulary or word list; and an unspecified book of logic.[4] Parish churches sometimes possessed Latin dictionaries for the use of their clergy, but it is unusual to find one holding so many grammatical works as these. It looks rather as though the churchwardens were acting as trustees of the books for the benefit of the local schoolmaster as, in similar instances, they did at Hedon and Wellington.[5]

CHIPPENHAM
Wiltshire

The grammatical miscellany which was probably used by Robert Londe in his Bristol school during the 1420s includes some tracts and exercises prefixed by the words 'Chyppnam' and 'Wotton'. Since Wotton-under-Edge possessed a grammar school in the early fifteenth century, it is possible that Chippenham also had one, and that an exchange of material went on between these schools and that of Bristol.[6]

CIRENCESTER
Gloucestershire

A few tenuous references suggest the continuity of education in Cirencester from the 1240s until the establishment of an endowed grammar school there in the middle of the fifteenth century.[7] The first allusion to a schoolmaster is in 1242 when he acted as an arbitrator in an ecclesiastical suit between the abbeys of Gloucester and Lire (in Normandy) over the tithes of two chapelries in Herefordshire.[8] Next in 1361 Walter Browning, a witness at the proof of age of John Willington of Sandhurst in Gloucestershire, claimed to remember Willington's birth in 1340 because on the day after the christening, being then aged twenty-one, he left for Cirencester to study in the school there and told the news to the abbot.[9] Again

---

1 Lincoln Cathedral MS 88 (A.3.15) fo 119v (*Cat. of the MSS of Lincoln Cathedral Chapter Library*, ed. R. M. Woolley (Oxford, 1927), p 49).
2 For Hugutio see *ESMA*, p 93.
3 For Thomas Hanney see ibid., p 96 and note 2.
4 J. Hutchins, *History of Dorset*, ii, 29.
5 For Hedon see *Testamenta Eboracensia*, ed. J. Raine, vol ii (Surtees Soc., xxx, 1855), p 270, and for Wellington, below, p 107.
6 Oxford, Lincoln College, MS lat. 129 pp 162, 199, and see also above, p 40.
7 For the endowed school see below, p 128.
8 *Historia et Cartularium Monasterii Gloucestriae*, ed. W. K. Hart, vol i (Rolls Series, 1863), p 281.
9 *Cal. Inquisitions Post Mortem*, xi, no 130.

almost a century passes before we encounter a chaplain of Cirencester named Stephen Scolemayster paying a contribution to the clerical subsidy of 1419.[1] Whether he was a practising schoolmaster at the time, or whether 'schoolmaster' was merely a surname unrelated to his work, is hard to say.[2] Finally in 1433 Thomas Polton, bishop of Worcester, bequeathed £4 to a boy protégé of his named William, who was studying at Cirencester, to enable him to continue at school. That the bishop should have chosen to place a boy there suggests that the school was then of some repute.[3]

CREDITON
Devon

The ecclesiastical centre of Crediton has always been the great collegiate church which remained there after the bishop departed for Exeter in 1050. The nominal establishment of the college during the later middle ages included eighteen prebendaries, often non-resident, and an equal number of vicars to sing the services. The standard of these services in the fourteenth century did not come up to the exacting demands of Bishop Grandisson, and in 1334 he ordered the resources of the choir to be augmented. The college was henceforth to maintain four clerks with men's voices and four choristers. The clerks, who were evidently in minor orders, had to give up their places when they became priests. Besides assisting in the choir they were each allotted duties in the church, and one of them was charged with teaching the choristers in song and manners. The choristers were to divide their time between choir and school, and they had to leave the choir when their voices broke. Each clerk received 26s. 8d. a year to support him, and each boy 17s. 4d.[4]

The arrangements which Grandisson made appear to have lasted until the dissolution of the college in 1545. During this period therefore we can reckon on the existence of at least a song school in Crediton for the benefit of the choristers. Casual references in visitation documents testify to their continuing presence. In 1361 Grandisson ordered that any boy who failed to appear in the choir, unless he were engaged in school, should receive seven or ten stripes on his bare bottom.[5] In 1439 Bishop Lacy again mentioned the choristers

---

1 PRO, Exch. KR, Clerical Subsidy Rolls, E 179/58/10.
2 Several people surnamed 'Schoolmaster' occur elsewhere in this work, including Dunster (below, p 99). Launceston (below, p 101), Stow-on-the-Wold (below, p 104) and Tiverton (below, p 106). Was the surname applied to men who were not or never had been schoolmasters? It was certainly used by women, perhaps the wives or widows of masters (see examples in *Gesta Abbatum Monasterii Sancti Albani*, ed. H. T. Riley, vol iii (Rolls Series, 1869), p 192; *Somerset Medieval Wills*, ed. F. W. Weaver, vol i (Somerset Record Soc., xvi, 1901), p 323). The comparative scarcity of the name suggests that it never became established as an independent surname, but it may have been used of people who had once been schoolmasters and were no longer.
3 *Reg. Chichele, Canterbury*, ed. E. F. Jacob & H. C. Johnson, vol ii (Canterbury & York Soc., xlii, 1937), p 492. The place is there spelt 'Sussetr'. The provenance of the bishop and the associated references to Bristol and Worcester make Cirencester much more likely than the editors' suggestion of Chichester. Similar spellings of Cirencester are found at that time.
4 *Reg. Grandisson, Exeter*, ed. F. C. Hingeston-Randolph, ii, 753; Oliver, *Monasticon*, pp 81-2.
5 *Reg. Grandisson*, Exeter, iii, 1222.

and forbade their absence from services.¹ In 1511 Bishop Oldham, finding the college in a decrepit condition, made some new ordinances for its life and worship. He reduced the number of clerks to two, but one of them was still expected to instruct the boys and play the organ in church. His salary was raised to £5. 6s. 8d., the stipend proper to an adult cleric, and he was excused attendance in choir between mass and vespers in order to teach the boys. Their emoluments were also increased to £1. 6s. 8d.² In 1523 Bishop Veysey made further modifications to what Oldham had laid down, raising the clerk-schoolmaster's salary to £6. 13s. 4d. and increasing the number of boys to six.³ In 1545 Philip Alcock was the master of the choristers, and he received a pension of £4 a year when the college was dissolved.⁴

So much for the song school in the college; what of the town? There was certainly a grammar school in Crediton by 1377 when Walter Cotel, vicar of St Veryan, Cornwall, received permission from the bishop to be absent from his parish for three years in order to teach it. The bishop's licence to Cotel tells us two things about the school. It was a general, public grammar school, and other people were forbidden to teach in the town without the permission of those to whom the appointment of schoolmasters belonged. Since the bishop, who was the lord of the manor, did not claim this patronage for himself, there can be little doubt that it belonged to the college.⁵ The subsequent history of the grammar school before the Reformation rests largely upon conjecture, but the likelihood is that such a school continued in being. The allusion to the patronage of the school in 1377 is important in this respect, for it shows that Cotel did not merely drift into Crediton of his own accord, but that a recognised authority existed to appoint schoolmasters and may therefore have done so on later occasions. Again, the request of John Clifton, sometime bailiff of Crediton, in 1449 that twelve boys should read the psalter about his body before its burial suggests that there were other literate boys in the town besides the choristers themselves.⁶ Finally there is the question why a new grammar school was founded in Crediton by the government of Edward VI on 2 April 1547.⁷ Although the foundation was carried out under the young king, it was an evident legacy from the reign of Henry VIII who had died in the previous January. It came two or three years before the main crop of Edwardian school foundations (which were linked with the dissolution of the chantries), and its title, 'The King's New Grammar School', was similar to the titles which Henry VIII gave to other old schools which he refounded. It would be very odd before about 1550 to find the crown establishing a new grammar school where one had not existed

1 *Reg. Lacy, Exeter,* ed. G. R. Dunstan, ii, 142.
2 Devon Record Office, Reg. Veysey, Exeter, ii, fos 10v–12.
3 Reg. Veysey, Exeter, ii, fos 28v–30; Oliver, *Monasticon,* p 84.
4 PRO, E 301/81; *LPFD,* xxi part i, p 778. He was apparently the composer of a setting of *Salve Regina* in British Museum, MSS Add. 17802–5 (F. Ll. Harrison, *Music in Medieval Britain* (2nd ed., 1963), p 454).
5 *Reg. Brantyngham, Exeter,* ed. F. C. Hingeston-Randolph, i, 378–9. This corrects the statement made in *ESMA,* p 145 and map p 147, that Crediton school was under episcopal patronage.
6 *Reg. Lacy, Exeter,* iv, 56.
7 *CPR 1547–8,* pp 43–4.

before, and we may reasonably presume that the new foundation of Crediton School, so similar to that at Ottery, was also intended to replace an earlier school. The dissolution of Crediton College in 1545 provides the obvious reason why a new foundation was necessary. Slight though they be, these indications make it likely that a public grammar school existed in Crediton between 1377 and 1545, the master being appointed by the college, teaching perhaps for fees, and possibly holding his school in the 'schoolhouse' in the college mentioned in 1547.[1]

DARTMOUTH
Devon

The churchwardens' accounts of St Saviour's Dartmouth, in 1490 include a payment of 3s. 4d. 'to the mayor, for a reward to the schoolmaster'. No other details of this man or his school are at present known.[2]

DEVIZES
Wiltshire

On 22 March 1463 Richard Beauchamp, bishop of Salisbury, granted licence to Walter Barber, clerk, to teach grammar and letters in the town of Devizes during his, the bishop's, pleasure. For ecclesiastical purposes Devizes was a peculiar jurisdiction under the bishop's control and this suggests the reason why Barber took care to secure Beauchamp's approval before he opened his school.[3]

DUNSTER
Somerset

Although no school as such is mentioned at Dunster in the middle ages, there are signs that schoolmasters were to be found there, perhaps under the patronage of the two families who held the manor and the castle—the Mohuns until 1404 and their successors the Luttrells. In 1355 a commission of oyer and terminer was issued on a complaint by John Mohun, lord of Dunster, that Philip Luccombe and others had driven away his deer and assaulted Richard le Scolemaister his servant, who had been deputed to collect the profits of Dunster fair.[4] Later in 1410 Richard the chaplain of Luxborough was charged with having drawn the blood of Lawrence Scolemayster with his fist, contrary to the peace.[5] Finally in 1424 an account roll of the Luttrell family mentions a certain John Scolemaystre, staying as a

1 Unless that was merely the building where the choristers were taught.
2 Exeter, East Devon Record Office, Dartmouth: St Saviour's Accounts, m 1489/90; H. R. Watkin, *Dartmouth,* vol i (Devonshire Association, 1935), pp 310–11.
3 Reg. Beauchamp, Sarum, vol i part ii, fo 153.
4 *CPR 1354–8,* p 231. For a discussion of 'Schoolmaster' as a surname see above, p 97.
5 H. C. Maxwell-Lyte, *History of Dunster* (1909), i, 303.

guest in the household for ten weeks.¹ His services however are more likely to have been intended for the boys and youths of the household itself.

GREAT TORRINGTON
Devon

Torrington may have had a school in the later fifteenth century, for in 1486 Anne, the widow of Sir Thomas Ormonde, held part of a messuage called the 'scolehouse' in Great Torrington.² There was certainly a short-lived school in 1524 when Thomas Bennet, the Protestant 'martyr', taught young children in Torrington after withdrawing from Cambridge. But, says John Foxe, 'that town not serving his expectation', he left after a year and went to Exeter.³

HEANTON PUNCHARDON
Devon

Heanton Punchardon is a village four and a half miles north west of Barnstaple. The rector in 1529 was John Bellamy, and it was he who first taught Bishop Jewel, then seven years old, the elements of learning. Bellamy was Jewel's uncle. It is not clear whether he had any other pupils.⁴

ILMINSTER
Somerset

The only reference to a medieval school in Ilminster comes in a letter of 1440 from Robert Lawrence, rector of St Martin, Wareham, to William Mills, an English merchant then dwelling at Rouen. In this the writer reminded his correspondent, 'that ye and I were schoolfellows sometime at Ilminster, ye being at board at More's house, the which he recommends me to you'.⁵ The presence of someone from a distance who had to board and of someone else who later became a priest, suggests that this was a grammar school.

LAUNCESTON
Cornwall

Launceston was the county town of Cornwall in the middle ages and one of the likeliest places to have possessed a permanent school, but as usual the references to education are

1 Ibid., p 101; Taunton, Somerset Record Office, Luttrell MSS, box 37, no 10.
2 *Cal. Inquisitions Post Mortem, Henry VII*, vol i (1898), p 65.
3 J. Foxe, *Acts & Monuments* ed. J. Pratt (1870), v, 18–26. The information was supplied to Foxe by John Hooker of Exeter.
4 Laurence Humfrey, *Joannis Juelli Angli Episcopi Sarisburiensis Vita et Mors* (London, 1573), p 17.
5 *Letters & Papers Illustrative of the Wars of the English in France*, ed. J. Stevenson, vol ii (Rolls Series, 1864), p 307.

few. In 1342 when Bishop Grandisson made his visitation of the Augustinian priory in the town, he ordered the canons to invite poor boys 'suitable and apt to learn grammar' to partake of the daily meal which they gave to the poor in their hall.[1] Since the priory, if it had been maintaining and teaching boys in its almonry would have made its own arrangements for feeding them, the boys mentioned by Grandisson must have belonged to a grammar school in the town. Parallels to the feeding of poor scholars by local religious houses can be found at Bridgwater, Bristol and other places.[2]

Teaching probably continued, for in 1462 the corporation was involved in a legal dispute in the mayor's court against Mr Simon Scolemayester.[3] We next hear of the school as an endowed chantry foundation in 1548, and this is discussed below.[4]

MALMESBURY
Wiltshire

The registers of Malmesbury Abbey indicate the existence of a school in the town during the thirteenth century, most probably in the 1260s. It stood on a corner site in Griffin's Lane, and the master, Master Richard 'rector of the school of Malmesbury', was also vicar of the town church of St Paul.[5]

MARLBOROUGH
Wiltshire

There was a school at Marlborough in 1232 when the master was appointed a papal judge delegate in a dispute between Luke, archdeacon of Surrey, and Elias of Derham, canon of Salisbury, about the tithes of Potterne in Wiltshire.[6] Judicial functions of this kind were often deputed to schoolmasters at this period.[7] The town was still a centre of education in 1301, when Bartholomew de Plecyz, rector of Wimborne St Giles in Dorset, was licensed to study for a year with the schoolmaster of Malmesbury. The rector appears to have been a young man of knightly birth, who had only recently secured a benefice.[8] Whether schooling continued to be available during the fourteenth and fifteenth centuries is likely, but not known. Marlborough was always one of the major Wiltshire towns: in 1377 it was fifth in size with 402 taxpayers, and in 1548 it is described as a 'great town' with three parish

1 *Reg. Grandisson, Exeter,* ii, 955.
2 See above, pp 37 and 94, and *ESMA,* pp 1179–80.
3 R. & O. B. Peter, *The Histories of Launceston and Dunheved* (Plymouth, 1885), p 143. For 'Schoolmaster' as a surname see above, p 97.
4 Below, p 148.
5 *Registrum Malmesburiense,* ed. J. S. Brewer, vol i (Rolls Series, 1879), pp 128, 132; Bodleian Library, MS Bodley 191 fo 41-v.
6 *Sarum Charters and Documents,* ed. W. R. Jones and W. D. Macray (Rolls Series 1891), pp 250–1.
7 Compare the examples at Wells (above, p 85) and Shaftesbury and Wilton (below, pp 103, 108).
8 *Reg. Simon de Gandavo, Sarum,* ed. C. T. Flower and M. C. B. Dawes, vol ii (Canterbury & York Soc., xli, 1914), p 849.

churches and 1056 communicants.¹ The chantry certificate of 1548 included a request from the mayor and corporation that the endowments of the hospital of St John might be converted to support a free school, 'for the inducement of youth within the same town, and in the country near abouts'.² This does not rule out the existence at that time of a schoolmaster teaching for fees.

MELLS
Somerset

In the early sixteenth century Mells was a prosperous village of clothiers and belonged to Glastonbury Abbey. The large church attracted benefactions and there was also a grammar school. In his will of 1524 John Robbins, a wealthy man of the place, bequeathed 10s. to the grammar schoolmaster and 3s. 4d. each to ten of his poor scholars. Robbins died shortly after making his will, and was buried in the parish church.³

MENHENIOT
Cornwall

In his description of Devon and Cornwall, the 'Synopsis Corographicall', the historian John Hooker, who was born in Exeter, explains how his parents died and left him an orphan at the age of ten, in about 1535. In this predicament he was put under the care of John Moreman, doctor of divinity, sometime fellow of Exeter College, Oxford, and after 1529 vicar of Menheniot in Cornwall. The connection may have come about during Moreman's brief tenure of the rectory of Holy Trinity, Exeter, between 1528 and 1530. Hooker goes on to inform us that he 'was brought up to school' under Moreman at Menheniot until he was able to leave for Oxford to study civil law. Like John Jewel at Heanton Punchardon, Hooker was probably the beneficiary of a private arrangement, for although he praises Moreman as a religious teacher of his parishioners, he says nothing of any other pupils.⁴

MITCHELDEAN
Gloucestershire

A rental of the manor of Mitcheldean made in 1545 for William Baynham by the bailiff, James Wynston, lists William Sargeant as paying 3s. for a tenement 'sometime a schoolhouse and parcel of the chantry'.⁵ The chantry was presumably that of the Holy Trinity and St George, but it did not claim to provide education in 1548.

1 *VCH Wilts.*, iv, 306–11, PRO, Chantry Certificates, E 301/58 no 54; *ESR*, part ii, pp 260–1.
2 Ibid.
3 PRO, Prob 11/21 (PCC 19 Bodfelde); *Somerset Medieval Wills,* ed. F. W. Weaver, vol ii (Somerset Record Soc., xix, 1903), p 225.
4 John Hooker, Synopsis Corographicall (Exeter, East Devon Record Office, pp 105, 115; British Museum, MS Harley 5827, fo 45v). For Moreman's biography see *BRUO*, iv, 400.
5 The rental is contained in a seventeenth-century MS journal made by Richard Colchester (Gloucestershire Record Office, Colchester MSS, D 36 iv, fo 22v).

PLYMOUTH
Devon

The only reference so far discovered to education in Plymouth before the foundation of the free grammar school in 1561 is a casual allusion to 'James the schoolmaster' in 1507.[1]

PLYMPTON
Devon

An inquisition after the death of Baldwin de Reviers, earl of Devon, in 1263 recorded that he had possessed the castle and township of Plympton 'with the advowson of the school'.[2] So the local school had a recognised patron responsible for appointing masters. Lay patrons of schools are not very common until the fifteenth century, and this instance appears to be one of the earliest known.[3]

SHAFTESBURY
Dorset

In 1234 the schoolmaster of Shaftesbury acted as a papal judge-delegate in a case concerning Reading Abbey and the church of 'Compton' in Salisbury diocese.[4]

SHERBORNE
Dorset

It is just possible, as we shall see, that the history of Sherborne school can be traced back to the twelfth century, but it is not mentioned in contemporary records until much later. The earliest evidence at present available comes from 1419 when the schoolmaster appears in a taxation list of Dorset clergymen. The reference informs us that his Christian name was Peter, he was master of a grammar school, and he was also a chaplain in priest's orders.[5] Another master, named Thomas Copeland, survives as the donor of 3s. 4d. to the hospital of St John, Sherborne, in 1438.[6] Whether he was a priest or a layman is not recorded. The evidence is slender, but it proves the existence of a grammar school in the town during the first half of the fifteenth century.

1 R. N. Worth, *History of Plymouth* (Plymouth, 1890), p 269.
2 *Cal. Inquisitions Post Mortem*, i, 174.
3 For other examples see *ESMA*, pp 146–8.
4 British Museum, MS Cotton Vespasian xxv, fo 114v.
5 PRO, Clerical Subsidy Rolls, E 179/52/96. The schoolmaster is listed among parishes in the rural deanery of Shaftesbury under the heading 'Shirlton'. This seems to be a confusion of 'Shirborne' and Shilton. Shilton cannot have had a school, and since the clergy of Shaftesbury itself are listed separately, this leaves Sherborne as the obvious place where the master was working.
6 A. F. Leach, 'Sherborne School before, under, and after Edward VI', *Archaeological Journal*, lv (1898), pp 7–8.

There was still a grammar school in Sherborne on the eve of the Reformation, probably in continuous descent from its predecessor. In 1524 the wardens of the parish church paid £1 to the schoolmaster for looking after the organs during one year. In 1535 the wife of the master (not necessarily the same man) is noted giving an altar cloth to the church, and in the following year there is a reference to his seat.[1] The school was a grammar school, and in 1535 the abbey was paying the sum of £3. 18s. per annum out of its lands and tenements in Sherborne to support three of the scholars.[2] The benefaction was said to have been made by Aelfric of Thornecombe. If this is true, it was an ancient one, for Aelfric was the father of Clement and William of Thornecombe, abbot and sacristan of Sherborne in about 1160 and 1170 respectively.[3] Unfortunately we cannot be sure that the foundation dated back so far in its educational form, and it remains evidence only for the sixteenth century. Nor do we know enough about the relationship between the school and the abbey. The school was evidently taught by secular masters, both priests and laymen, and was open to the public. The role of the abbey was (probably) to appoint the masters and (more certainly) to provide three exhibitions for the scholars.

SOUTH MOLTON
Devon

Bishop Jewel went to school at South Molton for a short time in the early 1530s under a master named Anthony Simon. This was after he left Braunton and before he went on to study at Barnstaple.[4]

STOW-ON-THE-WOLD
Gloucestershire

Among those who paid the poll-tax at Stow in 1381 appears a John Scolmarster, a layman keeping a servant.[5]

STRATTON
Cornwall

There was a school at Stratton during the middle of the sixteenth century, though the range of studies is not clear. In 1548 the wardens of the parish church, who drew up their accounts every 2 February, accounted for 4d. received from 'the schoolmaster' for occupying the church house. This suggests that the school existed by 1547. The master paid 5d. rent to

---

1 J. Fowler, 'Sherborne All Hallows Church Wardens Accounts', *Somerset & Dorset Notes & Queries*, xxiii (1938–42), p 312; xxiv (1943–6), pp 105, 121, 144, 162, 304.
2 *Valor Ecclesiasticus*, i, 284.
3 British Museum, MS Add. 46487, fo 74; F. Wormald, 'The Sherborne Cartulary', *Fritz Saxl Memorial Essays*, ed. D. J. Gordon (London, 1957), pp 118–19.
4 Laurence Humphrey, *Joannis Juelli Angli Episcopi Sariburiensis Vita et Mors* (1573), p 17.
5 *VCH Gloucs.*, vi, 163, quoting PRO, Exch. KR, Lay Subsidy Rolls, E 179/113/21 rot. 2. For other people surnamed 'Schoolmaster' see above, p 97.

the wardens during the following year, 1548–9, but no other payments are recorded until 1554–5, when the rent rose to 12d. In the last entry of all, 1555–6, it was 2s.[1] Stratton is not far from Week St Mary, and it is interesting that so apparently remote an area of the countryside could support two schools in 1548. If the rise in the master's rent is any guide to the size and success of his undertaking, he may well have profited from the closure of Week school which took place shortly after his own is first mentioned.

TAUNTON
Somerset

A school existed in Taunton by the reign of Edward I when Master Walter de Tolre (probably of Toller in Dorset), schoolmaster of the town, occurs as a witness in an action for assault relating to Christmas 1286.[2] Further evidence on the subject comes in testimony submitted by a man named John of Kent at the proving of the age of Hugh de la Tour, a Somerset heir in 1310. He claimed that his son had accompanied the five-year-old Hugh to Taunton school in about 1293.[3] Nothing more is heard of education in the town until 1523 when a new schoolhouse was built inside the castle precinct by Richard Fox, bishop of Winchester and founder of Corpus Christi College, Oxford, at the considerable cost of £226. 5s. 10d. The building measured sixty feet long by twenty wide and thirty in height, with the bishop's crest and initials above the door. With this benefaction Fox demonstrated his personal interest in education and showed, as bishop of Winchester, a proper solicitude for the borough which was under the government of his see.[4]

In 1548 the inhabitants of Taunton reported to the chantry commissioners that Roger Hill, a merchant of the town, had paid for a schoolmaster and usher from about 1533 onwards and that they had instructed between 120 and 140 scholars. It must be remembered that the figures for school attendance given in the chantry certificates were always produced by interested parties and are never susceptible of proof.[5] The benefaction did not survive Hill's death. His will was dated 6 January 1545 and proved on 8 April 1546, but although he gave generously to the poor of the district and patronised the local chantries, he offered no further aid to the school.[6] 'Since the death of the same Roger Hill', said the men of Taunton, 'the said schoolhouse standeth void, without either master, usher or scholars, to the great prejudice, hurt and discommodity of the commonwealth of the said shire'. They therefore requested the king to grant lands for the permanent support of a master and usher to teach in Fox's schoolhouse. This evoked no response, and it remained for

1 Accounts of the High Wardens of Stratton, 1512–77 (British Museum, MS Add. 32,243), fos 45v, 47v, 54, 56. The master may have been Nicholas Bond, who paid 2d. rent for the church house in 1546–7 (ibid., fo 42). I am grateful to Mr R. J. Whiting for drawing my attention to this source.
2 *Cat. Ancient Deeds,* i, 232.
3 *Cal. Inquisitions Post Mortem,* v, 126.
4 Winchester Pipe Rolls, 1523, m 2.
5 *Somerset Chantries,* ed. E. Green, p 25; *ESR,* part ii, p 190.
6 PRO, Prob 11/31 (PCC 7 Alen).

William Walby, a fellow of Fox's college, to endow the school with twenty marks a year in 1554.[1]

TAVISTOCK
Devon

In the history of his family which he wrote in 1593, Robert Furse of Moreshead describes how his uncle Edward Furse, while at school in Tavistock, wounded his knee as he sharpened some wood with a knife, and subsequently died of the wound. Edward was one of the sons of John Furse of Great Weeks in Torrington, a small landowner and the steward of several local lordships including Tavistock Abbey. The accident probably took place in about 1530. The reference suggests that education was available to the laity in Tavistock, either through the admission of outsiders to an almonry school within the abbey or at some other more public establishment in the town.[2]

TIVERTON
Devon

There are two slight indications of a school at Tiverton at the end of the fourteenth century. A list of expenses of the sons of Edward Courtenay, earl of Devon, in the 1390s includes the payment of 2d. 'to the scholars of St Nicholas at Tiverton'.[3] This suggests a school taking part in its chief annual festival, the celebration of St Nicholas Day, complete with a boy-bishop. The master may have been the John Scolemaystre who witnessed the grant of a tenement in Tiverton along with the provost and bailiff of the town in 1400.[4]

TOTNES
Devon

Totnes, in the early sixteenth century, was a flourishing centre of the cloth trade. Its wealth in 1523 was second only to Exeter among the Devon towns, and sixteenth in England as a whole—well ahead of Plymouth, Tavistock and Barnstaple. The population may have reached 2–3,000.[5] The first reference to a school in the town comes from a petition of 1509 recorded by the late Mr T. Kelly, but now untraceable. Accordingly to Mr Kelly, the petition was addressed to the archbishop of Canterbury by William Giles, MA, the vicar of Totnes. In it he stated 'that he was a serving priest keeping a grammar school and song

1 *VCH Som.*, ii, 445.
2 Devon Record Office, 2507B (Robert Furse, MS History of the Furse Family), fo 25.
3 Exeter, East Devon Record Office, Courtenay Accounts, CR 1466.
4 E. S. Chalk, *A History of the Church of St Peter, Tiverton* (Tiverton 1905), p 78. For the surname 'Schoolmaster' see above, p 97.
5 W. G. Hoskins, *Provincial England* (1963), pp 70–2. See also Laura M. Nicholls, The Trading Communities of Totnes and Dartmouth in the Late 15th and Early 16th Centuries (University of Exeter, MA Thesis, 1960).

school in Totnes' at which 'a great number of the children of the town and the country round had been sufficiently instructed, and by occasion thereof the divine service within the town of Totnes was solemnly done and kept'. He concluded by asking to be appointed as chaplain of the chantry of St Edmund on the town bridge.[1] It is difficult, however, to accept Mr Kelly's account completely. One man would not normally have combined the offices of vicar, schoolmaster and chantry priest in his own person.[2] It seems more likely that the petition was made on behalf of another priest who was serving the community as schoolmaster, and whom the vicar wished to reward with a benefice. Be that as it may, we know at any rate that a school existed in 1509; it taught song and grammar, it was kept by a priest, and it was probably not endowed.

The continuance of schooling in the town is suggested by an interesting document now in the departmental archives of Seine-Inférieure in France. This is an agreement in French, dated 6 February 1526, between Richard Savery and Michel Vimont, merchants respectively of Totnes and Rouen. Savery belonged to one of the wealthiest families of Totnes and was mayor in 1537 and 1544. The agreement provided that he should receive Vimont's son Nicolas, aged fourteen, for one year, give him board and lodging, and send him to school. In return Vimont was to take Savery's apprentice Thomas Russell, aged eighteen, and show him how 'to deal and traffic in merchandise'.[3] In short, the two merchants, who were doubtless both involved in the same trade, exchanged members of their families so that each could gain experience of life on the other side of the Channel. Since it appears that Nicholas Vimont was to live with Savery, the school he attended must also have been in Totnes. The next reference to a school in the town comes from 1553.[4]

WELLINGTON
Somerset

The town of Wellington belonged to the bishop of Bath and Wells who held two of the adjoining manors including the borough, while a third was owned by the dean of Wells. On 14 August 1371 Nicholas Pontesbury, subdean of the cathedral, bequeathed in his will a copy of Hugutio to the parish church of St Mary, Wellington, to be kept by the vicar and churchwardens and delivered, upon good security, to the schoolmaster 'that he and his boys may specially pray for me'.[5] The book in question was almost certainly the *Derivationes* of Hugutio, the popular Latin dictionary, and shows the schoolmaster to have been teaching

1 T. Kelly, *The History of King Edward VI Grammar School, Totnes* (Totnes, 1947), p 1. Mr Kelly gave no reference.
2 William Giles was vicar of Totnes from 1505 until his death in 1537 (Devon Record Office, Reg. Oldham, Exeter, fo 6; Reg. Veysey, Exeter, ii, fo 87v).
3 M. Mollat, *Le Commerce maritime normand à la fin du moyen age* (Paris, 1952), p 174.
4 *CPR 1553*, pp 227–8.
5 The best text of Pontesbury's will is given by J. Coleman, 'Four Wells Wills of the Fourteenth Century', *Somerset & Dorset Notes & Queries*, viii (1903), pp 151–3. The will was proved on 24 October 1372.

grammar.[1] This is the only reference to a school in medieval Wellington, which had an estimated 808 communicants in 1548, and a population, presumably, of about a thousand.

WILTON
Wiltshire

Wilton, rather than Salisbury, was the chief town of Wiltshire in the twelfth and thirteenth centuries, and the meeting place of the county court. It was an ecclesiastical centre of importance with its famous abbey of nuns, eight parish churches, two hospitals, and latterly a Dominican friary.[2] The school is first mentioned in 1238 when the master was appointed a papal judge-delegate in a suit between the chancellor of Salisbury and the monks of Tutbury Priory, Staffordshire, concerning the tithes of Fifield in the county of Oxford.[3] After the middle of the thirteenth century Wilton began to lose ground to New Salisbury, and by the fifteenth the town was in a depressed condition. Later still, in Tudor times, it experienced something of a recovery due to the rise of the cloth industry, and a school again appears on the eve of the Reformation.[4] Whether it had a continuous descent from its predecessor is a matter of speculation. The master, Nicholas Hartwell, was a Londoner by origin, born in about 1504. He entered Winchester College as a scholar in 1517, proceeded to New College, Oxford, in 1521 and was admitted a fellow in 1523. He took his BA four years later and his MA in 1529. A note to the effect that he subsequently became schoolmaster of Wilton survives in the registers of Winchester College. In view of Hartwell's qualifications his school must have been one of grammar, and since schoolmastering was usually a young man's avocation, he was probably teaching in Wilton during the 1530s.[5]

WOOLAVINGTON
Somerset

An unusual fragment of biography describing the origins of the Hody family in the late fourteenth century relates that

> Adam Hody was a bondeman to my Lorde of Awdeley and heywarde of Woolavyngton, and he had ii sonnys, John and Thomas. Thys John went to scole with a chawntery prest in Wolavyngton and fro that to Oxford, and so he hadde lycens of the Lorde of Awdely, and was i-made a prest, and after that be fortune he was a chanon yn Wellys and Chawnceler yn Wellys.

The account goes on to describe how John Hody found his nephews to school, secured their manumission, and when he died left goods with his younger nephew, Sir Alexander

---

1 On the *Derivationes* see *ESMA*, p 93.
2 *VCH Wilts.*, vi, 15.
3 *The Cartulary of Tutbury Priory,* ed. A. Saltman (Hist. MSS Commission, Joint Publications, ii, 1962), pp 48–50.
4 *VCH Wilts.*, vi, 15–16, 24.
5 For his career see *BRUO,* iv, 272.

Hody, to purchase lands for the chantry priests of Woolavington, 'for the love that he had to it, for there he began his first learning.'[1]

John Hody, who became chancellor of Wells and archdeacon of Dorset, was born in about 1375, so that he was of school age in the late 1380s and 90s.[2] The story of his origins and education, on the other hand, was not written until the late fifteenth century, and it comes from a hostile source. The Pym family of Brymore were then engaged in a fierce dispute with the Hodys over the patronage of the three chantries of Woolavington, and were putting about documents such as this to discredit their enemies. The existence of a chantry school at Woolavington is not impossible but the source, setting aside its hostility, is rather late to be accepted without question.

WOTTON-UNDER-EDGE
Gloucestershire

The borough of Wotton possessed a schoolmaster as early as 1291–2 and the schoolhouse is mentioned in the earliest account roll of the borough, which dates from the same period.[3] We next hear of the school in 1349 when the first attempts were being made to endow it, and these are discussed below.[4]

WRINGTON
Somerset

Evidence of teaching at Wrington in the early sixteenth century comes from a tithe dispute of 1537. One of the witnesses, Paul Taverner of Wrington, aged forty and described as a gentleman, recalled seeing tithe cheeses brought into the parish church when he was about ten or twelve years of age, 'going then to the school at the parish church at Wrington'. This must have been in about 1507–9. Since the incumbent at that time, William Fitzherbert, was a wealthy and probably non-resident pluralist, it is likely that the teaching was provided by the parish chaplain or the parish clerk.[5]

---

1 H. C. Maxwell-Lyte, 'The Hody Family', *Somerset & Dorset Notes & Queries,* xviii (1925), pp 127–9.
2 He was aged about sixty in 1435 (*Cal. Papal Registers,* viii, 527). For his life see *BRUO*, ii, 941–2.
3 E. S. Lindley, *Wotton under Edge* (1962), p 224, quoting MSS from Berkeley Castle. He dates the account roll between 1292 and 1323.
4 Below, pp 190, 192.
5 Taunton, Somerset Record Office, Diocesan MSS, Deposition Book 4. The reference, for which I am indebted to the kindness of Mr R. W. Dunning, arrived too late to include Wrington on the distribution maps.

3
Endowed Schools and Chantry Schools

ASHBURTON
Devon

The early history of education in Ashburton has been the subject of many speculations by local historians which, it must regretfully be said, do not possess any sound basis of fact.[1] In reality, very little is known of the history of schooling in the town before 1546, and what little evidence survives is largely confined to the early sixteenth century. The two centres of education in the town before the Reformation were the parish church and the guild of St Laurence. Ashburton was the type of large and wealthy parish which maintained a small amateur choir during the later middle ages to assist the clergy in singing the services. In 1481 the choral establishment consisted of four men singers and four boys, their numbers rising by the 1530s to five and six respectively. Allusions to the boys as 'scholars' suggest that here, as in some other important churches[2], they were taught to read and sing as part of their choral training. Their instructor may have been the parish clerk, or more probably one of the choirmen. A 'rector of the choir' is mentioned in 1499, and a man named William White was paid 3s. 4d. a year from 1547 until 1552 for discharging the office of cantor.[3] A small number of boys may thus have learnt or practised reading and song through membership of the church choir, from the 1480s to the 1550s. That the church maintained a public song school is a larger assumption, and one which cannot be justified from the evidence at present available.

The major source of education in the town was provided by the guild or chantry of St Laurence, a foundation originated by Bishop Stapledon of Exeter. In 1314 he granted the offerings and revenues of the chapel of St Laurence in Ashburton to support a chantry priest, appointed by the portreeve and burgesses of the town and bound to pray for the bishops of Exeter.[4] By the first survey of the chantries in 1546, the chantry had come to be called the guild of St Laurence, and possessed revenues amounting to over £10, of

---

1 Some of these are mentioned in the article of Dom J. Stephan, 'Some Notes on Ashburton Grammar School', *Devonshire Association Transactions*, xci (1959), pp 112–23.
2 E.g. Bristol and Cirencester, (above, p 38; below, p 130).
3 *Churchwardens' Accounts of Ashburton, 1479–1580*, ed. Alison Hanham (Devon & Cornwall Record Soc., new series xv, 1970), pp 26, 88, 90, 118–26, 191. John Bartlet, Stephen Mayne and Richard Turpin are all mentioned as boys of the choir in 1532.
4 Dom. J. Stephan, op.cit., pp 113, 118–20.

which part was applied to maintain the town's water supply. The parishioners who furnished these details also claimed that the foundation was intended 'to keep a school for the erudition of children freely for ever', the incumbent, John Farell, receiving a salary of £6. 13s. 4d. The chantry certificate of 1548 is not extant, but an abstract survives which confirms the educational side of the guild and identifies the school as a grammar school.[1] The chapel stood in South Street, and the school may have been held nearby, where the eighteenth-century schoolroom still survives.

It has usually been assumed, on the basis of the chantry certificates, that the school was coeval with the chantry and owed its origin to the founder of Exeter College, Oxford, himself. There are no grounds for the assumption. Guild or chantry schools had not evolved in 1314, the earliest example being probably that of Wotton-under-Edge, founded seventy years later. As things stand at present we know only that the chantry priest came to teach grammar at some point before 1546. The existence of the school after this date is another matter. The Edwardian chantry commissioners recognised its status and ordered that it continue. John Farell thereafter received his salary from the crown, payments to him being recorded until at least 1553.[2]

BARNSTAPLE
Devon

Barnstaple school achieved a rare fame in the sixteenth century, even beyond Devon, for having educated two of the leading writers of the English Reformation. 'Out of this town's school', wrote William Camden in 1590, 'there issued two right learned men and most renowned divines: John Jewel, bishop of Salisbury, and Thomas Harding, the public professor in Louvain, who most hotly contended and wrote learnedly one against the other concerning the truth of religion'.[3] The elder of the two was Harding, who was born at Combe Martin in 1516.[4] He must have been studying at Barnstaple before 1528, the year in which he proceeded to Winchester College, a not uncommon transition from a local school to one of national importance. Jewel was younger and cannot have known Harding at school. He first saw the light at Buden near Berrynarbor in 1522 and did not begin his education until he was seven.[5] Between 1529 and 1535, when he went up to Merton College, Oxford, he attended four local schools in turn, of which Barnstaple was the last. His master there was Walter Bowen, and although Jewel cannot have been under his tuition for long, he always held his old master, says his biographer, in great love and respect.[6] Whether Bowen also tutored Harding is not recorded.

1 PRO, E 301/15 no 35, E 301/80; *The Chantry Certificates for Devon,* ed. L. S. Snell, pp 39, 69; *ESR,* part ii, pp 46, 48.
2 PRO, Exch. Land Revenue, LR 6/104/3–4.
3 Camden, *Britannia,* 4th ed. (London, 1590), p 143. The passage is not in the earlier editions. The translation is by P. Holland (1610), p 206.
4 For his life see *BRUO,* iv, 265–6.
5 For his life see ibid., pp 317–18.
6 Laurence Humfrey, *Joannis Juelli Angli Episcopi Sariburiensis Vita et Mors* (1573), p 17. The other schools were Heanton Punchardon, Braunton and South Molton.

These biographical details confirm the existence of a grammar school at Barnstaple between at least 1528 and 1535. Its constitutional basis at this time is not clear, but the Henrician chantry certificate of 1546, after listing the guild and chantry priests in the borough, notes that 'one of the said priests doth teach school'.[1] Two years later the Edwardian chantry certificate reports specifically that the guild of St Nicholas 'was founded to keep a grammar school'. Its income at this time was reckoned as £7. 18s. 3d., but the name of the priest has not survived.[2] The guild was an ancient one dating back to at least 1303, so that it could not have been *founded* with the purpose of keeping a school which must, as at Ashburton, have been a much later addition. The chantry commissioners followed their usual policy by ordering the school to continue, the master's salary being paid by the crown. Payments to an unnamed schoolmaster appear in the accounts of the local receiver-general of crown lands until at least 1553.[3]

BLANDFORD FORUM
Dorset

The village of West Hemsworth near Wimborne Minster had a free chapel dating back to the thirteenth century, to which a series of 'rectors' were instituted during the later middle ages.[4] The value in 1548 was £2. 13s. 4d. The chantry certificate of that year makes the curious statement that 'the said chapel was ordained for a schoolmaster to be maintained in Blandford', citing as evidence 'an exemplification under the seal of the court of Augmentations'. The chapel however is not known to have had any educational connections, and the chantry commissioners themselves observed 'no cause of continuance there'.[5] The existence of a school in Blandford, though likely, cannot be deduced from this.

BODMIN
Cornwall

The chantry certificate of 1548 described Bodmin as the greatest market town in Cornwall and estimated the number of communicants in the parish at 2,000. The chantry of St John the Baptist, also called Nayler's Chantry, was located in the parish church of St Petrock and had been founded in 1474 by John Nayler, a married clerk of the royal chancery who probably came from Bodmin.[6] The annual income was £6, of which the chaplain received £5. 6s. 8d. while the remaining 13s. 4d. was distributed among the poor. The incumbent in 1548 was Nicholas Taprell, aged 57, a man of local origin. The people of the parish, it was further alleged, were 'very ignorante'.[7]

1 PRO, E 301/15 no 56; *The Chantry Certificates for Devon*, ed. L. S. Snell, p 51; *ESR*, part ii, p 319.
2 PRO, E 301/80; Snell, op. cit., p 69; *ESR*, part ii, pp 47–8.
3 PRO, Exch. Land Revenue, LR 6/104/4.
4 J. Hutchins, *History of Dorset*, iii, 168.
5 PRO, E 301/16 no 115; *ESR*, part ii, p 57.
6 *CPR 1467–76*, pp 468–9.
7 PRO, E 301/9 no 23; Bodleian Library, MS Rawl. D 363 fos 255–6; *The Chantry Certificates for Cornwall*, ed. L. S. Snell (1953), p 11; *ESR* part ii, pp 38–9. Nicholas Taprell was ordained subdeacon on 27 February and priest on 3 April 1518 to the title of Bodmin Priory (Reg. Oldham, Exeter, fo 120–v).

Nothing is said of any teaching by the chantry priest, either in the licence for the foundation of 1474 or in the chantry certificates of 1546 or 1548. Only in the enrolments of the 1548 certificates made for the purpose of awarding pensions do we find the note, 'a school there, the schoolmaster being the said Nicholas'. He was evidently teaching grammar, for the chantry commissioners ordered his 'grammar school' to continue and arranged for him to receive his former salary from the crown.[1] There is at present however no evidence about the school's existence before 1548, and no sign of when it began. Nicholas Taprell continued to be paid his salary until 1555.[2] Later he became rector of St Mellion near Callington. In 1561 he was described as a non-graduate priest, not married or in concubinage, moderately learned, keeping residence and hospitality, but not a preacher.[3] He probably died in the spring of 1565.[4]

BRADFORD-ON-AVON
Wiltshire

Bradford school was a product of the cloth industry which brought so much prosperity to the border towns of Somerset and Wiltshire in the early sixteenth century. The founder was one of the three sons of John Horton, a clothmaker of Iford, two miles south-west of Bradford on the county boundary, who died in 1497.[5] The eldest brother, William, followed his father's trade and settled at Lullington near Frome where he died in 1508.[6] The second son, Thomas, who founded Bradford school, was born in about 1470 and also began his adult life as a clothmaker. The youngest brother, James, was born in 1472–3 and educated for the Church. He was sent to school at Winchester College as a fee-paying commoner until 1485 when he was given a scholarship. He went on to New College Oxford, in 1489, received a fellowship there two years later, and finally graduated as a bachelor of civil law. In 1507 he was instituted as rector of Horsington, a moderately wealthy benefice in south Somerset, where he stayed for the rest of his life, until his death in 1526.[7]

Although Thomas Horton followed the same trade as his father and his elder brother, the scale of his activities was clearly much larger, and so too were his profits. In 1510 when, like hundreds of others, he purchased a general pardon from the new king Henry VIII, he was described as a clothmaker not only of Iford and Bradford but also of London, and in later life he called himself 'merchant'.[8] His activities must have involved him in buying and selling as far afield as the capital, as well as producing cloth in Wiltshire. Besides retaining his father's dwelling at Iford, he built the 'goodly large house of squared stone'

1 E 301/10 no 26; Snell, op. cit., pp 11–12; *ESR*, part ii, pp 41, 42.
2 PRO, Exch. Land Revenue, LR 6/104/2–4, LR 6/1/1–2.
3 Cambridge, Corpus Christi College, MS 97; photocopy in Exeter, East Devon Record Office, p 35.
4 Reg. Alley, Exeter, fo 9.
5 For his will see PRO, Prob 11/11 fo 140v (PCC 17 Horne).
6 His will is registered in PRO, Prob 11/15 fo 277-v (PCC 35 Adeane).
7 For his career see *BRUO*, ii, 968.
8 *LPFD*, i, no 438 (1) m 15.

which still stands at the east end of Bradford churchyard. According to John Leland, he also erected 'divers fair houses of stone' in Trowbridge,[1] and the inquisitions *post mortem* which were held after his death show that he possessed property both there and at Chippenham. He also held a scattering of farms and fields in the villages of east Somerset and west Wiltshire, amounting to more than 400 acres of land and valued at over £40 per annum.[2] This, of course, was after the alienation of property worth £10 a year to endow his school. His will, made on 26 July 1530, confirms the impression of modest wealth, since the specified bequests alone amounted to almost £200. He left £43 to Bradford church to purchase vestments and finance repairs, £20 to the Carthusian priory of Hinton, and £6 to the rebuilding of Freshford bridge. The residue of his property went to his wife Mary for the rest of her life, and afterwards to his nephew Thomas Horton the younger, the son of his elder brother William.[3] Horton himself died on 14 August 1530 at about the age of sixty, and was buried as he requested near his father's grave in the Lady chapel of Bradford church. The memorial brass survives, bearing his effigy and that of his wife.

Thomas Horton was thus in the same position as most of the other founders of schools whom we shall encounter. He was a prosperous man, free of the claims of children, who could afford to devote his wealth to the endowment of charity. The foundation of Bradford school was a project which occupied the last years of his life. On 14 September 1524 he received the king's licence to found a chantry of one chaplain to say mass at the altar of the Lady chapel in Bradford church, and to endow the chantry with property to the value of £10 a year. In choosing the site Horton was doubtless moved by the presence of his father's grave in the Lady chapel and by his own intention to be buried there. A similar licence issued on the same day authorised William Bird, the vicar of Bradford, to found a second chantry at the altar of the Holy Trinity, with endowments at the same rate.[4] Horton chose as the first chaplain of his chantry a priest named William Furbner, who had been born in

---

1 Leland, *Itinerary*, ed. Lucy Toulmin Smith, vol i (1907), p 135.
2 In Somerset he held 20 tenements, 2 tofts, 5 cottages, 50 acres of land and 16 acres of meadow at Rode, rent 2s. 7d. per annum, income £10 clear per annum; 1 toft, 30 acres of land, 2 acres of meadow, and 2 closes of pasture in Rode and Woolverton, rent 4s., income 5s.; a messuage in Rode without land or tenement, rent 2d., income 8s.; 2 messuages, 1 toft, 40 acres of land, 4 acres of meadow and 4 of pasture at Tellisford, rent one rose, income 24s. (PRO, Inquisitions Post Mortem, C 142/81/285; E 150/922/6). In Wiltshire he held 4 messuages, 1 cottage, 20 acres of arable land, 4 acres of pasture and 2 acres of meadow in Rode, rent unknown, income £1. 6s.; 8 acres of meadow in North Bradley, rent 18d., income 20s.; 6 messuages, 80 acres of arable, 4 acres of meadow, 4 acres of pasture, 2 shambles and 6 gardens in Trowbridge, rent 21s. 6d., income £9; 20 acres of arable and pasture for 40 sheep in Tilshead, rent 9s., income 5s.; another messuage, 1 toft, 5 acres of pasture, 100 acres of arable and pasture for 300 sheep in Tilshead, rent 20s., income £4; 1 curtilage and garden in Iford, rent 3d., income 6s.; 4 acres of pasture in Great Cheverell, rent unknown, income 8s.; 1 messuage and 20 acres of pasture in Chippenham, rent 2s., income £10; 6 acres of pasture in Foxham, rent unknown, income 10s.; and 9s. of rent in Sevington (PRO, E 150/983/2).
3 PRO, Prob 11/23 fos 156v–7 (PCC F20 Jankyn).
4 *LPFD*, iv part i, no 693 (14).

about 1492 and was then in his mid thirties. He continued to hold office throughout the whole period that the chantry existed, until its dissolution in 1548.[1]

The royal licence makes no mention of a school, and not until the chantry certificate of 1548 are we told directly that the priest was bound to teach. This naturally raises the question whether Thomas Horton did indeed originate the school, or whether the teaching of grammar was instituted after his death through the initiative of other people. The available evidence strongly suggests that Horton was responsible. It convinced the chantry commissioners who stated that the chantry 'was founded purposely for the maintenance of a free school', and it is supported by William Furbner's long tenure of the chantry. A man who was teaching in 1548 was able and likely to have done so in 1524. The statutes of the chantry no longer survive, but such details as have been preserved also indicate that a school was provided for. In February 1540 Thomas Cromwell wrote to his friend Walter Lord Hungerford, a leading local agent of the crown, to say that certain licences, foundation statutes and other writings deposited by Thomas Horton at Hinton Priory had been embezzled and removed. Hungerford was asked to summon before him Horton's widow Mary, his nephew Thomas Horton the younger, the vicar of Bradford (William Bird), and the chantry priest (William Furbner), to examine them on oath about the matter. Hungerford duly began his enquiries and wrote a report to Cromwell on 17 March. The evidence he gathered shows that Thomas Horton arranged for statutes to be drawn up for the chantry in the form of a quadripartite, or four-sided, indenture between himself and the three neighbouring priories of Hinton, Witham and Bath. The text was drafted by Sir John FitzJames. It provided that the patronage of the chantry, including the right to appoint the chaplain, should be exercised by the prior of Hinton, or by the other two priors in his default. This explains why the documents were stolen from Hinton and why Cromwell was anxious to recover them. The dissolution of the monasteries caused all their property, including the patronage of schools, to pass to the crown, and the Horton family had evidently tried to recover control of the Bradford chantry for themselves by stealing the evidence.[2]

The inquisition of 1540 also fails to mention the school as such, but it further strengthens the likelihood that Horton founded one. Sir John FitzJames was one of the three co-founders of Bruton grammar school, Somerset, in 1520.[3] Bruton was the most recent and also the most novel school foundation in Somerset or Wiltshire when Horton was planning his own scheme in 1524, and was an obvious model to be copied. Its own statutes took the same form of a quadripartite indenture with three monasteries, involving the patronage of the school by one of them, with the other two acting as safeguards if the first failed to discharge its responsibilities. The choice of Hinton as the patron of Horton's chantry was unusual in that Carthusian monks did not often undertake this role, but it reflected a long-standing family connection with the house. The prior had been a witness and a beneficiary of Horton's father's will. Horton did not follow FitzJames in one important respect, since

1 PRO, E 301/58 no 43; *ESR*, part ii, pp 258–9.
2 *LPFD*, xv, nos 185, 353; PRO, State Papers, SP 1/158 no 353.
3 For Bruton school see below, pp 117–22.

Bruton did not include a chantry, and the master could be a layman as well as a priest. But he may well have copied another of the Bruton provisions: that the schoolmaster should confine himself to teaching grammar, rather than waste his time on elementary work such as the alphabet, reading or song. According to the chantry certificate of 1548, Horton's chaplain had to give 20s. a year to the parish clerk of Bradford to teach children to sing, and this probably means that he was also restricted to teaching grammar. Bruton school was bound to use 'the good new form' of grammar taught at St Paul's, London, and Magdalen College, Oxford, and it is possible that this was also the case at Bradford.

The total weight of the evidence is therefore to suggest that in about 1524 Thomas Horton established a chantry grammar school in Bradford under the government of the Carthusian monks of Hinton, to give free tuition in grammar to all comers. In 1548 the income of the chantry, according to the chantry certificate, was £11. 5s. 11d. gross, or £10. 12s. 7d. after the deduction of the mandatory tenths which the clergy had to pay to the crown. The chaplain did not get the whole of this sum as his salary, since he had to pay £1 to the clerk and 13s. 4d. to the poor, so that his own share was just under £9.[1] The chantry commissioners ordered the school to be continued, but seized the lands, which were bought in 1549 along with those of several other Wiltshire chantries by the founder's nephew, Thomas Horton the younger.[2] Following the usual arrangement the schoolmaster was paid a salary after 1548 by the local receiver-general of crown lands, at the rate he had enjoyed before the chantry was dissolved. But as elsewhere (at Launceston for example) confusion arose as to how much Bradford should receive. The chantry commissioners ruled that the schoolmaster was entitled to £11. 5s. 11d., but in the end the tenths were deducted and he got only £10. 12s. 7d.[3] The school remained entitled to this sum until 1569 when, by a disgraceful theft, the citizens of Salisbury induced the crown to transfer the annuities of both Bradford and Trowbridge schools to provide a second grammar school for their own city. The excuse was 'that the said towns of Trowbridge and Bradford were upland towns, wherein did inhabit but few people, having small resort of gentlemen or merchants, by reason whereof there was neither need for such schools and less profiting in good learning.'[4] It was no compliment either to Horton or to the people of Bradford, but as so often in Tudor England the gospel precept was observed that 'unto every one that hath shall be given, and he shall have abundance, but from him that hath not shall be taken away even that which he hath'.

BRUTON
Somerset

Bruton School was founded in 1520 by the combined efforts of three men, all of local origin. The senior of them, Richard FitzJames, was born in the mid 1440s, the son of John

1 E 301/58 no 43; *ESR,* part ii, pp 258–9.
2 *CPR 1548–9,* p 248.
3 *ESR,* part ii, pp 265–6.
4 *Report of Charity Commissioners* (*House of Commons Papers,* 1833, vol xix), p 366.

FitzJames and Alice his wife of Redlynch, two miles south-east of Bruton.[1] In 1465 he was elected a bachelor fellow of Merton College, Oxford, becoming a full fellow in about 1468. He subsequently held various offices in the college until on 20 March 1483 he was appointed warden. It was customary for the college to recommend three candidates to the archbishop of Canterbury who chose the warden, but the fellows on this occasion expressed a definite preference for FitzJames, and a commendatory letter from the sub-warden and seniors on his behalf eulogised his blood, his learning and his character.[2] He had indeed completed his academic career by securing the doctorate in theology and had already been senior proctor of the university. His promotion from the world of the university to a career in public life came about through the favour of Henry VII, who had made him one of his chaplains by 1489.[3] He preached before the king on several occasions (notably at the funeral of Queen Elizabeth in 1503), and was one of the executors of Henry's will. After 1485 he was able to supplement his wardenship with a canonry and treasurership of St Paul's as well as with two Somerset parishes, Minehead and Aller. In 1497 he was promoted to be bishop of Rochester, was translated to Chichester in 1503 and to London in 1506, the see which he filled for the sixteen years that remained of his life.

FitzJames did not forget his obligations to those who had made his career possible. In 1489 the names of his father and mother were admitted to the list of the brethren receiving prayers at Merton College.[4] His continued connection with Somerset is suggested by his execution of at least two local wills in the 1490s.[5] At Merton his rule was as distinguished as the fellows had prophesied, and the warden's lodgings with the still surviving gateway were completed by him in 1497.[6] When he resigned from Merton on 7 April 1507 the fellows were so saddened that most of them could not restrain their tears, and they agreed to observe an anniversary in his honour to be celebrated by warden, fellows and chaplains while he lived, and to keep his obit after his death.[7] He had already given volumes to the college library in 1494 and others were added later, at least nineteen such gifts being recorded, as well as two of vestments for the chapel in 1504 and 1516. In 1517 the college received £12 for beautifying the nave of the college chapel from FitzJames and his associates, including John Edmunds the co-founder of Bruton School, and three old Mertonians to whom the bishop had given canonries to St Paul's.[8]

1 For notes on the family see C. H. Mayo, 'The FitzJames Family of Somerset', *Somerset & Dorset Notes & Queries,* xvi (1918–20), pp 54–68. Biographies of Richard will be found in *BRUO*, ii, 691, and in *DNB*.
2 *Registrum Annalium Collegii Mertonensis,* ed. H. E. Salter (Oxford Historical Soc., lxxvi, 1923), p 10.
3 *Epistolae Academiae Oxoniensis,* ed. H. Anstey, vol ii (ibid., xxxvi, 1898), p 558.
4 *Reg. Ann. Coll. Merton.*, p 125. They were probably both dead by this time.
5 The wills of Henry Burnell and William Adice (*Somerset Medieval Wills,* ed. F. W. Weaver, vol i (Somerset Record Soc., xvi, 1901), pp 293, 358–9).
6 *VCH Oxon.*, iii, 102.
7 *Reg. Ann. Coll. Merton.*, p 330. Compare also the will of his successor as warden, Thomas Harper, who said of him "quem inter omnes mortales vnice diligo" (PRO, Prob. 11/16 (PCC 10 Bennett)).
8 *Reg. Ann. Coll. Merton.*, p 476.

As bishop of London, however, FitzJames was involved in two affairs which have proved fatal to his reputation. There was the notorious case of Richard Hunne in 1514–15, who after posing as a champion against ecclesiastical abuses was tried for heresy before the bishop and finally died in prison at the instigation (so it was said) of his chancellor, William Horsey.[1] Hardly less unhappy were his relations with his more famous dean, John Colet. FitzJames was apparently a conservative theologian and Colet was certainly an innovator. His teaching on image worship so angered the bishop, Erasmus tells us, that he cited the dean before the archbishop himself on a charge of heresy. So FitzJames lives in the letters of Colet and Erasmus as 'a superstitious and unconquerable Scotist', and their estimate of his character has prevailed.[2] Perhaps something should be said on the other side. FitzJames was responsible for the restoration of regular lectures in theology at his cathedral.[3] He imitated his dean in founding a grammar school dedicated to the New, not the Old, learning. He carried out much rebuilding in the episcopal palace at Fulham. And when he drew up his will on 11 April 1518 he made the charitable gestures expected of men in his position. He bequeathed 30 marks to the canons who attended his funeral and 'month's mind', and the same amount in doles to the poor. He left all the goods in his chapel at London, in his palace, and in the manors of Fulham, Hadham and Wickham, to remain for the use of his successors. The residue of his goods was assigned to his executors for disposal and his will therefore contains few personal details.[4] His death took place on 15 January 1522 and he was buried in the chapel of St Paul which he had erected in his cathedral church.

The second founder of Bruton School was Sir John FitzJames, son of the bishop's brother John and Isabel his wife, who had succeeded to the Redlynch property and had begotten this one son and some three daughters.[5] The younger John is mentioned at the Middle Temple in 1504, and six years later he occurs as recorder of Bristol.[6] His rise to prominence in the law was marked by his appointment in 1519 as attorney-general in all courts of record in England and in 1522 as chief baron of the exchequer. In 1526 he became chief justice of the king's bench and was afterwards knighted.[7] He had already undertaken delicate royal business,[8] and later took a prominent part in the state trials which accompanied the Henrician Reformation, until his retirement shortly before January 1539. He is said to have first married Joan, the daughter of Thomas More of Melplash in Netherbury, Dorset, by whom he had four children, and his second wife was Elizabeth, the daughter

---

1 On the affair see A. Ogle, *The Tragedy of the Lollards' Tower* (Oxford, 1949).
2 See for example Erasmus, *Opus Epistolarum,* ed. P. S. Allen (1906–58), ii, 37; iv, 523–4.
3 Reg. FitzJames, London, fos 127v–8, quoted in *Registrum Statutorum Sancti Pauli Londinensis,* ed. W. S. Simpson (1873), pp 413–15.
4 PRO, Prob 11/19 (PCC 3 Ayloffe). The executors were Sir Henry Wyot, Sir Richard Brook, John FitzJames, Dr Hugh Sanders, and Dr John Adams, with Sir John Fyneux, CJKB, and Dr John Edmunds as supervisors.
5 For Sir John FitzJames's life see the article by J. M. Rigg in *DNB*. This incorrectly supposes that it was John's father who aided Richard in founding Bruton School.
6 *LPFD,* i, part i, no 485 (40).
7 *LPFD,* iii part i, no 46; part ii no 2034.
8 Ibid., no 3322.

of Sir Humphrey Coningsby (who founded the grammar school of Rock in Worcestershire). She was the widow of Richard Berkeley of Stoke Gifford, by whom she had three daughters and two sons before his death in 1514–15. She gave her second husband no issue, although she survived him. Sir John's eldest son John pre-deceased his father, who made over his manors of Knole and Redlynch in his will to his son's widow for life. The second son James was a doctor of theology of Oxford who held various canonries of Wells and other benefices, dying in 1541.[1] As for Sir John himself, he made his will on 23 October 1538, still sufficiently optimistic about the future to leave money for prayers to the two Somerset charterhouses. His law books went to his cousins Aldred and Nicholas, and he also left 20s. apiece to Redlynch and four neighbouring churches.[2] The date of his death is unknown but took place before his will was proved on 12 May 1542.

The third of the co-founders was John Edmunds. His family, which lived in Bruton, was much less eminent than were the FitzJameses, but it achieved notability in its way for producing scholars and ecclesiastics. The oldest of them, also named John Edmunds, who seems to have been born in the 1450s, took degrees in canon and civil law and ended his life as a canon of Wells in 1521.[3] Another, Richard Edmunds, became a fellow of Merton College in 1490 but appears to have died in the early sixteenth century.[4] John the founder of Bruton school was probably born in the 1460s. He became a fellow of Lincoln College, Oxford, in 1485 and of Eton College seven years later. At Oxford he graduated in succession as MA, bachelor and doctor of theology, achieving the latter distinction in about 1500. He was a protégé of Richard FitzJames by 1499 when Richard, as bishop of Rochester, presented him to the rectory of Woolwich in Kent. A second rectory, Southfleet, was added in 1501. Edmunds followed his patron to St Paul's where FitzJames promoted him to a canonry in 1510 and to the office of chancellor in 1517. In 1530 and 1531 he resigned his benefices, and that is the last we hear of him. He doubtless died soon afterwards.[5]

The co-founders were probably maintaining a free school at Bruton during the 1510s, before the formal foundation had been carried out. In 1515 William Bailey of Wareham bequeathed £20 to his godson, William Chyke, whose father lived at Bruton and was on good terms with the FitzJames family. He ordered the boy to be sent home to his father, 'for at Bruton is a free school'.[6] The legal foundation of the school was made on 29 September 1520 by a quadripartite indenture between the three founders on the one part, and the abbots of Bruton and Glastonbury and the prior of Witham on the others. The abbot of Bruton was intended to be the trustee and patron of the school, and the other two prelates

---

1 For Sir John's relatives see C. H. Mayo, op. cit., and J. Smith, *Lives of the Berkeleys,* ed. J. Maclean, i, 263.
2 PRO, Prob 11/29 (PCC 5 Spert); *Somerset Medieval Wills,* ed. F. W. Weaver, vol iii (Somerset Record Soc., xxi, 1905), pp 48–51.
3 See *BRUO,* i, 626. He was of Bruton when ordained subdeacon, deacon and priest in 1482–3 (Taunton, Somerset Record Office, Reg. Stillington, Wells, fos 210–11).
4 See *BRUO,* i, 626.
5 For his career see ibid., pp 625–6.
6 *Somerset Medieval Wills,* ed. F. W. Weaver, vol ii (Somerset Record Soc., xix, 1903), pp 181–3.

were to act as guardians and overseers.[1] By their indenture the founders agreed to amortise to the abbot of Bruton and his successors the manor of Blintesfield in the parish of Shaftesbury, Dorset, together with lands and tenements recently purchased by John FitzJames at Warminster, and a tenement in Bruton where Edmunds's father had once dwelt. During their lives the founders were to have the patronage and government of the new school, but after the death of the last survivor the rights would pass to the abbots of Bruton. Thereafter the abbots would appoint an able and sufficient person, either priest or layman, to teach grammar at a salary of £10, within eight weeks of the mastership becoming vacant. If they failed to do so, the heirs of John FitzJames and after them the abbot of Glastonbury or the prior of Witham had the right to fill the vacancy. The schoolmaster could also be ejected by the abbot of Bruton for vicious living, with the co-operation of one of the other two religious, but in any case the latter were to be informed of the schoolmaster's defaults within a month of the abbot of Bruton's hearing of them. The abbot of Bruton, William Gilbert, on his part promised to build a schoolhouse in Bruton at his own expense within two years, as well as a house for the master, on the site of a tenement formerly belonging to William Carpenter and at present inhabited by David Howell, which had been handed over to the abbot by Dr Edmunds in September 1518. He also agreed to keep the buildings in repair.

The indenture proceeded to define the conduct of the new grammar school. Teaching was to be given continually in the schoolhouse except in time of plague, when it would be lawful to move to some place of clean air near Bruton chosen by the abbot. The master should not be hindered from teaching by the abbot, unless his personal presence was required on the special business of the monastery. He was to receive all the scholars who came to him, 'indifferently after their capacities, as well the poor man's child as the rich', taking no fees for his labour, although he was allowed to accept rewards if they were freely given. He might not teach his pupils song or any other petty learning such as the 'crisscross-row' or alphabet, reading from the mattins book and psalter, or even the reading of English, but only what properly concerned the learning of grammar. 'For the founders of the said school intend, with Our Lord's mercy, only to have the grammar of Latin tongue so sufficiently taught that the scholars of the same, profiting and proving, shall in times to come, forever be, after their capacities, perfect Latin men'. They were to study their grammar 'after the good new form used in Magdalen College in Oxford, or in the school at Paul's in London, or after such good form as for the time shall be used.' Every morning the master was to gather the scholars together to pray for the founders and benefactors of the school, and for its increase in virtue and learning. At the end of the day they had to say the psalm *De Profundis* and another general prayer for the founders. The master was warned to be discreet about correcting his scholars, and was not to strike them on the head or the face with his rod or palmer. No holidays were specified, but teaching was to be

---

1 The statutes (in English) are printed by F. W. Weaver, 'Foundation Deed of Bruton School', *Somerset & Dorset Notes & Queries*, iii (1892–3), pp 241–8. Other important sources for the history of the school are listed in T. D. Tremlett, *Calendar of the MSS belonging to the King's School, Bruton, 1297–1826* (Bruton, 1939).

given on the days and at the times accustomed to be used in other good schools. One extra holiday might be granted in a week for play, but no more, unless the abbot gave permission.

The statutes show the founders to have been concerned with more than the mere transmission of information. The moderation of discipline and the care against plague show a humane consideration for the proper development of the pupils entrusted to the schoolmaster's care. The acceptance of the reformed grammar of Oxford and St Paul's ought certainly to mitigate the bishop of London's reputation as one who merely persecuted Colet and was unsympathetic to the New Learning. Bruton also accorded with the new fashion for founding schools without the traditional accompaniment of a chantry, so that the master might be a layman as well as a priest. Nevertheless the founders still valued the old, the life of the Austin canons, enough to extract a promise in the statutes that the abbots of Bruton would take into their religion some of the scholars who promised well in virtue and learning.

Little is recorded of the history of the school before the dissolution of the monasteries. Its good reputation, however, is suggested by the likelihood that Bradford-on-Avon grammar school (1524) was modelled on Bruton, since Sir John FitzJames was asked to help in drawing up the Bradford statutes.[1] In Bruton itself Sir John, who was apparently the only one of the co-founders to remain active after 1530, spent the early 1530s in falling out with Abbot Gilbert. Writing to Thomas Cromwell in 1532 he complained that the abbot had been 'an unkind neighbour, and I would gladly have a better one'. In the following summer Abbot Gilbert died or resigned, and Sir John's candidate, John Ely, filled his place, Cromwell writing to say that he 'would as fain that ye were neighboured as ye would yourself'.[2] For the next few years the affairs of the abbey and school were probably conducted to Sir John's satisfaction, but with the dissolution of the abbey on 1 April 1539 the founders' arrangements for governing and financing the school were suddenly put into jeopardy. Sir John was still alive at this point, but he was now elderly, and he does not seem to have affected the subsequent course of events.

The reigning master in 1539 was Hugh Sherwood. He is almost certainly to be identified with a man of the same name who was born in Dorset in about 1504, entered Winchester College as a scholar in 1516, and was usher of the college school from 1521 to 1525.[3] On 10 February 1542 he secured a pension from the court of Augmentations in recompense for his salary, which he had probably not received since the dissolution of the abbey. The court granted him the school-house with the adjoining close and garden of four acres and an annuity of £5 for life. It also exonerated him from keeping the free grammar school and allowed him to charge his scholars the fees that were commonly taken elsewhere.[4] As in other similar cases, the schoolmaster represented himself, or the court regarded him, not as the incumbent of an independent foundation of which the abbot was merely trustee,

1 See above, p 116.
2 *LPFD*, v, nos 1304, 1340.
3 For his life see *BRUO,* iv, 515.
4 PRO, Exch. Augm., Miscellaneous Books, E 315/101, fo 122v.

but as a simple official of the monastery with a life interest. The decision was bound to be unpopular in Bruton, since the free school now came to an end, and the continued presence of even a schoolmaster charging fees was left to depend on Sherwood's pleasure. Still, the situation was not of his own making, and it is difficult to see what else he could have done for himself.

Not long afterwards legal proceedings were begun against Sherwood by Robert Bishop, a husbandman of Mere in Wiltshire, who claimed that four acres of the close adjoining the school had been granted to him by Abbot Ely in 1538, but which the schoolmaster firmly denied. Both sides brought witnesses to support their claims, and the affair dragged on through the 1540s.[1] On 21 April 1548 the inhabitants of Bruton made a bitter complaint about the school to the chantry commissioners declaring, not wholly accurately, that the schoolhouse had been built in 1524–5, that the master had received a salary of £12, and that Hugh Sherwood, 'late schoolmaster', had surrendered the lands into the king's hands, 'endeavouring himself rather to live licentiously at will than to travail in good education of youth'. The cessation of free education, they said, had resulted in 'the great decay, as well of virtuous bringing up of youth in the said shire in all good learning, as also of the inhabitants of the king's said town of Bruton of great relief that came thereby'. The petitioners concluded by asking for the restoration of the free school as its founders had intended.[2] A second petition was made to the chancellor of the court of Augmentations on behalf of the inhabitants of Bruton by two of their number, Stephen Chyke and William North, the first of whom had been on good terms with the FitzJames family. This further alleged that Hugh Sherwood had ceased to teach the school and had turned its building into a malt-house.[3]

The petitioners received the answer they wanted in 1550 when the government of Edward VI refounded the school and returned to it the original endowments. A board of governors was set up to administer the foundation in place of the abbot of Bruton, and North and Chyke were among the first men to be appointed.[4] The refoundation does not seem at first to have affected Sherwood's position. He remained in receipt of his pension[5] and continued even to occupy the schoolhouse until at last the governors drove him out in exasperation. There is a last glimpse of the old master in 1573 petitioning the court of the Exchequer in a vain attempt to obtain redress.[6]

CHELTENHAM
Gloucestershire

In 1548 the town of Cheltenham had a parish church, an estimated population of 600 communicants, and two chantries. St Katherine's, the more valuable of the two, was

1 Exch. Augm., Proceedings, E 321/14/65; Misc. Books, E 315/113, fo 110; Proceedings, E 321/38/14.
2 PRO, Exch. Augm., Chantry Certificates, E 301/42 no 172; *Somerset Chantries*, ed. E. Green, p 131; *ESR,* part ii, p 191.
3 E. H. Fairbrother, 'The Foundation of Bruton School, Somerset', *Somerset & Dorset Notes & Queries,* xii (1910), pp 49–52.
4 *CPR 1549–51*, pp 191–2.
5 PRO, Exch. Land Revenue, LR 6/15/2 lists his pension as being paid in 1554.
6 Tremlett, *Cal. of the MSS of the King's School, Bruton,* p 20.

worth £5. 18s. 11d., of which the incumbent Edward Grove, aged 60, had £5 for his yearly stipend. He 'was charged by special covenant between the parishioners of the said town of Cheltenham and him, always to teach their children', the town being 'a market town and much youth within the same, near whereunto is no school kept'.[1] It seems likely that here as elsewhere the chantry priest had come to be expected to teach as well during the years just before the Reformation.

The school was evidently a grammar school, for the chantry commissioners ordered that it should continue, and Grove went on receiving his stipend of £5 from the crown until at least 1554.[2] He himself was a typical member of the lower ranks of the parish clergy, having been curate of Charlton Kings in 1532 and of Cheltenham itself in 1540.[3]

CHIPPING CAMPDEN
Gloucestershire

In the fifteenth century the town of Chipping Campden was a prosperous community engaged in the wool trade, and in 1548 there were estimated to be 600 communicants in the parish. Its grammar school however was not the benefaction of a local wool merchant, but of a royal clerk who passed most of his life away from Gloucestershire. The early life of John Ferriby is obscure, but the dates of his later career suggest that he was born in the last quarter of the fourteenth century, and since benefactions like his school were invariably made in places with which the donor felt strong ties of birth and interest, it is reasonable to suppose that he came either from Campden itself or from the surrounding countryside. This was also the conclusion of the inhabitants of the town in a petition to the lord chancellor in 1627, when they said that the founder of their school 'was born near the said town of Campden (as the complainants had heard) which was one of the motives that stirred him up to so good and charitable a work.'[4] It is partly justified by a reference to Ferriby in 1425 as of Worcester diocese[5] and by the knowledge that he died holding property in Cutsdean and the neighbouring hamlet of Hinchwick, a few miles south of Campden.[6]

Ferriby made his career as an officer in the king's household, and in 1415 he appears in the counting house as one of the two clerks of the greencloth.[7] Their duty was to supervise the provisioning of the household and to keep accounts of the payments and receipts which this involved. All the higher officials of the counting house had specified liveries of food, clothes, light and fuel, and the two clerks also received an allowance of 7½d. for every day

---

1 PRO, Exch. Augm., Chantry Certificates, E 301/23 no 53; *ESR,* part ii, pp 85–6; Sir J. Maclean, 'Chantry Certificates, Gloucestershire', *TBGAS,* viii (1883–4), pp 283–4.
2 PRO, Exch. Land Revenue, LR 6/28/1.
3 HWRO, MS ref. 802, pp 53, 93.
4 Gloucestershire Record Office, Deeds, D 253/11; British Museum, MS Lansdown 227 fo 280.
5 *Cal. Papal Letters,* vii, 420.
6 *Reg. Chichele, Canterbury,* ed. E. F. Jacob, vol ii (Canterbury & York Soc., xlii, 1937), p 578.
7 N. H. Nicolas, *The Battle of Agincourt* (1832), p 349.

that they were present at court.¹ Ferriby followed Henry V on the Agincourt campaign with the rest of the household, but took no part in the battle, for he fell sick and was left behind in the castle of Miramont.² By 1419 he is described as 'cofferer' which probably means that he had risen one step to become cofferer of the household, with larger allowances but the same daily wage, and with the responsibility of paying out all fees, wages and rewards in the household.³ In about 1438 he was again promoted to be controller—the third dignity in the counting house, and began his office by taking an oath before the king himself.⁴ It was now his duty to supervise the work of his subordinates, but in fact the controllers were often absent on royal business. He was still controller on 5 January 1439, but by 26 April he had given way to Sir Thomas Stanley. He was back in office by 9 March 1441 and probably continued there until his death in the following October.⁵ He received several rewards for his services, notably a grant of 12d. a day in January 1415,⁶ and the reversion in 1421 of the manor of Witley in Surrey for the term of his life. It was worth £40 a year and then lay in the withered hands of Richard II's old nurse.⁷ To this was added in February 1423 the office of parker of Witley with the usual profits, and Ferriby was holding both manor and park when he died.⁸ In 1438 he was able to purchase the wardship of the young son of Sir William Ingleby at an annual render of £120,⁹ and in the following January he was awarded a tun of Gascon wine each year for the Easter celebrations.¹⁰

Early in 1420 Ferriby married by a special licence Margery, the only daughter of Sir Richard Berners of West Horsley in Surrey and his wife Philippa *née* Dallingridge, the father having died in 1412.¹¹ At the time of her marriage Margery was aged about fifteen.¹² She brought her husband several manors including Barnsbury in Islington (Middlesex), Beaumont, Springfield and Berners Berwick (Essex) and Icklingham (Suffolk), together with West Horsley itself where it is probable that he and his wife usually lived. It was committed to his keeping in November 1420, and he swore fealty for it to the king in 1423.¹³ As a result of his marriage his standing and influence in Surrey became considerable. He was put on the commission of the peace for the county in 1424 and sat upon it continuously

---

1 For the duties and perquisites of the officers of the royal household see A. R. Myers, *The Household of Edward IV* (1959).
2 Nicolas, op. cit., p 379.
3 F. Devon, *Issues of the Exchequer, Henry III–Henry VI* (London, 1837), p 360.
4 He occurs as controller on 12 February 1438 (*CPR 1436–41*, p 195), but there is extant an account of his controllership which runs from 17 April 1437 to 30 September 1438 (PRO, Exch. KR, Accounts Various, E 101/408/24, fo 44v).
5 *CPR 1436–41*, pp 232, 286, 486, 511.
6 *CPR 1413–16*, p 272; *CPR 1436–41*, p 486.
7 *CPR 1416–22*, p 397.
8 *CPR 1422–29*, p 80; *CPR 1436–41*, pp 195, 511.
9 *CPR 1437–45*, pp 47, 61.
10 *CPR 1436–41*, p 232.
11 *Reg. Chichele, Canterbury*, ed. E. F. Jacob, vol iv (Canterbury & York Soc., xlvii, 1947), pp 200–1.
12 She was said to be aged seven in 1412 (*CCR 1419–22*, p 2).
13 *CFR 1413–22*, p 360; *CCR 1422–29*, p 88.

from 1427 until his death, as well as serving on numerous other commissions *ad hoc* during the same period.¹ He was three times returned as knight of the shire for Surrey in the parliaments of 1425, 1429 and 1433, this being not unusual for a household official. In 1426 and again ten years later he was appointed sheriff of Surrey and Sussex, the two counties being usually administered together.² Of his religious and charitable interests much less is known; his great benefaction was his school, but he and his wife also granted a spring and some land at Islington, where they were lord and lady of the manor, to the London Charterhouse.³

John Ferriby made his will on 1 October 1441, shortly before his death.⁴ He asked to be buried in Chertsey Abbey, which was the chief religious house of the neighbourhood, and bequeathed twenty marks for the performance of his obsequies and the attendant alms. He left sums of money to four of his own relations, including a namesake who was then a Carthusian of Sheen and a nephew, Richard Ferriby, BCL, who had been presented by his uncle to the church of West Horsley of which he was patron in his wife's right, and who survived to run through ten benefices in less than thirty years without ever attaining great distinction.⁵ Ten of the servants received small gratuities, and the archbishop of York, John Kempe, a distant cousin of Margery, was remembered with a gift of plate. All the residue of the estate was left to Margery who was designated the sole executrix. It included her husband's farms in the Cotswolds, his reversion of the manor and advowson of Heythrop in Oxfordshire, a messuage in Thames Street, London, and more significantly the sum of £400, 'to be disposed for my soul by Margery my wife in the manner and form which I ordered her'. This seems likely to have been the resources with which the intended grammar school at Campden was to be established and endowed.

Soon after making this will Ferriby was dead,⁶ and Margery did not long remain a widow. By May Day 1442⁷ she had taken as her second husband Sir John Bourchier, one of four brothers who all got peerages: the eldest by inheritance, the second as archbishop of Canterbury, and the third and himself through their marriages. The rise of the Bourchiers had scarcely begun in 1442, but for the rest of her life Margery belonged to a family of increasing power and influence. Her husband was first summoned to parliament by name in 1455 as 'John Bourchier of Berners', doubtless in recognition of the union of two important families which his marriage represented, as well as of his personal services. His activities were mostly of a political kind, but he assisted in the foundation of chantries at Lanthony Priory near Gloucester and in the parish church of Staines.⁸ The marriage probably produced several children, but only two sons survived, and it was a grandson who became a courtier of note under Henry VIII and is remembered as the author of a

1 *CPR, passim.*
2 *CFR 1422–30*, p 156; *CFR 1430–7*, p 303.
3 *Cat. Ancient Deeds*, i, no B 1507; *CPR 1429–36*, p 105.
4 *Reg. Chichele, Canterbury*, ii, 577–8.
5 For the career of Richard Ferriby see *BRUO*, ii, 678.
6 The writ of *diem clausit extremum* was issued on 20 October 1441 (*CFR 1437–45*, p 196).
7 *CPR 1441–46*, p 81.
8 For Sir John Bourchier's life see G. E. Cockayne, *The Complete Peerage*, ed. V. Gibbs & others, ii, 153. For the chantries see *CPR 1452–61*, pp 153, 287.

great English translation of Froissart's chronicles. Margery's second husband died in May 1474 and was also buried in Chertsey Abbey.[1] His widow survived him only until 18 December 1475, and was doubtless laid in the same church as her two spouses.[2]

None of this gives us any sign of who founded the school which bears Ferriby's name, or in what year this took place. In 1627 the inhabitants of Campden in their petition to the lord chancellor believed that the endowment had been made by John Ferriby, 'about one hundred and forty years then last past', although they admitted that they had not seen any deeds or muniments of the school.[3] This date of 1487 is much too late for it falls outside the lifetimes of both Ferriby and his wife. Since the chantry commissioners of 1548 who were probably better informed noted that the school was founded by both John and Margery, it is likely that he intended to endow the school to benefit the district from which he had come, and that she executed the scheme after his death, probably employing the sum of £400 set aside in his will. To assign the foundation to about 1441 is to make the best of the unsatisfactory evidence.

Unlike the founders of other Gloucestershire grammar schools such as Wotton and Newland, John and Margery lived far from the town which would benefit from the school, and had few interests there. It is likely therefore that they did not retain the control of the school for themselves and their heirs but, as the inhabitants of Campden later believed, enfeoffed several persons of the town with the lands of the endowment. These included a moiety of the manor of Lyneham near Chipping Norton, which had come into Ferriby's possession in 1425, and is said to have contained nineteen yard-lands of arable, meadow and pasture, together with 'one great close' called Fiennes Court.[4] In 1548 the income was worth twenty marks a year. The endowment supported a free grammar school and an annual distribution of money to the poor of the parish on Good Friday, known as 'Ferriby's Dole'. In 1546 the chantry commissioners were told that the schoolmaster had to be a priest, and that he received £8 a year for his salary; £2 was spent on the dole.[5] The commissioners of 1548 received slightly different information, which may have reflected local fears about the possible fate of the school. It was not made clear on this occasion that the master had to be a priest, nor were any chantry duties specified. His salary was now claimed to be sometimes £10, sometimes £12, according to his learning, qualities and behaviour. Three or four score scholars were said to attend the school.[6] The commissioners treated the foundation as a school without a chantry, and its lands consequently escaped confiscation. The school survived the Reformation and has continued.

Two of the schoolmasters of Chipping Campden during the 1540s are known by name. The first of them, James Dodwell, occurs in 1542, when he was ordained priest. An

1 For Sir John Bourchier's will see PRO, Prob 11/6 (PCC 15 Wattys), and *Testamenta Vetusta*, ed. N. H. Nicolas (London, 1826), p 328.
2 G. E. Cockayne, *The Complete Peerage*, ed. V. Gibbs & others, ii, 153.
3 Gloucestershire Record Office, Deeds, D 253/11; British Museum, MS Lansdown 227 fo 280.
4 *CCR 1422–9*, p 345.
5 PRO, Exch. Augm., Chantry Certificates, E 301/21 no 31; *ESR*, part ii, p 78.
6 Chantry Certificates, E 301/22 no 37; *ESR*, part ii, pp 80–1; Sir J. Maclean, 'Chantry Certificates, Gloucestershire', *TBGAS*, viii (1883–4), p 280.

Oxfordshire man by origin, he had graduated from Oxford as an MA in the previous year, having been a demy, or undergraduate scholar, of Magdalen College. He must have left Campden by 1548, and after a lapse of several years turns up again as rector of of Stogursey, Somerset, in 1556. He died in 1569.[1] Dodwell's successor was probably Robert Glassman, who is mentioned in the chantry certificate of 1548 and was still teaching the school three years later. Glassman was not a graduate, but as curate of Saintbury near Campden he had been assistant to its notable rector William Latimer, the humanist scholar, friend of Erasmus and tutor of Cardinal Pole.[2] It seems unlikely that so learned a man as Latimer would have hired an ignorant mass priest to assist him. On the whole, what we know of these two masters and their biographies reflects credit both upon themselves and upon the school which employed them.

CIRENCESTER
Gloucestershire

Cirencester, which possessed facilities for learning at an early date, was also one of the first English towns to acquire an endowed grammar school.[3] The founder was John Chedworth, bishop of Lincoln. Nothing is known of his early life, but his choice of Cirencester as the site of his school, together with his surname, makes it likely that he came from the town itself or one of the neighbouring villages. He was probably born a year or two after 1400, since he first appears as a bachelor of Merton College, Oxford, in 1422, where he graduated as an MA and became a fellow. From arts he went on to study theology and emerged in due course as a doctor of divinity. His rise in the Church can be traced to the help of three great men. The first was William Gray, bishop of Lincoln, who gave him his earliest benefice, Stoke Hamond in Bucks., in 1434. After Gray's death two years later he was fortunate enough to attract the attention of Walter Lord Hungerford, whose grandson Robert went up to Oxford in 1437 as part of his training as a nobleman. Chedworth became his tutor, and evidently did so well that Hungerford gave him the rectory of Okeford Fitzpaine in Dorset as a reward. Later, perhaps with his backing, Chedworth acquired other benefices in the area, including a canonry of Salisbury. Hungerford was a senior councillor of Henry VI, and he may also have assisted in getting Chedworth made a fellow of the king's new college at Cambridge in 1443. Once he reached King's, Chedworth soon rose in Henry's favour. He was made provost of the college in 1447, archdeacon of Wiltshire in 1449, and bishop of Lincoln in 1451. He held the see for twenty years until his death on 25 November 1471, and was buried in his cathedral.[4]

1 For Dodwell's career see *BRUO*, iv, 170.
2 Robert Glassman (also Glaseman and Glasyer) was born *c.* 1495 and was curate of Saintbury in 1540 (HWRO, ref. 802, p 212). He probably left there after the death of Latimer in 1545, who bequeathed him 40s. in his will of that year (PRO, Prob 11/30 (PCC 38 Pynnyng)). He was still schoolmaster of Campden in 1551 (Gloucester Public Library, Hockaday Abstracts, General, 1551).
3 On the earlier history of education in Cirencester see above, p 96.
4 On Chedworth's career see *BRUO*, i, 401–2, and also below, p 142.

Chedworth was one of the circle of ecclesiastics whom Henry VI gathered about him in the 1440s, who assisted the king with his educational projects and who founded grammar schools on their own account.[1] He himself was commissioned by Henry in 1455 to assist William Wainfleet in reforming the statutes of Eton and King's.[2] His subsequent reputation as an educational reformer is shown in a letter addressed to him by the university of Oxford in December 1466. The university masters recall how saddened Chedworth has been by the contemporary decline of learning, especially because grammar, 'which stands as the root of the other sciences, has departed from the kingdom as if sent into exile'. The bishop, it appears, has reflected how to provide a remedy, and is praised for his interest in the study of grammar and for some unspecified schemes to prevent its decay. The letter ends with polite offers of assistance if necessary.[3] So it is not surprising that Chedworth, like others of Henry's associates, tried to strengthen the teaching of grammar at a local level by founding an endowed grammar school. Exactly when he made his foundation at Cirencester remains obscure. The school does not appear in records until a dozen years after his death, and not until 1535 is it linked with his name. But on 1 March 1457 Chedworth received a royal licence (in return for a fee of £40) to found a chantry of two, three or four chaplains in the chapel of St Nicholas and St Katherine in the parish church of Cirencester. The foundation, called 'Bishop Chedworth's Chantry', was to be endowed with lands up to the value of £40 a year. This may have been an early form of the scheme which ended as an endowment for a single chantry-chaplain and grammar master.[4]

The first allusion to the school comes in 1483 when £10 was paid to the churchwardens of Cirencester by the abbot and convent of Winchcombe out of their manor of Sherborne in Gloucestershire. A second payment to the same wardens in 1485 was specified for the 'free school for the time of its duration'.[5] This is the earliest evidence for what is confirmed later, that the monks of Winchcombe were trustees of the school endowment, and paid out the master's salary at the usual rate of £10 in quarterly instalments. In 1487 the schoolmaster paid 13s. 4d. towards a clerical subsidy.[6] His name was Simon Molland, and he was an Oxford MA and fellow of Chedworth's old college, Merton. Molland must have returned to Merton by 1488, for he subsequently filled several college offices there, his pedagogic leanings being particularly shown by his appointment in 1490 as grammar master of the college. He left it finally in 1499 for the Oxford vicarage of St Peter-in-the-East which he held till he died in 1520, and was buried in Merton chapel.[7]

Chedworth was not the only bishop to be connected with Cirencester. His footsteps were followed by Thomas Ruthall, who was born and brought up in the town in the 1460s, studied at both the universities, and rose to be bishop of Durham from 1509 until

1 Some of their names are given in *ESMA*, p 200.
2 *CPR 1452–61*, p 241.
3 *Epistolae Academiae Oxoniensis*, ed. H. Anstey, vol ii (Oxford Historical Soc., xxxvi, 1898), p 381.
4 *CPR 1452–61*, pp 338–9.
5 Gloucestershire Record Office, Sherborne MSS, Compoti nos 87, 88.
6 HWRO, Reg. Morton, Worcester, fo 14v.
7 For Molland's biography see *BRUO*, ii, 1291.

his death in 1523.¹ According to Anthony Wood in the seventeenth century, 'towards his latter end he founded a free school at the place of his nativity, and gave a house and seven pounds per annum for the maintenance of a master'.² Wood was certainly wrong to ascribe the foundation of the school to Ruthall, and the endowment of which he is thinking was not applied to its support until after 1540. But it is not impossible that Ruthall intended making benefactions to both school and parish church. As for the latter, Leland reported that 'he promised much, but prevented by death gave nothing'.³ Two undoubted benefactors of education in Cirencester, on the other hand, were Robert Richards, a clothier of the town who died in 1518, and his wife Elizabeth who later married Christopher Toll. Richards bequeathed his lands in the hundred of Berkeley to establish a chantry at the altar of St Anthony in Cirencester church. The foundation was carried out by his wife after his death. The chaplain, who was to be experienced in plainsong, pricksong, and descant, was charged with instructing four children in these subjects *gratis*, the children being chosen by the churchwardens with the advice of the abbot of Cirencester. The chaplain's salary was to be £8 a year.⁴ This is an example of an endowed song school, albeit on a small scale, and was no doubt intended to assist the worship in the parish church. In 1548 when it was dissolved, it was supporting two children and the incumbent, William Wilson, had just over £6 for his salary.⁵ As for Elizabeth, in her will of 1534 she left the modest but useful sum of £10 to repair the buildings of the grammar school.⁶

The *Valor Ecclesiasticus* of 1535 provides the only information about the origins of Chedworth's school. It records that Humphrey, master of the grammar school, received an annuity of £10 from the monastery of Winchcombe by ordinance of John Chedworth, sometime bishop of Lincoln.⁷ 'Humphrey' can be identified as Humphrey Horton, who occurs as a stipendiary priest in Cirencester church in 1532 and 1534.⁸ He was probably an Oxford graduate. In 1536 he was presented to the rectory of Rendcombe by Henry VIII, but obtained permission to be non-resident. In 1556, by then an MA, he also acquired the vicarage of Tetbury, which he administered honourably, it seems, for in 1563 the churchwardens reported that although their vicar held two benefices, they had service at due times. They merely complained that Horton had not preached against the bishop of Rome in his sermons.⁹ In 1564 Horton paid the first-fruits of the vicarage of Fairford but he never gained full possession, and in 1570 he was presented to Colesbourne, the next parish to Rendcombe. At the archbishop's visitation in 1576 he was still holding the three parishes, but he seems shortly afterwards to have been deprived of Rendcombe, Archbishop Grindall

---

1 Ibid., iii, 1612.
2 Wood, *Athenae Oxonienses* (1691–2), i, cols 565–6.
3 Leland, *Itinerary*, i, 129.
4 For his will see PRO, Prob 11/19 (PCC 8 Ayloffe).
5 PRO, Exch. Augm., Chantry Certificates, E 301/22 no 64; *ESR*, part ii, p 81; *VCH Gloucs.*, ii, 389.
6 For her will see PRO, Prob 11/25 (PCC 17 Hogen).
7 *Valor Ecclesiasticus*, ii, 447, 459.
8 HWRO, MS ref. 802, pp 55, 95.
9 Gloucester Public Library, Hockaday Abstracts, General, 1563.

admitting another cleric to be rector there despite Horton's claim that he was still lawfully in possession. He died early in 1578.[1]

On 23 December 1539 the abbey of Winchcombe was dissolved, and the schoolmaster's annuity apparently ceased. There is nothing to show that it continued to be paid by the king's receiver-general of the abbey lands, as happened at Evesham, or to suggest why the schoolmaster did not sue for a new grant in the court of Augmentations, like the masters of Bruton and Winchcombe who found themselves in a similar position. The last schoolmaster, Michael Simpson, certainly outlasted the dissolution by a little, for he was present when Bishop Bell visited Cirencester church on 30 April 1540.[2] But when in due course he left, no school was kept until about 1545 when the inhabitants of the town, 'driven thereunto of great necessity', arranged for the chantry priest of Our Lady in the parish church to teach grammar instead. The incumbent was Thomas Taylor, and the endowments of the chantry were £7 per annum and a house. The chantry commissioners of 1548, to whom these particulars were related, found Taylor satisfactory, and arranged for his salary to be paid in future by the crown.[3] So Cirencester survived the Reformation with a partially endowed school worth £3 less than the original foundation of John Chedworth, but the latter, with its distinctive endowments and unknown ordinances, came to an end.

CREWKERNE
Somerset

The free grammar school of Crewkerne is said to have been founded by John Combe in a deed dated 20 January 1499.[4] Of the founder's origins it is remembered only that his ancestors, 'gentlemen of good note, formerly took that name from Combe, a place lying within the parish [of Crewkerne]'.[5] He first appears to us in 1448 when he supplicated at Oxford for the degree of BCL, which makes it likely that he was born in the early 1420s.[6] Although he is not known to have been a fellow or scholar of any university foundation, he had special associations with Exeter College. He appears in a deed of 1451 in the company of two of the fellows, and in 1478 he acted as proctor for the college in its suit before the archbishop of Canterbury for the appropriation of the church of Menheniot.[7] In 1483 he gave it 30s. to help complete a great set of volumes of the sermons of Hugh of Vienne.

1 For Horton the Oxford graduate see *BRUO*, iv, 299–300. It is possible however that the *BRUO* entry conflates two careers, the occupant of the Staffordshire and Derbyshire benefices being a different man. Reason, on the other hand, suggests that the schoolmaster of Cirencester was the same as the rector of the neighbouring parishes.
2 HWRO, MS ref. 802, p 299.
3 Chantry Certificates, E 301/23 no 40; *ESR,* part ii, pp 84–5. Thomas Taylor was still receiving his salary as schoolmaster in 1555 (PRO, Exch. Land Revenue, LR 6/28/2).
4 R. Grosvenor Bartelot, *History of Crewkerne School* (1899), p 24.
5 Thomas Gerard, *Description of the County of Somerset,* ed. E. H. Bates (Somerset Record Soc., xv, 1900), p 67.
6 For this and for Combe's career see *BRUO*, i, 473.
7 *Hist. MSS Commission, Report on Various Collections,* iv, 87.

Combe's connection with Exeter College was facilitated because much of his life was spent at Exeter Cathedral. He was a canon there by 1477 and rose to be treasurer and then precentor, holding the latter office from 1486 until his death. As a lawyer it is not surprising to find him acting as vicar-general for his diocesan bishop in 1478. All the evidence suggests that Combe kept continual residence in Exeter from the time he secured his canonry until he died.[1] His connection with Crewkerne on the other hand was strengthened when in 1472 he was instituted to the first and wealthiest of the three portions into which the rectory there was divided, which he kept until 1496.[2] He thus had a double obligation to the village, once as his birthplace and once for providing him with his living. The foundation of a school in recompense was his last major act, for he was dead by the spring of 1499.

There is no contemporary record of the school until the end of Henry VIII's reign when Leland noted that 'the church standeth on the hill and by it is a grammar school, endowed with lands for an annual stipend'.[3] According to the chantry certificates of 1548 the school was 'sometime called the chantry of the Trinity', but the schoolmaster is not described as a priest, and the chantry origin of the foundation, though likely, is not clear. The master, John Bird, 'a man of honest conversation, well learned and of goodly judgment', received the whole profits of a little over £8. The number of his scholars was estimated at six or seven score, but the same figure is given for the school in the much larger Taunton, and it may reflect an anxiety to stress the usefulness of the foundation. This would have been an intractable class for one man. At some time before 1538 lands called 'Crafte' had been granted out of the manor of Crewkerne by copy of court roll to Sir Hugh Paulet and Henry Cricke for the term of their lives for the use of the chantry and maintenance of the school, and these produced 40s. in 1548. The inhabitants of Crewkerne requested that the school might remain, and this was approved by the chantry commissioners, the foundation apparently keeping its original endowments.[4]

ENFORD

Wiltshire

Enford lies in the Avon valley, seven miles north of Amesbury. The chantry certificate of 1548 relates that John Westley, then deceased, founded a chantry there and gave a thousand sheep as the endowment. After the flock had dwindled in size William Bird, the neighbouring rector of Fittleton who was attainted in 1540, added a further 578. In 1548 there were 886 sheep, which were let 'to diverse men' for £7. 14s. 6d. The incumbent of the chantry, William Morris, aged 56, is described as 'a very honest poor man' who 'hath

---

1 Exeter Cathedral Library, Dean & Chapter 3754.
2 *Regg. Stillington & Fox, Wells*, ed. H. C. Maxwell-Lyte (Somerset Record Soc., lii, 1937), p 41; *Regg. King & Hadrian, Wells*, ed. H. C. Maxwell-Lyte (ibid., liv, 1939), p 2.
3 J. Leland, *Itinerary*, i, 160.
4 PRO, Exch. Augm., Chantry Certificates, E 301/42; *Somerset Chantries*, ed. E. Green, p 7; *ESR*, part ii, pp 189–90.

always occupied himself in teaching of children there'. The chantry commissioners made no order for the school to continue, which suggests that the teaching was confined to reading or song.[1]

GLOUCESTER: ST NICHOLAS SCHOOL

The first attempt to endow a free grammar school in Gloucester was made by Thomas Gloucester, cofferer of the king's household, in the middle of the fifteenth century. Nothing is known of his origins and his career was largely passed away from Gloucester. Only his name and the regard he showed for the town in his will, especially for the parish of St Nicholas, suggest that he was born or brought up there or elsewhere in the town during the last quarter of the fourteenth century. At the time of his death in 1447 he still had a young niece in Gloucester and owned some unspecified property in the countryside nearby.[2] The details of his later life are not much clearer. In 1452 he was said to have done good service to all three of the Lancastrian kings on both sides of the Channel, which puts back his career to at least 1412.[3] Most of his life was passed in the king's household, where the earliest likely reference to him occurs in 1418 when he accounted at the exchequer in place of the treasurer and the controller.[4] By 1437 he had risen to be cofferer of the household and on 4 November 1439 he was also appointed receiver-general of the duchy of Cornwall, to hold the office in person or by deputy. He kept both appointments until his death.[5] As cofferer he was a colleague of John Ferriby, controller of the household and founder of the grammar school at Chipping Campden.[6] Gloucester's wife Anne, to whom he was married by 1431, may have been the sister of John Edward who appears in documents as Gloucester's 'brother'. She predeceased her husband and was buried in the church of the Greyfriars in London.[7] There were no surviving children. Gloucester also acknowledged some 'cousins', the two daughters of Alice Poynings, heiress of Warnford in Hampshire, and with this family he was on good terms. But having few close relatives with claims upon him, he was free at his death to devote his wealth to charitable schemes.

Gloucester invested his income by purchasing lands in Hertfordshire. In 1426 William Rotse of York quitclaimed the manor of Baas and other lands in Broxbourne and Cheshunt to a group of royal clerks including himself, Ferriby and John Edward.[8] After this date Gloucester's interests in Broxbourne grew steadily. He held lands at Cheshunt nearby in 1428 and also acquired the manor of Langtons in Broxbourne, where he was holding

1 PRO, Chantry Certificates, E 301/58 no 26; *ESR*, part ii, 257–8.
2 These personal details come from his will (Lambeth Palace Library, Reg. Stafford, Canterbury, fos 146v–7).
3 *CPR 1452–61*, pp 30–1.
4 *CPR 1416–22*, p 182.
5 *CPR 1436–41*, p 345. He was cofferer by 14 May 1437 (PRO, Exch. KR, Accounts Various, E 101/408/24).
6 See above, p 125.
7 C. L. Kingsford, *The Grey Friars of London* (British Society of Franciscan Studies, vi, 1915), p 80.
8 *CCR 1422–9*, p 315.

courts by about 1442.¹ Periers manor came to him from William Perriers in 1431 and in the same year with William Cantelowe, his friend and associate, he secured from the king a lease of lands further away at Abbots Langley for ten years at an appropriate rent.² By 1433 Gloucester was holding courts at Baas although the manor was not formally conveyed to him alone until 1438.³ He was 'of Broxbourne' by 1428 and remembered the parish church in his will by ordering his executors to pay £40 for a new bell. As a landowner in the county he naturally sat on commissions of the peace, twice in 1435 and 1437 and once in 1439.⁴ Either through his local or his official status he sat on five commissions to keep the River Lea near London free from weirs (1433–1440). At his death he also owned the manor of Hokes in Essex.⁵

Something is known of Gloucester's circle of friends. One of the most important was William Cantelowe, mercer and alderman of London. They occur together in 1428 giving a recognisance for two hundred marks to Sir Walter Hungerford.⁶ Three years later they were both leasing crown lands at Abbots Langley and in 1444 are mentioned as joint owners of a tenement called the 'Crown' in West Cheap, London.⁷ Cantelowe was not mentioned in Gloucester's will but their friendship is apparent from later events. The merchant was associated in the disputes over Gloucester's debts which followed his death,⁸ and in 1458 when the latter had been dead for over ten years, Cantelowe arranged for masses to be said for both their own and their wives' souls at the Greyfriars in London where the Gloucesters lay buried.⁹ But the heights of Cantelowe's career as alderman, sheriff and burgess for London in Parliament, together with his knighting at Edward IV's coronation, belong to the period after Gloucester's death. Others of his friends were Alice Kingston of Warnford in Hampshire and her daughters, to whom he was in some way related. Alice was a grand-daughter and co-heiress of Thomas Poynings, Lord St John of Basing, who died in 1429, and her daughters were the children of her first marriage with John Orell.¹⁰ In March 1439 she was a widow from her second marriage when, wishing to safeguard the future of her three-year-old son by her second husband, Sir Thomas Kingston, she made over the manor and advowson of Warnford to Gloucester and to Thomas Batell, another relative, for the term of their lives with remainder to the child.¹¹ Batell was the survivor and the heir succeeded in 1457. She also entrusted jewels and various other goods to Gloucester. In the following May, after Alice's death, he was able to purchase the wardship of the heir

1 *Inquisitions and Assessments relating to Feudal Aids,* vol ii (London, 1900), p 450; *VCH Herts.,* iii, 436.
2 Ibid., pp 451–2; *CFR 1430–7,* pp 38, 147–8.
3 *VCH Herts.,* iii, 433–4.
4 *CPR 1429–36,* p 618; *CPR 1436–41,* p 583.
5 *CPR 1429–36,* pp 350, 356; *CPR 1436–41,* pp 83, 371, 453, 'Hokes' is perhaps Hooks in Dagenham.
6 *CCR 1422–9,* p 451.
7 *Cat. Ancient Deeds,* iii, C 3414.
8 *CPR 1446–52,* pp 134–5.
9 *Cat. Ancient Deeds,* v, A 11, 314.
10 *VCH Hants.,* iii, 269.
11 *CPR 1436–41,* p 248.

for five hundred marks.[1] Gloucester dealt faithfully with the affairs entrusted to him and when he made his own will in 1447 he ordered that all the goods belonging to his cousins Elizabeth and Eleanor Orell which were in his keeping should be delivered to them according to their mother's wishes, 'so that the said two children lack no pennyworth of goods that ever came to my hands'. He also bequeathed to them from his own resources an unspecified but competent sum of money and a flock of 700 sheep which he had at Warnford, to help make up their marriage portions.

Gloucester's will was made on 31 January 1447 a little before his death.[2] He asked to be buried beside his wife in the church of the Greyfriars within Newgate, London, and to have a tomb erected there before the altar of Our Lady. He bequeathed all his lands and tenements to his 'brother', John Edward, who was to endow therewith a perpetual chantry of one priest singing in the Greyfriars for the souls of Thomas and his wife and taking an annual stipend of ten marks. More important from our point of view was the second chantry which Edward was ordered to establish in the church of St Nicholas in Gloucester. A suitable priest was to celebrate masses for ever for Thomas and his wife, and was to give instruction in grammar freely and without payment to all who came to him. For this he was to receive a salary of twenty marks a year (£13. 6s. 8d.) and to have a suitable house provided for his use. The salary alone, in the absence of other details, suggests that the scheme was ambitious, for the usual salary of a chantry schoolmaster at this time and for long afterwards was only £10, so that the endowment of the St Nicholas school ought to have attracted a good series of incumbents. Gloucester must have been aware of the serious problem of circumventing the educational monopoly which Lanthony Priory still exercised in the town and we cannot tell how he hoped to overcome it; perhaps he reckoned on the support of the municipal authorities.

After his will had been drawn up in Latin the testator added a codicil in English which showed his confidence in the reality of his wealth by planning a third benefaction. He ordered that all the moneys owing to him should be collected and that his own debts should also be paid, those which he owed to the king by reason of his receivership being settled first. He then willed that a fund of 500 marks or more should be established in Gloucester by his executors so that poor men and young men who were making their way in business could borrow up to £100 for a year if they had sufficient sureties. The idea was suggested by a similar stock of money kept in the Guildhall in London and lent out in loans without interest. His two executors were his 'brother', John Edward, who had been his associate since at least 1426, but of whom little is known, and Walter Gorfen who knew Gloucester by 1440 when they were both enfeoffed with lands by Thomas Fisher of Nazeing in Essex.[3] In 1441 he was appointed steward of a duchy of Cornwall lordship in Essex and would have had dealings with Gloucester as receiver-general of the duchy.[4] He survived his friend until at least 1464, mainly appearing as an auditor of the accounts of the king's

1 Ibid., p 256.
2 Reg. Stafford, Canterbury, fos 146v-7.
3 *CCR 1435–41*, p 352.
4 *CPR 1436–41*, p 554.

ministers in south Wales. Gloucester himself was dead by the middle of February 1447 and his will was proved on 15 April.[1]

Difficulties soon arose because, when Gloucester died, money which he was holding as cofferer of the household and as receiver-general had not yet been paid to the proper recipients. Sir John Popham, the treasurer of the household, and John Parke, one of the clerks of the greencloth, having apparently approached the executors and friends of the deceased without effect, complained to the court of Chancery that before his death Gloucester had held the large sum of £858. 5s. 9½d. owing to the king's creditors. Although some had been paid out, a great part was still unpaid, and these officials were aware that he had ordered the king's debts to be settled first, which the executors could not deny. On 19 April 1448 Parke brought into the court of Chancery the book of the names of the king's creditors and John Edward promised to make the outstanding payments which amounted to £585. 14s. 9d. This promise was formally repeated by both executors on 7 May.[2] But not until December 1452 was Edward pardoned of all actions which the king could have against him for the debts and liabilities of Gloucester, and those which related to his time as receiver-general were excepted. He was however specifically pardoned of a sum of £127. 19s. 2d. still due from Gloucester.[3] Another petition was made to the chancellor against Walter Gorfen by Guy Ketteridge, the executor of Richard Ketteridge, who had bound himself by certain obligations to Gloucester for a sum of £60. Guy claimed that although the money had been repaid, the obligations had been retained by Gloucester during his life and were now held by his executors who still refused to deliver them. The chancellor's intervention was sought because the plaintiff could not secure the obligations by any process in the common law.[4]

Edward began to dispose of Gloucester's property in Hertfordshire in 1448, either to realise the wealth to pay his legacies and establish his chantries, or else to settle the debts for which liability had been admitted. All the manors around Broxbourne were therefore demised, principally to Sir John Say.[5] This raises the question whether the settlement of Gloucester's debts swallowed up all his capital and made it impossible for the executors to carry out their friend's designs. It looks to have been the case, for there is no sign that any of the intended charities were ever established, although news of them reached the town of Gloucester and a copy of the testator's will still survives among the corporation records.[6] Thomas and his wife were regarded as special benefactors at the Greyfriars, but it was William Cantelowe who in 1458 agreed with the friars, in return for a gift of £200 to repair their church, that a daily mass should be said for their souls. If Gloucester's own chantry had been established there such an arrangement would have been unnecessary.[7]

---

1 Writs of *diem clausit extremum* were issued on 18 February and 1 May (*CFR 1445–52*, pp 44–5).
2 The process was exemplified on 5 June 1448 (*CPR 1446–52*, pp 134–5).
3 *CPR 1452–61*, pp 30–1.
4 PRO, Early Chancery Proceedings, C 1/19/10, C 1/15/338, C 1/19/188.
5 *Cat. Ancient Deeds*, i, B 241; *VCH Herts.*, iii, 433–4, 436, 451–2; *CPR 1446–52*, p 253.
6 *Calendar of the Records of the Corporation of Gloucester*, ed. W. H. Stevenson (Gloucester, 1893), p 398, no 1134.
7 Kingsford, *The Grey Friars of London*, pp 80, 208–11; *Cat. Ancient Deeds*, v, A 11, 314.

Not for over eighty years was an endowed school to be founded in Gloucester as its namesake had planned.

GLOUCESTER: CRYPT SCHOOL

The Crypt School, the first free school to be successfully established in Gloucester, was endowed by John Cook, who was born at Minsterworth five miles west of the town in the middle of the fifteenth century, the son of Thomas and Alice Cook. Although the details of his life are few, he was certainly one of the wealthiest and most powerful burgesses in Gloucester between 1500 and 1528.[1] A mercer by trade, he was sheriff of the town in 1493, 1494 and 1498, and mayor four times—in 1501, 1507, 1512 and 1519.[2] He was frequently a justice of gaol delivery and in 1523 he served as a collector of the parliamentary subsidy.[3] In the subsidy roll itself he was placed at the beginning of the list for Gloucester next to the mayor, his goods being rated at £300 and his contribution at £15.[4] His wife Joan, née Messenger, belonged to a leading family in the town and her brother Thomas was also mayor in his turn; the marriage however was childless. Little is known of John's business activities, but he was buying land in the villages outside Gloucester in 1512 and purchased mills and other tenements at Ebley and Stonehouse from Giles Kyn during 1524–6.[5] He was also holding lands in Minsterworth at his death. His wealth is suggested by his will, where the specified monetary bequests alone amount to about £440, and the real total was obviously larger.

John made his will on 18 May 1528 when he was sick in body, although he did not die until 13 September. It exemplifies the largesse which a rich and childless burgess could dispense in his town. Besides the alms provided for his funeral (£35), he bequeathed a pair of vestments to every parish church and religious house in Gloucester. He asked to be buried in Christ Church (the usual sixteenth-century name for St Mary Crypt), before the altar of St John the Baptist, his patron and favourite saint. To this altar he gave a tablet showing the life of the saint in alabaster and he arranged, as we shall see, for a chantry priest to sing there for his soul for ever. Another priest was to sing for him in St Nicholas church for two years, replacing the chaplain maintained there by the wardens of Our Lady service so that they could save the income meanwhile. His obit was to be observed annually in both churches. He left £23 to repair St Bartholomew's Hospital, the inmates of which were endangered by floods in winter time. The prior of this house, Andrew Whitmay, titular bishop of Chrysopolis, was John Cook's confessor and the supervisor of his will. To improve the state of the town itself he left £45 to repair highroads and the great west bridge. One of his

---

1 Most of the surviving information about John Cook and his wife Joan is to be gathered from their wills, PRO, Prob 11/22 (PCC 38 Porche), and Prob 11/31 (PCC 4 Alen), respectively.
2 *List of Sheriffs for England and Wales* (PRO, Lists & Indexes, ix, 1898), p 184; R. Furney, History of Gloucester, vol i (Bodleian Library, MS Top. Glouc. c. 4).
3 *CPR 1404–1509*, pp 322, 437, 488, 560; *LPFD*, i part i, 1662 (1), iii part ii, pp 1367, 1458.
4 PRO, Exch. KR, Lay Subsidy Rolls, E 179/113/189.
5 *Calendar of Records of the Corporation of Gloucester*, ed. W. H. Stevenson (1893) nos 1194, 1202–4.

lesser bequests was to arrange for the education of Thomas Stewe, a relative, until he should be ordained priest, and this was later carried out.

John also declared in his will that he intended to endow a free school in Gloucester but that lack of time prevented him from setting out his plans in detail. He had therefore to rely on his wife Joan, whom he made his sole executrix, to carry out his intentions in this respect. Six days before making his will, on 12 May, he had enfeoffed Thomas Messenger, Thomas Bell the elder, and others with his lands and tenements in Gloucester, Badgeworth, Chaxhill, Ebley, Oxlinch, Rodley, Stonehouse and Westbury to the use of his wife so that she could purchase lands and tenements after his death to the annual value of £20 for purposes with which he had already made her familiar.[1] These included the establishment of a chantry grammar school of the usual kind. The schoolmaster was to be a priest, to keep school every day and to teach grammar freely in a schoolhouse to be built on a chosen site within the parish of Christ Church. He was also to say a daily mass in the parish church before the altar of St John for the souls of John, his wife and their parents. Other alms, obsequies and deeds of charity were to be established and continued in Christ Church daily and yearly for ever.

About a year after his death these plans began to be put into effect. On 6 October 1529 Richard Hart the prior of Lanthony, patron of Christ Church, and the rector Robert Stinchcombe conveyed part of the burial ground to Thomas Messenger, Thomas Bell the elder and three other burgesses for the erection of a schoolhouse, at the nominal rent of a red rose.[2] Since the canons of Lanthony were also the patrons of the existing, fee-paying grammar school in Gloucester, they had obviously been won over to supporting the scheme for an endowed foundation—either as an alternative or more probably as the successor to their own school. The new school building had been finished by 1540 and consisted of a schoolroom fronting on to Southgate Street with chambers for the master overhead. The endowment of the school on the other hand was delayed for some years, probably because of the difficulty of buying suitable land for the purpose. It is likely that Joan Cook paid a master to teach during the 1530s out of her own pocket, since Richard Fletcher occurs as a schoolmaster in Christ Church parish in 1534, when he made a contribution to the clerical subsidy.[3]

The school did not long remain a private venture of the Cooks. It was a natural result of their leading position in the town that the corporation should have become involved, several of John's feoffees and associates being its members. An institution was needed to guard the school's endowments and appoint masters, and the corporation was eminently

---

1 John Cook's will; R. Austin, *The Crypt School, Gloucester* (1939), p 18. Mr Austin's book prints most of the important deeds bearing on the foundation and early history of the school.
2 Ibid., pp 27–8, 30, 147ff.
3 HWRO, MS ref. 802, p 104. He is to be distinguished from the chantry priest of the same name at St Briavels in 1548 but may well be the Richard Fletcher admitted M Gram at Oxford on 21 June 1531 after two years of study and five of teaching boys (Bodleian Library, University Archives, Reg. H fo 251), or the Richard Fletcher admitted to the rectory of St Aldates, Gloucester, on 23 October 1534 (Reg. Ghinucci, Worcester, fo 69v).

suitable in this respect. The canons of Lanthony may have intended becoming the patrons of the new school as they had been of the old, but by 1536 the monasteries were coming under strong pressure from the crown and on 10 March 1538 Lanthony itself was dissolved.[1] So on the following 12 May we find the mayor and burgesses of Gloucester being licensed to acquire lands up to the value of £50 a year to support the school and to repair the bridge and causeway over the Severn. Joan Cook however paid for the licence.[2] The dissolution of Lanthony also suggested the possibility of endowing the school with monastic land, and the bishop of Worcester, Hugh Latimer, who was interested in fostering endowed schools, exerted himself to write to Thomas Cromwell on Joan's behalf. In an undated letter subsequent to the grant of 12 May he relayed her request to buy the manor of Podsmead in Hempstead parish, a possession of Lanthony, at the usual purchase price of twenty times the annual value. He also sent his chaplain to discuss the matter with both parties.[3] His intervention was successful, and on 5 September 1539 the treasurer of the court of Augmentations acknowledged the receipt of £266. 6s. 8d. from Joan Cook by the hands of John Partridge as the purchase price of Podsmead. Letters patent were issued the next day to confirm the grant of the manor, and it was leased shortly afterwards by Joan to Partridge at a rent of twenty marks a year.[4]

Once the endowment had been arranged, a tripartite indenture was drawn up on 11 January 1540 between Joan Cook on the first part, the mayor and burgesses of Gloucester on the second, and the bailiffs and citizens of Worcester on the third. The latter were meant to check on negligence by the mayor and burgesses, who were liable to pay a fine of £10 for breaches of covenant or failure to observe the terms of the indenture.[5] Joan made over to the mayor and burgesses her lands and tenements in Podsmead, Brockworth and other places, with a tenement in Westgate Street, Gloucester, the total annual value of which did not exceed forty marks. The corporation covenanted in return to pay her during her life all the rents and profits arising from the properties. While Joan lived she was to pay the schoolmaster and support the school, and after her death the whole responsibility would pass to the corporation. Once a year the mayor, recorder, two senior aldermen, the two sheriffs, town clerk, four stewards, the swordbearer, four serjeants of the mace and five porters of the town gates were to go in procession to view the schoolhouse and cause any defects and disrepairs to be amended, all receiving a modest fee for their pains. The indenture also provided for a weekly distribution of 3s. 4d. among the poor folk of the hospital of St Bartholomew and an annual payment of £5 to maintain the causeway between the town and the river.

The mayor and burgesses convenanted to find a schoolmaster who was to be chosen, and if necessary removed, by the mayor acting with the advice of the recorder and two

1 *LPFD*, xiii part i, no 482.
2 Ibid., no 1115 (17).
3 Ibid., no 1179.
4 Austin, *The Crypt School*, pp 29, 145–6.
5 Ibid., pp 147–58. Joan also granted an annuity to the bailiffs and citizens of Worcester on 20 November 1540 in recompense for their overseeing the provisions of the indenture for ever (ibid., pp 158–61).

senior aldermen. The master was to be honest, well-learned and a priest, 'if any such may conveniently be had', in which case his yearly stipend was £10, but if he were a layman only £9. Nevertheless by opening the mastership to laymen a significant departure was made from John Cook's original plan for a chantry school, and a foundation was made more in accordance with the times—wisely as it turned out, for the chantries were dissolved only eight years later. The master was to occupy a chamber above the school, 'which is appointed for him and his scholars only and not for his wife or his family or strangers'. He was to teach grammar freely to all the children and scholars who resorted to him and, if a priest, he was also to say mass two or three times a week in Christ Church, no intercessions being specified. In consequence the school never came within the scope of the Chantry Acts of 1545 and 1547. The first schoolmaster who is known for certain was Thomas Young, who held the post by April 1540, when he was called 'Master Young'.[1] He probably continued at the school until he was presented on 27 February 1543 to be rector of Christ Church itself, where he remained for three years.[2] Joan bequeathed him 10s. in her will, of which he was one of the witnesses.

Joan also made further arrangements for the perpetuation of her own and her husband's memory on 12 January 1540 when she enfeoffed Thomas Bell, Thomas Payne and others with lands and tenements in Brockworth. They were to pay from these 40s. a year for a solemn obit to be kept on 13 September (the anniversary of John's death) in Christ Church together with a mass on the following day. Seven priests, boy choristers and candles were to be hired; prayers were to be said for John, Joan and their families; and 13s. 4d. was to be given to the poor.[3] Yet more arrangements for prayers appear in Joan's will, dated 1 May 1544. She desired to be buried by her husband in the chancel of Christ Church, where masses were to be said for her soul every month for a year by at least eight priests. She made bequests to the church itself and its clergy, to the highways of Gloucester and the poor in the town, as well as legacies in money and goods to several of her Messenger relatives. Her executors were William and Thomas Messenger, with Thomas Bell as overseer, and the will was proved on 20 February 1546, so she presumably died in the winter of 1545–6.[4]

A glimpse of Joan in her last years comes in a lawsuit of 1550 in which the mayor and burgesses sued William Messenger to recover deeds and evidences relating to her affairs which were still in his possession. Witnesses in the suit recalled that Joan was unable to attend in person to take formal possession of her new property in 1540. 'She was such an unwieldy woman for age and unwieldiness that she could not ride nor go herself to such places out of the town of Gloucester where the said lands and tenements lay'. So she authorised Richard Parkins, a chaplain known to her husband, and the schoolmaster Thomas Young to go as her attorneys to Podsmead where they solemnly took possession, the latter

1 HWRO, MS ref. 802, pp 253, 189.
2 Gloucester Public Library, Hockaday Abstracts, Gloucester: St Mary Crypt, 1543, 1546, quoting Gloucester Diocesan Records, 2a doc. 170, and PRO, Exch. First Fruits, Composition Books, E 334/3 fo 9.
3 PRO, Prob 11/31 (PCC 4 Alen).
4 Ibid.

—it was said—accompanied by his scholars.[1] Something of Joan's character also survives in the documents she has left behind. Her evident fondness for intercessory masses suggests that, like her husband, she was a religious conservative at a time when some people were losing interest in such things. She also appears to have been a stubborn person to deal with. She always refused to hand over the evidences and deeds of her Podsmead property to the corporation during her lifetime and insisted on retaining a measure of control over her school until she died.

When the foundation of the Crypt School was begun in 1529 the old grammar school of the town under the patronage of Lanthony Priory was still in existence. By 1535 however the old school appears to have been discontinued[2] and for a short period the Crypt School became the only grammar school of the town. Then in 1541 Henry VIII established a new cathedral in the former abbey of St Peter's, and the statutes issued for it in 1544 provided for a second grammar school, free to all comers. In this way Gloucester, like Bristol and Worcester, emerged from the Reformation with two new endowed schools, and the 1540s marked the beginning of a new era in the local history of education.

HEYTESBURY
Wiltshire

The history of Heytesbury school is largely that of its founders, the Hungerford family. It lay at the centre of their power, reflecting their wealth and benevolence, and when they suffered their notable series of disasters, so did the school. The rise of the Hungerfords needs no discussion here. The first generation achieved some prominence in Wiltshire during the early fourteenth century as landowners, members of parliament, and servants of the earldom of Lancaster. In the second generation Sir Thomas Hungerford (d. 1397) bought the two major properties of Farleigh and Heytesbury, served as chief steward of the duchy of Lancaster in southern England, and sat in the House of Commons on sixteen occasions. In 1377 he became the second person to fill the new office of speaker.[3] With his son Walter Lord Hungerford (c. 1378–1449) the third generation of the family achieved national prominence and elevation to the peerage. Walter, through marriage and purchase, became one of the greatest landowners in the west of England. His family's loyalty to Lancaster stood him in good stead when Henry IV ascended the throne in 1399. He was elected to six Lancastrian parliaments, he recovered his father's old post as a chief steward of the duchy, and Henry V entrusted him with several foreign embassies. He fought at Agincourt with nineteen men-at-arms and sixty archers, and was subsequently rewarded with lands and offices in France. In 1417 he became steward of the royal household and a member of the privy council, on which he continued to sit for twenty years. The Garter was conferred upon him, and in 1421 he was appointed one of Henry V's executors and nominated to

---

1 R. Austin, 'John and Joan Cook's Gift to Gloucester', *TBGAS*, lxv (1944), pp 199–219.
2 See above, p 65.
3 On the career of Sir Thomas Hungerford and the origins of his family see J. S. Roskell, 'Three Wiltshire Speakers', *Wilts. Archaeological and Natural History Magazine*, lvi (1955–6), pp 274–300.

attend on the person of his infant son. During the royal minority after 1422 Walter was a leading member of the council. In 1426 he became a parliamentary peer and a great officer of state as treasurer of England, a post he retained until 1432. He was an influential figure in government until the late 1430s, after which he withdrew into gradual retirement. He died, in his early seventies, on 9 August 1449.[1]

During the course of his life Walter distinguished himself as a landowner, warrior, administrator, diplomatist and statesman. Nor were these varied roles the sum of his interests. Like many of the Lancastrian aristocracy he was clearly a literate and cultivated man, well acquainted with the world of literature. The victors of Agincourt were such amateurs of reading for pleasure that it is no surprise to find *The Siege of Troy* and *The Golden Legend* in French among Walter's possessions. More serious studies are suggested by the great Bible in two volumes, probably in Latin, 'with all my books of theology', which he bequeathed to a clerical grandson destined for university, and it is possible that he himself was originally schooled for the Church.[2] He was, after all, a younger son by birth and only came to his inheritance after the death of two elder brothers. Be that as it may, he took a special interest during his later life in education, both that of school and university. The Oxford masters evidently viewed him as a potential patron in 1434 when they sent him a letter of recommendation on behalf of one of their number, a former proctor.[3] His close relations with Merton College are indicated by the gift of 100 marks which he made towards building the bell-tower, and to which he added another fifty in his will.[4] It is also likely that Walter conceived the idea of sending his eldest grandson Robert to study at Oxford in 1437. Robert was heir apparent, after his father, to the family lands and title, and there is no likelihood that he was ever intended for the Church. On the contrary, his stay in Oxford is one of the earliest examples of what became common in England only after the Reformation: the sending of noble boys to university as part of their aristocratic training. Robert's tutor, John Chedworth, was a former fellow of Merton and the two of them spent at least three terms together in Chedworth's rooms at University College.[5] Shortly afterwards Walter rewarded Chedworth with the rectory of Okeford Fitzpaine in Dorset, and he may well have done more for him than this. Chedworth's subsequent rise in the Church (he became bishop of Lincoln in 1451) came about through the patronage of Henry VI, after Chedworth had become a fellow of the king's new college at Cambridge in 1443. It is not impossible that Hungerford was responsible for bringing Chedworth to Henry's notice and for getting him the fellowship through which he eventually rose in the king's favour.[6]

1 Walter Lord Hungerford's career is well covered in a subsequent section of the same article, pp 301–41.
2 These books are mentioned in his will of 1449 (Lambeth Palace Library, Reg. Stafford, Canterbury, fos 114–117v).
3 *Epistolae Academicae Oxon.*, ed. H. Anstey, vol i (Oxford Historical Soc., xxxv, 1898), p 112.
4 *Oxford City Documents*, ed. J. E. Thorold Rogers (ibid., xviii, 1891), p 314; Reg. Stafford, Canterbury, fos 114v–15.
5 BRUO, ii, 985.
6 For Chedworth's career see ibid., i, 401–2, and above, p 128.

Besides his connections with Oxford, Walter was the founder of Heytesbury school. According to his daughter-in-law, Margaret Lady Hungerford and Botreaux, he built 'an almshouse of twelve poor men and a woman, and a house for a schoolmaster, being a priest, as well to teach grammar as to have the rule and oversight of the said poor men and woman, at Heytesbury in Wiltshire, and ordained and declared by his last will that the manors of Cheverell Burnell and Great Cheverell [should] be amortised to the said schoolmaster, poor men and woman and their successors, for their sustentation, for ever more'.[1] The date of the project, since it was not completed, appears to belong near Walter's death in 1449. This would connect it with the spate of new schools which followed upon Henry VI's foundation of Eton in 1440, when benefactions of this kind were fashionable in court circles. Whether or not this is true, it is equally possible that the origin of the scheme preceded Eton, and that Henry got his interest in education from Hungerford and his other senior courtiers, rather than vice versa. The Heytesbury foundation has obvious affinities with the college at Higham Ferrers which Archbishop Chicheley founded in 1422 for eight priests, a grammar school, and an almshouse of twelve poor men and a woman.[2] Ewelme Hospital, founded by the earl of Suffolk, William de la Pole, in 1437 is another comparable foundation. It supported two chaplains, thirteen poor men, and by 1450 if not earlier, one of the chaplains was ordered to teach grammar.[3] Similar features also appear at Tattershall College, founded by Sir Ralph Cromwell in 1439 with the help of five other trustees, Hungerford himself being one. Tattershall included a college of priests, a house of thirteen almsfolk, and eventually a grammar master.[4] All four of these founders—Chicheley, Cromwell, de la Pole and Hungerford—were contemporaries, and all were involved in Henry's minority government during the 1420s and 30s. It looks as though chantry colleges, almshouses and grammar schools were a common interest among them before Henry grew up, though it must be admitted that the grammar schools, except for Higham Ferrers, cannot be dated for certain before the foundation of Eton.

Lady Hungerford's evidence attests that Walter built the school, planned its management and allocated lands. But it was not until 1472, when he had been dead for over twenty-two years, that the foundation was set on a permanent footing with endowments, statutes and a royal licence. The interval was due to the catastrophes which struck the family after Walter's death, of which Lady Hungerford herself has left us such an eloquent account.[5] The first was the capture of Robert Lord Moleyns, the boy who had studied at Oxford, in the Gascon campaign of 1453. He was held in France for seven years, and his capture laid a heavy burden on the family's resources. A ransom of £6,000 had to be paid, and the costs of maintenance and raising loans amounted to nearly £4,000. No sooner had Lord Moleyns come home in 1460, having just succeeded to the Hungerford title, than he threw himself into the English civil war on the side of Lancaster, in the loyal tradition of his ancestors.

1 Sir R. C. Hoare, *The Modern History of South Wiltshire: Heytesbury* (1824), pp 100–2.
2 *VCH Northants.*, ii, 177–9.
3 *CPR 1436–41*, p 80; *Hist. MSS Commission, IXth Report,* Appendix p 217.
4 *CPR 1436–41*, p 292; *Hist. MSS Commission, MSS of Lord De L'Isle and Dudley*, vol i (1925), p 182.
5 Sir R. C. Hoare, op. cit., pp 100–2.

It was the losing side. Hungerford had to flee to France, and when he was attainted by the Yorkist parliament in 1461, he forfeited the whole of his property. The effective patron of the Hungerford interest now became his mother Margaret, Lady Hungerford and Botreaux. Not that her own position was very strong in 1461. She was confined by the Yorkists in Amesbury Priory and it took her much trouble to recover her dower share of the Hungerford lands. Her son met his end in 1464 on the battlefield of Hexham, where he was caught and executed. His own son Thomas was attainted and beheaded in Wiltshire five years later. The final victory of Edward IV over the Lancastrians in 1471 saw the Hungerford fortunes at their lowest ebb, and the heirs did not recover their lost lands and titles until the Lancastrians returned to power in 1485. On the other hand, the years after 1471 were years of peace. Margaret herself retained enough wealth, and was sufficiently free from other pre-occupations, to be able to settle some of the projects left unfinished by her family. One of these was the uncompleted school and almshouse. Whether the school was open from the time it was built is not certain, but the almshouse seems to have been, since the second Lord Hungerford bequeathed it 20s. in 1459, presumably for the benefit of the inmates.[1] The schoolmaster and the almsfolk may well have been supported out of Hungerford revenues until the alienation of the proposed endowment became possible.

The refoundation of the school and almshouse was sanctioned by a royal licence of 20 February 1472, for which Margaret paid £80. This permitted her to establish an almshouse at Heytesbury for a chaplain, twelve poor men and one poor woman, and also to endow the foundation with the manors of Cheverell Burnell and Great Cheverell.[2] Six weeks later on 4 April Lady Hungerford issued a deed of foundation[3] and she also drew up a detailed body of statutes, the date of which has not survived.[4] The foundation was officially entitled 'The Almshouse of Walter and Robert Hungerford, Lords of Hungerford and Heytesbury', but in later times it was generally known as the Hospital of St John. A warden or keeper in priest's orders was to be placed in charge and the deed appointed Robert Stephens, chaplain, to hold this office. He was expected to keep continual residence and could not leave the house (except to go for walks) without permission from the lord of the manor. Even then his absence was not to exceed a month at a time, and he was not allowed to hold any other office or benefice. His salary, or so it appears from later evidence, was £10 a year and his duties were twofold. He was to say mass every day in the almshouse chapel or the parish church for the souls of Margaret, her husband Robert Lord Hungerford, and their parents. He was also to attend mattins, high mass and evensong in the parish church on Sundays and festivals. On all other days he was to teach children and others who came to his school, 'from the beginning of learning unto such season as they have sufficient or competent [knowledge] of grammar'. This must have involved

---

1 This is in the will of Robert Lord Hungerford (PRO Prob 11/4 fo 132 (PCC 17 Stokton)); printed in *Somerset Medieval Wills,* ed. F. W. Weaver, vol i (Somerset Record Soc., xvi, 1901), pp 186–93.
2 *CPR 1467–77,* p 306; Sir R. C. Hoare, op. cit., pp 128–30.
3 Ibid., pp 130–1.
4 J. E. Jackson, 'Ancient Statutes of Heytesbury Almshouse', *Wilts. Archaeological and Natural History Magazine,* vol xi (1869), pp 289–308.

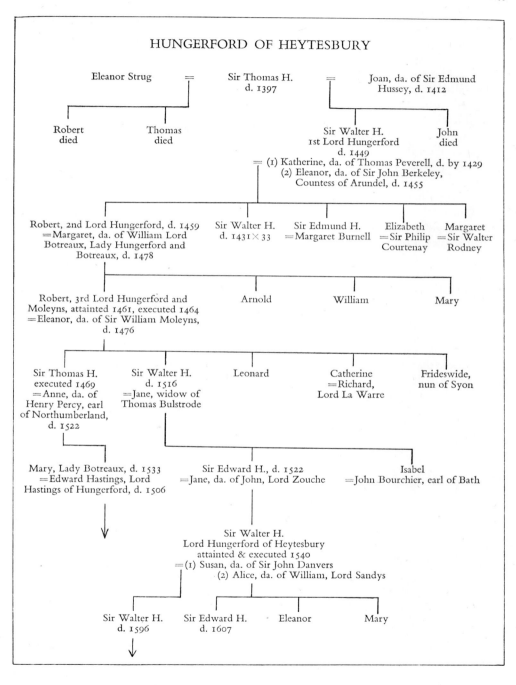

him in the whole range of school subjects, from the alphabet to advanced grammar. He was not to take fees from his scholars unless their friends and relatives could spend £10 or more a year, or were prepared to pay him voluntarily. Future wardens were to be appointed by Lady Margaret during her lifetime and afterwards by the chancellor of Salisbury Cathedral, or by the chapter in his absence. The Hungerford family was intimately connected with the cathedral, in which several of its members were buried, and the chancellor was the dignitary with special charge of education. He was thus an appropriate person to choose the schoolmaster-warden. No other provisions were made about the conduct of the school, the vast majority of the statutes being concerned with the government and well-being of the twelve poor men and the woman who was retained to look after them.

Like most schools, Heytesbury reveals little of its history after the act of foundation. Only four of the wardens are known by name before the Reformation, and the study of their careers does not shed very much light upon the school they ran. Nothing is known of the first master, Robert Stephens,[1] and John Lucas who held office in 1498–9 is an equally shadowy figure.[2] The other two wardens, William Raven (1503–4)[3] and Robert Balfront (1535)[4] are better known, but their activities are not easily reconciled with the requirements of the hospital statutes. Both men were protégés of the Hungerford family, which became once more a powerful force with the accession of Henry VII, and it looks as though the Hungerfords, rather than the chancellor of Salisbury, came to wield the decisive power over the appointments. Both held a parochial benefice in breach of the statutes, but since the benefices concerned were Hungerford ones, the arrangement evidently had the approval of the power that mattered. Raven was rector of Tellisford in Somerset during his term of office, while Balfront was rector of Upton Scudamore and chaplain of Frome Selwood. Each went on to become a moderately wealthy clerical pluralist, and did rather better in

1 Unless he is the Robert Stephens, MA of Oxford in 1450 (*BRUO*, iii, 1772).
2 The name appears in one of the two surviving account rolls of the hospital (PRO, Ministers' Accounts, SC 6/Hen VII/1697). He is possibly the same as John Lucas, BCL, of Worcester diocese (*BRUO*, ii, 1170).
3 Named in the other account roll, SC 6/Hen VII/1698. He was definitely an Oxford MA and fellow of Magdalen College. For his career see *BRUO*, iii, 1549–50.
4 Robert Balfront, apparently not a graduate, was chaplain of the chantry of Our Lady in the castle of Farleigh Hungerford, Somerset, instituted 7 November 1524, resigned by August 1526 (*Reg. Wolsey, Wells*, pp 37, 45); rector of Tellisford, Somerset, instituted 5 September 1531, resigned by 1535 (ibid., p 64; *Valor Ecclesiasticus*, i, 162); chaplain of St Katherine, Frome Selwood, Somerset, instituted 14 February 1533, till death (*Reg. Wolsey*, pp 67, 109); chaplain of Atworth Parva, Wilts., instituted 26 November 1533 (Reg. Campeggio, Sarum, fo 44); rector of Little Cheverell, Wilts., instituted 12 December, resigned by 30 December 1534 (ibid., fos 49v, 50v); and rector of Upton Scudamore, Wilts., instituted 30 December 1534, till death (ibid., fo 50v; Reg. Capon, Sarum, fo 22v). Excepting Atworth, these were all Hungerford benefices. He occurs as warden of Heytesbury in 1535 (*Valor Ecclesiasticus*, ii, 103), and was given a dispensation to reside away from Upton Scudamore on 16 February 1535 (*Faculty Office Registers*, ed. D. S. Chambers (1966), pp 21, 39). His will, dated 21 October, was proved on 20 December 1544 (PRO, Prob 11/30 fos 156–7 (PCC 20 Pynnyng)).

this respect than most ex-schoolmasters. Their other affairs were such that one wonders how much time they gave to their functions in the hospital. It is not impossible that the office of warden became something of a sinecure, and that the duty of teaching (which we have reason to believe continued) was carried out by a deputy.

This quiet period came to an end in 1540 when once again the school fell into jeopardy as the result of a crisis in the Hungerford family. The current head of the Heytesbury branch, Walter Lord Hungerford, was a close associate of Thomas Cromwell. He was raised to the peerage in 1536, but he evidently made himself powerful enemies and his fall in June 1540 followed swiftly upon that of Cromwell. The charges against him were political and personal. He was said to have comforted one of the king's enemies, to have employed conjurors to estimate how long the king should live, and to have practised sodomy with members of his household. His property was confiscated by a bill of attainder, and he shared the fate of Cromwell upon Tower Hill on 28 July 1540.[1] Heytesbury school and its endowments were much too closely linked with the Hungerford family not to suffer from the new seizure of its property. In June 1541 the manor of Heytesbury, now in the hands of the crown, was leased to William Sharington, page of the king's wardrobe, and he became the dominant figure in the district for the next seven years.[2] The manors of Cheverell Burnell and Great Cheverell, which had been granted to the hospital by royal licence, were also leased by the crown with no legality to John Lute and Ralph Erle in 1544 and 1545 respectively.[3]

The last known warden, Robert Balfront, died in the autumn of 1544. Whether he was still in office remains uncertain, but the school appears to have been open since his will, which was made on 21 October, included a bequest of 13s. 4d. 'to the schoolmaster of Heytesbury'.[4] At about this time, however, and possibly as a consequence of Balfront's death, Sharington intruded himself into the office of warden. He continued to maintain the almsfolk but allowed the school to disappear, and filched the surplus revenues. This was the situation when the first survey of chantries and hospitals was made in 1546. The chantry commissioners of Henry VIII, after noting the presence of the thirteen poor, reported that an abuse was apparent, 'in that a grammar school was established by the original foundation, over and above the maintenance of the twelve poor men, the schoolmaster of which should receive £10 a year for his salary, but now there remain neither schoolmaster nor scholars in the place'.[5] The Edwardian chantry commissioners of 1548 found a similar state of affairs. There had been no schoolmaster for the last five or six years and Sharington received the revenues of the hospital, 'but by what authority we know not'.[6]

1 *LPFD*, xv, nos 498 c. 61, 784, 926.
2 Ibid., xvi no 459 (24).
3 Ibid., xix part ii, no 340 (16); xx part i, no 620 (7).
4 PRO, Prob 11/30 fos 156–7.
5 PRO, Chantry Certificates, E 301/56 no 8; *ESR*, part ii, pp 256–7.
6 PRO, E 301/58 no 88; E 301/105 no 16; *ESR*, part ii, pp 262, 265. The estimate of 'five or six years' need not be taken literally, such observations being often subjective.

Heytesbury school, then, ceased to operate in about 1544 and remained suspended for some thirteen years. The abuse was notorious, but Sharington was too powerful to be disciplined. He was knighted at Edward VI's coronation in 1547, and he had friends in high places including Hugh Latimer the Reformer and the politician Thomas Lord Seymour. He was nearly ruined after Seymour's fall in January 1549 when he was himself imprisoned for monetary frauds committed while he was vice-treasurer of the Bristol mint. But he was pardoned later in the year, and after paying a fine of £12,000 to recover his property, he died in 1553 still tenant of Heytesbury and its school.[1] His death, and the collapse of the Protestant regime, then opened the way for the restoration of the status quo. In May 1554 the Hungerford heir recovered Heytesbury and others of the Wiltshire properties, including the two manors of Cheverell.[2] Three years later, on the initiative of William Geoffrey, chancellor of Salisbury, the hospital was given back into clerical hands by the orders of Cardinal Pole. On 3 April 1557 the bishop of Salisbury, William Capon, instituted John Lybbe, bachelor of canon law, to the wardenship of the hospital, 'vacant by the death of Sir William Sharington, a married layman who intruded himself into the rule of the hospital *de facto* since he could not do so *de jure*, against the institution of the founder and the will of the Highest, and took upon himself to be ruler or administrator of the same'.[3] With this short sketch of recent events, the hospital was restored into the care of a resident grammar master and the school, after its peculiar experience of Reformation spoliation, resumed the tranquil life of its earlier days.

LAUNCESTON

Cornwall

There was a grammar school at Launceston by the fourteenth century,[4] but it is not until the middle of the sixteenth that the existence of a continuous foundation endowed with lands becomes clear. In 1548 the chantry commissioners of Edward VI were told that lands in Bamham by Launceston had been given to the mayor by John Cory, Richard Cobbethorn and others to support a priest celebrating in the church of St Mary Magdalen and teaching children grammar.[5] The assertion has some historical basis. The parties concerned did indeed transfer the lands to the mayor and corporation in 1409, but the objects of the benefaction were only stated to be the maintenance of chaplains and the upkeep of the

---

1 For Sharington's life see the article by A. F. Pollard in the *DNB*. He seems to have been a rogue, but Latimer thought well of him.
2 *CPR 1553–4*, pp 92, 94.
3 Reg. Capon, Sarum, fos 76–77v. There is a good general sketch of the hospital's later history in *VCH Wilts.*, iii, 337–40.
4 See above, p 100. For a general history of the school see H. Spencer Toy, *A History of Education at Launceston* (Marazion, 1966).
5 PRO, E 301/9 no 7; *The Chantry Certificates for Cornwall*, ed. L. S. Snell, pp 29–30; *ESR*, part ii, pp 34–5; Bodleian Library, MS Rawl. D 363 fos 230–2.

church.[1] Teaching was not mentioned, and was probably a much later addition, the foundation of endowed schools being still unusual in the early fifteenth century.

The Bamham lands supported two schoolmasters in 1548, one teaching reading and the other grammar, an arrangement similar to that at Penryn, another major centre of education in Tudor Cornwall.[2] The elementary teacher, John Bannek, 'an aged man chosen by the mayor to teach young children the ABC', was 60 years old and received 13s. 4d. for his pains. The grammar master was Stephen Gourge, aged 40, whom the chantry certificate described as 'a man well learned, meet for the education of youth in the Latin tongue'. He had been canon and sub-prior of Launceston Priory until the house was dissolved in 1539, and enjoyed a pension of £10 besides his salary as grammar master which was £6. The inhabitants of Launceston were evidently concerned for the fate of their school, and a memorandum attached to the chantry certificate not only stressed the need for a grammar school in the locality but suggested that Week St Mary school, allegedly in decay, might properly be transferred to Launceston, the two places lying only seven miles apart.[3]

This suggestion, duly transmitted to the crown, received favourable attention. The government consulted with leading men of the area and on learning of their approval the protector, Edward duke of Somerset, ordered the school of Week to be transferred to Launceston.[4] Its staff consisted of William Cholwell the schoolmaster with a salary of £11. 13s. 3½d., an usher with £1. 6s. 8d., a manciple with £4 and a laundress with 13s. 4d. Since the crown had taken over the responsibility of paying the salaries its local receiver-general should have disbursed a total sum of £17. 13s. 3½d. each year to the school, now settled in Launceston.[5] But what of Bannek and Gourge? Bannek, as a mere elementary master, should have been pensioned off with 13s. 4d., the salary he had previously received.[6] Gourge appears to have been considered redundant, and a note in the chantry certificates ordered him to be pensioned at the expense of the inhabitants of Launceston because Week school had been transferred at their request.[7] It looks as if the crown's intention was to discontinue Launceston's own school, it having been replaced by that of Week.

We cannot unfortunately be sure that this intention took effect. The accounts of Anthony Aylworth, the local receiver-general of crown lands, show that from 1548 until 1555 an annual sum was paid not of £17. 13s. 3½d. but £18. 19s. 11½d., made up of £11. 13s. 3½d. to Cholwell, £1. 6s. 8d. to his usher, and £6 to Gourge.[8] This may indicate that Cholwell and Gourge both taught grammar in Launceston during Edward VI's reign. After Michael-

---

1 *CPR 1408–13*, p 53.
2 See below, p 168.
3 E 301/9 no 7; Snell, op. cit., pp 29–30; *ESR*, part ii, pp 34–5; MS Rawl. D 363 fo 230.
4 A. F. Robbins, 'John Aylworth and the Launceston Free School', *Notes & Gleanings for Devon & Cornwall*, iii (Exeter, 1890), pp 161–7. On Week school see below, p 181.
5 Snell, op. cit., pp 51–3; *ESR*, part ii, pp 40–2.
6 He went on being paid this sum until at least 1555, though whether as a pension or as a salary is not clear (PRO, Exch. Land Revenue, LR 6/1/2).
7 Snell, op. cit., p 31; *ESR*, part ii, p 41.
8 PRO, LR 6/104/2–4, LR 6/1/1–3.

mas 1556 however Aylworth refused to make any further payments, not only to Launceston but apparently to the other three Cornish schools entitled to receive them—Bodmin, Penryn and Saltash. This refusal, which was shared by the receivers-general of some but not all the other English counties, may have been influenced by the transference of responsibility for ecclesiastical pensions from the crown to the Church in 1555.[1] No more money was paid to Launceston school until in the spring of 1560 the matter was brought to the attention of the court of the Exchequer, probably by the corporation. The court gave a judgment in favour of the school and Aylworth was ordered not only to continue the annuity but to pay the arrears due from Michaelmas 1556 until Lady Day 1560. The sum however was fixed once more at £17. 13s. 3½d., which may mean that Gourge was no longer on the scene. In this way Launceston regained a school endowment, that of Week, which it continued to enjoy under Elizabeth's regime.[2]

LYME REGIS
Dorset

The chantry certificate of 1548 alleges that the lands of Our Lady service in Lyme Regis, worth only £1. 18s. 11d., were given for 'the finding of a clerk and children'.[3] This probably indicates the existence of a choir school such as existed at Ashburton, Cirencester and some of the other major churches in the west country.

MALMESBURY
Wiltshire

In 1548 the town of Malmesbury, which is known to have possessed a school in the thirteenth century,[4] was estimated to contain 860 communicants in its two parishes. One of the two, St Mary Westport, included a stipendary priest maintained by an income of £5. 14s. 9d. from land; the foundation is not specified. The incumbent, John Wimbolle, aged 54, was described as a 'very honest man, well learned', who occupied himself in 'bringing up young children in learning'. As well as his stipend from Westport, he held a pension of £6 out of the former abbey, dissolved in 1540.[5] This suggests that he should be identified with John Horsley, chanter of the monastery, who probably adopted the name Horsley from his native village near Stroud when he entered the abbey in the 1520s.[6] The chantry commissioners did not preserve the school, which makes it likely that Wimbolle only taught reading and song, with which they were not concerned. There may well have been a separate grammar school in Malmesbury at this time.

1 *Statutes of the Realm,* iv part i, pp 275ff.
2 *Notes & Gleanings for Devon & Cornwall,* iii (1890), pp 161–7; PRO, LR 6/1/8.
3 PRO, E 301/16 no 73; *ESR,* part ii, pp 54–5.
4 See above, p 101.
5 PRO, Chantry Certificates, E 301/58 no 36; *ESR,* part ii, pp 258–9.
6 John Horsley occurs as a monk of Malmesbury in 1527 (*Chapters of the Black Monks,* ed. W. A. Pantin, vol iii (Royal Historical Soc., Camden third series, liv, 1937), p 131). He was pensioned with £6 in 1540 (*LPFD,* xiv part ii, no 687).

MARLDON
Devon

A chantry was founded at Marldon near Paignton in 1485 by Otes or Oto Gilbert, a local esquire, to support a chantry priest and two poor men receiving 8d. a week or thereabouts.[1] In the chantry certificate of 1546 it still figures as a foundation for a priest and poor relief, but an abstract of the certificate of 1548 includes a note that the endowments were also given 'for the maintenance of a grammar school for the children inhabiting at Marldon'.[2] This statement is at variance with all that is known of the chantry's history, and the chantry commissioners evidently thought so too, for they merely pensioned off the incumbent, Thomas Harris, like an ordinary chantry priest. It is not impossible that he or one of his predecessors had once taught grammar on a personal initiative, but even this must at present be regarded as unproven.

MILTON ABBAS
Dorset

The credit for founding Milton Abbas grammar school is difficult to assign with certainty, since the two accounts of the foundation which we possess give the honour to different people. The earlier of them, the chantry certificate of 1548, ascribed the foundation to John Loder, priest, 'with others'.[3] Loder was a Dorset rector who died in 1533, the incumbent of five parishes in the county at different times. Two of them, Bingham's Melcombe and Winterborne Whitchurch, were close to Milton Abbas.[4] Half a century later than the chantry certificate, an inquisition was held at Blandford in 1600 concerning the history of the school. It told a different story, based on deeds and conveyances.[5] The school, it declared, was founded by William Middleton, abbot of Milton from 1482 to 1525.[6] He was said to have purchased the manor, farm and free chapel of Little Mayne in Dorset from Thomas Kirton, and to have granted it back to him on 10 February 1521 with the consent of his convent, for the maintenance of a free grammar school. These accounts could be reconciled if the enterprise was in fact a cooperative one. Loder's benefices were not very lucrative and he was lower in status than most of the people who endowed free schools

---

1 *CPR 1476–85*, p 522; *Valor Ecclesiasticus*, ii, 360.
2 PRO, E 301/15 no 30, E 301/80; *The Chantry Certificates for Devon*, ed. L. S. Snell, pp 36–7, 69; *ESR*, part ii, p 48.
3 PRO, E 301/16 no 81; *ESR*, part ii, p 55.
4 John Loder was rector of Winterborne Came, instituted 28 February 1503, resigned by November 1520 (Hutchins, *History of Dorset*, ii, 291); rector of West Stafford, instituted 21 April 1503, exchanged January 1522 (ibid., p 517); rector of Bingham's Melcombe by exchange, instituted 27 January 1522, resigned by May 1523 (ibid., iv, 381); rector of Hammoon, instituted 4 April 1525, resigned by July 1531 (ibid., i, 274); and vicar of Winterborne Whitchurch, instituted 9 November 1529, till death. He was dead by January 1534 (ibid., p 202).
5 Ibid., iv, 396.
6 On Middleton see also ibid., iv, 392, 402–5.

at this time. Perhaps he contributed money along with others towards the foundation, which was then carried out by Abbot Middleton. In any case a school could hardly have been founded in Milton without the abbot's goodwill.

Little else is known of the early history of the school. Thomas Kirton held the lands at Little Mayne until 1536–7 when he granted them to seventeen feoffees, all local knights and gentlemen. The surviving feoffee, Matthew Arundel, made a fresh enfeoffment to eight others in 1599. By Abbot Middleton's deed of 1521 the profits of the lands were to maintain a school for 97 years, and if within that time a licence in mortmain might be obtained from the crown, the feoffees had to convey the lands to the school. If not, they were to sell the manor at the expiration of the term and continue supporting the school while the money lasted. It is not clear why no licence was forthcoming during the sixteenth century. In 1548 the lands were being leased to Robert Best of Little Mayne at a rent of £8 a year, which was paid to the schoolmaster for his stipend. The master does not appear to have been a chantry priest. In this respect the school of Milton, like those of Bruton and Winchcombe, belongs to a new phase of educational benefactions in which schools were at last being founded for their own sake and not, as hitherto in association with chantries.[1] In consequence Milton school was not affected by the Edwardian chantry act.

NETHERBURY
Dorset

The origins of Netherbury grammar school appear to belong to the 1540s. In a petition of 1564 to the lord chancellor, the churchwardens and parishioners of the village stated that the income of two tenements in the manor, called 'Bodnam' and 'Paradise', totalling fifty acres, had been applied for about the last hundred years either to support a priest or to maintain a schoolmaster. As we shall see, the schoolmaster was a recent innovation. The petitioners went on to say that the lands had been leased by the lord of the manor to a succession of tenants who paid the profits, some £7 a year, to the churchwardens of Netherbury. The money was used to pay a priest to serve in the church, or else a clerk to play the organ. Then in about 1542 the wardens, instead of the priest, appointed a schoolmaster whom they had since maintained.[2] This evidence is quite credible. Many such villages had acquired endowments to support a chantry priest or parish chaplain, and not a few, like Netherbury, went over to supporting a schoolmaster as interest in education grew during the early sixteenth century.

This must be the school which appears in the Netherbury chantry certificate of 1548, when Martin Smith, priest, was schoolmaster with a stipend of £5. 6s. 8d. It was a grammar school. The chantry commissioners ordered the school to be continued, but they do not appear to have confiscated the endowments, hence the chancery suit of 1564, which concerned the tenancy of the lands.[3]

1 On this development see *ESMA*, pp 156, 196.
2 PRO, Early Chancery Proceedings, C2/55/4; F. J. Pope, 'The Founder of Netherbury School', *Somerset & Dorset Notes & Queries*, x (1906–7), pp 2–3.
3 PRO, E 301/16 no 57, E 301/23; *ESR*, part ii, pp 54, 57.

NEWLAND

Gloucestershire

THE GREYNDOUR FAMILY

The medieval grammar school of Newland commemorated the name of Robert Greyndour, a prominent Gloucestershire landowner of the first half of the fifteenth century. His family, which may have originated at Hadnock near Monmouth, emerged from obscurity in the 1350s when Laurence Greyndour married Margaret Abenhall, heiress of the manor of that name near Mitcheldean.[1] John, the son of their marriage, who was probably born in 1356, had a distinguished military and civil career. He accompanied Richard II to Ireland in 1394 and was knighted soon afterwards. Under Henry IV he was keeper of the castles of Radnor and Chepstow, and represented Herefordshire in parliament on two occasions. He saw service with the prince of Wales against the Welsh in 1407, and at the end of his life joined the prince—now Henry V—in France. He was present on the Agincourt campaign of 1415 with ten men-at-arms, thirty foot archers, and 120 miners—doubtless from the Forest of Dean. His death took place sometime between then and October 1416.[2]

Sir John married twice but left only two surviving children. His first wife Marion Hatheway, of a local family, bore him his son and heir Robert, and by his second wife Isabel he had a daughter Joan. Robert was born at least before 1390 since he appears as a witness to deeds in 1403 and 1408. Before his father's death he was described as constable of the Forest of Dean.[3] The family inheritance lay on the borders of Gloucestershire and Herefordshire, including the manors and advowsons of Abenhall and Aston Ingham with a moiety of Mitcheldean and the right to present the rector there at every third turn. There were also the manors of Littledean, Clearwell and its neighbour Noxon, and smaller pieces of farmland and woodland in four of the Forest parishes. The manor of Abenhall carried with it the office of woodward, and some family lands in St Briavels called 'Hatheways', which probably came to Robert through his mother, were held by the service of being chief forester. Robert also owned a certain amount of town property. In 1427 he exchanged his tenements in the 'Corvisers' Row' in Hereford with Thomas Bromwich, who conveyed to him in return lands in and around Staunton and St Briavels. From his father he inherited at least one burgage in Chepstow, and at his death he is said to have held

---

1 *Cal. Inquisitions Post Mortem,* ix no 13, x no 449, xiv no 143.
2 For references to Sir John's career see the calendars of patent and close rolls, 1385–1413 *passim;* *The St Albans Chronicle, 1406–1420,* ed. V. H. Galbraith (1937), p 23; and Sir N. H. Nicolas, *The Battle of Agincourt* (1832), pp 380, 386. He was dead by 30 October 1416 (*CFR 1413–22,* p 144). There is at present no evidence for Prof. E. F. Jacob's suggestion that Sir John was a Lollard (*The Fifteenth Century* (1961), p 103), but Henry Greyndour, who was, must have been related to him (*Memorials of Henry V,* ed. C. A. Cole (Rolls Series, 1858), p 148).
3 Gloucestershire Record Office, MS Calendar of Gage Deeds *penes* Sussex Archaeological Trust, Lewes.

forty acres and ten and a half burgages there. In Monmouth he held 18 messuages of the king by burgage tenure.[1]

His wife, whom he probably married before 1419, was Joan, the daughter and heiress of Thomas and Katherine Rigge. The father, who was still alive in 1428, held land in Chicklade, Wiltshire, where he was patron of the living and may have taken his name from Ridge nearby. The mother was the daughter of Sir John Bitton and had inherited several manors and advowsons beside the Bristol Avon, so that Joan brought a good deal of property to her husband. It included the manors and churches of Charlcombe and Norton Malreward in north Somerset, together with lesser possessions in the Quantocks, including an annual fair in Perry near Nether Stowey. In Gloucestershire she brought him the manors of Nass in Lydney and, across the river, East Hanham, with lands in the neighbouring hamlets of Upton Cheyney (reputed a manor in 1485) and Churchley, with other smaller holdings further north in Stone and Berkeley. To this may be added Sharpness Park, a pasture which Robert and Joan held jointly by the gift of James, Lord Berkeley.[2]

Robert Greyndour's activities were less notable than his father's and more restricted to local affairs. He was never knighted. He served on various commissions of array and other inquisitions between 1418 and 1434, was never pricked for sheriff, but represented Gloucestershire in parliament on three occasions: 1417, 1420 and 1433. He was a joint steward of the Mowbray manors of Chepstow and Tidenham during the heir's minority in 1433 and on the death of the duke of Bedford in 1435 he was appointed steward and constable of the Forest of Dean and St Briavels.[3] At this time he was engaged in a suit with the king which he lost through the pains of John Vampage, the royal attorney.[4] His ecclesiastical interests included the right to present to five parish churches and at every third turn to another. He and his wife had papal licences to keep a portable altar and to receive plenary indulgence from their own confessor when they died.[5] Their domestic chaplain is mentioned in 1436.[6] Apart from presiding over his own and his wife's manors and advowsons, Robert owned at least one ship, the 'Trinity' of Chepstow, which had been bequeathed to him by his near relative, John Chin, in 1415.[7]

Robert Greyndour died on 19 or 20 November 1443 and was buried in Newland church.[8] His widow continued to possess most of their property. As well as retaining her own inheri-

1 For Robert Greyndour's property see *CCR 1413–19*, pp 338; *Calendarium Inquisitionum post Mortem*, vol iv (Record Commission, 1828), p 220; *CCR 1441–7*, pp 177–9, and Gloucestershire Records Office, Machen Deeds, 278/89.
2 For Joan's property see *Calendarium Inquisitionum*, iv, 220, 419; *Cal. Inquisitions post Mortem: Henry VII*, i, p 3 no 7, p 47 no 116; and H. T. Ellacombe, *The History of the Parish of Bitton, Gloucs.* (1881), pp 302–18 *et passim*.
3 *CPR 1429–36*, pp 252, 499.
4 F. Devon, *Issues of the Exchequer, Henry III–VI* (London, 1835), p 429.
5 *Cal. Papal Letters*, vii, 414, 532.
6 *Reg. Spofford, Hereford*, ed. A. T. Bannister (Canterbury & York Soc., xxiii, 1919), p 210.
7 PRO, Prob 11/2B (PCC 37 Marche); *CCR 1413–19*, p 397. I cannot help suspecting that John Chin's will is really that of Sir John Greyndour.
8 According to the inquisition post mortem, he died on 19 November 22 Henry VI (1443) but his obit at Newland church was kept on 20, St Edmund's Day.

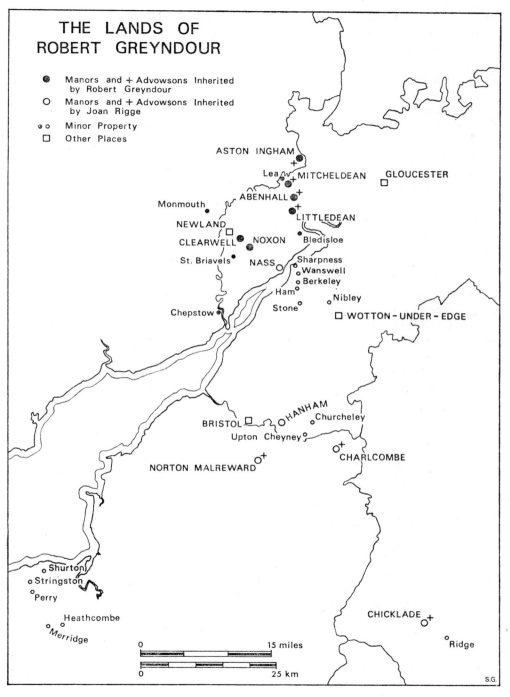

tance, she received one third of her husband's possessions in dower,[1] while the manors of Clearwell and Noxton in the Forest, which Robert had arranged for her to hold jointly, were to remain in her possession while she lived and then pass to his heirs. Their only surviving child was a daughter, Elizabeth, born in about 1421. Sustained by the prospect of a good inheritance she became the second wife of Reynold West, Lord de la Warr, but they had no surviving issue. He died in August 1450 and she, doubly enriched with her father's lands and her own dower, gave her hand to John Tiptoft, earl of Worcester, a year later. She died giving birth to their first child on 1 September 1452 and her baby with her, but by English custom her husband was permitted to keep her property for the rest of his life.[2] He was executed at Tower Hill on 18 October 1470. His share of the Greyndour lands then passed to William Walweyn, whose mother Joan was Robert's half-sister. She had died in 1461. Walweyn came into possession in February 1471 but had little time to enjoy his inheritance for he fell sick on a journey to Rochester and died in the autumn.[3] His only daughter Alice was the wife of Thomas Baynham of Mitcheldean, and it was into this family that all the Greyndour lands ultimately came.

Joan Greyndour spent the first years of her widowhood in establishing a chantry and a school in her husband's memory. In the absence of personal records such as a will, it is difficult to be sure which of them first conceived the idea. Since the chantry school bore Robert's name and was set up at Newland in the middle of his own hereditary possessions as soon as conveniently possible after his death, it is likely to have reflected his interests as well as hers. Newland was probably chosen for two reasons. It was the nearest village to Clearwell where Joan lived, and lay within her sphere of influence. It was also an important local centre. The parish church served a large area on the western side of the Forest of Dean including the settlements at Coleford, Clearwell and Bream. The village itself was a place of some resort. It stood in an area where much iron was mined, and the trading which went on in the churchyard on holidays and even on Sundays drew censures from the bishop of Hereford on more than one occasion.[4]

The first stages of founding the chantry school were completed with the publication of the first set of statutes on 21 March 1446, the school then beginning its work under the first master, John Clifford. At some time between August 1447 and March 1449 Joan married Sir John Barre of Rotherwas in Herefordshire, a knight of distinction, who already had a daughter by a previous marriage. His political career was a more striking one than that of Robert Greyndour. He was knight of the shire for Herefordshire in three parliaments of Henry VI, and once for Gloucestershire after his second marriage. He supported the king in the disorders of 1459, when some of the fighting took place on the borders of Hereford-

---

1 For a rental of her dower lands dated 8 May 1458 see Gloucestershire Record Office, MS Calendar of Colchester MSS, D 36 (iv) fo 22v.
2 G. E. Cockayne, *Complete Peerage,* ed. V. Gibbs and others, iv, 153–4; xii part ii, p 845.
3 William Walweyn's will is dated 30 September, proved 23 November, 1471 (PRO, Prob 11/6 (PCC 4 Wattys)). For his succession to the lands see *CFR 1461–71,* pp 295–6; *CCR 1468–76* no 584.
4 On Newland in medieval times see Sir C. Fortescue-Brickdale, 'Newland in the Middle Ages', *TBGAS,* lv (1933), pp 191–233; lvi (1934), pp 179–96; and *Reg. Spofford, Hereford,* pp 96–7, 231.

shire, and on 21 May 1460 was granted twenty marks a year out of forfeited Yorkist lands as a reward for good service against Salisbury, Warwick and York. When the Yorkists returned to power in July after the battle of Northampton, they ordered his arrest (13 August 1460) and he did not receive a pardon until 1468. When Henry VI was restored to power in 1470, Sir John seems to have sat in the Lancastrian parliament then summoned as a member for Gloucestershire, and after the return of Edward IV he had again to secure pardons. Thereafter he engaged himself quietly in founding a chantry at Clehonger in Herefordshire, where he was buried beside his first wife after his death on 14 January 1483.[1]

During the period of their marriage Sir John exercised the patronage of the Newland chantry school in the right of his wife and presented five schoolmasters (1449–1466). But it was Joan who carried through two successive revisions of the chantry statutes in 1454 and

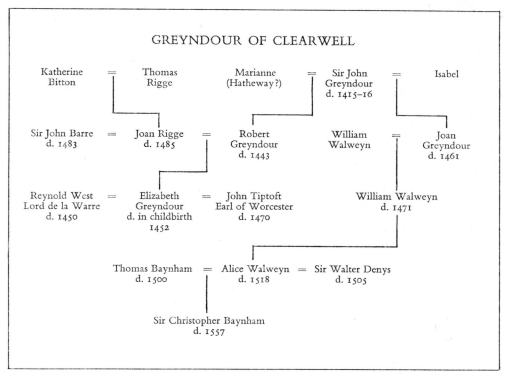

1465. Her meticulous attention to detail and her unwearied endeavour to legalise the present and safeguard the future display something of her character. So too does her lengthy will with its careful descriptions of all her property and the long lists of friends and dependents whom she wished to remember and assuredly did not forget. The will was

1 J. C. Wedgwood and A. D. Holt, *History of Parliament 1439–1509* (1936): *Biographies*, p 44; *Register*, p 386.

made on 3 February 1485,[1] and began with a request to be buried with her first husband in their chapel in Newland church. Like many of her class she left complicated directions for the celebration of large numbers of masses for her soul and those of her family. One priest was to sing for three years in the Newland chapel, and another to be hired for a year especially to repeat St George's trental with all the due fasts and observances. A thousand masses at a penny apiece were to be completed as soon as possible after her death, as well as seven varieties of the mass in sets of fifty, and other appropriate prayers. Twenty-eight poor men were to attend her funeral with torches and tapers, and fifty others were to requite her gifts of shirts and smocks by saying fifty psalters of the Virgin, while a hundred gowns, cloaks and coats were also to be distributed among the poor for their prayers. She bequeathed vestments, ornaments and other goods to the Greyndour chantry and to her second husband's foundation at Clehonger. Gifts were made to Flaxley Abbey, to the anchoress of Gloucester and to eleven religious houses of which Joan counted herself a sister, in return for all their prayers. She did not forget the chapel of St Katherine in Bitton church where her ancestors lay, nor the parish church of Charlcombe where she had been christened. Her literary possessions included two mattins books, while a small portuous and the *Pupilla Oculi* were left to Philip ap Eynon, the chantry schoolmaster of Newland. Joan's solicitude for the neighbouring clergy was displayed in fifteen small bequests and the list of her servants reaches twenty-nine, including William Walker of High Meadow her bailiff, her gentleman Richard Rede, two gentlewomen and a chamberlain, the butler, pantler, two clerks, cook, slaughterman, baker, two yeomen of the brewerne and the stable, and the laundress. All the residue of her goods was ordered to be sold and bequeathed to poor churches and for mending highways and bridges. The four executors, who each received £10, included Philip ap Eynon schoolmaster of Newland, John Skinner rector of English Bicknor, Thomas Morgan a Gloucester gentleman, and John Caerwent of Newent. The overseer was Thomas Baynham.

The will included a detailed inventory of all the furnishings in the house at Clearwell which was due to pass to Robert Greyndour's great-niece Alice and her husband Thomas Baynham. The great chamber contained the principal bed of red say cloth with coverlet and curtains, while the adjoining room held a white hanging bed stained with branches, roses and ivy leaves. The hall was decorated with two hangings of stained cloth of which one showed the wheel of Fortune and the other the romance of Sir Guy of Warwick. Next door was a parlour containing another hanging bed, and a fourth bed stood inside another chamber off the parlour. The private chapel boasted an alabaster tablet above the altar, with images of St John and St Anne, all the usual ornaments and vestments, a portuous and a great mass book with a box to keep them in, and a little pair of organs. The rest of the inventory described the kitchen, the brewerne and the pantry with their appropriate

---

[1] PRO, Prob 11/7 (PCC 16 Logge), printed in Ellacombe, *The History of the Parish of Bitton*, pp 309–16. It was proved on 22 July 1485.

fittings. Joan Greyndour died on 17 June 1485,[1] and her lands were thereupon dispersed. Her father's property at Chicklade passed to one of his relations, Margaret the daughter of John Rigge, and her mother's to five different heirs, of whom Robert Basset obtained the manor of Norton Malreward. Her dower portion of Sir John Barre's property was returned to his daughter Isabel, countess of Devon, and that of the Greyndour lands, including the patronage of Newland school, passed to Robert's heirs Alice Walweyn and her husband Thomas Baynham, esquire. Baynham presented to the school only once before his death in 1500 and the patronage then returned to his widow who married Sir Walter Denys and died again a widow in 1518. She was sufficiently interested in education to bequeath £10 to her relative Christopher Walweyn to help him proceed BCL at Oxford, and eight marks to her chaplain, Sir William, for his studies.[2] The patronage then descended to her son, Sir Christopher Baynham, who presented the last four chaplain-schoolmasters between 1521 and 1538.

THE SCHOOL

Robert Greyndour had died in November 1443 and the foundation of his school began two years later, the escheators not having been ordered to lift the king's hand from his properties until the summer of 1444.[3] On 6 November 1445 Joan received the king's licence to set up a chantry in Newland church, to be called 'the chantry of Robert Greyndour', and to endow it with lands to the value of £12 *per annum*. The licence cost her £35.[4] The lands of the proposed endowment had next to be approved. The king's order to the escheator of Gloucestershire to enquire as to these went out on 20 November, and the escheator's inquisition, giving a favourable reply, was held on 9 February.[5] Accordingly on 28 February 1446 Joan was licensed to grant specified lands to the chaplain whom she had by now engaged to serve the new chantry.[6] These lands lay in Lydney, Aylburton and Newland and were rated at £4. 5s. 6d. *per annum*, to be held as of the value of £6. Their exact site is unknown and they cannot represent the whole endowment of an annual income of £12. When the chantry lands were sold in 1559 they were valued at £11. 12s. and stated to have lain in Newland, Clearwell and Lydney.[7]

The chantry statutes were issued on 21 March 1446.[8] After a preamble acknowledging the importance of the mass, the foundress provided for the establishment of a perpetual

---

1 Two dates are given for her death in the inquisitions post mortem: 17 June 1485, and in *Cal. Inquisitions post mortem, Henry VII*, i, p 3, no 7, 10 August 2 Richard III (1484). Neither the month nor the year of this latter agree with the dates of the making and the proving of her will.
2 PRO, Prob 11/19 (14 Ayloffe).
3 *CCR 1441–7*, pp 177–9.
4 *CPR 1441–6*, p 388. The whole licence is printed in Ellacombe, *The History of the Parish of Bitton*, pp 307–8.
5 PRO, Chancery, Inquisitions *ad quod Dampnum*, C 143/450/19.
6 *CPR 1441–6*, pp 446–7. The property is specified as a messuage, three tofts, a dovecote, 203 acres of arable land, 38 acres of meadow and three acres of wood in the three above-mentioned places.
7 PRO, Exch. Augm., Particulars for grants, E 318/2560; *CPR 1558–60*, p 359.
8 *Reg. Spofford, Hereford*, pp 281 ff.

chantry of one chaplain and one clerk serving under him, to be held before the altar of St John the Baptist and St Nicholas in Newland church. The chaplain was to be suitably educated in song, reading and the art of grammar, as well as being of holy life, good morals and in priest's orders. It was his responsibility to administer the endowments. His own salary was £12 a year, but out of this he was obliged to make certain payments. The most important of these were the wages of a clerk, not specified in value but large enough to be found burdensome later on. The clerk, who was also to be learned in grammar, was evidently to act as second master in the school as well as assisting in the chantry. He would probably have been in minor orders. The chaplain held office for life, but if incapacitated by old age or sickness he was either to find a suitable deputy or resign and receive an annual pension of five marks charged upon his successor. Only one of the chaplains of Newland is known to have retired in this way.

The patronage of the chantry was retained by Joan for herself and her heirs, and for lack of these was to pass to the descendants of Robert's half-sister, the Walweyns. Presentations were to be made to the bishop of Hereford within a month of a vacancy by death or resignation. If the patron neglected to make a presentation within six weeks, or if the patron was a minor in the king's wardship, the right of presentation for that turn passed to the prior and convent of Lanthony by Gloucester. They were probably chosen for their experience of appointing schoolmasters in Gloucester. An interesting clause reserved to John Clifford, the first master, the right to nominate his successor—perhaps because he had more experience or contacts than the foundress herself.[1] During vacancies the chantry goods and revenues were to be administered by the churchwardens of Newland, so that the clerk should be supported and the school maintained until the arrival of the next incumbent. The daily services to be said by the chaplain were set out in detail, with the variations to be observed on different days of the week. At the introit of the daily mass the priest had to read out in English the list of those for whom prayers were said. Those still living included Joan, her daughter Elizabeth and son-in-law Reynold West, Lord de la Warr. The dead were headed by Robert Greyndour, his father and his father's wives, Joan's parents Thomas and Katherine Rigge, and her mother's ancestors the Bittons. If the school was Robert's idea, the chantry stood a memorial to Joan no less than to her husband. The annual commemoration of Robert and Joan, the chief event of the year, was to be held on St Edmund's day (20 November) with as many priests and clerks as could be found in Newland church.

A house was provided for the chaplain and clerk to live in. It was called 'Blackbrook' and stood near Newland church, quite possibly on the site of the surviving seventeenth-century grammar school. The school seems also to have been held there, since in 1548 the building was known indifferently as the chantry house and schoolhouse. It was open, in the usual phrase, to all who came, but fees were charged and at not much less than the usual rate. In the lower class those who learnt the alphabet, mattins book and psalter were not to pay more than 4d. a term, while those who studied grammar paid not more than

---

[1] *Reg. Spofford, Hereford,* p 283.

8d.¹ The scholars were not to be put to other duties but to be free for continual study. There appears to have been an upper age limit of eighteen for those admitted to the school but this was later removed. Scholars who were disobedient could be removed if they would not amend themselves. School evidently began early in the morning. At nine o'clock the scholars broke off to say the psalm *Deus misereatur nobis*, the *Paternoster* and the *Ave Maria* for the souls of Robert and Joan, and then went out to breakfast. At five they repeated the antiphon *Sancta Maria, virgo, intercede*, the psalm *De profundis*, the *Paternoster* and *Ave*, and the collect *Inclina aurem tuam, Domine*, upon their knees before going home to supper. There were regular school holidays modelled on the system in use at Wotton-under-Edge. They lasted from Palm Sunday until the octave of Easter, from the vigil of Pentecost until the morrow of the Holy Trinity, from 1 August until 14 September, and from 21 December until 6 January, a total of about eleven weeks. The schoolmaster himself was restricted, with the patron's permission, to a month each year.

Of John Clifford, the first schoolmaster, we know only that he was a priest and was instituted to the chantry at an unknown date in 1446.² He resigned three years later to be succeeded by William Coburley, who had been ordained priest seven years before.³ During his mastership the foundress decided to amend the statutes, and a new and expanded version was drawn up, dated 12 October 1454, and recorded as before in the bishop's register.⁴ The chief reason for the change was to abolish the clerk, whom the chaplains had found it a burden to support, so that in future they had only to find and maintain a scholar or literate, competent in grammar, to assist in the teaching and live in the chantry house. The other changes of 1454 were minor ones. The time within which presentations had to be made after a vacancy was increased to three months. The chaplain was permitted to occupy another benefice which did not require personal residence of more than a week at a time or a month altogether. The pension on which an aged chaplain could retire was raised to six marks. School books were mentioned for the first time, the chaplain being obliged to keep them in good repair, but the earlier reference to an age limit for the scholars was now omitted.

William Coburley, dying in office, was followed by Richard Dering,⁵ who soon resigned,

---

1 School fees were usually 8d. a quarter at this time (*ESMA*, p 118).
2 John Clifford (Clyfford) was designated chantry priest of Newland by 28 February 1446 (*CPR 1441–6*, pp 446–7), and instituted the same year being in priest's orders (*Reg. Stanbury, Hereford*, p 106), resigned by March 1449 (*Reg. Beauchamp, Hereford*, p 15). Possibly the same as John or Philip Clifford, rector of Staunton near Newland, instituted 21 April 1428, resigned by June 1449 (*Reg. Spofford, Hereford*, p 354, *Reg. Beauchamp, Hereford*, p 15).
3 William Coburley was ordained acolyte 8 March 1438; subdeacon 31 March, deacon 26 May, priest 22 September 1442, to a title provided by Richard Grey, sixth Lord Grey of Wilton-on-Wye, Herefordshire (*Reg. Spofford, Hereford*, pp 328, 338–40). Chaplain of Newland, instituted 4 March 1449, till death. Died by October 1457 (*Reg. Beauchamp, Hereford*, p 15, *Reg. Stanbury, Hereford*, p 189).
4 Ibid., p 21.
5 Richard Dering (Deryng) was ordained acolyte 16 September 1454, subdeacon 18 September 1456, deacon 6 June 1457, to the title of Hereford Cathedral (ibid., pp 137, 141–2). Chaplain of Newland, instituted 30 October 1457, resigned by July 1459 (ibid., pp 189, 176).

to be succeeded by Edward Janyns. Janyns was only beginning his career. He stayed four years at Newland, and after a short spell as vicar of Diddlebury in Shropshire, he secured the vicarage of Lydney, gaining a wealthier benefice at each removal. There he led more than the life of a country parson, for in October 1468 he was given leave of absence from his parish for a year, probably to study at a university, since by 1476 he had gained the degree of bachelor of canon law. In that year he returned to Newland as vicar of the well-endowed living. Between 1478 and 1490 he was also rural dean of Ross.[1] Janyns was followed in 1463 by William Phillips, during whose mastership the foundress issued a third and revised set of statutes, dated from Newland on 3 August 1465.[2] She apologised for making further changes by recalling that even God had changed in the New Testament some of the things which he had established in the Old. The new statutes were occasioned by Joan's fear that the patronage of the chantry might pass into the hands of distant and unknown relatives after her death. The Walweyn relatives who were the next heirs were now represented only by William Walweyn and his daughter Anne, who married Thomas Baynham. The statutes therefore provided that if William had no heirs, the patronage of the chantry should pass to Flaxley Abbey, the local Cistercian house, for which Joan had some regard since she made it gifts in her will in exchange for prayers. This clause was never fulfilled, for the patronage passed peacefully into the Baynham family. The opportunity was also taken to make other changes of detail. The chaplain was permitted to deputise for the vicar of Newland, and his annual leave of absence was increased to six weeks, except during principal feasts. More importantly, he was allowed to make leases of the chantry lands for the term of a life or forty years.

Phillips died in office in 1466.[3] Next came Philip ap Eynon or Beynon, who may have

---

[1] Edward Janyns (Jenyns) was ordained subdeacon 10 March 1458, priest 19 May 1459 to the title of Monmouth Priory (ibid., pp 144–5). Chaplain of Newland, instituted 20 July 1459, resigned by December 1463 (ibid., pp 176, 179). Vicar of Diddlebury (patrons, dean and chapter of Hereford), instituted 5 March 1464, resigned by June 1466 (ibid., p 191). Vicar of Lydney (patrons, the same) instituted 4 June 1466, resigned by October 1476 (ibid., p 183; *Reg. Myllyng, Hereford,* p 187). Licensed to be absent for one year, residing at Christmas, Easter and Pentecost, October 1468 (*Reg. Stanbury, Hereford,* p 195). Vicar of Newland, instituted 2 October 1476, still on 6 March 1490 (*Reg. Myllyng, Hereford,* pp 186, 125). B Can L by October 1476. Commissioner to inquire into the patronage of Pyrton Chantry, Lydney, 25 May 1478, when evidently dean of Ross, since he appended the decanal seal to the report (*Reg. Myllyng, Hereford,* p 37). As rural dean in 1490 he reported with Thomas Stokes to the bishop as commissioners appointed to enquire into the vacancy and patronage of Goodrich church, Herefs. (ibid., p 125). On 22 June 1485 he was pardoned for not appearing with Isabel Hyet when sued as executors of the will of Robert Hyet (*CPR 1476–85,* p 469).

[2] *Reg. Stanbury, Hereford,* pp 105–10.

[3] William Phillips was instituted chaplain of Newland on 7 December 1463, till death. Died by June 1466 (ibid., pp 179, 183). A dispute over his will is mentioned on 18 June 1468 in the Hereford rural consistory court (Gloucester Public Library, Hockaday Abstracts, Newland, 1468). Several clerics of this name appear in the bishops' registers.

been a member of the Baynham family.¹ He was on good terms with the foundress who bequeathed him in her will (dated 3 February 1485) a portuous of the use of Sarum, the *Pupilla Oculi* or manual for priests, Friar John Somer's edition of the calendar,² a silver dish and cover, and £10. He was also designated an executor. Joan died in the summer, and on 2 December Philip exchanged the chantry with Thomas Stokes, who had succeeded Janyns at Lydney.³ Stokes was a man of some standing since he was often referred to as *magister*, although it is not known whether he was a graduate. In 1490 he was a commissioner with Janyns to enquire into the vacancy and patronage of Goodrich church. A benefaction to the scholars of Newland belongs to this period. It was made by Isabel the wife of Robert Hyet of Littledean, serjeant of St Briavels castle and holder of several other offices in the government of the Forest, who died in about 1480.⁴ In 1481 his widow took a vow of chastity before the bishop of Hereford at Whitbourne.⁵ Her benefaction, according to the chantry certificate of 1548, was of land and rent for an annual obit in Newland and for distributing money to the poor scholars and other poor of the parish. In 1548 the value was 18s. 4d., of which 10s. was given away.⁶

The gap in the series of bishops' registers at Hereford between 1492 and 1504 prevents us knowing how long after 1490 Stokes remained as schoolmaster. The next person who certainly held the office was Richard Norton, of a Newland family, who was a priest in the parish church by 19 September 1501.⁷ When he resigned the Greyndour chantry on 16 May 1521 he was allowed the statutory pension of six marks. He was dead by 1536. His successor John Bolter, BA, is the first known graduate schoolmaster. In 1527 he leased a

1 Philip ap Eynon (Beynon) was ordained acolyte 2 April 1457, subdeacon 27 May 1458 to the title of Hereford Cathedral (*Reg. Stanbury, Hereford*, pp 141, 143). Chaplain of Newland, instituted 4 June 1466, exchanged 2 December 1485 for the vicarage of Lydney, Gloucestershire, resigned by June 1488 for another benefice (ibid., p 183; *Reg. Myllyng, Hereford*, pp 201, 196). Executor of the will of Lady Joan Barre, dated 3 February 1485. Bequeathed a gilt salt-cellar by Elizabeth Cornwell of Bristol in her will dated 3 January 1489 (PRO, Prob 11/8 (PCC 23 Milles)).
2 On this work see *BRUO*, iii, 1727.
3 Thomas Stokes was instituted vicar of Lydney, 14 October 1476, exchanged 2 December 1485 for Newland chantry, where still incumbent on 6 March 1490 (*Reg. Myllyng, Hereford*, pp 181, 201, 125). Referred to as *magister* in 1478, 1484 and 1490 (ibid., pp 37, 200, 125).
4 *CPR 1476–85*, p 469.
5 *Reg. Myllyng, Hereford*, p 62.
6 PRO, Exch. Augm., Chantry Certificates, E 301/22; *TBGAS*, viii (1883–4), p 292.
7 Richard Norton was a chantry priest in Newland, probably of the Greyndour chantry, by 19 September 1501 (Gloucestershire Record Office, MS Cal. of Gage Deeds, GG 298). He also occurs as a chantry priest at Newland in 1502 in the same calendar (GG 302) and as a witness to the will of William Walker of Newland (PRO, Prob 11/13 (PCC 22 Blamyr)). He resigned the chantry on 16 May 1521 (*Reg. Bothe, Hereford*, p 334; Gloucester Public Library, Hockaday Abstracts, Newland, 1521). The early references to Norton at Newland make more doubtful Sir John Maclean's discovery of a Greyndour chantry priest named John Alexander, said to have sealed a lease in 1502 (*TBGAS*, vii (1882–3), p 122, followed by *VCH Gloucs.*, ii, 415). But Maclean did not know of Norton for he, and Leach after him, mistook the 1521 resignation as being that of Sir Thomas Poumphrey, who was in fact only Norton's proctor. For Norton's death and family see Cal. of Gage Deeds, GG 381.

M

piece of arable land lying in 'le Clowre' in Staunton to William Hall of High Meadow for forty years, at an annual rent of 16d.[1] Bolter was followed by David Smith, BA, who was instituted on 12 January 1531 but had died by the following September when the administration of his goods was granted to the patron, Sir Christopher Baynham.[2] Next came Roger Winter, an Oxford MA and fellow of Oriel College, elected for Shropshire.[3] A lease survives from 1533 by which he granted a grove called Brownhill to William Mathyn of Mork for forty years at a rent of 2s. 8d. a year.[4] In September 1537 while he was still schoolmaster, Winter became vicar of Woolaston some ten miles off. In the following year he also secured the rectory of Staunton, leaving the school soon afterwards. Winter was apparently a conservative in religious matters. In August 1551 as rector of Staunton he was ordered not to affirm the real presence of Christ in the sacrament, and in October as vicar of Woolaston he was enjoined to preach more often against pilgrimages, relics and other superstitions.[5] He held Staunton until his death, but in 1563 the parishioners complained that he was not always resident in the parish.[6] He died in the spring of 1582.

Roger Ford, the last of the chaplain-schoolmasters, was instituted on 6 November 1538, at about the age of forty-five.[7] Ten years later when the chantry commissioners extended their inquiries to Newland, the school appears to have been in a flourishing condition. As we have seen, three of the recent schoolmasters had been graduates. Ford himself was characterised as 'a man of honest conversation and good learning and wholly given and applying himself in the virtuous bringing up of the same scholars, whereof are at this present good store and the school very well haunted, to the great commodity of the country thereabouts'. The master's salary had fallen slightly to between £10 and £11. He was still maintaining the scholar, and the teaching was still only 'half-free', some fees being paid by the pupils.[8] The school was ordered to be continued, Roger Ford being still resident in Newland in 1551 and still receiving his old stipend in 1554, but the ultimate fate of the

---

1 John Bolter (Bolthar) was admitted BA, Oxon., in 1514 (*BRUO*, iv, 56). He was instituted chaplain of Newland on 16 May 1521, and resigned by January 1531 (*Reg. Bothe, Hereford*, pp 334, 345). The lease made by him is among the Gage Deeds, GG 338. He may be the same as John Bolthar, instituted chaplain of the chantry of St John Baptist, Chipping Norton, Oxon., between 1535 and 1538, said to be worth over £9 a year (PRO, Early Chancery Proceedings, C1/742/48).

2 David Smith was chaplain of Newland, instituted 12 January 1531, till death. Died by 20 September 1531 (*Reg. Bothe, Hereford*, p 345; Gloucester Public Library, Hockaday Abstracts, Newland, 1531). BA by 1531 but not certainly identified as an Oxford man.

3 For his career see *BRUO*, iv, 649.

4 *Historical MSS Commission, Reports on Various Collections*, iv, 185.

5 Ibid., vii, 55, 56.

6 Hockaday Abstracts, Staunton, 1563, quoting Gloucs. Dioc. Records, 20/32.

7 Roger Ford was born *c*. 1493 since he was aged 55 in 1548. He was instituted chaplain of Newland on 16 November 1538 (*Reg. Bothe, Hereford*, p 382), and occurs as chaplain at Newland in 1551 (Hockaday Abstracts, General, 1551, during Bishop Hooper's visitation). He may well be the Roger Ford who was admitted M Gram at Oxford on 30 January 1532 after fifteen years study of grammar and twelve years practice (Bodleian Library, University Archives, Reg. H fo 259).

8 PRO, Exch. Augm., Chantry Certificates, E 301/23 no 34; *ESR*, part ii, pp 83-4.

institution is mysterious.[1] The endowment was certainly taken by the crown and included in a large quantity of lands for which William Winter, 'the queen's servant', and Edward Baeshe of London paid over £2,000 in 1559.[2] It is most likely that as in some other places the crown neglected to pay the master's salary during Mary's reign, and it is possible that for a time the school ceased to exist. There was however a schoolmaster in the parish again by 1576,[3] at about which time Edward Bell re-endowed the grammar school, which subsequently bore his name.

OTTERY ST MARY
Devon

The collegiate church and grammar school at Ottery St Mary were founded by John Grandisson, bishop of Exeter, in 1338. On the founder's life a whole volume could be written, describing his noble birth, his studies at Paris and Oxford, and his long and diligent episcopate of 42 years, still unsurpassed by any of his successors.[4] We need only note his strong interest in school education, to a degree unusual among his contemporaries. Not only did he realise Stapledon's scheme for founding grammar scholarships at St John's Hospital, Exeter,[5] but he provided the scholars of Launceston with meals in the local priory,[6] and in 1357 he issued an almost unique set of instructions to the schoolmasters of his diocese about how and what they should teach.[7] It is less surprising that such a man, when founding a collegiate body to perform religious services, should also have made careful arrangements for the education of its members. Grandisson's models in this respect were probably the secular cathedrals and some of the ancient prebendal churches like Beverley, Southwell and Warwick. Many of these foundations had a grammar master loosely associated with them by the early fourteenth century. He was usually expected to instruct the clerks and choristers of the establishment in return for a small stipend, besides teaching for fees such members of the public who asked for his services. Ottery College had choristers in need of education and its town, though small, was something of a local centre with a potential number of schoolboys—hence the point of the grammar master.

The scale of the college, as fitted so great a bishop, was a large one, including no less than forty clerics.[8] There were eight canons headed by a warden; an equal number of vicars, secondaries and choristers; three chaplains; four other clerks, and the grammar master. The secondaries received 8d. a week if they kept residence and an extra 12s. *per annum*;

1 PRO, Exch. Land Revenue, LR 6/28/1.
2 *CPR 1558–60,* p 359.
3 Hockaday Abstracts, General, 1576–7.
4 For Grandisson's life see *BRUO,* ii, 800–1, and the introduction to *Reg. Grandisson, Exeter,* ed. F. C. Hingeston-Randolph, vol iii.
5 See above, pp 48–9.
6 See above, p 101.
7 *Reg. Grandisson, Exeter,* ii, 1192–3.
8 For the history of the college see J. N. Dalton, *The Collegiate Church of Ottery St Mary* (Cambridge, 1917), especially p 93, and G. Oliver, *Monasticon Dioecesis Exoniensis,* pp 259–86.

the choristers likewise 4d. and 6s. 8d. Only the latter were specifically mentioned as attending school, but it is likely that the secondaries did so too.[1] The chaplain of the Lady chapel was responsible for teaching song and organ-playing in the college, and the schoolmaster for teaching grammar. The college statutes have little to say about the master, but from random allusions elsewhere we learn that he was expected to attend services and that a chamber, garden and schoolhouse were put at his disposal. He was appointed by the canons in chapter and received a stipend of £1. 6s. 8d. 'besides the emoluments of the school'.[2] This gives us an insight into his position. The stipend was evidently his recompense for teaching the choristers, and the emoluments must have been the fees which he took from pupils who came to him from outside. The grammar school was therefore open to the public, but it was not free. Grandisson provided the locality with a schoolmaster, but he did not subsidise the teaching which the master gave.

The subsequent history of the college appears on the whole to have been calm and uneventful. The grammar school continued its existence until the 1540s and there are regular references to it or its master during the fourteenth and fifteenth centuries. John Weymon, for example, is mentioned as schoolmaster in 1438.[3] An exception to this occurs in 1380 when we are told that the school had been vacant for over a year and that the chapter had rented out the schoolmaster's garden to a layman. Bishop Brantingham ordered its restoration.[4] But in general the school shared in the growing prosperity which the college achieved through its annexations of parish churches and their revenues. In 1343 the master's stipend was raised by 6s. 8d. following the appropriation of Ilsington and by a similar sum in 1361 after that of Northam. By 1380 it stood at £2, increased to £4 when Ipplepen was appropriated in 1439, although at the Reformation in 1544 it seems to have been only £3. 13s. 4d.[5] Besides the grammar master, the chaplain of the Lady chapel continued to do duty as song master, the post being held in the early sixteenth century by the well-known poet and translator, Alexander Barclay. His version of Sebastian Brant's satirical poem, *The Ship of Fools,* was completed at Ottery in 1508 and includes a playful suggestion that the fools should give place in their ship to the eight secondaries, his pupils:

> I have eyght neyghbours that firste shall have a place
> Within this my shyp, for they most worthy be;
> They may theyr lernynge receyve costeles and fre,
> Theyr wallys abuttynge and joynynge to the scoles.
> No thing they can[6], yet nought will they lerne nor se,
> Therfore shall they gyde this one shyp of foles.[7]

1 In view of Barclay's remarks, below.
2 Dalton, op. cit., pp 98, 100.
3 Oliver, *Monasticon,* p 282. There are other references to the school on pp 280–4.
4 *Reg. Brantyngham, Exeter,* ed. F. C. Hingeston-Randolph, i, 435.
5 Dalton, op. cit., pp 262, 267, 272–3, 282, 296.
6 I.e. 'know'.
7 Sebastian Brant, *The Shyp of Folys,* trans. A. Barclay (London, Richard Pynson, 1509), fo 74; *The Eclogues of Alexander Barclay,* ed. Beatrice White (Early English Text Soc., original series, clxxv, 1928), pp xi–xv.

Barclay later abandoned his post at Ottery and became a monk of Ely, but he returned to teaching at the end of his chequered career, as grammar master of Wells in 1548.[1]

Ottery College was surrendered to the king on 28 May 1545 while apparently in full working order, with 38 members still on the foundation. There were still eight choristers and the grammar master was a priest, John Chubbe.[2] While anxious to take over the secular colleges and their possessions, Henry VIII was not unmindful of the public schools and parochial services which some of them had provided, and in most cases he made arrangements for these to continue.[3] In this instance the dissolution of the college was followed by the immediate grant of a pension of £10 to Chubbe, the usual stipend of an endowed schoolmaster at this time, which strongly suggests that he remained in office teaching the school.[4] Five months later on 16 October the king gave orders for the refoundation of Ottery school, and letters patent to this effect were issued on 24 December. A corporation of four governors was set up from among the inhabitants of Ottery; they were provided with revenues, and given possession of the old college including the schoolhouse. The governors were to appoint schoolmasters in future and pay them £10 a year. The school, if it were not already so, became free of fees and was given the title of 'The King's New Grammar School of Ottery St Mary'.[5] In this way Grandisson's school survived the fall of his college, and began a new era of its existence on its ancient site, but with a new name and new resources.

PENRYN
Cornwall

The town of Penryn was fortunate in possessing one of the most important religious houses of medieval Cornwall, the college of Glasney. Founded in 1267 by Walter Branscombe, bishop of Exeter, it boasted a provost, twelve canons and thirteen vicars, while the statutes, which date from about 1276, mention four clerks as well as 'the boys of the choir'.[6] We hear intermittently of both clerks and boys during later years. In 1355 Bishop Grandisson appropriated the church of St Just to Glasney to maintain two clerks receiving 8d. a week and two choristers receiving 4d.[7] In 1445 Bishop Lacy, on hearing that the choristers had been turned out of their chamber to wander by day and night in the town without masters, ordered it to be restored to them.[8] In 1535 there were six 'choristers',[9] but two of these may

1 See above, p 87.
2 Dalton, op. cit., pp 296, 300–1. A John Chube was ordained subdeacon on 15 April and deacon on 10 July 1525 (Taunton, Somerset Record Office, Reg. Clerke, Wells, ordination lists).
3 On this subject see *ESMA*, pp 268–70.
4 Dalton, op. cit., pp 300–1.
5 *LPFD*, xx part ii, p 320; no 1068(45). There is a complete transcript of the refoundation document in Oliver, *Monasticon*, pp 417–21.
6 Oliver, *Monasticon Dioecesis Exoniensis*, p 48; T. C. Peter, *The History of Glasney Collegiate Church, Cornwall* (1903), pp 42–3.
7 *Reg. Grandisson, Exeter*, ed. F. C. Hingeston-Randolph, ii, 1154.
8 *Reg. Lacy, Exeter*, ed. G. R. Dunstan, ii, 331.
9 *Valor Ecclesiasticus*, ii, 392.

have been clerks, since the establishment of the college at its dissolution in 1548 included a chapel clerk, bellringer and four choristers aged between ten and thirteen.

No surviving documents mention a school in the medieval college, but some arrangements must have been made for teaching the choristers, at least in song. Moreover by the time of its dissolution Glasney had undoubtedly come to provide public education for the locality. The chantry certificates of 1548 reveal two schools. John Pounde, the college bellringer, received £2 for teaching the ABC 'to poor men's children', which may indicate that he took fees from the better off. Grammar had been taught by one of the vicars, but he had recently died, for which the people of Penryn, according to the certificate, 'make great lamentations, and it is meet to have another learned man, for there is much youth in the town'. The chantry commissioners accordingly authorised the school to continue with an annual stipend of £6. 18s., presumably what the vicar had received.[1] At the same time they gave permission for a new schoolmaster, John Arscote, MA, to teach grammar in the town as well. This man had been since at least 1537 the senior chaplain or 'archpriest' of the chantry on St Michael's Mount.[2] The chantry was dissolved like all the rest in 1548 but Arscote appears to have been allowed to keep his old stipend of £10 a year in return for teaching grammar at Penryn[3]. As an MA he was no doubt regarded as a useful candidate to fill the vacancy. He went on receiving his stipend until Michaelmas 1555, but at the following Michaelmas the local receiver-general of crown lands paid two years' salary to an unnamed schoolmaster of Penryn at £6. 18s. *per annum*. It looks as if Arscote may have ceased to teach in 1554, and that after an interval of two years the arrangements originally visualised by the chantry commissioners in 1548 came into effect. No payments then appear to have been made to the schoolmaster of Glasney from 1556 until 1561, doubtless because of the receiver-general's refusal to do so—a decision paralleled at Launceston and in other English counties during Mary's reign. In 1561 however the payment was restored and Penryn grammar school, stemming from the old college, continued its history into Elizabeth's reign as an endowed foundation.[4]

ST BRIAVELS

Gloucestershire

St Briavels with its castle was the medieval centre of government of the Forest of Dean, and the parish was reckoned in 1548 to include 160 communicants. In that year it was reported that certain lands and tenements belonging to Our Lady Service, of unknown foundation, maintained a priest singing in the parish church and bringing up children in virtue and learning. The incumbent, Richard Fletcher, had £6. 3s. 9d. for his stipend. The

1 PRO, E 301/9 no 1, E 301/10 no 1; *The Chantry Certificates for Cornwall*, ed. L. S. Snell, pp 36–40; *ESR*, part ii, pp 29–32, 39–40, 42.
2 Oliver, *Monasticon Dioecesis Exoniensis*, p 38; *Faculty Office Registers*, ed. D. S. Chambers (1966), p 114.
3 *ESR*, part ii, p 42.
4 PRO, Exch. Land Revenue, LR 6/104/3–4, LR 6/1/1–8.

chantry commissioners did not judge it necessary to continue what was evidently only an elementary school, and simply assigned the priest a pension of £4.[1]

SALTASH
Cornwall

The inhabitants of Saltash, which lay almost a mile distant from its parish church of St Stephen, enjoyed by at least the fourteenth century the convenience of a chapel of ease in the town itself, dedicated to St Nicholas. In 1546 they reported to the chantry commissioners of Henry VIII that a certain John Smith had endowed a stipendiary priest to serve the chapel and also to teach children freely in a school 'built within the town'. The endowments, administered by the mayor and burgesses, produced over £10 a year of which the incumbent had £7.[2] The chantry certificate of 1548 adds that there were 600 communicants in the parish, that the priest's name was Andrew Furlong, and that he was aged 40.[3] A little is known about Furlong's antecedents. He was ordained priest in 1534 and had already become schoolmaster of Saltash by the autumn of 1538. At that time he was under suspicion of questioning the king's authority over the Church of England, and even lay for a space in prison, after the discovery in his chamber of an English Bible, from which some lines in praise of the royal supremacy had been rubbed out. The episode does not seem to have had an adverse effect upon his subsequent career.[4]

The antiquity of the school, as usual in these cases, remains obscure, since John Smith's endowment, whenever it was made, may only have been meant to support a priest, the duty of teaching freely being added later as education became more popular. The school was evidently one of grammar, for the chantry commissioners ordered that it should continue[5] and Furlong went on receiving his stipend of £7 from the crown until 1555.[6]

1 PRO, Exch. Augm., Chantry Certificates, E 301/22 no 73, /23 no 37; *TBGAS*, viii (1883–4), pp 295–6, missed by Leach from *ESR*. Richard Fletcher was born *c*. 1494 since he was aged 54 in 1548. One of his name from Hereford diocese was ordained priest to the title of Monmouth Priory on 16 March 1522 (Reg. Ghinucci, Worcester, fo 85v). He was at St Briavels by September 1530 when he witnessed the will of Matthew Whittynton of that place (PRO, Prob 11/23 (21 Jankyn)). Still in receipt of his pension in 1554 (*TBGAS*, xxix (1906), p 123), he is said to have been rector of 'Abnoll' (? Abenhall) in 1559, but no episcopal records confirm this (Gloucester Public Library, Hockaday Abstracts, St Briavels, 1559).He must be distinguished from his namesake and contemporary, schoolmaster in Gloucester in 1534 (see above, p 138).
2 PRO, E 301/15 no 83; *The Chantry Certificates for Cornwall*, ed. L. S. Snell, pp 46–7; *ESR*, part ii, p 28; Bodleian Library, MS Rawl. D 363 fo 243.
3 Ibid., E 301/9 no 19; Snell, op. cit., p 46; *ESR*, part ii, p 37. Andrew Furlong was ordained subdeacon on 20 December 1533, deacon 28 February, priest 4 April 1534, to the title of Barnstaple Priory (Reg. Veysey, Exeter, i, ordination lists).
4 *LPFD*, Addenda i part ii, no 1370.
5 E 301/10 no 20; Snell, op. cit., p 46; *ESR*, part ii, p 41.
6 PRO, Exch. Land Revenue, LR 6/104/2–4, LR 6/1/1–2.

STOW-ON-THE-WOLD
Gloucestershire

The foundation of an endowed school in medieval Stow-on-the-Wold rests on the statement of Sir Robert Atkyns, the historian of Gloucestershire who died in 1711, that Sir William Martin gave lands in St Olave's parish, Southwark, for this purpose in the late fifteenth century.[1] The endowment of which Atkyns was writing originated, however, with William Chester, a scion of Stow who prospered to become both a merchant of the staple of Calais and a citizen and skinner in London. He bequeathed in his will of 1476 certain lands and rents in Southwark called the 'Gleane' to augment the guild of the Holy Trinity in Stow, originally founded by his father Robert Chester but since fallen into decay. In particular the properties were to support a chantry chaplain appointed by the guild warden, and an almshouse for eight poor men and women.[2] The premises, which included twenty-five messuages, six cottages and thirty-six gardens, were recovered from William's niece Joan Bullisdon and her husband by William Martin in 1487. He was an alderman of London, knighted in 1494, who died in 1505. Having recovered the Southwark lands, he released them to nine feoffees of Stow in 1488, doubtless to fulfil the provisions of William Chester's will, and the two surviving feoffees made a new enfeoffment to eighteen others in 1516.[3] In 1535 the value of the lands was estimated at £25. 4s. 4d. a year, and at the Henrician chantry survey of 1546 the almsfolk numbered nine and the chaplain had £6 for his salary.[4] The guild and chantry do not appear in the Edwardian chantry certificates and were later regarded as concealed lands, for in 1564 the guild lands in Stow were leased by the crown to John Jenever by whose industry they had been recovered after their concealment.[5] In 1583 an inquisition was held to discover whether the incumbent in 1548 had been a chantry priest or a mere chaplain; it concluded that he had been a chantry priest, but made no mention of him teaching a school.[6]

There is therefore no contemporary evidence to support Atkyns's assertion that the guild or chantry included a school. It has however been repeated by later historians. Samuel Rudder, who records the 1488 release to the feoffees of Stow, implies that the school was Martin's addition to the scheme.[7] According to A. F. Leach, a tenement called 'le Schole Howse' next to the churchyard lay ruined in Elizabeth's reign.[8] The 'Gleane' lands in Southwark somehow came into the hands of Theophilus and Robert Adams of London,

---

1 Sir R. Atkyns, *The Ancient and Present State of Gloucestershire* (1712), p 366.
2 Chester's will is in PRO, Prob 11/6 (PCC 23 Wattys). See also R. E. Chester-Waters, *Memoirs of the Chesters of Chicheley* (2 vols, London, 1878), i, 9–10.
3 Gloucestershire Record Office, Deeds, D 1375/174–5.
4 *Valor Ecclesiasticus*, ii, 436; PRO, Exch. Augm., Chant. Certs., E 301/21 no 34. Chester's foundation was indifferently called a guild, hospital and chantry. The only chaplain whose name survives is William Cowley in 1540 (HWRO, ref. 802 p 201).
5 *CPR 1563–6*, no 790.
6 PRO, Exch. KR., Special Commissions, E 178/886.
7 S. Rudder, *New History of Gloucestershire* (1779), p 706.
8 *VCH Gloucs.*, ii, 420.

who sold them in 1583 to Richard Shepham, himself a citizen and merchant tailor in the capital, who applied them towards founding a grammar school in Stow on his own account in 1604.[1] The existence of an earlier grammar school remains doubtful.

TROWBRIDGE
Wiltshire

Trowbridge school, like that of Bradford, grew out of the wealth and interest in education of the prosperous clothiers of west Wiltshire. Its basis was a chantry founded in Trowbridge church by James Terumber, clothier and merchant of the parish in the late fifteenth century. On 14 January 1484 he enfeoffed thirty-four men of the neighbourhood with lands in and around Trowbridge to support a chantry priest at the altar of Jesus in the parish church, saying masses for his soul and those of his two wives.[2] The priest was to be nominated by the feoffees and the churchwardens, and had the duty of managing the endowments. He was to act as governor of the nearby almshouse also founded by Terumber, and to pay £4 a year to support the inmates. He had to hold an annual obit for the founder's soul and to pay fees to the rector, the curate, three other chaplains, the parish clerk, the bedesman and five choristers for their attendance. His own salary was fixed at £6. 13s. 4d. The detailed chantry ordinances make no mention of the school, and there is no reason to believe that Terumber intended to endow one. The only point of educational interest in the ordinances is their reference to the choristers, who are described as 'five children being in their surplices at the said dirges and masses there, singing and reading'.[3] Similar boys are found at other large parish churches in the west of England, such as Ashburton, Bristol and Cirencester, and may be regarded as a small educational unit, in so far as they learnt or practised reading and singing.[4] There may well have been other means of acquiring education in early Tudor Trowbridge of which nothing is now known.

The conversion of Terumber's chantry into a chantry grammar school was probably made in 1542. This is to be inferred from the evidence offered six years later at the survey of the chantries. The chantry certificate for Trowbridge informs us that Robert Wheteacre was the priest of Terumber's chantry, 'a very honest man, well learned and right able to serve a cure', in other words a cure of souls. 'And furthermore he hath occupied himself in teaching a school there ever since he came first hitherto'. Further information establishes that the school was a free grammar school.[5] The tone of the certificate suggests that the school was not of ancient origin but began with Wheteacre's arrival in Trowbridge. The date of this can be guessed from his biography. Robert Whetacre was born in 1505–6

---

1 Gloucestershire Record Office, Deeds, D 1375/176.
2 W. H. Jones, 'Terumber's Chantry at Trowbridge', *Wilts. Archaeological and Natural History Magazine*, x (1867), pp 240–52.
3 Ibid., p 249.
4 On these churches, see above, pp 38, 111, 130.
5 PRO, E 301/58 no 45, E 301/105; *ESR,* part ii, pp 260, 264.

and probably came from one of the numerous Wiltshire families of that name.[1] He was a priest by 1537 when he became chaplain of Magdalen College, Oxford, and proceeded, rather late in life, to undertake an academic career. He graduated in 1539 as a BA, as an MA in the following year, and was admitted a probationary fellow of Magdalen in 1542, but left the college almost at once—probably in order to come to Trowbridge. A university master with the chance of a fellowship, one feels, would not have left for a chantry in the country unless he had been invited to do so on good terms. No doubt the churchwardens and feoffees who governed Terumber's chantry were anxious to provide their community with a free school and to safeguard the chantry endowments at a time when all religious property seemed in danger of confiscation. They may have offered Wheteacre a higher salary than his predecessors. The net value of the chantry in 1548 was £15.9s. 1d., and even the expenses of the obit and the almsfolk could still have left the chaplain with the £10 which was the accepted salary for schoolmasters at that time.

The chantry commissioners ordered the school to continue and arranged for Wheteacre to receive an annual stipend from the crown equal to the whole £15.9s. 1d. of the chantry income. Terumber's endowments would then have been confiscated and sold. The master himself apparently remained at Trowbridge until 1554 when, like most of his colleagues who had endured a dozen years of teaching, he took the opportunity to move into a parochial benefice. He was admitted to the rectory of Hilperton near Trowbridge in July, but seems not to have kept it, for in the following September he became rector of Priston in north Somerset, where he died some five years later. As for Trowbridge school, it shared the fate of Bradford in 1569 when both their annuities were appropriated by the citizens of Salisbury on the pretext that they were unnecessary in their previous location. If Trowbridge school continued, it must have done so by relying wholly upon fees.[2]

TRURO
Cornwall

Truro possessed educational facilities in 1548 when the chantry commissioners found lands worth £6.13s. 4d. a year supporting a priest to minister in the parish church and keep a school. The lands were under the control of the corporation, and the incumbent, who received the whole income, was Richard Fosse aged fifty. The town at that time was reckoned to include 600 communicants, but there is no evidence to show when the school began. The commissioners moreover made no arrangements for it to continue, and Fosse

---

[1] On Wheteacre's career, see *BRUO*, iv, 620. He is probably the Robert Wheteacre who was ordained subdeacon on 7 March 1528 to the title of the college of Westbury-on-Trym, Gloucs. (Reg. Campeggio, Sarum, fo 62v). The wills of John Wheteacre of Westbury (1530) and Richard Wheteacre of Edington (1538) survive in PRO Prob 11/24 fos 10v–11 (PCC 2 Thower) and Prob 11/27 fo 154v (PCC F19 Dyngeley) respectively.
[2] *Reports of Charity Commissioners* (House of Commons Papers, 1833, vol xix), p 366 and see above p 75.

was awarded a pension of £6 as if he had been a mere chantry priest.[1] This suggests that he taught reading or song, subjects which the commissioners were not concerned to foster, although they generally went out of their way to preserve grammar schools. It is possible however that after this decision the corporation of Truro made arrangements of their own for education to continue in the town. There is a late seventeenth-century reference to an indenture of 1549 between the corporation and Walter Borlase for the building of a school, and there was certainly a schoolmaster in the town by 1600.[2]

WEEK ST MARY
Cornwall

The grammar school of Week St Mary was one of the most distinctive educational foundations to be made in the South West during the sixteenth century. Though not the earliest grammar school to operate in Cornwall, it was the first free school to be endowed in the county. Its constitution included unusual features not found elsewhere in the region. Though it stood in a remote village and lasted for only forty years, it was one of the leading Cornish schools of its day and seems to have enjoyed a high reputation. The foundress of Week school was also an unusual woman. Her rise from rags to riches became legendary, and was retold until recently with all the fanciful embellishments that legends acquire. It has taken the careful researches of Mr P. L. Hull to separate the truth from the fiction, and to provide a definitive account of her life and benefactions. The following pages are largely based upon his valuable work.[3]

Thomasine Bonaventure was born at Week in about the middle of the fifteenth century, although the exact decade remains uncertain. Her parents were John and Joan Bonaventure. They do not seem to have been quite as humble as later tradition portrayed them. Joan was a coheiress of John Westlake, a man of armigerous status, and her sister married one of the Dinhams of Lifton, a local family of gentry.[4] Thomasine's rise in the world probably began well up the social scale, rather than right at the bottom. The story of how it occurred is first preserved in Richard Carew's *Survey of Cornwall*, published in 1602. The details are picturesque, but they are not absolutely improbable. 'While in her girlish age', so Carew tells us, and keeping sheep upon the village moor, 'it chanced that a London merchant passing by saw her, heeded her, liked her, begged her of her poor parents, and carried her to his home', in other words to enter his service in London. 'In process of time her mistress

---

1 PRO, E 301/9 no 26, E 301/10 no 30; *The Chantry Certificates for Cornwall*, ed. L. S. Snell, pp 50–1; *ESR*, part ii, pp 39, 41–2 Bodleian Library, MS Rawl. D 363 fo 262-v. A Richard Fosse was ordained priest on 15 June 1527 to the title of Barnstaple Priory; another was collated as rector of Truro on 12 May 1558 (Reg. Veysey, Exeter, i, ordination lists; Reg. Turberville, Exeter, fo 36).
2 R. E. Davidson, *The History of Truro Grammar and Cathedral School* (Mevagissey, 1970). This work misdates the chantry certificates.
3 P. L. Hull, 'The Endowment and Foundation of a Grammar School at Week St Mary by Dame Thomasine Percival', *Journal of the Royal Institution of Cornwall*, new series vii part i (1973), pp 21–54.
4 Ibid., p 39. Was Thomasine Dinham, prioress of Cornworthy, Devon, c. 1470–1519, one of her namesake's relations?

was summoned by death to appear in the other world, and her good thews, no less than her seemly personage, so much contented her master, that he advanced her from a servant to a wife, and left her a wealthy widow'.[1] From this point onwards the story is corroborated by other evidence.[2] The name of Thomasine's benefactor and first husband was Thomas Barnaby. After his death she married Henry Gall. He also predeceased her, and she then gave her hand for the third and last time to John Percival. The dates of her weddings are not known, but presumably lie in the third quarter of the fifteenth century.

The last of Thomasine's three marriages was also the most important. Compared with her first two husbands, of whom nothing is now known, John Percival was much wealthier and became far more famous. He was also her favourite spouse, with whom she chose to be buried, and it was through his company that she acquired the interest in education which led her to found a school in her native village. Like Thomasine, John Percival was a countryman by birth. He was born 'hard by' the town of Macclesfield in Cheshire, and came to London where he took up the trade of a merchant taylor.[3] He evidently prospered, and duly extended his activities to other kinds of merchandise. In 1487 he was licensed to import 500 quarters of corn, and a further 100 gallons of wine from Gascony in the following year. Transactions with a Spanish iron merchant, Ochoa Martines, are mentioned in his will. His London residence was 71 Lombard Street, in the parish of St Mary Woolnoth, and something of the size of his household is suggested by his wife's will, which mentions fourteen servants and apprentices. Private wealth led to public offices, first in the company of merchant taylors and then in the government of the city. He was successively renter and upper warden of the company, and finally its master in 1485. In the same year he was elected an alderman of the city, and from 1486 to 1487 he also served as sheriff. His knighthood followed shortly afterwards, between 21 September and 16 October 1488.[4] The next step for such a man was to become lord mayor, and the merchant taylors were particularly anxious for Sir John's election to this office because none of their company had yet enjoyed it. They put him forward in the late 1480s and again in 1493, but the rest of the corporation repeatedly passed him over, allegedly 'because of his hot appetite' to be lord mayor 'in other manner than his predecessors'. More probably the delay arose from a long-standing feud within the London cloth trade between the drapers and mercers on the one hand, and the taylors, fullers and dyers on the other. At length Sir John's exclusion became so notorious that the king himself and the bishop of London sent letters of recommendation to the corporation on his behalf. His colleagues were obliged to give way, and in 1499 he was belatedly elected to the coveted post of honour.[5]

1 Richard Carew, *The Survey of Cornwall* (London, 1602), pp 118–19.
2 E.g. Thomasine's will and the foundation deed of her chantry.
3 For details of his life see C. M. Clode, *The Early History of the Guild of Merchant Taylors* (London, 1888), ii, 8–21, and P. L. Hull, op. cit., p 41.
4 *Calendar of Letter Books of the City of London: L,* ed. R. R. Sharpe (1912), pp 260, 264. The meaning of John Stow's remark (*Survey of London,* ed. C. L. Kingsford (1908), ii, 179) that he was knighted 'in the field' is not clear.
5 *The Great Chronicle of London,* ed. A. H. Thomas & I. D. Thornley (London, 1938), pp 245–6, 288.

The Percivals thus ended their married life as wealthy members of the city élite. The only reasonable ambition which eluded them was a family of children, since there is nothing to show that Thomasine had issue by any of her three husbands. So like other rich and childless people of their age, they turned their attention instead to the support of charity and religion. Shortly before his death in 1503 Sir John began to carry out a number of charitable benefactions. First on 25 January he arranged for the establishment of a free grammar school at Macclesfield, of which more anon. Next on 21 February he conveyed twelve messuages in Lombard Street and Cornhill to the merchant taylors to maintain two chantry priests in the church of St Mary Woolnoth where he worshipped.[1] Finally on 4 March he made his last will and testament.[2] He arranged to be buried in St Mary's, and gave copious directions for an elaborate funeral. He made bequests to a large number of London churches and religious houses, and arranged for alms and doles to the poor. The residue of his goods went to his wife. His death on 19 April left Thomasine a widow for the third time. She passed the remaining nine years of her life in London, engaging in similar works of charity to those of her late husband. We learn from her will that she brought up five poor children in her household. In 1506 she began to establish her own grammar school at Week St Mary. In 1509 she granted seven more messuages to augment her husband's chantry, and to provide 5d. a week for five poor householders of Woolnoth parish.[3] Finally on 26 March 1512 she made her own lengthy will, full of complicated directions for her funeral and for almsdeeds when she died.[4] She arranged to be buried in Sir John's tomb, and provided for a chantry priest to sing masses for five years in the chapel of Scala Celi at Westminster. She gave monetary donations to eleven London hospitals, ten churches and nine prisons. She left bequests to her surviving brother and his wife, and to various other relatives, servants and apprentices. Her two charity girls were promised their maintenance until they were fourteen, and the three boys were enabled to train as priests if they so desired. The residue of her property was bequeathed to John Dinham of Lifton. He was both Thomasine's cousin on her mother's side and the husband of her sister's daughter Margery. Thomasine herself died at some point between 10 April and 30 July 1512.

The gifts of money which the Percivals made to churches, chantries, the sick and the poor were generous acts of charity, but there is nothing distinctive about them. Hundreds of men and women of similar rank and wealth left money for these purposes. The distinction of the Percivals lies rather in their school foundations. Schools still competed for attention with many other charitable causes, and even in 1503 endowing a school was a more original and unusual benefaction than founding a chantry or feeding the poor. The Percivals' interest in education probably arose from Sir John's friendship with Thomas Savage and Sir Richard Sutton. All three were Cheshire men. Savage was the bishop of London who pressed for Sir John's election as lord mayor, and afterwards became archbishop of York.[5]

1 *Calendar of Wills in the Court of Husting, London,* ed. R. R. Sharpe, vol ii (1890), p 605.
2 PRO, Prob 11/13 (PCC 23 Blamyr).
3 *Calendar of Wills in the Court of Husting,* ii, 618–19.
4 PRO, Prob 11/17 (PCC 28 Fettiplace).
5 For his career see *BRUO,* iii, 1646–7.

Sutton was a country gentleman from the Macclesfield area, and is best known as the co-founder of Brasenose College, Oxford, in 1512.[1] The idea of founding Macclesfield school, according to Sir John, originated from a suggestion of Savage's, and both he and Sutton gave generous help with the foundation. Since Macclesfield was the principal model available to Thomasine when she came to plan her own school, a brief review of its features will not be out of place. The deed of foundation was issued by Sir John on 25 January 1503.[2] It established a chantry grammar school of the type still usually founded at that date. The lands of the endowment were entrusted to a body of eighteen lay feoffees. The four chief members of this body were empowered to appoint the schoolmaster, and also to choose a suitable rent collector to administer the endowments. The master had to be a priest and a university graduate, the latter stipulation being uncommon at this time and possibly another of Savage's suggestions.[3] He was to keep a free grammar school and to say a daily mass in the parish church for the souls of John and Thomasine. On holy days the pupils were also to attend the parish church for mattins, mass and evensong. As Mr Hull has pointed out, these provisions were all copied by Thomasine when she founded her own grammar school three years later.[4]

The foundation of Week school was begun in the spring of 1506. The main endowment was purchased by Thomasine in May of that year from Sir John Lisle for £220. It consisted of the manor of Simpson and 270 acres of land in the parish of Holsworthy, Devon.[5] Not long afterwards on 10 July she issued a deed establishing the school.[6] The influence of Macclesfield is clear, not only in the provisions, but in the word for word transcription of some of Sir John's original phrases. Like him she established a body of nineteen lay feoffees, including two local knights (Sir John Trevelyan and Sir Thomas Greenfield), her cousin and heir John Dinham, and several other gentlemen of the neighbourhood. The feoffees were to hold the endowments and employ the profits to support the school. When in due course their numbers were reduced to four, the survivors were to make a new enfeoffment of the school lands to the male heirs of the original feoffees, or to other suitable persons. The four senior feoffees appointed the schoolmaster, and could also remove him from office when necessary. If they failed to appoint a new master within three weeks of a vacancy arising, the right for that occasion devolved upon the abbot of Hartland. If he neglected his duty, it passed to the prior of Bodmin. The four senior feoffees were also to nominate a rent gatherer, as at Macclesfield, to supervise the endowments and collect the income. After meeting certain prescribed expenses, he was to pay the whole of the residue to the schoolmaster for his salary.

The master was to be a priest, of virtuous character and sufficiently learned in grammar. Like her husband, Thomasine laid down the unusual condition that he should be a university

1 For his biography see R. Churton, *The Lives of William Smyth, Bishop of Lincoln, and Sir Richard Sutton* (Oxford, 1800).
2 D. Wilmot, *A Short History of the Grammar School, Macclesfield* (Macclesfield, 1910), pp xli–l.
3 For a list of foundations closed to graduates see *ESMA*, p 154 n 1.
4 P. L. Hull, op. cit., p 25.
5 Ibid., p 26.
6 Ibid., pp 43–8.

graduate—either of grammar or arts.[1] His duties, as in all chantry schools, were twofold—liturgical and educational. He was to say mass every day in the parish church of Week for the souls of the foundress and her relatives. Once a year, on 19 April, he was to keep a solemn obit in their memory, assisted by his scholars and by the local clergy. For the rest of the time he was to teach grammar in a new house at Week, built specially for the purpose. Parts of this building survive near the church, behind a battlemented wall.[2] The school was free and open to all comers. Teaching appears to have been given all the year round, except on Sundays and holy days. But like most contemporary founders, Thomasine gave no directions for the conduct of her school beyond regulating its worship. Every morning the master and scholars were to say specified prayers in Latin 'in the worship of the Father, the Son and the Holy Ghost'. Every afternoon before school broke up, they were to sing a Latin anthem to the Virgin and the psalm of intercession, *De Profundis,* for the soul of Thomasine. On holy days, when teaching was suspended, all the available scholars were ordered to attend mattins, mass and evensong in the parish church, and there to refrain from 'jangling, or talking or other idle occupation'.[3]

The deed of foundation, however, did not establish the school in its final form. Two important additions were subsequently made to the provisions it contained. The first came on 6 November 1508 when Thomasine improved the legal status of her school by securing a royal licence for its foundation. The licence permitted her to establish a chantry at Week and to convey lands worth £20 a year to the chaplain, under the law of mortmain.[4] Accordingly on 1 December the foundress granted the schoolmaster (John Andrew) possession of the manor of Simpson together with other lands at Wicott in North Petherwin and at Week itself.[5] The master thus replaced the lay feoffees as the legal owner of the endowments, though the feoffees retained their original powers to appoint and dismiss him. As a result we find the masters granting leases of the school lands on their own initiative during the 1520s and 30s.[6] The question of the endowments, however, is more complicated than this. In 1507 Thomasine purchased the manor of Bradworthy, Devon, from Henry Thorne for £100 and left it by will to her executors to use as they thought fit. Part of this property was later applied to her foundation, for the chantry survey of 1548 discovered John Dinham of Lifton in possession of a piece of land called Ash in Bradworthy, from which he paid £4. 13s. 4d. a year to support the school. But it never came under the schoolmaster's direct control, and remained a separate endowment, the legal status of which was open to dispute.[7]

1 For degrees in grammar see *ESMA,* pp 151–3.
2 For illustrations of the building see P. L. Hull, op. cit., pp 36–7.
3 Ibid., pp 44–5, 49–51. For similar regulations about school prayers at Bruton and Newland, see above, pp 121, 161.
4 *CPR 1494–1509,* p 604.
5 P. L. Hull, op. cit., p 29.
6 Ibid., pp 27–8.
7 Ibid., p 27; PRO E 301/9 no 6; *The Chantry Certificates for Cornwall,* ed. L. S. Snell (1953), pp 51–2; *ESR,* part ii, pp 33–4.

The other major development after 1506 arose from the nature of the school's location. Ethically considered, Week St Mary was a right and proper place to choose. Custom demanded that one's birthplace and the kith and kin who lived there should receive the chief honour and benefit from one's charity. From the educational point of view, the village was far less suitable. It was not a large community. The estimate of 150 communicants in the chantry certificate of 1548 points to a total population of little more than 200. The countryside in which it lay, from Bodmin Moor to Barnstaple Bay, was a land of small villages and hamlets with hardly one sizeable settlement. Launceston, the nearest important town, was ten miles away. Nowhere else in the South West, except perhaps at Newland, was an endowed grammar school established in so underpopulated an area. The disadvantages of the site were eventually to prove fatal to Thomasine's foundation, but they were offset in the early days by the high standard of the education she provided. Free schooling in grammar under a university graduate was not easily to be found elsewhere in Cornwall or even in Devon, and in this respect Week offered a valuable amenity. As a result the school seems to have been well frequented. The chantry certificate of 1546 described it as 'a great comfort to all the country there', and Richard Carew suggests that is also attracted people of quality, 'for divers the best gentlemen's sons of Devon and Cornwall were there virtuously trained up'.[1] Many of the pupils must therefore have come from well outside the immediate neighbourhood.

There was nothing unusual in boys travelling away from home in order to be educated. But medieval schools, with one or two important exceptions like Eton and Winchester, did not provide for boarders on their own premises. The normal practice was for boys to take lodgings in private houses nearby. At Ledbury, Herefordshire, in 1548 the local inhabitants particularly mentioned the advantages they gained from lodging scholars and supplying them with victuals.[2] Similar arrangements are recorded in the South West at Exeter, Ilminster and possibly also Bruton.[3] But at Week St Mary the supply of lodgings must have been limited—especially of lodgings suitable for the children of the gentry. As a result the school had to take the unusual step for a small foundation at that time, and provide its own boarding facilities. When this happened is uncertain. It is not mentioned in the deed of foundation, but it probably developed during the early days of the school. Carew asserted that the *foundress* provided 'fair lodgings for the schoolmaster, scholars and officers, and added twenty pounds of yearly revenues for supporting the incident charges'.[4] Thomasine certainly endowed her foundation with £20 a year, and the generous scale of the endowment may well have been intended to support the larger household necessary for a boarding school. At all events, Week was boarding its pupils by 1546, when we are told that 'they that list may set their children to board there and have them taught

1 *The Chantry Certificates for Cornwall*, ed. L. Snell, p 52; *ESR*, part ii, pp 25–6; Carew, *The Survey of Cornwall*, pp 118–19.
2 *ESR*, part ii, p 92.
3 See above, pp 50–1, 100, 123.
4 Carew, *The Survey of Cornwall*, pp 118–19.

freely, for the which purpose there is a house and officers appointed by the foundation'.[1] Although, as we shall see, the records disagree about the number and functions of these officers, there were probably three of them besides the schoolmaster: a manciple, an usher and a laundress. The manciple presumably arranged the supply of provisions, and may also have cooked them; there was a well-equipped kitchen in the house in 1548.[2] The principal duty of the laundress was to wash the clothes of the master and the manciple, but doubtless she was able to take in the boys' linen for an extra sum.

The most important officer, of course, was the schoolmaster. Four men are known to have filled the post during the forty years that the school survived. The first of them, the man chosen by the foundress to open the school in 1506, was John Andrew.[3] He was born at West Dean, Wiltshire, in about 1474, and entered Winchester College as a scholar ten years later. He went on to New College, Oxford, in 1490, but left after taking his BA degree in 1495. He spent the next five years at Winchester as usher of the college school. Andrew was thus well qualified to inaugurate Thomasine's foundation, a fact which she acknowledged by granting him tenure for life, unlike his successors who were all removable by the feoffees. The second master, David Smith, occurs in 1526. He was an MA, and probably left the school in 1529 when he became rector of Week—a more lucrative benefice.[4] In 1535 the post was held by Thomas Row, who is not known to have been a graduate.[5] Three years later, when he was rumoured to be on the point of resigning, the king's minister Thomas Cromwell wrote to the feoffees to solicit the appointment of John Poynt, an Oxford BA of 1529.[6] Cromwell's wishes opened most doors, but there is nothing to show that Poynt ever arrived to teach at Week. The last of the masters was William Cholwell, who occurs from 1546 until the school was moved in 1548. His graduate status, like that of Row, is doubtful, but this did not make him unqualified to teach.[7] The chantry certificate of 1548 described him as 'a man well learned', 'a great setter forth of God's word', and Richard Carew praised him in similar terms as 'an honest and religious teacher'.[8]

In 1536 the school became involved in disputes over clerical taxation. The taxes concerned were the first fruits and tenths,[9] which had recently been imposed upon the clergy by a statute of 1534. Tenths were an income tax of ten per cent per annum upon every benefice, while first fruits involved paying the whole of the first year's income of any new benefice which any cleric subsequently acquired. A new valuation of church property, the well-

---

1 *The Chantry Certificates for Cornwall*, ed. L. Snell, p 52; *ESR*, part ii, pp 25–6.
2 Bodleian Library, MS Rawl. D 363 pp 9–10; P. L. Hull, op. cit., p 52.
3 For his career see *BRUO*, i, 34.
4 For a possible identification see *BRUO*, iv, 521. The rectory was worth £17 in 1535, as against the £11–£12 of the school (*Valor Ecclesiasticus*, ii, 403).
5 P. L. Hull, op. cit., p 28.
6 *LPFD*, xiii part i, no 105; *BRUO*, iv, 461.
7 Born probably in 1488, he is too old to be identified with William Cholwell, fellow of Exeter College, Oxford, 1527–36, and later a beneficed clergyman in Devon and Cornwall (*BRUO*, iv, 116).
8 P. L. Hull, op. cit., p 52; *ESR*, part ii, pp 33–4; Carew, *Survey of Cornwall*, pp 118–19.
9 Not tithes, as Mr Hull suggests, op. cit., p 38 n 154.

known *Valor Ecclesiasticus*, was made for this purpose in 1535. This estimated the income of Week school at £11. 11s. 3d. net, after the payment of £1. 1s. 9d. in rents and charges. The tenths were fixed at £1. 3s. 1½d.[1] No mention was made, however, of the additional sum of £4. 13s. 4d. which we have reason to believe that the Dinham family was paying out of the Bradworthy lands. According to letters from John and William Dinham to Thomas Cromwell in October 1536, the schoolmaster (Thomas Row) had difficulty in paying his tenths because some of the school lands were 'wrongfully occupied' by other people, and he had not yet gained full possession of them. The Dinhams wanted Cromwell to stop the bishop of Exeter, the local collector of ecclesiastical taxation, from pressing the master for immediate payment.[2] The outcome is not known, but the episode had a sequel. The state papers of this period include the draft of a parliamentary bill, in very rustic spelling, endorsed 'Cornubia: for the school of Week and others like'. It proposes that chantry schools such as Week, which it names specifically, should be excluded from the imposition of first fruits and tenths, because the new taxes diminish the masters' salaries and discourage good men from taking up posts in such schools.[3] The bill may have been formally introduced into parliament by a Cornish member, or submitted to the crown informally as a suggestion for future legislation. It is another indication of the interest which the school aroused in local circles. At the same time it failed to achieve its object. Clerical schoolmasters continued to be subject to first fruits and tenths until the taxes were abolished by Mary in 1555. Only when Elizabeth revived them in 1559 were educational foundations finally granted statutory exemption.

We come next to the dissolution of the chantries and the consequent destruction of the school of Week in its original form. During the 1540s the school came under the scrutiny of two chantry commissions—that of Henry VIII in 1546 and that of Edward VI in 1548. Each commission produced a report or certificate describing the school, and these certificates differ considerably, thus raising problems of accuracy and interpretation.[4] The Henrician certificate gives the net income of the school as £14. 13s. 1d. Three officers of the school are mentioned: the master, manciple and laundress. The manciple is described as an usher with the duty of teaching children under the schoolmaster. The salaries of the three officers are stated to be £12. 6s., 26s. 8d., and 13s. 4d. respectively. The impression is given of a flourishing school, providing a useful amenity to the neighbourhood. The Edwardian certificate differs in several respects. Four officers are now identified: master, usher, manciple and laundress. The manciple is clearly distinguished from the usher, and no mention is made of him doing any teaching. His name, by the way, was George Sprye, and his wife Alice was the laundress. The income of the school (£16. 11s. 4d.), the schoolmaster

---

1 *Valor Ecclesiasticus*, ii, 403.
2 *LPFD*, ix, nos 679, 810, 954.
3 Ibid., x, no 1092; PRO, State Papers, SP 1/104 pp 151–4.
4 The Henrician certificate is PRO, E 301/15 no 73. The Edwardian one, E 301/9 no 6, is based on material collected in Bodleian Library, MS Rawl. D 363 pp 9–10. E 301/10 no 9 is an adjusted abstract of E 301/9 no 6. For printed versions see P. L. Hull, op. cit., p 52; *The Chantry Certificates for Cornwall*, ed. L. Snell, pp 51–2; *ESR*, part ii, pp 25–6, 33–4, 40.

(£12. 16s. 5d.) and the usher (26s. 8d.) are much the same as before, barring minor fluctuations.[1] But the manciple (£4) and the laundress (13s. 4d.) are paid separately by John Dinham out of lands at Bradworthy 'given for the maintenance of the said school of Week'. The total income of the school is thus in excess of £21. Its condition, on the other hand, is not at all flourishing. It is, rather, in decay because it stands in such a desolate part of the country, and so far from a market for furnishing the scholars with food.

The Edwardian account is undoubtedly to be preferred to the Henrician one. The Henrician commissioners appear to have gathered their information largely through sending questionnaires to the clergy and churchwardens of each parish.[2] This enabled the parishes to send back inaccurate and incomplete returns. The Edwardian commissioners probably relied on questionnaires as well, but they seem to have been more active in probing and checking the information they received. A good deal of their detective work in Cornwall was done by John Greenfield, who was both a commissioner and the local surveyor of crown lands. As a result the Edwardian account of Week is fuller than the Henrician, and probably more accurate as to the endowments, the officers and even the condition of the school. The favourable picture of the school in 1546 must have been drawn by the parishioners, who naturally wished to keep the school at Week. The more critical account of 1548 was presumably added by the commissioners, from a more detached point of view. There is no reason to doubt the impression they give of a school well-endowed and well-conducted, but hampered from functioning efficiently by the nature of its site.

The proposal that the school should be transferred to Launceston seems to have been first made to the Edwardian commissioners by the people of the town.[3] The commissioners agreed with the proposal, and sent an appropriate memorandum to the central government. The lord protector, Edward Seymour, duly took action. He consulted a number of leading men in the county as to whether they thought the school should remain at Week or be moved to Launceston. The people he approached took the same view as the commissioners, and the protector then issued a formal order for the school to be transferred.[4] The transfer thus reflected local opinion, at any rate within the governing class and the county town. It had the effect, however, of destroying the distinctive foundation which Lady Percival had set up. The Week establishment was not taken up *in toto* and deposited in its old form at Launceston. Launceston already had an endowed grammar school, and Cholwell and his usher simply joined the staff of this foundation. Like all ex-chantry masters they were paid salaries by the crown after 1548, at the rates laid down in the chantry certificates. The chantry buildings and the endowments were seized by the crown, and subsequently sold off in 1549.[5] The manciple and his wife received pensions, and the feoffees lost their remaining

---

1 There was however an outstanding claim to a rent charge of 13s. by the duke of Suffolk. This, and perhaps other claims, finally reduced the master's residual income to £11. 13s. 3½d.
2 For their procedure see *ESMA*, p 274.
3 E 301/9 no 7; *The Chantry Certificates for Cornwall*, ed. L. Snell, pp 29–30; *ESR*, part ii, pp 34–5.
4 On the sequence of events see A. F. Robbins, 'John Aylworth and the Launceston Free School', *Notes & Gleanings for Devon & Cornwall*, iii (Exeter, 1890), pp 161–7.
5 *CPR 1548–9*, pp 314, 362, 364–5.

rights and powers over the school. The new situation can be seen from the account of the local receiver of crown lands, rendered at Michaelmas 1552. He paid £11. 13s. 3½d. to Cholwell, £6 to Launceston's own master Stephen Gourge, and 26s. 8d. to Cholwell's usher.[1] Cholwell was still at Launceston in 1556.[2] Nothing remained at Week, except the remains of the old buildings and the memory of the lost benefaction. It was left for Richard Carew to record the inhabitants' resentment at losing their school, 'through a petty smack only of popery', as they later, mistakenly, came to believe.[3]

WESTBURY-ON-TRYM

Gloucestershire

The grammar school at Westbury-on-Trym near Bristol was founded in 1463 by John Carpenter, bishop of Worcester, who was currently engaged in reorganising and augmenting the old college of secular priests which lay there. On 17 December he appropriated the revenues of the parish church of Clifton to provide a master at Westbury to teach the staff of the college and any others who wished to come, without charge.[4] Although the letter of appropriation represents the bishop as granting a long-standing request from the dean and chapter of Westbury, Carpenter was a notable patron of education and a school was a characteristic addition to his scheme for reforming and enlarging the foundation. He intended Westbury to be a residence for the bishop and a centre of Christian life for the largest town in his diocese, which was remote from the cathedral and the episcopal manors in Worcestershire. Westbury was only three miles north of Bristol, and Carpenter probably expected that scholars would come from the town to frequent his free school. The choristers of the college, of whom there were twelve, would have needed instruction as well.[5] The master's salary was £10 and he ranked next to the subdean among the clergy usually resident in the college.

Carpenter's choice as the first schoolmaster of Westbury was Roger Fabell, rector of Beckington in Somerset. Fabell, who already held the degree of 'master of grammar' when he took holy orders in 1450, had probably started life as a schoolmaster but, like many of his profession, deserted it for a cure of souls when opportunity offered itself. He subsequently held five moderately wealthy west-country benefices in turn, of which Beckington was the last.[6] On 28 September 1463 the bishop of Bath and Wells, at Carpenter's request, granted him four years' leave of absence from his parish in order to teach grammar at Westbury.[7] It is not clear how long he remained at the school, but he had

---

1 PRO, Exch. Land Revenue, LR 6/104/3. For Cholwell's salary see above, p 181 n 1.
2 LR 6/1/3.
3 Carew, *Survey of Cornwall*, pp 118–19.
4 Reg. Carpenter, Worcester, i, fo 183v.
5 *Bristol Great Orphan Book of Wills*, ed. T. Wadley, p 151.
6 For Fabell's career see *BRUO*, ii, 663. It should be added that he was rector of Manningford Abbots, Wilts., resigning by September 1488 (Reg. Langton, Sarum, fo 22).
7 *Reg. Bekynton, Wells*, ed. H. C. Maxwell-Lyte, i, 400–1, and for another reference to his teaching activities see ibid., ii, 540.

resigned Beckington by 1473 and re-appears briefly as vicar of White Waltham near Maidenhead from 1477 until about February 1479. In 1494 he was chaplain of Bessels Leigh near Oxford when, by an indenture dated 20 May 1495, he entered into a contract with Osney Abbey to teach grammar to the novices in return for his board, lodging and a salary of 40s. He was also to be the convent physician, to diagnose sickness and administer medicine, and was permitted to receive private patients. He must by this time have been at least in his sixties, and the agreement with Osney provided for his burial in the conventual churchyard.[1] Fabell was evidently a man of some reputation and several qualifications. At Westbury he received an adequate stipend and could also draw on the profits of his rectory. His influence probably spread wider than the country parishes which he occupied.

Five of Fabell's successors at Westbury are known by name. They occur as follows: Nicholas Barber (1498),[2] John More (1513),[3] Richard Brode (appointed in 1521),[4] John Blount (1532),[5] and John Gold (1534–5).[6] All are styled 'master' in the records where they appear, but only Barber and Brode were definitely masters of arts. Like Fabell they both seem to have held the schoolmastership with another benefice, Barber being prebendary of Kemenhall in the parish church of Leigh near Worcester, while Brode was vicar of Tytherington, Gloucestershire, at his death in 1523. Pluralities of this kind, which appear to have been tolerated in Bishop Carpenter's educational foundations, may have helped to make Westbury school more attractive to men of ambition and learning. To judge from the list of masters, which is now our only guide to the quality of the school, it compared well with the other foundations in Gloucestershire, perhaps better.

One other of Bishop Carpenter's educational benefactions was linked with Westbury College. He founded six exhibitions out of the revenues of St Anthony's Hospital, London (where he was once master) to support scholars at Oriel College, Oxford. These 'St Anthony' exhibitioners were lodged in St Mary Hall and batelled in college, receiving an allowance of 8d. a week. By 1533 when their elections are first recorded, the dean of Westbury had the nomination of at least one exhibitioner; he exercised the right for the last time in 1543.[7] It is therefore possible that a few of the scholars of Westbury proceeded to Oxford by this means. On 10 February 1544 the dean and prebendaries surrendered the college 'voluntarily' to Henry VIII, who was now bent on dissolving the collegiate churches as he had earlier done the monasteries.[8] In the case of other colleges surrendered at this time,

---

1 *Snappe's Formulary*, ed. H. E. Salter (Oxford Historical Soc., lxxx, 1924), pp 228–9.
2 To the account of his career in *BRUO*, i, 106 add his ordination as deacon on 5 June 1490 (*Reg. Myllyng, Hereford*, p 179).
3 Reg. Silvestro de Gigli, Worcester, fo 99v. He was probably still there in 1515 (ibid., fo 140v).
4 For his career see *BRUO*, iv, 71.
5 HWRO, ref. 802 (BA 2764), p 62. He is not designated as schoolmaster but appears in the right place making the appropriate contribution to the clerical subsidy.
6 Ibid., p 101; *Valor Ecclesiasticus*, ii, 434–5.
7 C. L. Shadwell, *Registrum Orielense* (2 vols, London, 1893–1902), *passim*. The dean's nominees were James Bond (1533 and 1538), Thomas Watson (1539), Thomas Abbot (1541) and Thomas Lewis (1543).
8 *Report of the Deputy Keeper of the Public Records*, vol viii appendix ii (London, 1847), p 48.

such as Ottery St Mary, arrangements were made for the preservation of public grammar schools where they existed, but this did not happen at Westbury. The reason, if not due to negligence, may have been the foundation of Bristol Cathedral School by the king in 1542. This, following hard upon Robert Thorne's benefaction, gave the city two endowed grammar schools and thereby greatly diminished the need for Westbury school to continue.[1] While admitting the fact, it is nevertheless sad to record the disappearance of what had been effectively Bristol's first endowed school, which had made, almost certainly, a valuable contribution to local education during the eighty years of its existence.

WIMBORNE MINSTER
Dorset

Wimborne Minster before the Reformation was a market town, 'meetly good and reasonably well-inhabited', on the main road from Winchester to Dorchester and a chief centre of eastern Dorset.[2] Its ancient minster had also a local importance. It was the parish church of the town and of a large surrounding area, as well as the seat of a college of secular clergy the origins of which went back to Saxon times.[3] The collegiate establishment in the later middle ages consisted of a dean and four prebendaries (not necessarily resident), a sacrist, four vicars who served the church and its dependent chapels, four secondary clerks, and four or five chantry priests. By the sixteenth century some of the chantry priests doubled as vicars. There is no evidence that the college provided education before 1500 and the foundation of an endowed school, though associated with the minster, was a private benefaction by Lady Margaret Beaufort. Her name, of course, is justly famous for educational projects. The foundress of St John's College, Cambridge, and the refoundress of Christ's, she is equally remembered for the divinity lectureships which she endowed in the two ancient universities.[4] Wimborne was her only benefaction for school education, the choice of the town being prompted by family associations. Her father John Beaufort, duke of Somerset, and her mother Margaret, née Beauchamp, were both buried in the minster, and the school their daughter founded was also a chantry dedicated to intercessions for their souls.

It was on 1 March 1497 that Lady Margaret first received licence to found a perpetual chantry in Wimborne church dedicated to Jesus and the Virgin Mary, and to endow it with lands to the value of £10 a year.[5] This sum, the salary of a schoolmaster rather than that of a simple chantry priest, suggests that she had in mind the foundation of a chantry school from the very beginning. The endowment was being assembled in 1504 when the foundress granted lands at Bourton, Curry Rivel and Langport Weston in Somerset to

1 The last dean of Westbury, John Barlow, was later associated with the founding of Robert Thorne's benefaction, Bristol Grammar School (*VCH Gloucs.*, ii, 366).
2 Leland, *Itinerary*, i, 256.
3 For the history of the college see *VCH Dorset*, ii, 107–13.
4 For her life see the *DNB* article by H. A. Tipping.
5 *CPR 1494–1509*, p 79.

two of her agents, Hugh Oldham and Sir William Knyvett, from whom they ultimately passed to the school.[1] But the foundation had not been completed when Lady Margaret died on 29 June 1509, and the task in consequence fell upon her executors, led by the bishops of Rochester and Winchester, John Fisher and Richard Fox. On 7 August 1509 Henry VIII confirmed the licence of 1497 and permitted the executors to grant lands to the chantry to the additional value of £6.[2] In the following autumn the dean of Wimborne, Henry Hornby, who was also one of the executors, paid £5 or half a year's wages to William Cox, priest and 'master of my lady's free grammar school at Wimborne'.[3] This shows that the school was open by Easter 1510, a year before its formal foundation. Hornby noted that the master would have to be paid another £5 at the following Easter, but Cox did not survive so long and Richard Hodgkins, BA, was named as chaplain and schoolmaster in the foundation deed of the school on 12 March 1511.[4]

The deed of foundation took the form of a tripartite indenture between the executors, the dean and chapter, and the chantry priests of Wimborne who probably constituted the resident clergy at the minster. The foundation was both a chantry and a school. The deed does not explain who appointed the chaplain, but other evidence suggests that the duty belonged to the dean. He was to celebrate mass each day at the altar on the south side of the Beaufort tomb for the souls of Henry VII, Lady Margaret and her parents. A solemn obit was to be kept each year on the anniversary of her death. The chaplain was also to teach grammar freely in a building opposite the house of the sacrist, according to the mode and form in use at Eton and Winchester. His stipend was to be £10 a year, and another £2 was reserved for his usher. He was given the power of administering the chantry endowments and required to render an account each year to the sacrist. Formal possession of the chantry lands in Somerset was given to Hodgkins in the following May.[5]

Little, as usual, remains of the subsequent history of the school. The next known schoolmaster, Edward Laborne, was appointed by the eighteen-year-old dean, Reginald Pole, in 1518 or 1519. A letter survives which he wrote to Pole's mother, the countess of Salisbury, on 7 August 1519 to complain about quarrels in the parish which he alleged to be the fault of the college sexton.[6] Laborne was still in office in 1535, when the clear annual

---

1 PRO, Exch. KR, E 135/3/21 fo 3. This is a register of ten deeds relating to the foundation of the school and chantry.
2 *LPFD*, i part i, no 158 (25).
3 R. F. Scott, 'Notes from the College Records', *The Eagle* (magazine of St John's College, Cambridge), xxxi (1910), pp 283–5. A William Cox was usher of Winchester College from 1500 to 1507 (*BRUO*, i, 507). Another was ordained subdeacon 3 March, deacon 24 March, priest 7 April 1509 to the title of Cerne Abbey, Dorset (Reg. Audley, Sarum, ordination lists, fos 10–11v). All three *could* be the same man.
4 E 135/3/21 fos 5–9; Dorchester, Dorset Record Office, P 204/GN1; J. Hutchins, *History of Dorset*, iii, 270–3. A Richard Hodgkins was ordained subdeacon 8 March, deacon 20 September 1505, priest 28 March 1506 to the title of Bruton Priory (Taunton, Somerset Record Office, Reg. Hadrian de Castello, Wells, fos 140, 142a).
5 E 135/3/21 fos 3v–4.
6 *LPFD*, iii part i, no 411.

value of the chantry was returned as £9. 11s. 2d.[1] When we next hear of the school in the spring of 1548 it was vacant, and the coincidental vacancy of the deanery, at a time when colleges and chantries in general were being dissolved, made the prospect of appointing a new master seem poor. Local opinion was naturally concerned for the future of the school. A memorandum attached to the Edwardian chantry certificate drew attention to the importance of the town as a thoroughfare and market, and asserted that there was no other grammar school within twelve miles.[2] The churchwardens of Wimborne, as their accounts for 1548 reveal, exerted themselves considerably on behalf of the school. References are made to a schoolmaster named Willcher who seems to have been appointed and paid on the initiative of the local community. Money was spent on the school, apparently in building repairs, and £7. 11s. 9d. was paid towards the expenses of two representatives at London 'for the suit of the school to the council'.[3]

In the event the minster survived the dissolution of colleges and chantries without much harm. The college was indeed dissolved, but the four vicars and secondaries were allowed to remain in order to serve the church and its dependent chapels. The grammar school was also preserved, but its lands were confiscated and the crown took over the duty of paying the master's stipend which was rated in 1548 as £10. 2s. 11d.[4] Willcher did not get the vacant mastership because Edward VI's tutor, John Cheke, had a candidate of his own to recommend. This was Simon Smith, a Cambridge MA and an adherent of the Reformation, which gave him a considerable advantage. He was appointed as from Lady Day 1548, but he did not occupy the position for long.[5] By Michaelmas 1551 he had been succeeded by Michael Everton who was paid for the next twelve months.[6] Everton in turn gave way at Michaelmas 1552 to William Gibson, who continued to hold office until at least 1559.[7] Finally in 1563 the inhabitants successfully petitioned the queen to establish church and school upon a new foundation. A corporation of twelve governors was set up, lands were granted to them, and they were made responsible for appointing the grammar masters. Something of Lady Margaret's foundation nevertheless survived, both in the use of the old schoolhouse and in the stipulation that the teaching there should follow the usage of Eton or Winchester.[8]

WINCHCOMBE
Gloucestershire

The grammar school at Winchcombe was founded from a stock of money originally designed for quite different purposes by Lady Joan Huddleston in 1518. The younger

1 *Valor Ecclesiasticus*, i, 275.
2 E 301/16 no 106; *ESR*, part ii, p 56.
3 Dorset Record Office, Wimborne Minster Churchwardens' Accounts, P 204/CW35 p 152; Hutchins, *History of Dorset*, iii, 261.
4 E 301/23; *ESR*, part ii, p 57.
5 PRO, Exch. Land Revenue, LR 6/104/2.
6 LR 6/104/3.
7 LR 6/104/4; LR 6/12/1-5.
8 *CPR 1560-3*, pp 577-9.

daughter and co-heiress of Sir Miles Stapleton of Ingham, Norfolk, she was twice married: first to Christopher Harcourt of Long Combe, Oxfordshire,[1] and afterwards to Sir John Huddleston, by each of whom she had male issue. Her second husband, originally of Millom Castle in Cumberland, moved south to become constable of Sudeley Castle near Winchcombe from 1478 to 1486, and again from 1505 to 1510, serving also as sheriff of his newly adopted county. He died on 1 January 1512 in the abbey of Hailes near Sudeley and was buried there.[2] As he lay on his deathbed, he made a final nuncupative will expressing remorse for having induced his wife to give her inherited lands to their son John, contrary to the entails made by her ancestors, and he besought his son to renounce his claim to the property.[3] He also ordered that his wife should have a life interest in his manor of Temple Guiting, unless she remarried, and that on her death or remarriage it should be sold by his executors and the profits applied for the health of their two souls. The will was proved by two of the executors, Sir Robert Southwell and Christopher Urswick, archdeacon of Oxford, on 30 January, but the third, John Daston, renounced, and caused much trouble by disputing what was done later.

Southwell dying soon afterwards, Urswick and Lady Joan made over the manor of Guiting to Richard Fox, bishop of Winchester, who was then assembling properties with which to endow his new college of Corpus Christi in Oxford. Fox and Urswick were old acquaintances who had both attended Henry VII during his insecure exile in France. They followed him to Bosworth Field, and afterwards rose high in his service.[4] On 5 December 1514 Fox bought Lady Joan's life interest in Guiting for £200 and agreed to pay £750 to Urswick for the reversion of the manor after her death. Urswick however accepted only £550 and waived the balance of £200 on condition that one of the monks of Winchester (for whom Corpus Christi was at that time intended) should say a daily mass in the college chapel for the souls of Sir John and Lady Joan. It was also agreed that the president and scholars of the college should keep an obit for them each 2 January and sing a requiem mass on the following day.[5] Although Fox paid a large sum for Guiting and had to engage in further litigation with Sir John's heirs and the recalcitrant executor, the purchase was of considerable value[6] and the £200 which Urswick remitted to the college entitles it to be

1 *CFR 1461–71*, p 193.
2 For the lives of John and Joan Huddleston see C. R. Huddleston, 'Sir John Huddleston, Constable of Sudeley', *TBGAS*, xlviii (1926), pp 117–132, and H. S. Cowper, 'Millom Castle and the Hudlestons', *Trans. Cumberland & Westmorland Antiquarian & Archaeological Soc.*, new series xxiv (1924), pp 181–234.
3 For Sir John's will see PRO, Prob 11/17 (PCC 21 Fettiplace).
4 For Urswick see *BRUO*, iii, 1935–6. He was himself a benefactor of education, leaving money by his will in 1521 to Lancaster school and to provide exhibitions for poor scholars (PRO, Prob 11/20 (PCC 23 Maynwaryng)). There also survives in the cathedral library at Wells a beautiful psalter which Urswick commissioned at his own expense in 1514 from Peter Meghen of Hertogenbosch, and presented to Hailes Abbey in memory of Sir John and Lady Joan Huddleston.
5 Oxford, Corpus Christi College, Twyne Transcripts, vol xxi, pp 93–111.
6 In 1535 the manor of Temple Guiting with its outlying properties was worth over £52 a year, but this probably included additional purchases of land to that of 1514 (*Valor Ecclesiasticus*, ii, 244–5).

regarded as a benefaction. His part in the transaction however makes it difficult to determine whether the Huddlestons themselves had much interest in education. Corpus Christi was ultimately established as a college of secular clerks, but in 1535 two priests were singing there daily for the souls of the Huddlestons at a salary of £4 each.[1]

Lady Joan continued her husband's association with Hailes Abbey. She paid for the repair of the church roof and maintained good relations both with the abbot, Anthony Melton, and his Benedictine neighbour, Richard Kidderminster, who ruled at Winchcombe. When she made her will on 18 April 1518, Melton was named supervisor, and Kidderminster an executor together with William Tracy of Toddington, a local gentleman who later gained notoriety as a heretic.[2] In her will she left a hundred marks (£66. 13s. 4d.) to build and maintain an almshouse in Winchcombe for thirteen poor men, but after her death in the summer of 1519, the executors found their resources too small for the project. She had provided no site for the almshouse, nor given any lands to endow it, and although they had in hand a further £400 as the residue of her goods after the discharge of legacies and funeral expenses, the annual income of the sum could not amount to much more than £20, and was clearly inadequate. Hence the executors, acting as they said on the advice of learned men in both the laws spiritual and temporal, and with the consent of the ordinary, decided to apply the money in hand to some other good deed of charity as a memorial to her soul.[3] The decision to found a grammar school may be properly ascribed to Richard Kidderminster, the enlightened and capable abbot of Winchcombe.[4] His house was already trustee of the grammar school at Cirencester.[5] With the agreement of Hailes Abbey, Kidderminster and his monks by an indenture dated 7 September 1521, undertook to purchase lands and tenements to the yearly value of £21. 6s. 8d., and to obtain the king's licence for the foundation of a school and schoolhouse in Winchcombe and the maintenance of six choristers in the abbey.[6] The abbot and convent of Hailes were named as conservators of the endowment and had the duty of seeing that the terms of the indenture were properly observed.

The indenture provided for a schoolmaster appointed and removable by the abbots of Winchcombe. He was to rule the school according to such statutes as they might devise, and to teach all who came to him for nothing, except for rewards freely offered. He was to be continually resident, apparently teaching the school at all times except for the four weeks of his annual holiday or if school attendance was disrupted by plague or

---

1 Ibid., p 245. Their obits were also observed at Rewley Abbey (ibid., p 255).
2 For Lady Joan's will see PRO, Prob 11/19 (PCC 18 Ayloffe).
3 The action of the executors is explained in the indenture founding the school, preserved in PRO, Exch. Land Revenue, LR 6/29/2. William Tracy proved Lady Joan's will on 10 June 1519, and a second probate was granted on 4 August to Richard Kidderminster.
4 For Kidderminster's life see *BRUO*, ii, 1047. The educational reforms he made in the abbey are described by W. A. Pantin, 'Abbot Kidderminster and Monastic Studies', *Downside Review*, xlvii (1929), pp 199–211.
5 See above, p 129.
6 The indenture survives from the enrolment of 1567 (PRO, Exch. Land Revenue, LR 6/29/2).

sickness.[1] His stipend was fixed at £6. 13s. 4d. *per annum* together with an annual gown or else 20s. He was also promised a chamber, either within or without the monastery, four loads of firewood, and meat and drink in the abbey according to his degree. The abbot covenanted that £10 of the endowment should always be applied to the grammar school and its master, and this is doubtless the cause of the apparent disparity between references to the master's salary, which is sometimes said to be ten marks and sometimes £10, which would include the value of the board and lodging provided. In 1535 the sum of £21.6s. 8d. was being duly expended to support the master of the grammar school and six boys of the monastery who were being taught in grammar and song. They probably received instruction in song from the master of the choristers in the abbey, who was paid something from the endowment as well. Obits for Sir John and Lady Joan were also maintained at Hailes and Winchcombe with distributions of bread to the poor.[2]

One 'Sir Christopher' was schoolmaster in 1532.[3] This was Christopher Glanfield, instituted as chaplain of St Mary's chantry in the parish church on 4 March 1533, from which he resigned shortly before September 1542.[4] We learn from a letter of 1536 to Thomas Cromwell from the Reformist curate of Winchcombe, Anthony Saunders, that Glanfield fell foul of Richard Mounslow, Kidderminster's successor as abbot. In Saunders' view the schoolmaster, who 'hath a chantry in the parish church', was a man 'discreet and well-learned in the truth', who had been of great assistance in setting forth the gospel and edifying the people. The abbot however, it was alleged, had retaliated by diminishing the schoolmaster's wage, 'which was wont to be as good as £10 stipend by the year, to bare 40s'. Moreover he had set the parish against him and forbidden him to deputise for the parish priest at services in Winchcombe church on pain of a shilling fine for each occasion. Cromwell's assistance was solicited in the matter, but the abbot could fairly have replied that the duties of a schoolmaster should lie first and foremost in his school.[5]

The abbey of Winchcombe was dissolved on 23 December 1539. Nothing is then heard of the school until on 13 February 1542 George Broke, master of the free grammar school of Winchcombe, having recited the emoluments of his office in similar terms to the indenture of 1521, secured a pension from the court of Augmentations, as if he had been retained for life like the other monastic servants. The court awarded him the schoolhouse of Winchcombe, the master's chamber and an annuity of £5 for life. Furthermore he was exonerated from teaching for nothing and permitted to charge his pupils the fees that were usually taken in other schools. The grant mentions that Broke had taught the school since Michael-

---

1 The enrolment is not clear about the master's period of residence, owing to the loss of a line or two from the original.
2 *Valor Ecclesiasticus*, ii, 459.
3 HWRO, ref. 802, pp 52, 93.
4 Reg Ghinucci, Worcester, fo 56; Reg. Bell, Worcester, fo 25v. Christopher Glanfield was ordained subdeacon on 28 March, deacon 22 May, 1529 (Reg. Morton, Worcester, appended folios).
5 PRO, State Papers Domestic, SP 1/89 no 171; *LPFD*, viii, no 171. The suggested date, 3 February 1535, is almost certainly a year too early, since the circumstances of Saunders' appointment by Cromwell to be curate and lecturer at Winchcombe are characteristic of the summer of 1535.

mas 1541 and recompensed him accordingly, but how it had survived during the previous two years is uncertain.[1]

This curious decision, which had an exact parallel at Bruton in Somerset,[2] failed to recognise the separate existence of the school from the monastery. The contemporary schoolmaster received personal compensation, but free schooling ceased and schooling of any kind was made dependent on Broke's own pleasure. The sequel—which remains equally enigmatical—is that the decision was never carried out. At Michaelmas 1543 Anthony Aylworth, the king's bailiff of the lands of the late monastery of Winchcombe, accounted for £20, paid not to Broke but to a new figure, Humphrey Dick, master of the 'common school' of Winchcombe, in respect of two years of teaching. The authority for the grant is given as a decree in the court of Augmentations during the thirty-third year of Henry VIII (April 1541 to April 1542), but no sign of this remains except the grant to Broke.[3] By some means unknown the school was therefore saved, although the schoolhouse which is later stated to have been alienated was probably lost at this time. Humphrey Dick continued to be paid an annual stipend of £10 by the king's receiver until Michaelmas 1560. He then apparently resigned his place to Robert Hide, who was paid from 1561 to 1563. Dick returned from Michaelmas 1563 to Michaelmas 1566 when he was finally succeeded by Thomas Angel, on whose appointment the whole of the original indenture of 1521 was engrossed upon the account roll of the receiver of the Winchcombe lands. This shows that the incumbency of Dick and his successors represents the true continuation of the old school.[4]

WOTTON-UNDER-EDGE

Gloucestershire

The free grammar school of Wotton-under-Edge, which we have seen possessed a school as early as the late thirteenth century,[5] was founded by Lady Katherine Berkeley who died in 1385. Probably born in the second decade of the fourteenth century, she was the daughter of Sir John Clevedon by his second wife Emma. Her inheritance seems to have comprised some modest property at Clevelode in Worcestershire, the manors of Low Ham, Ham Burci and a quarter of Exton in Somerset, and the patronage of Clevelode chapel and Exton church.[6] Her first husband was Sir Peter Veel, lord of the manor of Charfield in Gloucester-

1 PRO, Exch. Augm., Misc. Books, E 315/101 fo 152.
2 See above, pp 122–3.
3 PRO, Special Collections, Ministers Accounts, SC 6, Henry VIII/1243 fo 68. See also /1244 fo 65, /1245 fo 46, /1246 fo 35.
4 PRO, Exch. Land Revenue, LR 6/28/1–11, 6/29/1–2. Robert Hide first appears in 1561-2 (LR 6/28/8), but the previous year's account seems to be missing, and it is not known whether Hide or Dick was then master. A. F. Leach (*VCH Gloucs.*, ii, 421), although one of the first to use these accounts, is quite inaccurate in his references to the schoolmasters and their salaries.
5 See above, p 109.
6 John Smith, *Lives of the Berkeleys*, ed. Sir J. Maclean, i, 346. See also Katherine's inquisition *post mortem* (PRO, C 136/38/8; *Calendarium Inquisitionum post mortem*, vol iii (Record Commission, 1821), p 64).

shire and of other lands in Wiltshire, Somerset and Devon, who already had an heir by a former wife. His son by Katherine, named John, was born in 1337 and there was also a daughter, Joan. But early in 1343 Sir Peter was drowned in the sea, and his lands were thereupon divided between his elder son who took Charfield, and Katherine who received property in Wiltshire as her dower, including the manors of Ablington and Alton as well as lands in Plympton, Devon. All these ultimately passed to the elder son, the younger Peter Veel. She also held the manor of Penleigh and the patronage of Alton church for life, with reversion to her children. After her son's death in childhood the heiress was her daughter Joan, who married Henry Moigne and whose son Sir John Moigne received them after his grandmother's death.[1]

Katherine remained a widow for a little over four years before she married Thomas, Lord Berkeley, on 30 May 1347 at Charfield.[2] Like her first husband, Sir Thomas, who was then in his mid-fifties, was a widower with a son nearly out of his nonage, and Katherine could offer him the double attraction of her own inheritance and her dower lands. The marriage lasted fourteen years and produced four sons, but only the youngest, John Berkeley, survived childhood. He was born at Wotton on 21 January 1352.[3] Sir Thomas died on 27 October 1361 and for the remaining twenty-three years of her life Katherine lived as a widow at Wotton. She held several Gloucestershire manors by way of dower, including those of Wotton, Symond's Hall and Cam, a moiety of Compton Greenfield, the chapel there and the patronage of Wotton church. Other lands had been settled upon her for life by Sir Thomas with remainder to their children, and these comprised the manors of Tockington with a chapel, Over with a chantry, and Beverstone with a castle. They eventually formed the endowment of her son John and his descendants.[4]

Her widowhood, like that of many of her class, was characterised by devotional and charitable projects. In 1363 we hear of her going on a pilgrimage beyond the seas—to Spain, perhaps, or Rome.[5] To the Cistercian monks of Kingswood near Wotton she is said to have given a yearly pension of six marks, 'and when she died many rich gifts, and endowed them with fair possessions of her own purchase'.[6] In 1384 she paid twenty marks for a royal licence to found a chantry at the altar of St Andrew in Berkeley church for a chaplain praying for her good estate and for the souls of her ancestors.[7] But the 'House of Scholars' which she founded in Wotton is for us her most important achievement. Not only was it an unusual benefaction for its time, compared with which her other activities were merely commonplace. It also gives her credit from the probability that it was the

---

1 *Cal. Inquisitions Post Mortem*, viii, no 466, pp 311–12.
2 Smith, op. cit., i, 346.
3 Smith, *Lives of the Berkeleys*, i, 348. The other children were Thomas, born 7 June 1348 who died the same year; Maurice, born 27 May 1349; and Edmund, born at Berkeley on 10 July 1350. Both the latter were still alive in 1355 but died in youth.
4 PRO, Chancery, Inquisitions Post Mortem, C 136/38/8; *Calendarium Inquisitionum post mortem*, iii, 64.
5 *CPR 1361–4*, p 335.
6 Smith, op. cit., i, 347, quoting a register of Kingswood Abbey then in Berkeley castle.
7 PRO, Chancery, Inquisitions ad quod Dampnum, C 143/402/15; *CPR 1381–5*, p 415.

earliest example of that characteristic educational benefaction of the later middle ages—the endowed chantry school. It is worth our while to pause and ask how such a foundation came to be made.

We know too little about Katherine herself to penetrate the origins of her interests in schools. But it is not a surprising interest for one of her class. The Berkeleys, like other noble families of the time, were cultivated, literate people. Katherine's step-grandson Thomas, head of the family from 1368 to 1417, was an avid reader not merely of light literature but of the learned treatises on history, war and science which John Trevisa translated from Latin into English for his use.[1] The Berkeleys kept company with important clerics and men of affairs, and must have been well acquainted with the world of learning. Wotton, strange though it now may seem, was an obvious place for an educational benefaction. Its thirteenth-century school may still have been in existence. One attempt had already been made to put it on a sound footing shortly after Katherine's marriage into the Berkeley family. On 3 March 1349 a royal licence was given to certain 'chaplains and brethren of the order of the Holy Cross' to acquire a dwelling place in Wotton, together with land and rent worth £10 a year, in order to establish religious worship and to keep a free school.[2] These brethren have usually been identified with the small international order of Crutched Friars, but this order had no special connection either with the area or with education. The clerics concerned may have come from any of the numerous communities who wore the cross as a badge and lived under the rule of St Augustine.[3] The projected foundation, of which by the way nothing else is ever heard, can hardly have been planned without the knowledge and consent of the Berkeleys. This in turn suggests that the interest in Wotton school was shared by the family as a whole, not by Katherine alone.

Her foundation occupies an important place in the constitutional development of English schools. Endowments for school education in the thirteenth century had generally taken the form of exhibitions to provide scholars with all or some of the cost of their board, lodging and clothes while attending school. During the fourteenth century a new kind of benefaction was evolving, whereby instead a schoolmaster was endowed to teach for nothing. Katherine's foundation followed the new development but retained something of the old. There was a schoolmaster who taught gratis, but also two scholars who received the cost of their board and lodging. The schoolmasters hitherto endowed by fourteenth-century benefactors had all been attached to colleges, at the universities or elsewhere, and had been primarily intended for the members of those colleges. The originality of Katherine's scheme was that the endowed schoolmaster became at last an entity in his own right and offered free education to *any* member of the public who cared to come to his school. This kind of small endowed school became one of the models, perhaps the

1 On Trevisa see *BRUO*, iii, 1903–4.
2 PRO, Chancery, Patent Rolls, C 66/227 m 21; *CPR 1348–50*, p 268.
3 E.g. St Mark's Hospital, Bristol, a house with which the Berkeleys had connections, the members of which were sometimes called 'crutched friars' (*Somerset Medieval Wills*, ed. F. W. Weaver, vol i (Somerset Record Soc., xvi, 1901), p 329).

archetype itself, for dozens of similar foundations all over England during the following centuries.[1]

The endowment of Wotton school took place in 1384. It was carried out by Katherine and her two agents, the chaplains Walter Burnell and William Pendock, with the approval of Lord Berkeley. Application having been made for a licence to grant land in mortmain, the inquisition *ad quod dampnum* was held on 16 May and returned a favourable verdict.[2] Accordingly on 16 June the two chaplains secured the royal licence for a fee of £20 to build a schoolhouse in Wotton and to alienate certain lands to a master and scholars, to be held by them according to ordinances yet to be made.[3] The endowment included a curtilage of two acres in Wotton near the church, upon which the schoolhouse was to be built, and a total of 145 acres of lands with tofts and messuages, a mill and 10s. 7½d. in rent, lying in Nibley, Stancombe and Woodmancote two or three miles north of Wotton. The charter founding the school was issued on 20 October, and it was witnessed by the local chivalry: Thomas Lord Berkeley; John Berkeley, Katherine's surviving son; Peter and Thomas Veel, her relatives by her first marriage; Thomas Fitz-Nichol and Edmund Bradestone. The bishop of Worcester did not give his confirmation to the foundation until 29 December 1390.[4]

Katherine justified her foundation by remarking that many who wished to be taught grammar, the foundation of all the liberal arts, were hindered by poverty and lack of means. The schoolmaster of Wotton and his successors were therefore to receive with kindness all who came to them and give teaching without taking any fees. Two poor scholars who wished to learn grammar were also to be supported on the foundation. The master was to be a priest so that he could carry out the chantry duties, which involved the celebration of mass in the chapel of St Katherine in the manor house of Wotton whenever the lord and lady of the manor were in residence, and in the parish church during their absence. He was to pray for the souls of Katherine, her parents, her husbands, her stepson Thomas, Lord Berkeley, her own son Sir John Berkeley, and all their wives. The master was to have control of the possessions of the house, but might not alienate them save in the full court of the homage of the lordship, with the assent of the patron of the school or his steward. The master was to keep the lands and their buildings in good repair and maintain the two poor scholars in food and drink, lodging and any other necessaries except shoes and clothing. The rest of the income was reserved for his own use and that of the foundation, but his exact salary was not specified.

The patronage of the chantry was reserved to Thomas, Lord Berkeley, the head of the family, and his descendants in the male line. If these failed it was to pass to Katherine's son

---

1 Further to this subject see *ESMA*, pp 184–90.
2 PRO, C 143/402/14.
3 *CPR 1381–5*, pp 413–14.
4 The documents concerning the foundation are calendared and partly transcribed in *Reg. Wakefeld, Worcester*, ed. W. P. Marett (Worcestershire Historical Soc., new series, viii, 1972), pp 80–9. Extracts from the statutes are printed and translated in A. F. Leach, *Educational Charters and Documents, 598–1909* (Cambridge, 1911), pp 330–41.

John and his heirs. Careful clauses made provision for yet other possibilities. If the heirs failed entirely, the patronage was to belong to the lord of the manor of Wotton. If the patron was a minor in the king's wardship, the right passed to the abbot of St Augustine's, Bristol, during the interim, this being a house with which the Berkeley family had close connections. On the death or resignation of the master, the patron was to present a qualified successor quickly, and some other suitable person, not necessarily a priest, should rule the school in the meantime. During vacancies the possessions of the school were entrusted to the reeve of Wotton, who was to maintain the two poor scholars from the profits. The master could also be removed for persistent disobedience to the statutes, but if he were unable through age or infirmity either to discharge his duties or provide a deputy, he was to retire with a pension of five marks a year.

The two 'poor and indigent scholars wishing to learn grammar' were not to be aged more than ten at their admission, although they might in exceptional cases be admitted when older. The first two scholars were named as John Beenleye and Walter Morkyn. They and their successors were to stay at school for six years, and to be obedient to the master. He was not to put them to any office or service but to compel them to devote all their time to study and learning. They could be expelled only under the supervision of the patron or his steward, and only then if continually disobedient. The two scholars had in fact more status than mere schoolboys, and they were joined with the master 'as in a college' (*collegialiter*). In later times the foundation was usually called 'The House of Scholars of Wotton'. No other directions were given about the management of the school except with respect to terms and holidays. The year was arranged to include four vacations, instead of the customary practice of teaching on all except holy days. The vacations lasted from 21 December until 7 January; from Palm Sunday until Low Sunday; from the vigil of Pentecost until the morrow of the Trinity; and from 1 August until 14 September, a total of eleven weeks in all. The holidays are strikingly similar to those of today.

Katherine's choice as the first schoolmaster was a cleric named John Stone. He seems to have been a protégé of hers, and may have been educated specifically in order to teach the school. In 1380, when he was still only a clerk in minor orders, she presented him to the rectory of Alton near Figheldean in Wiltshire, a small parish and possibly only a sinecure. Since he is termed an MA four years later, it is likely that he was currently reading the arts course at Oxford. He probably started to teach at Wotton in the autumn of 1384, since he is mentioned in the foundation statutes and had resigned from Alton by the following January. His formal institution, however, as master of the House of Scholars did not take place until August 1387.[1] Katherine herself survived the inauguration of her school by less than a year, for she died on 13 March 1385 and was buried beside her second husband in

---

[1] John Stone (Stones), 'clerk', was instituted as rector of Alton on 18 March 1380 and resigned by January 1385 (Reg. Erghum, Sarum, institutions fos 33, 66). He was ordained deacon and priest, probably in 1380, to the title of Alton (*Reg. Wakefield, Worcester*, pp 179, 181, where Alton is incorrectly identified with Alton Barnes). He is mentioned as master of Wotton and MA in the statutes of October 1384 (ibid., p 81), was formally instituted on 3 August 1387 (ibid., p 57), and resigned by September 1404 (Reg. Clifford, Worcester, fo 79).

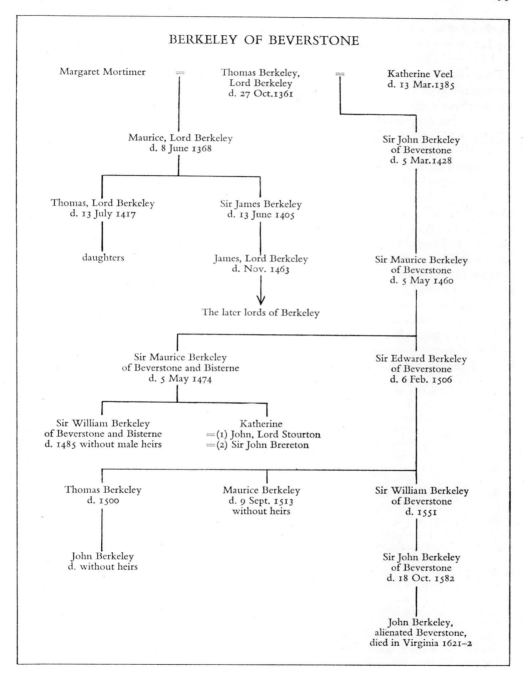

Berkeley church. Her dower lands were then dispersed, but her own property was inherited by her only surviving son, John Berkeley, who established himself at Beverstone Castle and fathered a line of heirs. It was to this branch of the Berkeley family that the patronage of the school passed in 1417, when Lord Thomas died without leaving male issue. Its members continued to exercise the right until after the Reformation, except in 1511 when the heir was a minor.

John Stone resigned after twenty years of service in 1404, and was succeeded by William Hazleton. He was merely a clerk and did not proceed to major orders until the following year.[1] Very little can be said of him or any of his pre-Reformation successors, except that they were chaplains who differed little from the other secular clergy of the area, and that several of them left over the years to occupy rectories and vicarages of their own. Thus John James resigned the school in 1416 on securing the neighbouring rectory of Newington Bagpath,[2] and in 1423 William Hogyn exchanged benefices with Thomas Joye, rector of Bromham in Wiltshire.[3] John Paradise was already a local chaplain when he was instituted in 1427, but he held the school for thirty years before retiring with a pension.[4] His two successors, Walter Frocester[5] and Robert Haynes,[6] were probably also local men. The former was an Oxford master who had studied canon law. Another graduate was Master John Packer who ruled the school from 1487 to 1493. The patron, Sir Edward Berkeley, then presented him to the free chapel of Tockington, but Packer was by this time a bachelor of both laws and these small benefices cannot represent the whole of his activities.[7] He was followed by John Chilcote, an Oxford MA and formerly a fellow of All Souls where he had been elected for Somerset. He remained at Wotton for seventeen years and ultimately secured another benefice at Shilton in Oxfordshire.[8]

1 William Hazleton was ordained acolyte and subdeacon on 19 September 1405, deacon on 18 December 1406, to the title of the House of Scholars of Wotton, of which he was styled warden or master (ibid., fos 42v, 43, 47).
2 John James was instituted as rector of Newington Bagpath on 16 February 1416, and resigned by April 1433 (Reg. Peverel, Worcester, fo 75; Reg. Polton, Worcester, fo 144v).
3 Thomas Joye was instituted as rector of Bromham on 25 November 1419 and exchanged with William Hogyn on 21 August 1423 (Reg. Chandler, Sarum, fos 27v, 65; Reg. Morgan, Worcester, ii, fo 23). Hogyn is probably the same as William Hoghton, rector of Bromham, who had died by the next institution in October 1451 (Reg. Beauchamp, Sarum, fo 8v).
4 John Paradise, chaplain, was granted lands in Sapperton, Gloucs., by John and Christina Evesham on 18 February 1410 (*Cat. Ancient Deeds*, ii, 376).
5 Walter Frocester supplicated for B Can L at Oxford on 11 November 1449 (*BRUO*, ii, p 732). On 24 October 1456 he was commissioned to prove the testament of John Bailey of Wotton (*Reg. Bourgchier, Canterbury*, ed. F. R. du Boulay (Canterbury & York Soc., liv, 1957), p 178).
6 Robert Haynes was ordained subdeacon to the title of Longbridge Hospital, Berkeley, on 26 May 1453 (*Reg. Bekynton, Wells*, ii, 498).
7 John Packer (or Parker) was B Can & C L by 24 January 1493 when instituted to the free chapel of Tockington, Gloucs., resigned by April 1499 (Reg. Morton, Worcester, fo 47v; Reg. Silvestro de Gigli, Worcester, fo 10). A John Parker, B Can & C L was instituted to the vicarage of Batheaston, Som., 11 July 1503, still there in 1535 (*Reg. King, Wells*, p 81; *Valor Ecclesiasticus*, i, 179). Another was vicar of Thame, Oxon., 7 March 1504, resigned by February 1536 (*BRUO*, iii, 1427).
8 For John Chilcote see *BRUO*, i, 414.

There can be little doubt that the school flourished for most of the fifteenth century. It was able to attract graduate masters and the average length of service was about ten years, longer than at Winchester or Eton. Two other pieces of evidence suggest that Wotton had an influence upon schools elsewhere in Gloucestershire. A grammatical miscellany used in the New Gate grammar school in Bristol during the 1420s includes some sentences for translation headed 'Wotton' which may have come from Wotton school.[1] Furthermore in 1446, the statutes of Newland, the second school to be endowed in Gloucestershire, reproduced those of Wotton at several points.[2]

Robert Coldwell, the last of the pre-Reformation masters, was born in about 1488 and instituted on 24 April 1511 probably soon after coming down from university with a BA degree. As the statutes provided, he was presented by the abbot of St Augustine's because of the minority of the Berkeley heir. The rest of his life was spent at Wotton where he was schoolmaster for over forty years. In 1546 the chantry commissioners of Henry VIII investigated the school, which was then called the Katherine Veel Free School, probably to distinguish the foundress from the other Katherines of the Berkeley family. The income was said to be £17. 15s. 2d. of which the master received £10 and a single scholar £4.[3] Neither the commissioners of 1546 nor those who followed them two years later were told of the chantry duties which the statutes had prescribed. Although the Chantry Act of 1547 guaranteed the continuity of foundations like Wotton, the real character of the school was not made clear at the time, and this later made possible the charge that it was a concealed chantry. When such allegations were made early in Elizabeth's reign, the patron, Sir John Berkeley of Beverstone, was able to protect the school, but they continued into the seventeenth century and seriously troubled its subsequent history.

The chantry certificate of 1548 was not complimentary about Coldwell, then aged sixty. He was described as 'unwieldy' or infirm and 'neither meet in discipline nor behaviour'.[4] Indeed his long career was about to end in scandal. On 12 July 1552 he was accused in Gloucester Consistory Court of fornication with Lycetta Hedges, a young woman whom he was rumoured to be keeping secretly in the schoolhouse. Coldwell denied the charge but did not appear and was then suspended on 22 September. His brother William came in his place to plead that he was ill and suffering from paralysis, so the court gave Robert a further fortnight to appear and restored him in the meantime. In the end Coldwell was either put out or resigned, for his successor Robert Knight had been installed by May 1553 and we are told that the old schoolmaster retired to live with the Adams family, dying sometime during Queen Mary's reign.[5]

1 See above, p 40.
2 See above, p 161.
3 In 1535 the House of Scholars was worth £11. 12s. 6½d. (*Valor Ecclesiasticus*, ii, 494). In 1546 the master's income was £10. 1s. 7¼d., and rents and tenths amounted to £3. 13s. 6¾d. (PRO, Exch. Augm., Chantry Certificates, E 301/21 no 49; *ESR,* part ii, p 79).
4 E 301/22 no 37; *ESR,* part ii, pp 79–80.
5 Gloucester Public Library, Hockaday Abstracts, Wotton, 1552–3, quoting Gloucester Diocesan Records 6, pp 141, 143, 153; and PRO, Exch. First Fruits, Composition Books, E 334 vol 4 fo 118.

In 1616 attempts were once more being made to prove that Wotton School was a chantry under the act of 1547, and a few octogenarian survivors who had been at school in Coldwell's time were assembled to give evidence on the matter.[1] One of the erstwhile scholars had become parish clerk of Wotton while another filled the same position at Berkeley. A third was clerk to Sir Thomas Throgmorton. There were two broadweavers (Leland had found Wotton occupied with the cloth trade), a chapman and two unspecified yeomen. Their evidence gives a last glimpse of life in the school in the days before the dissolution of the chantries. According to John More the first and fullest witness, the schoolhouse had been formerly called the chantry-house and Sir Robert Coldwell the 'morrow mass priest'. He had been accustomed to say mass on Wednesdays, Fridays, Sundays and holy days at ten o'clock in winter and at six or seven in summer within the north-east aisle of Wotton church, which was enclosed and had a door leading into it. On All Souls Day a solemn mass for 'divers spirits' was said in another chapel for all the founders and benefactors of the school. More justified his recollections by asserting that he had often been one of the two boys who assisted Sir Robert in his masses, especially in the *Confiteor* and *Oremus pro Animabus*, kneeling in their surplices on cushions on either side of the master. For a penny Sir Robert would include the names of any other persons in his intercessions, and the boys were given the odd penny. He also remembered that the tenants of the school lands came to a court held by the master in the schoolhouse once every two years or so, where they paid their rents and fines. Thomas Cole of Wotton alleged that he had also helped in the masses, and that the school had usually numbered about twenty or thirty scholars, who seldom stayed for more than seven or eight years but were then placed abroad. Another deponent recalled that Sir Robert was held in greater estimation than the other two priests in Wotton, and Thomas Hughes, who remembered the old schoolmaster's burial, claimed to have held part of his books and papers for some time afterwards. With these last recollections the history of Wotton school before the Reformation comes to an end.

[1] PRO, Exch. KR, Depositions, E 134/14 James I, Mich. no 28, Gloucester. The depositions were taken at Stone, Gloucs., on 14 July 1616 and at Wotton on 5 September 1616.

SCHOOLMASTERS OF WOTTON-UNDER-EDGE

		Instituted	Patron
1	John Stone, MA	3 Aug 1387 res. by Sept 1404	Thomas, Lord Berkeley
2	William Hazleton	23 Sept 1404 died by Oct 1407	The same
3	John Seman	26 Oct 1407	The same
4	John James	res. by Feb 1416	
5	William Clifton, *Mag.*	16 Feb 1416	The same

6	William Hogyn	res. by Aug 1423	
7	Thomas Joye	21 Aug 1423 res. by Jun 1427	Sir John Berkeley
8	John Paradise	2 Jun 1427 res. by Dec 1456	The same
9	Walter Frocester, *Mag.*	18 Dec 1456 died by Sept 1460	Sir Maurice Berkeley (the elder)
10	Robert Haynes	30 Sept 1460 died by Jan 1461	Maurice Berkeley, esq. (the younger)
11	John Dale	7 Jan 1461 res. by Nov 1462	The same
12	John Towen	5 Nov 1462 res. by Jul 1465	The same
13	Richard West	30 Jul 1465 res. by Jul 1487	The same
14	John Packer, B Can & C L	2 Jul 1487 res. by Jul 1493	Edward Berkeley, esq.
15	John Chilcote, MA	23 Jul 1493 res. by Apr 1511	The same
16	Robert Coldwell, BA	24 Apr 1511 res. by May 1553	Abbot of St Augustine's, Bristol.

1 *Reg. Wakefeld, Worcester,* ed. W. P. Marett, p 57.
2 Reg. Clifford, Worcester, fo 79.
3 *Reg. Sede Vacante, Worcester,* ed. J. W. Willis-Bund, part iv, 387.
4 Reg. Peverel, Worcester, fo 75.
5 Ibid.
6 Reg. Morgan, Worcester, ii, fo 23.
7 Ibid.
8 Reg. Polton, Worcester, fo 19.
9 Reg. Carpenter, Worcester, i, fo 140.
10 Ibid., fo 155v.
11 Ibid., fo 157.
12 Ibid., fo 175.
13 Ibid., fo 189v.
14 Reg. Morton, Worcester, fo 19.
15 Ibid., fo 52.
16 Reg. Silvestro de Gigli, Worcester, fo 68; PRO, Exch. First Fruits, Composition Books, E **334/4** fo 118.

4
Education in Religious Houses

AMESBURY, Wiltshire,
Priory of Benedictine Nuns

The priory boarded several children of noble birth during the early fourteenth century. Eleanor, daughter of Edward I, aged four, died in the priory in 1311 and Joan, daughter of Piers Gaveston, did so in 1325 at the age of fifteen. Later, in 1333–4, Isabel, daughter of Henry earl of Lancaster had several children living with her in the priory.[1]

BATH, Somerset
Benedictine Cathedral Priory

On 8 January 1532 William Holloway, prior of Bath appointed John Pitt, a senior monk of the house, to the vacant office of schoolmaster (of the novices) at an annual stipend of £4. On 10 February 1543 he was awarded a pension of the same sum by the court of Augmentations.[2]

BRIDGWATER, Somerset
Franciscan Friars

Foreign friars, probably students, appear at the convent during the fifteenth century.[3]

BRIDGWATER
St John's Hospital

In 1298 the master and brethren undertook to maintain thirteen scholars fit for instruction in grammar, who probably attended the town school, and to feed seven poor scholars daily from that school. Thirteen boys were still being supported in the house in 1535.[4]

---

1 *VCH Wilts.*, iii, 248–9.
2 PRO, Exch. Augm., Miscellaneous Books, E 315/103 fo 128-v.
3 J. R. H. Moorman, 'The Foreign Element among the English Franciscans', *English Historical Review*, lxii (1947), p 298.
4 See above, p 94.

BRISTOL, Gloucestershire
Augustinian Friars

This house was a *studium particulare* of philosophy for the eight friaries of the 'limit' or district of Oxford. On 18 December 1385 John Huel was appointed principal lector in the house for three years, and John Broxmowth in May 1415, reappointed on 29 April 1423.[1]

BRISTOL
Dominican Friars

Gilbert Leddride occurs as lector of the house on 18 January 1337.[2] John Poseris, ordained subdeacon from the convent in 1443, and Vincent Benest, ordained priest in 1468, were probably foreign friars studying there.[3]

BRISTOL
Franciscan Friars

Gilbert Cranfort was appointed lector in the convent, *c.* 1240.[4] At least six foreign friars, probably students, appear in the house during the fifteenth century.[5]

BRISTOL
St Augustine's, Augustinian Abbey

In 1384 the abbot of St Augustine's was given responsibility for appointing masters of Wotton-under-Edge grammar school if the usual patron should be a minor in the king's wardship. The right was only once exercised, in 1511.[6]

There was a cloister school for the novices, with a grammar master, between 1491 and 1512. The master's stipend was £1. 6s. 8d. The office seems usually to have been shared between the succentor and the master of the boys, both canons. John Griffith, vicar of St Augustine the Less, is mentioned as teaching grammar to the novices and other boys in 1491–2.

Boys of the Lady chapel, varying in number from three to six, are also recorded between 1491 and 1512. They received food and clothing from the house. The office of master of the boys was held by William Thorne in 1491–2, John Rawlins in 1503–4, William Mulder

---

1 F. Roth, *The English Austin Friars, 1249–1538, I: History* (New York, 1966), p 144; *II: Sources* (New York, 1961), pp 229, 301.
2 *Reg. Shrewsbury, Wells,* ed. T. S. Holmes, vol i (Somerset Record Soc., ix, 1896), p 329.
3 A. B. Emden, *A Survey of Dominicans in England* (1967), pp 277, 427.
4 Thomas of Eccleston, *Tractatus de Adventu Fratrum Minorum in Angliam,* ed. A. G. Little (Manchester, 1951), p 49.
5 *English Historical Review,* lxii (1947), p 298.
6 See above, p 199.

in 1504, William Lentall in 1506–7, and Richard Brampeston in 1511–12. The salary appears to have been £2. 13s. 4d. The masters probably taught singing, besides doubling as grammar masters to the canons. The boys were also learning grammar in 1491–2.[1]

BRISTOL
St Mark's Hospital

The ordinances of the hospital, confirmed in 1259, provided for the house to maintain twelve scholars, one of whom was chosen to teach the others, probably in their choral work. The scholars may have been intended to frequent the town grammar school, but it is not certain if they ever actually existed.[2]

BRUTON, Somerset
Augustinian Priory, later Abbey

On 19 April 1452 Bishop Beckington ordered that the young canons should receive daily instruction in grammar.[3] In 1520 the abbot of Bruton was made trustee of the endowments of Bruton grammar school and given the responsibility of appointing masters.[4]

BUCKLAND, Devon
Cistercian Abbey

On 28 May 1522 Thomas White, abbot of Buckland, and his convent contracted with Robert Derkeham, organist, that he should assist in the choir of the abbey and teach the art of music and organ playing to four boys, as well as to any of the monks who wished to learn. In return Derkeham was to receive a salary of £2. 13s. 4d., board, lodging, fuel and one gown each year. He evidently held this post until the dissolution of the abbey in 1539 and was awarded a pension as compensation by the court of Augmentations on 18 December 1540.[5]

CIRENCESTER, Gloucestershire
Augustinian Abbey

The abbot of Cirencester was named in 1518 as an advisor to choose children for instruction in song by the priest of Robert Richards' chantry in Cirencester.[6]

On 14 March 1538 the abbot and canons appointed Henry Edmunds as master of the children of the Lady chapel in the monastery. His duties were to teach them pricksong and

---

1 A. Sabin, 'Compotus Rolls of St Augustine's Abbey, Bristol', *TBGAS*, lxxiii (1954), pp 195–7.
2 See above, p 37.
3 *Reg. Bekynton, Wells,* ed. H. C. Maxwell-Lyte, i, 180.
4 See above, p 121.
5 Oliver, *Monasticon Dioecesis Exoniensis,* p 381.
6 See above, p 130.

Latin accidence, and he had also to sing and play the organ in the chapel. His annual stipend included £3. 6s. 8d., 13s. 4d. in lieu of a gown, meat and drink among the abbey servants or else £2, four loads of wood and one of hay. On 11 February 1540 the court of Augmentations granted him in recompense a pension of £8. 10s.[1]

CLEEVE, Somerset
Cistercian Abbey

In about 1500 the abbot of Cleeve appointed one of his kinsmen as grammar master in the abbey.[2]

CORNWORTHY, Devon
Priory of Augustinian Canonesses

In the late 1450s Margaret Wortham, prioress of Cornworthy, agreed with Laurence Knight, a gentleman of Devon, to board his daughters in the priory and 'to teche them to scole'. The girls were Elizabeth, aged seven, and Jane, aged ten. Their father promised to pay 20d. a week for their expenses, and since they remained in the priory for over five years the bill rose to £21. 13s. 4d. Knight never paid the bill during his lifetime and after his death his widow refused to do so. These, at any rate, were the allegations of Thomasine Dinham who became prioress of Cornworthy in about 1470, and petitioned the chancellor of England for redress since there was apparently no remedy under common law.[3]

CRANTOCK, Cornwall
Collegiate Church

On 1 February 1352 Bishop Grandisson ordered the college to maintain two clerks and two or three boys competently instructed, to carry out the divine office. The clerks and boys were to be chosen by the dean, fed and housed in the college, and paid 16s. (clerks) and 8s. (boys).[4] In 1492 a visitation made on behalf of the archbishop of Canterbury disclosed that no clerks and boys were being maintained. The college was ordered to provide them by the following Michaelmas.[5]

CREDITON, Devon
Collegiate Church

In 1334 the college was ordered to maintain four choristers, raised to six in 1523, who were trained in song by one of the clerks until the dissolution of the house in 1545. The college seems also to have been responsible for appointing the schoolmaster of the town.[6]

1 PRO, Exch. Augm., Miscellaneous Books, E 315/94 fos 159v–61.
2 British Museum, MS Arundel 249 fo 86.
3 Eileen Power, *Medieval English Nunneries* (1922), p 269, quoting PRO, Early Chancery Proceedings, C 1/44/227, dating from between 1467 and 1472.
4 *Reg. Grandisson, Exeter*, ed. F. C. Hingeston-Randolph, ii, 1113–14.
5 Lambeth Palace Library, Reg. Morton, Canterbury, fo 125.
6 See above, pp 97–8.

DORCHESTER, Dorset
Franciscan Friars

In 1485 Sir John Byconill, knight, gave the friars some water mills beside their convent so that the profits might be used, among other things, to bring boys into the order and educate them in good manners and learning. The bequest also mentions the 'cursors' or lecturers of the convent teaching their scholars.[1]

EXETER, Devon
Dominican Friars

A few years before 1410, David Russell, an Irishman professed at Dublin, was admitted to the Exeter convent as a student.[2] Thirteen other foreign friars probably students, were ordained from the house during the later middle ages.[3]

EXETER
Franciscan Friars

The Exeter convent was a recognised centre of the study of theology for friars of the order in 1337.[4]

EXETER
St John's Hospital

In 1332 Bishop Grandisson established a foundation by which twelve poor scholars and a tutor were boarded in the hospital, while receiving their education in the high school of the city. Nine scholars were still being supported in 1535, and the house was dissolved four years later.[5]

FORDE, Devon
Cistercian Abbey

On 3 September 1537 Thomas Chard, abbot of Forde, appointed William Tyler, MA, 'late of Axminster', to teach grammar to the boys of the monastery and to lecture on holy scripture in the refectory, at an annual salary of £3. 6s. 8d., together with a furnished chamber in the house, a gown and food like one of the brethren. On 26 April 1539 the court of Augmentations awarded Tyler a pension of £3 instead.[6]

[1] Hutchins, *History of Dorset*, ii, 364–5; *VCH Dorset*, ii, 94.
[2] Reg. Stafford, Exeter, i, fo 101; Oliver, *Monasticon*, p 336.
[3] Emden, *A Survey of Dominicans*, p 24.
[4] A. G. Little, 'Educational Organisation of the Mendicant Friars in England', *Transactions of the Royal Historical Soc.*, new series viii (1894), p 68.
[5] See above, p 48.
[6] Oliver, *Monasticon*, pp 340–1. A fuller transcript from the lost original is in Exeter City Archives, DD, 22783.

GLASTONBURY, Somerset
Benedictine Abbey

The education of the novices in medieval Glastonbury is indicated by the appearance of John Totford as 'master of the school' in 1456 and of John Verney as master of the novices in 1525. They were both monks.[1] At Bishop Clerke's visitation of the abbey on 15 July 1538, several of the brethren complained about the state of the cloister school. Brother John Pantalion said that although the abbot was bound to provide a schoolmaster at his own expense, the brethren were made to pay contributions to his wages. Brother William Joseph alleged 'that the convent doth lack an instructor to teach them their grammar, and over against any visitation there they have an instructor, and when the visitation is done, then he is taken away'. He agreed that the young monks were made to pay the master's wages, and added that there had been no lecture of scripture in the house between Easter and Whitsunday. These assertions are not altogether consistent and should be treated cautiously. They also relate to a disturbed and untypical period.[2]

There was a large almonry school in the abbey by 1377 when 39 'clerks of the school' paid the clerical poll tax. This shows them to have been over the age of fourteen and under the degree of priests. Their duties probably included serving the monks who were priests at their private masses, their numbers being related to those of the monks, of whom there were 45 in 1377.[3] Such clerks still existed at Glastonbury in 1408 when Archbishop Arundel ordered that no brother should take one to himself without the abbot's permission, and that the clerks and other youths in the monastery under the age of twenty should not enter the monks' quarters but go straight from their table to church or school.[4]

On 10 August 1534 the abbot and convent appointed James Renynger of Glastonbury to be organist in the Lady chapel of the abbey and to teach six boys pricksong and descant. Two of the boys were also to be taught to play the organ for two years and afterwards to spend a further six singing and playing in the chapel. Renynger's stipend was fixed at £10 together with food, drink, lodging, fuel and a gown. He continued in office until the Dissolution, when he was awarded a pension of £10, which he was still receiving in 1569.[5]

GLOUCESTER
Franciscan Friars

On 2 August 1246 Henry III granted the Franciscan friars of Gloucester a tower on the

---

1 *Reg. Bekynton, Wells,* ed. H. C. Maxwell-Lyte, ii, 445–6; *Regg. Wolsey, Clerke, Knight & Bourne, Wells,* ed. Maxwell-Lyte, p 85.
2 *Dean Cosyn & Wells Cathedral Miscellanea,* ed. Dom A. Watkin (Somerset Record Soc., lvi, 1941), pp 159–64.
3 PRO, Clerical Subsidy Rolls, E 179/4/1 m 3.
4 *Reg. Bekynton, Wells,* ii, 555–6.
5 Dom A. Watkin, 'Last Glimpses of Glastonbury', *Downside Review* (1948–9), pp 76–9, quoting PRO, Exch. KR, Ecclesiastical Documents, E 135/2/31.

city wall adjacent to their convent, in which to hold a school of theology.[1] At least five German friars, probably students, appear at the convent during the fifteenth century.[2]

GLOUCESTER
St Oswald's, Augustinian Priory

Between 1096 and 1112 the house was granted control of Gloucester school, and was intermittently involved with public education in the town during later centuries. In 1400 the schoolmaster of Gloucester undertook to teach without charge eight boys sent by St Oswald's, apparently from its almonry.[3]

GLOUCESTER
St Peter's, Benedictine Abbey

Gerald of Wales studied at St Peter's during his youth under Master Hamo, c. 1160.[4] The schoolhouse of the abbey is mentioned in 1378.[5] On 16 April 1515 the monks appointed John Tucke, BA, to teach grammar to the young brethren and thirteen boys of the clerks' chamber, and plainsong and descant to five or six boys. With the latter he was to help celebrate a daily mass in honour of Our Lady, doubtless in the Lady chapel. His stipend included £6, a chamber, food and drink, fuel and a gown.[6] In 1535 the abbey was paying £6. 13s. 4d. to Robert Oldsworth, lecturer in theology; £13 to thirteen poor scholars of the almonry in food and clothes; and £5 to three men and five boys of the Lady chapel.[7] At the dissolution in 1540 a new lecturer appears in the person of Thomas Greenwood, a Cambridge STP and vicar of the abbey living of Standish, near Gloucester. John Tucke on the other hand was still 'master of the children' and the monastery still maintained ten choristers.[8]

HAILES, Gloucestershire
Cistercian Abbey

There does not seem to have been a working system of higher education at Hailes Abbey in 1535, when Thomas Cromwell ordered all monasteries to provide theology lectures for their brethren. According to the abbot, Stephen Sager, none of the resident monks was

---

1 *Close Rolls 1242–7*, p 447.
2 *English Historical Review*, lxii (1947), p 298.
3 See above, pp 57 and 62.
4 *Giraldi Cambrensis Opera*, ed. J. S. Brewer, vol iv (Rolls Series, 1873), p 107.
5 *Historia et Cartularium Monasterii Gloucestriae*, ed. W. H. Hart, vol i (Rolls Series, 1863), p 53.
6 Ibid., vol iii (Rolls Series, 1867), p 290.
7 *Valor Ecclesiasticus*, ii, 411, 418. Robert Oldsworth is an elusive figure. Nicholas Oldsworth, a scholar of Eton and Cambridge MA, may be meant. For his career see J. & J. A. Venn, *Alumni Cantabrigienses, part I:—1751*, vol iii (Cambridge, 1924), p 278.
8 PRO, Exch. Augm., Miscellaneous Books, E 315/494 pp 93–6; *LPFD*, xv, no 139. For Greenwood's career see *BRUO*, iv, 245–6.

learned enough to lecture and he was unwilling to call home any of those who were studying at Oxford. His Oxford friends recommended the name of George Cotes, bachelor of theology and fellow of Magdalen College.[1] Cotes came down to Hailes, read two or three lectures which met with approval, and accepted appointment as lecturer. He was sent to Cromwell on 31 August 1535 with a covering letter in order to swear to the royal supremacy, and took the oath before the minister himself two days later.[2]

During the autumn of 1535 Cotes, who eventually became Mary Tudor's bishop of Chester, made a stir in the district with sermons of a highly conservative nature. On 2 November Anthony Saunders, the Reformist lecturer in the neighbouring monastery of Winchcombe, reported to Cromwell that the abbot of Hailes, 'a valiant knight and soldier under Antichrist's banner', had hired 'a great Golias, a subtle Duns man, yea a great clerk as he saith' to catch him in his sermons. The reference was to Cotes. Saunders further alleged that the learned bachelor was neither expounding the word of God, asserting the royal supremacy, nor preaching against Rome.[3] Cromwell replied by calling Cotes before him, and the bishop of Worcester, Hugh Latimer, who had also been told of the matter, sent him the text of one of the sermons along with his comments. 'As far as I can learn', wrote Latimer, 'he is wilily witted, Duns-ly learned, More-ly affected, bold not a little, zealous more than enough'. He asked Cromwell either to warn him kindly and reform him, or else to send him away altogether.[4] In the event Cotes seems to have left the area. He was back in Magdalen College as lecturer in philosophy by the following year.[5]

HARTLAND, Devon
Augustinian Abbey

On 7 February 1310 Bishop Stapledon promised to provide the house with an instructor in the knowledge of letters as soon as the opportunity offered.[6] In 1506 the abbot of Hartland accepted certain duties relating to the oversight of Week St Mary grammar school in Cornwall.[7]

HINTON, Somerset
Carthusian Priory

The prior of Hinton was made responsible for appointing masters to Bradford-on-Avon grammar school, founded in 1524. The right was probably never exercised.[8]

---

1 For Cotes's career see ibid., p 140.
2 *LPFD*, vii, appendix no 35; ix, no 251. The suggested date of the first document, a year too early, should be corrected to that of the second.
3 Ibid., no 747.
4 Ibid., no 1118.
5 *BRUO*, iv, 140.
6 *Reg. Stapeldon, Exeter*, ed. F. C. Hingeston-Randolph, pp 172–3; Oliver, *Monasticon Dioecesis Exoniensis*, p 210.
7 See above, p 176.
8 See above, p 116.

ILCHESTER, Somerset
Dominican Friars

The names of two lectors of the friary survive from the fourteenth century: John of Ilchester, who held office in 1333, and William Sherborne, appointed on 7 April 1393.[1] John Fabri, ordained priest from the convent in 1451, was perhaps a foreign friar studying at the house.[2]

IVYCHURCH, Wiltshire
Augustinian Priory

At the dissolution of the priory in 1536 the staff consisted of five brethren, of whom one was a novice, and seventeen servants, including a schoolmaster and five 'children for the church'.[3]

KEYNSHAM, Somerset
Augustinian Abbey

In the twelfth century the canons may have held the patronage of Bristol school, but there is no evidence for this in later times.[4]

On 26 July 1526 at the visitation of the abbey by the vicar-general of the bishop of Bath and Wells, John Arnold the chancellor reported that the four novices were not taught letters but were 'almost illiterate'. Thomas Deverel, the refectuary, complained that no canon was studying at Oxford according to the laudable custom of the house. Thomas Bedford, John Browne, Thomas Parker and William Tybbat, the four professed novices, asked to have an instructor in grammar. On 30 July the visitor ordered the abbot to arrange for their instruction.[5]

LACOCK, Wiltshire
Abbey of Augustinian Canonesses

Lacock Abbey deserves to be mentioned for the late survival of the Anglo-French dialect there, long after it had ceased to be a vernacular language in England. On 23 August 1535 the king's visitor, John ap Rice, wrote to Thomas Cromwell, 'The house is well ordered. The ladies have their rules written in the French tongue, which they understand

---

1 *Reg. Shrewsbury, Wells,* ed. T. S. Holmes, i, 155; T. Kaeppeli, 'Registrum Litterarum Fr. Raymundi de Vineis Capuani', *Monumenta Ordinis Fratrum Praedicatorum Historia,* xix (Rome, 1937), p 178.
2 Emden, *A Survey of Dominicans,* pp 39, 335.
3 Sir H. Brakspear, 'Ivychurch Priory', *Wilts. Archaeological & Natural History Magazine,* xlvi (1932–4), pp 435–6.
4 See above, p 36.
5 H. C. Maxwell-Lyte, 'Visitation of Religious Houses and Hospitals, 1526', *Collectanea I* (Somerset Record Soc., xxxix, 1924), pp 216–17.

well, and are very perfect in the same. It varies from the French now used, and is more like the French of the common law'. This French must therefore have formed part of the training of the nuns and perhaps of their pupils also, if they had any.[1]

LANTHONY near Gloucester
Augustinian Priory

From the twelfth until the early sixteenth centuries the canons of Lanthony held the right of appointing schoolmasters in Gloucester and also owned the schoolhouse there.[2]

On 29 March 1533 Richard Hart, prior of Lanthony, appointed John Hogges, 'singing man', late of Coventry, and four children to sing, play the organs and keep Our Lady mass and anthem every day. Hogges was also to teach music, singing and organ playing to the canons and any other children the prior might send to him. In return he was to receive £8. 3s. 4d., bread and ale, and fodder for one cow. The four children were to be maintained in meat, drink, lodging and washing. On 20 November 1541 the court of Augmentations awarded Hogges a pension of £5. 6s. 8d.[3]

LAUNCESTON, Cornwall
Augustinian Priory

In 1342 Bishop Grandisson ordered the canons of Launceston to admit poor scholars of grammar to the daily meal which they provided in their hall for the poor.[4]

MILTON ABBAS, Dorset
Benedictine Abbey

In 1521 William Middleton, abbot of Milton, took a leading part in the establishment of a free grammar school in Milton Abbas.[5]

MUCHELNEY, Somerset
Benedictine Abbey

Ralph Drake was appointed by the monks, either between 1504 and 1522 or 1532 and 1538, to assist at masses of Our Lady in the abbey and to teach four boys and one monk to play the organ, besides any other monks who wished to learn. In return he was to receive £3. 6s. 8d., food, drink, fuel and a gown.[6]

1 *LPFD*, ix, no 160.
2 See above, p 58.
3 PRO, Exch. Augm., Miscellaneous Books, E 315/93 fos 231v–2.
4 See above, p 101.
5 See above, p 151.
6 Adam de Domerham, *Historia de Rebus Gestis Glastoniensibus,* ed. T. Hearne (1727), i, pp lxxx–ii. For his song 'Frere Gastkyn' see F. Ll. Harrison, *Music in Medieval Britain,* (2nd ed., 1963), p 457.

OTTERY ST MARY, Devon
Collegiate Church

The 1338 statutes of Ottery provided for eight choristers to be taught song and organ playing by the chaplain of the Lady chapel and grammar by a schoolmaster, appointed by the canons, who also taught the public. These arrangements appear to have lasted until the dissolution of the college in 1545.[1]

PENRYN, Cornwall
Glasney Collegiate Church

Glasney College maintained four clerks and some choristers by about 1276; there were four choristers in 1548. At about that date the college was supporting a public reading school in Penryn, and one of the vicars had been teaching a public grammar school.[2]

SALISBURY, Wiltshire
Dominican Friars

Twelve foreign friars, probably students, are known to have been ordained from this house during the later middle ages.[3]

SHERBORNE, Dorset
Benedictine Abbey

In 1535 the abbey was paying £3. 18s. *per annum* to support three scholars in the grammar school of Sherborne.[4]

SLAPTON, Devon
Collegiate Church

The collegiate church at Slapton was founded in 1373 by Sir Guy Brian, KG, lord of Slapton, for a rector, five priests, and four clerks 'sufficiently instructed in reading and song'.[5] By 1399 two of the clerks had been replaced by boys, and this was still the case in 1492.[6] By 1536 the number of choristers had risen to four. What arrangements, if any, were made for teaching and training these boys, remain unknown.

---

[1] See above, p 165.
[2] See above, p 167.
[3] Emden, *A Survey of Dominicans*, p 24.
[4] See above, p 104.
[5] Oliver, *Monasticon Dioecesis Exoniensis*, pp 322–30.
[6] *Reg. Stafford, Exeter,* ed. F. C. Hingeston-Randolph, p 381; Lambeth Palace Library, Reg. Morton, Canterbury, fo 127. In 1492 John Ewyn and John Phillip were the clerks, and John Toppe and Robert Stirche the choristers (ibid).

STANLEY, Wiltshire
Cistercian Abbey

On 29 April 1526 Thomas Calne, abbot of Stanley, and his convent appointed Thomas Counser to the office of schoolmaster in the abbey, to teach the brethren at the accustomed hours. His annual wages and perquisites were defined as a chamber in the monastery, victuals like one of the monks, food for his boy, four yards of cloth for his gown at 4s. the yard, two baskets of wood, and a salary of £4 charged on the manor of Loxwell.[1] Thomas Counser had been one of Cardinal Morton's scholars at Canterbury College, Oxford, in 1505. He graduated BA in 1506 and was still apparently in Oxford, renting a room at Lincoln College, between 1516 and 1521.[2] After the dissolution of Stanley Abbey in February 1536, he exhibited his contract in the court of Augmentations on 23 January 1537, and was awarded a pension of £2. 6s. 8d. in recompense.[3] He was still being paid in 1539.[4]

TAUNTON, Somerset
Augustinian Priory

There were probably choristers at Taunton in 1499.[5] On 16 September 1538 the prior, William Williams, and his canons appointed Thomas Foxe as cantor or clerk of the (Lady) chapel, with the duty of teaching song to the boys and the organ to any brother who wished to learn. His stipend was £5, a house, fuel and a gown. On 20 June 1539 he was awarded a pension instead by the court of Augmentations.[6]

TAVISTOCK, Devon
Benedictine Abbey

After a visitation of Tavistock in 1373 Bishop Brantingham ordered that the youths and novices in the abbey should be provided with at least one master to instruct them about divine service and the disciplines of the rule.[7] On 1 September 1529 the monks of Tavistock appointed John Elyctt to teach five boys of the Lady chapel, play the organ and arrange the singing there at an annual stipend of £3. 6s. 8d., together with food, drink, fuel and a gown. On 10 December 1539 he was awarded a pension of £6 by the court of Augmentations.[8]

1 PRO, Exch. Augm., Miscellaneous Books, E 315/91 fos 16v–17v.
2 *BRUO*, iv, 134.
3 E 315/91 fos 16v–17v.
4 E 315/442 fo 19; *LPFD*, xiv part ii, p 75.
5 *Regg. King & Hadrian, Wells*, ed. Sir H. C. Maxwell-Lyte, p 46.
6 E 315/101 fos 322v–3.
7 *Reg. Brantyngham, Exeter*, ed. F. C. Hingeston-Randolph, i, 313.
8 Oliver, *Monasticon Dioecesis Exoniensis*, pp 92–3.

TEWKESBURY, Gloucestershire
Benedictine Abbey

On 2 July 1378 Bishop Wakefield, finding that the young monks of Tewkesbury had no one to instruct them in letters, ordered the abbot to provide an instructor by Michaelmas next.[1] In 1535 the abbey was furnishing sixteen poor scholars with clothes costing £7. 13s. 4d. and giving food and drink worth £3. 11s. 8d. to an unspecified number of poor boys engaged in study. It seems likely that these references involve the monastic almonry rather than a public school.[2]

TORMARTON, Gloucestershire
Collegiate Church

A chantry college was founded at Tormarton by Sir John de la Rivere, the lord of the manor, between 1336 and 1344. The foundation ordinance of 1 May 1344 provided for a warden, four chaplains, two clerks (deacon and subdeacon), and three choristers. Choral services were evidently intended. The clerks received wages of 6s. a year and the boys 3s. 4d., besides their board and lodging; nothing was said about their education. In the event, the chantry was insufficiently endowed and in 1423 the pope sanctioned the abolition of the choral services, with a corresponding reduction of the staff to a warden and three chaplains only.[3]

TRURO, Cornwall
Dominican Friars

On 16 September 1397 Master Thomas Truro was appointed lector in the convent of Truro.[4]

TYWARDREATH, Cornwall
Benedictine Priory

On 20 December 1513 Bishop Oldham, after visiting the priory, ordered that the novices and other members of the house should be instructed in grammar.[5] At an inquisition held at Lostwithiel on 31 March 1584 concerning the patronage and tithes of the vicarage of Fowey, William Burnard of Lostwithiel, 'aged 90 and more', claimed to have been a scholar in the priory in the time of Walter Barnecot, prior 1450–96. Henry Tredenecke of Lostwithiel, barber, 'aged 60 or thereabouts', said he was a scholar in the priory under

---

1 *Reg. Wakefield, Worcester*, ed. W. P. Marett (Worcestershire Historical Soc., new series vii, 1972), p 159.
2 *Valor Ecclesiasticus*, ii, 483.
3 *Reg. Bransford, Worcester*, ed. R. M. Haines (Worcs. Historical Soc., new series, iv, 1966), pp xxxviii–ix, 84–6, 305–6, 474–80; *Cal. Papal Letters*, iii, 300–1; vii, 283.
4 *Monumenta Ordinis Fratrum Praedicatorum Historia*, xix (1937), p 196.
5 Oliver, *Monasticon Dioecesis Exoniensis*, p 35.

Thomas Rynd, chapel clerk, for two or three years before the resignation of Thomas Collins, prior from 1507 until about 1534. The latter reference suggests the existence of boys of the Lady chapel.[1]

WESTBURY-ON-TRYM, Gloucestershire
Collegiate Church

In 1463 Bishop Carpenter established an endowed grammar school in the college, the master being bound to give free instruction to the public and to the ministers of the college. There were twelve choristers at Westbury in 1474.[2]

WIMBORNE MINSTER, Dorset
Collegiate Church

Before its dissolution in 1548 the college supported four secondary clerks. The dean appears to have been responsible for appointing masters to the chantry grammar school privately established in association with the church in 1511.[3]

WINCHCOMBE, Gloucestershire
Benedictine Abbey

Under Richard Kidderminster, abbot from 1488 to 1525, an ambitious scheme of higher education was operated for the monks, then 28 in number. The abbot tells us that in his time there was scarcely one day of the week when a bachelor of theology did not lecture on the Old Testament and another on the New, while he himself held forth twice a week on the *Sentences* of Peter Lombard.[4] It may have been the reputation of Winchcombe as a centre of traditional theology that led Thomas Cromwell to appoint a lecturer from outside the house to instruct the monks in 1535. His name was Anthony Saunders, a former fellow of Merton College, Oxford, who had graduated MA two years earlier.[5] As we should expect, he 'held after the new world' in matters of religion. Two letters survive in which he complained to Cromwell of the difficulties he encountered at Winchcombe. On 2 November 1535 he asked his patron to establish a time each day for the monks to attend his lectures. 'They will not come in due time; they set so much by their popish services.'[6] Further complaints about the abbot's hostility to the Reformation followed on 3 February.[7] Notwithstanding, Saunders remained at Winchcombe where he died in May 1539, robbed by a few months from enjoying the final downfall of the abbey.

1 PRO, E 134/26 Eliz. Easter 14.
2 See above, p 182.
3 See above, p 184.
4 W. A. Pantin, 'Abbot Kidderminster and Monastic Studies', *Downside Review,* xlvii (1929), pp 199–200.
5 For his career see *BRUO,* iv, 506.
6 *LPFD,* ix, no 747.
7 Ibid., viii, no 171. For the dating see above, p 189 n 3.

There were probably almonry boys by the early sixteenth century. Hugh Cooper, monk of Winchcombe, writing to Cromwell in 1534 complained that he had been enticed into the monastery 'by fair promises' when aged fourteen. This can only have been as a boy of the almonry or chapel.[1] Abbot Kidderminster also established six choristers in the abbey in 1521, probably to serve the Lady chapel. The money used for this purpose was left by Lady Joan Huddleston.[2] In 1535 there was a 'master of the boys' and £21. 6s. 8d. was being spent on their maintenance and instruction in grammar and song.[3]

Finally the monks of Winchcombe acted as trustees of the endowments of two local grammar schools: Cirencester (founded between 1457 and 1483), and Winchcombe itself (founded in 1521).[4]

1 Ibid., vii, no 1367.
2 PRO, Exch. Land Revenue, LR 6/29/2, and see above, p 000.
3 *Valor Ecclesiasticus*, ii, 459.
4 See above, pp 129 and 188.

Bibliography

I. LIST OF UNPRINTED SOURCES CITED

Bridgwater, Town Hall
  Corporation MSS, vol x no 1.

Bristol, City Record Office
  All Saints' Church Book
  Mayors' Audit Books
  St John Baptist, Churchwardens' Accounts
  Thompson, E. M.   MS Calendar of Fox Deeds

Cambridge, Gonville and Caius College
  MS 417/447

Dorchester, Dorset Record Office
  Wimborne Minster, Churchwardens' Accounts, P 204/CW 35
  Wimborne Minster, Deeds, P 204 GN 1

Exeter, Cathedral Library
  Dean and Chapter MSS:
  Accounts of Excrescence, receipts and payments, 3754
  Chapter Act Books, 3500–1
  Deeds, Various, 600, 2109, 2228, 2477, 3625, 3674
  Fabric Rolls, 2648–2704/6
  Obit Ordinations and Mass of the Kalendar Book, 3675
  Payments of Ministers Accounts, 2758/1–2599/8

Exeter, Devon Record Office
  The Register of John Booth
  The Register of Hugh Oldham
  The Register of Edmund Stafford
  The Register of James Turberville
  The Register of John Veysey, 2 vols.
  Robert Furse, History of the Furse Family, 2507B

Exeter, East Devon (formerly City) Record Office
  Courtenay Accounts, CR 1466
  Deeds, DD 22783; ED/WA/2
  Mayor's Court Rolls, 16/17 Edward I
  St John's Hospital Cartulary
  John Hooker, Synopsis Corographicall

Gloucester, County Record Office
  MS Calendar of Colchester MSS
  MS Calendar of Gage Deeds
  Deeds, D 253/11; D 1735/174-5
  Machen Deeds
  Sherborne MSS

Gloucester, Central Library
  Hockaday Abstracts

Lincoln, Cathedral Library
  Dean and Chapter MS 88 (A.3.15.)

London, British Museum
  MS Add. 19046
  MS Add. 32243
  MS Add. 46487
  MS Arundel 249
  MS Cotton Vespasian xxv
  MS Harley 1027
  MS Harley 3300
  MS Harley 5827
  MS Lansdown 227
  MS Royal 1B XII

London, Guildhall Library
  The Register of Richard FitzJames

London, Lambeth Palace Library
  The Register of William Courtenay
  The Register of John Stafford
  The Register of John Morton

London, Public Record Office

  Chancery
  C 1   Early Chancery Proceedings
  C 2   Chancery Proceedings, Series I
  C 3   Chancery Proceedings, Series II
  C 66   Patent Rolls
  C 115 Chancery Masters' Exhibits
  C 136 Inquisitions Post Mortem, Series I, Richard II
  C 142 Inquisitions Post Mortem, Series II
  C 143 Inquisitions ad quod Damnum

  Exchequer, KR
  E 101 Accounts, Various
  E 134 Depositions taken by Commission

I. LIST OF UNPRINTED SOURCES

   E 135 Ecclesiastical Documents
   E 150 Inquisitions Post Mortem, Series II
   E 178 Special Commissions of Inquiry
   E 179 Subsidy Rolls

   Exchequer, Augmentation Office
   E 301 Certificates of Colleges and Chantries
   E 315 Miscellaneous Books
   E 318 Particulars for Grants of Crown Lands
   E 321 Proceedings

   Exchequer, First Fruits and Tenths
   E 334 Composition Books

   Exchequer, Land Revenue
   LR 6   Receivers' Accounts

   Court of King's Bench
   KB 27 Coram Rege Rolls

   Court of Common Pleas
   CP 40 Plea Rolls

   Prerogative Court of Canterbury
   Prob 11 Registered Copy Wills

   Special Collections
   SC 6   Ministers' Accounts

   State Paper Office
   SP 1   State Papers

Oxford, Bodleian Library
   MS Auct. D 1, 7
   MS Bodl. 191
   MS Bodl. 494
   MS Rawl. D 328
   MS Rawl. D 363
   MS Rawl. statutes 38
   MS Top. Glouc. c 4–5.
   MS Wood empt. 9
   University Archives: Registers G, H

Oxford, Corpus Christi College
   Twyne Transcripts

Oxford, Lincoln College
   MS lat. 129

Salisbury, Diocesan Record Office
    Choristers' Accounts
    Communars' Rolls
    Dean and Chapter Act Books:
        Hemingsby, Corffe, Dunham, Holmes, Draper, Vyryng,
        Pountney, Harding, Hutchins, Burgh, Newton, Machon,
        Harward's Memorials, Holt & Blacker
    Deeds, Various

Salisbury, Diocesan Registry
    The Register of Edmund Audley
    The Register of Richard Beauchamp
    The Register of Lorenzo Campeggio
    The Register of William Capon
    The Register of John Chandler
    The Register of Ralph Erghum
    The Register of Richard Mitford
    The Register of John Waltham

Stowell Park, Northleach
    Lanthony Cartulary, vol A 13

Taunton, Somerset Record Office
    The Register of Robert Stillington
    The Register of Oliver King
    The Register of Hadrian de Castello
    The Register of John Clerke
    Luttrell MSS
    Photostats of Winchester Pipe Rolls

Wells, Cathedral Library
    Communars' Books

Worcester, Hereford & Worcester Record Office
    Bishop Bell's Visitation Book, ref. 802
    Bishops' Register, 1516–1542
    The Register of John Alcock
    The Register of John Bell
    The Register of John Carpenter, 2 vols
    The Register of Richard Clifford
    The Register of Jeronimo Ghinucci
    The Register of Silvestro de Gigli
    The Register of Nicholas Heath
    The Register of Hugh Latimer, 2 parts

The Register of Philip Morgan, 2 parts
The Register of Robert Morton
The Register of Thomas Peverel
The Register of Thomas Polton

II. SELECT LIST OF PRINTED SOURCES

The Ancient Laws . . . for King's College, Cambridge and . . . Eton College, ed. Heywood, J., and Wright, Thomas, London, 1850

Atkyns, Sir Robert. *The Ancient and Present State of Glostershire,* London, 1712.

Austin, Roland. *The Crypt School, Gloucester, 1539–1939,* Gloucester, 1939.

Austin, Roland. John and Joan Cook's Gift to Gloucester, *Transactions of the Bristol and Gloucs. Archaeological Society,* lxv, 1944, pp 199–219.

Bartelot, R. Grosvenor. *History of Crewkerne School, 1499–1899,* Crewkerne, 1899.

Boucher, C. E. The Lond or Loud Brass in St Peter's Church, Bristol, *Transactions of the Bristol and Gloucs. Archaeological Society,* xxx, 1907, pp 265–72.

Boucher, C. E. St Peter's Church, Bristol, ibid., xxxii, 1909, pp 260–300.

Brickdale, Sir Charles Fortescue-. Newland in the Middle Ages, ibid., lv, 1933, pp 191–233; lvi, 1934, pp 179–96.

Calendar of Charter Rolls, 1226–1516, 6 vols, London, 1903–27.

Calendar of Close Rolls, 1272–1509, 47 vols, London, 1892–1963.

Calendar of Fine Rolls, 1272–1509, 22 vols, London, 1911–62.

Calendar of Inquisitions Post Mortem, 1216–1384, 15 vols, London, 1904–70.

Calendar of Inquisitions Post Mortem, Second Series, 1485–1509, 3 vols, London, 1898–1955.

Calendar of Letters and Papers, Foreign and Domestic, Henry VIII, ed. Brewer, S. J., Gairdner, J., and Brodie, R. H., vol a, 2nd edition, 1 vol in 3, London, 1920; vols 2–21, original edition, 20 vols in 32, London, 1864–1910; Addenda, 1 vol in 2, London, 1929–32.

Calendar of Papal Letters, 1198–1492, 14 vols in 15, London, 1894–1951.

Calendar of Papal Petitions, 1342–1419, London, 1896.

Calendar of Patent Rolls, 1216–1509, 1547–72, 68 vols, London, 1891–1966.

Calendar of Records of the Corporation of Gloucester, ed. Stevenson, W. H., Gloucester, 1893.

Calendarium Inquisitionum Post Mortem Sive Escaetarum, 4 vols, London, Record Commission, 1806–28.

Catalogue of Ancient Deeds, 6 vols, London, 1890–1915.

The Chantry Certificates for Cornwall, *Documents towards a History of the Reformation in Cornwall,* ed. Snell, L. S., vol i, Exeter, 1953.

The Chantry Certificates for Devon, *Documents towards a History of the Reformation in Devon,* ed. Snell, L. S., vol i, Exeter [1961].

Chapters of the English Black Monks, 1215–1540, ed. Pantin, W. A., 3 vols, London, Royal Historical Society, Camden third series, xlv, xlvii, liv, 1931–7.

Churchwardens' Accounts of Ashburton, 1479–1580, ed. Hanham, Alison, Devon and Cornwall Record Society, xv, 1970.

Close Rolls, 1227–1272, 14 vols, London, 1902–38.

Cockayne, G. E. *The Complete Peerage,* ed. Doublesday, H. A., and Gibbs, V., 14 vols in 15, London, 1910–59.

Councils and Synods with other documents relating to the English Church, Part II: 1205–1313, ed. Powicke, F. M., and Cheney, C. R., 2 vols, Oxford, 1964.

Dalton, J. N. *The Collegiate Church of Ottery St Mary,* Cambridge, 1917.

Davidson, R. E. *The History of Truro Grammar and Cathedral School,* Mevagissey, 1970.

Dean Cosyn and Wells Cathedral Miscellanea, ed. Watkin, Dom Aelred, Somerset Record Society, lvi, 1941.

Dictionary of National Biography, ed. Stephen, Leslie, and Lee, Sidney, 63 vols, London, 1885–1900.

Eccleston, Thomas of. *Tractatus de Adventu Fratrum Minorum in Angliam,* ed. Little, A. G., Manchester, 1951.

Edwards, Kathleen. Cathedral of Salisbury, *Victoria County History of Wiltshire,* iii, London, 1956, pp 156–210.

Edwards, Kathleen. College of De Vaux, Salisbury, ibid., pp 369–85.

Edwards, Kathleen. *The English Secular Cathedrals in the Middle Ages,* 2nd edition, Manchester, 1967.

Ellacombe, H. T. *The History of the Parish of Bitton, Gloucestershire,* Exeter, 1881.

Emden, A. B. *A Biographical Register of the University of Cambridge to 1500,* Cambridge, 1963.

Emden, A. B. *A Biographical Register of the University of Oxford to 1500,* 3 vols, Oxford, 1957–9.

Emden, A. B. *A Biographical Register of the University of Oxford, 1501–1540,* Oxford, 1974.

Emden, A. B. *A Survey of Dominicans in England, 1268–1538,* Rome, Istituto Storico Domenicano, Santa Sabina, Dissertationes Historicae, fasc. xviii, 1967.

Epistolae Academicae Oxon., ed. Anstey, H., 2 vols, Oxford Historical Society, xxxv–vi, 1898.

Faculty Office Registers, 1534–1549, ed. Chambers, D. C., Oxford, 1966.

Fairbrother, E. H. The Foundation of Bruton School, Somerset, *Somerset and Dorset Notes and Queries,* xii, 1910, pp 49–52.

Fowler, J. Sherborne All Hallows Church Wardens' Accounts, ibid., xxiii, 1939–42, pp 189–314 *passim;* xxiv, 1943–6, pp 6–166 *passim.*

Frere, W. H. *The Use of Sarum,* Cambridge, 1898.

The Great Red Book of Bristol, ed. Veale, E. W. W., 5 vols, Bristol Record Society, ii, iv, viii, xvi, xviii, 1931–53.

Harrison, F. Ll., *Music in Medieval Britain,* 2nd edition, London, 1963.

Hill, C. P. *Bristol Grammar School,* London, 1951.

Historia et Cartularium Monasterii Sancti Petri Gloucestriae, ed. Hart, W. K., 3 vols, London, Rolls Series, 1863–7.

Historical Manuscripts Commission, Reports and Calendars:
Third Report, London, 1872.
Sixth Report, 1 vol in 2, London, 1877–8.
Reports on Manuscripts in Various Collections, 8 vols, London, 1901–14.
Calendar of the Manuscripts of the Dean and Chapter of Wells, 2 vols, London, 1907–14.

Historic Towns, maps and plans of towns and cities in the British Isles, with historical commentaries, ed. Lobel, Mary D., vol i, London, 1969.

Hoare, Sir Richard Colt. *The History of Modern Wiltshire,* 14 parts, London, 1822–44.

Hull, P. L. The Endowment and Foundation of a Grammar School at Week St Mary by Dame Thomasine Percival, *Journal of the Royal Institution of Cornwall,* new series, vii part i, 1973, pp 21–54.

Humfrey, Laurence, *Joannis Juelli Angli Episcopi Sarisburiensis Vita et Mors,* London, 1573.

Hutchins, J. *The History and Antiquities of the County of Dorset,* ed. Shipp, W., and Hodson, J. W., 4 vols, Westminster, 1861–73.

Itineraria Simonis Simeonis et Willelmi de Worcestre, ed. Nasmith, J., Cambridge, 1778.

Jackson, J. E. Ancient Statutes of Heytesbury Almshouse, *Wiltshire Archaeological and National History Magazine,* xi, 1869, pp 289–308.

Jones, W. H. Terumber's Chantry at Trowbridge, ibid., x, 1867, pp 240–52.

Jordan, W. K. Charitable Institutions of the West of England, *Transactions of the American Philosophical Society,* new series, l part viii, 1960.

Kaeppeli, T. Registrum Litterarum Fr. Raymundi de Vineis Capuani, *Monumenta Ordinis Fratrum Praedicatorum Historica,* xix, Rome, 1937.

Kelly, T. *The History of King Edward VI Grammar School, Totnes,* Totnes, 1947.

Ker, N. R. *Medieval Libraries of Great Britain, a list of surviving books,* London, Royal Historical Society, 2nd edition, 1964.

Kirby, T. F. *Winchester Scholars, a list of the wardens, fellows and scholars,* London, 1888.

Knowles, M. D. *The Religious Orders in England,* 3 vols, Cambridge, 1948–59.

Knowles, M. D., and Hadcock, R. N. *Medieval Religious Houses, England and Wales,* 2nd edition, London, 1971.

Leach, A. F. *English Schools at the Reformation, 1546–8,* Westminster, 1896.

Leach, A. F. *The Schools of Medieval England,* 2nd edition, London, 1916.

Leach, A. F. Sherborne School before, under, and after Edward VI, *Archaeological Journal,* lv (second series, v), 1898, pp 1–83.

Leland, John. *The Itinerary of John Leland in or about the years 1535–1543,* ed. Smith, Lucy Toulmin, 5 vols, London, 1907–10.

Le Neve, John. *Fasti Ecclesiae Anglicanae, 1300–1541,* ed. Horn, Joyce M., Jones, B., and King, H. P. F., 12 vols, London, 1962–7.

Lindley, E. S. *Wotton under Edge, men and affairs of a Cotswold wool town,* London, 1962.

The Little Red Book of Bristol, ed. Bickley, F. B., 2 vols, Bristol, 1900.

Little, A. G. Educational Organisation of the Mendicant Friars in England (Dominicans and Franciscans), *Transactions of the Royal Historical Society,* new series, viii, 1894, pp 49–70.

Lyte, H. C. Maxwell-. *A History of Dunster and of the Families of Mohun and Luttrell,* 2 vols, London, 1909.

Lyte, H. C. Maxwell-. The Hody Family, *Somerset and Dorset Notes and Queries,* xviii, 1925, pp 127–9.

Lyte, H. C. Maxwell-. Visitations of Religious Houses and Hospitals [in Somerset], 1526, *Collectanea I,* Somerset Record Society, xxxix, 1924, pp 207–25.

Maclean, Sir John. Chantry Certificates, Gloucestershire, *Transactions of the Bristol and Gloucs. Archaeological Society,* viii, 1883–4, pp 229–308.

Mayo, C. H. The FitzJames Family of Somerset, *Somerset and Dorset Notes and Queries,* xvi, 1918–20, pp 54–68.

Moorman, J. R. H. The Foreign Element among the English Franciscans, *English Historical Review,* lxii, 1947, pp 289–303.

Notes or Abstracts of the Wills in the Great Orphan Book and Book of Wills, Bristol, ed. Wadley, T. P., Bristol and Gloucs. Archaeological Society, 1886.

Oliver George. *Lives of the Bishops of Exeter and a History of the Cathedral,* Exeter, 1861.

Oliver, George. *Monasticon Dioecesis Exoniensis,* Exeter and London, 1846.

Ordinale Exon., ed. Dalton, J. N., 3 vols, London, Henry Bradshaw Society, xxxvii, xxxviii, lxiii, 1909–26.

Orme, Nicholas. *English Schools in the Middle Ages,* London, 1973.

Pantin, W. A. Abbot Kidderminster and Monastic Studies, *Downside Review,* xlvii, 1929, pp 199–211.

Parry, H. Ll. *The Founding of Exeter School*, London, 1913.

Peter, R. and O. B. *The Histories of Launceston and Dunheved*, Plymouth, 1885.

Peter, T. C. *The History of Glasney Collegiate Church, Cornwall*, Camborne, 1903.

Pope, F. J. The Founder of Netherbury School, *Somerset and Dorset Notes and Queries*, x, 1906–7, pp 2–3.

Power, Eileen, *Medieval English Nunneries, c. 1275 to 1535*, Cambridge, 1922.

Registers of English Bishops:

Bath and Wells:

Calendar of the Register of John Drokensford, Bishop of Bath and Wells, 1309–1329, ed. Hobhouse, E., Somerset Record Society, i, 1887.

The Register of Ralph of Shrewsbury, Bishop of Bath and Wells, 1329–1363, ed. Holmes, T. Scott, 2 vols, ibid., ix–x, 1896.

The Register of Nicholas Bubwith, Bishop of Bath and Wells, 1407–1424, ed. Holmes, T. Scott, 2 vols, ibid., xxix–xxx, 1914.

The Register of Thomas Bekynton, Bishop of Bath and Wells, 1443–1465, ed. Lyte, Sir H. C. Maxwell-, and Dawes, M. C. B., 2 vols, ibid., xlix–l, 1934–5.

The Registers of Robert Stillington, Bishop of Bath and Wells, 1466–1491, and Richard Fox, Bishop of Bath and Wells, 1492–1494, ed. Lyte, Sir H. C. Maxwell-, ibid., lii, 1937.

The Registers of Oliver King, Bishop of Bath and Wells, 1496–1503, and Hadrian de Castello, Bishop of Bath and Wells, 1503–1518, ed. Lyte, Sir H. C. Maxwell-, ibid., liv, 1939.

The Registers of Thomas Wolsey, Bishop of Bath and Wells, 1518–1523, John Clerke . . . 1523–1541, William Knyght . . . 1541–1547, and Gilbert Bourne . . . 1554–1559, ed. Lyte, Sir H. C. Maxwell-, ibid., lv, 1940.

Canterbury:

The Register of Henry Chichele, Archbishop of Canterbury, 1414–1443, ed. Jacob, E. F., and Johnson, H. C., 4 vols, Canterbury and York Society, xlii, xlv–vii, 1937–47.

Registrum Thome Bourgchier, Cantuariensis Archiepiscopi, 1454–1486, ed. Du Boulay, F. R. H., ibid., liv, 1957.

Exeter:

The Registers of Walter Bronescome, 1257–1280, and Peter Quivil, 1280–1291, Bishops of Exeter, ed. Randolph, F. C. Hingeston-, London and Exeter, 1889.

The Register of Walter Stapeldon, Bishop of Exeter, 1307–1326, ed. Randolph, F. C. Hingeston-, London and Exeter, 1892.

The Register of John Grandisson, Bishop of Exeter, 1327–1369, ed. Randolph, F. C. Hingeston-, 3 vols, London and Exeter, 1894–9.

The Register of Thomas de Brantyngham, Bishop of Exeter, 1370–1394, ed. Randolph, F. C. Hingeston-, 2 vols, London and Exeter, 1901–6.

The Register of Edmund Stafford, [Bishop of Exeter,] 1395–1419, ed. Randolph, F. C. Hingeston-, London and Exeter, 1886.

The Register of Edmund Lacy, Bishop of Exeter, 1420–1455, Part I: The Register of Institutions, ed. Randolph, F. C. Hingeston-, London and Exeter, 1909.

The Register of Edmund Lacy, Bishop of Exeter, 1420–1455, ed. Dunstan, G. R., 4 vols, Canterbury and York Society, cxxix, cxxxii, cxxxiv, cxxxvii, 1963–71; Devon and Cornwall Record Society, new series, vii, x, xvi, xviii, 1963–71.

Hereford:

Registrum Johannis de Trillek, Episcopi Herefordensis, 1344–1361, ed. Parry, J. H., Canterbury and York Society, viii, 1912.

Registrum Thome Spofford, Episcopi Herefordensis, 1422–1448, ed. Bannister, A. T., ibid., xxiii, 1919.

Registrum Ricardi Beauchamp, Episcopi Herefordensis, 1449–1450, ed. Bannister, A. T., ibid., xxv, 1919.

Registrum Johannis Stanbury, Episcopi Herefordensis, 1453–1474, ed. Parry, J. H., and Bannister, A. T., ibid., xxv, 1919

Registrum Thome Myllyng, Episcopi Herefordensis, 1472–1492, ed. Bannister, A. T., ibid., xxvi, 1920.

Registrum Caroli Bothe, Episcopi Herefordensis, 1516–1535, ed. Bannister, A. T., ibid., xxviii, 1921.

Salisbury:

Registrum Simonis de Gandavo, diocesis Sarisburiensis, ed. Flower, C. T., and Dawes, M. C. B., 2 vols, Canterbury and York Society, xl-i, 1934.

The Registers of Roger Martival, Bishop of Salisbury, 1315–1330, ed. Edwards, Kathleen, Elrington, C. R., and Reynolds, Susan, 3 vols, ibid., lv, lvii, lix, 1959–65.

Worcester:

The Register of the Diocese of Worcester during the Vacancy of the See, usually called Registrum Sede Vacante, 1301–1435, ed. Bund, J. W. Willis, 1 vol in 2, Worcestershire Historical Society, 1893–7.

A Calendar of the Register of Henry Wakefield, Bishop of Worcester, 1375–95, ed. Marrett, W. P., ibid., new series, vii, 1972.

York:

The Register of John le Romeyn, Lord Archbishop of York, 1286–1296, ed. Brown, W., 2 vols, Surtees Society, cxxiii, cxxviii, 1913–17.

Register of the University of Oxford, ed. Boase, C. W., vol i: 1449–63, 1505–71, Oxford Historical Society, i, 1885.

Registrum Annalium Collegii Mertonensis, 1483–1521, ed. Salter, H. E., ibid., lxxvi, 1923.

Reports del Case en Ley que furent argues en le temps de . . . Henry le IV et Henry le V, London, 1679.

Reynolds, H. E. *Wells Cathedral, its foundation, constitutional history and statutes,* Leeds, c. 1881.

Robbins, A. F. John Aylworth and the Launceston Free School, Exeter, *Notes and Gleanings from Devon and Cornwall,* iii, 1890, pp 161–7.

Robertson, Dora H. Notes on some Buildings in the City and Close of Salisbury Connected with the Education and Maintenance of the Cathedral Choristers, *Wiltshire Archaeological and Natural History Magazine,* xlviii, 1937–9, pp 1–30.

Robertson, Dora H. *Sarum Close . . . the History of the Choristers for 900 years,* London, 1938.

Roskell, J. S. Three Wiltshire Speakers, *Wiltshire Archaeological and Natural History Magazine,* lvi, 1955–6, pp 274–341.

Roth, F. *The English Austin Friars, 1249–1538,* 2 vols, New York, 1961–6.

Rudder, Samuel. *A New History of Gloucestershire,* Cirencester, 1779.

Russell, J. C. *British Medieval Population,* Albuquerque, USA, 1948.

Sabin, Arthur. Compotus Rolls of St Augustine's Abbey, Bristol, *Transactions of the Bristol and Gloucs. Archaeological Society,* lxxiii, 1954, pp 192–207.

Sarum Charters and Documents, ed. Jones, W. R., and Macray, W. D., London, Rolls Series, 1891.

Smyth, John. *The Berkeley Manuscripts. The Lives of the Berkeleys . . . of Berkeley . . . from 1066 to 1618,* ed. Maclean, Sir John, 3 vols, Gloucester, Bristol and Gloucs. Archaeological Society, 1883–5.

Somerset Medieval Wills, ed. Weaver, F. W., 3 vols, Somerset Record Society, xvi, xix, xxi, 1901–5.

Statutes and Customs of the Cathedral Church . . . of Salisbury, ed. Wordsworth, C., and Macleane, D., London, 1915.

The Statutes of the Realm, from Magna Carta to the end of the Reign of Queen Anne, 10 vols, London, Record Commission, 1810–24.

Stephan, J. Some Notes on Ashburton Grammar School, *Devonshire Association Transactions,* xci, 1959, pp 112–23.

Sterry, Sir Wasey. *The Eton College Register, 1441–1698,* Eton, 1943.

The Survey and Rental of the Chantries, etc., in Somerset in 1548, ed. Green, E., Somerset Record Society, ii, 1888.

Thompson, A. Hamilton. The Jurisdiction of the Archbishops of York in Gloucestershire, *Transactions of the Bristol and Gloucs. Archaeological Society,* xliii, 1921, pp 85–180.

Toy, H. Spencer. *A History of Education at Launceston,* Marazion, 1966.

Tremlett, T. D. *Calendar of the Manuscripts belonging to the King's School, Bruton, 1297–1826,* Bruton, 1939.

Valor Ecclesiasticus tempore Henrici VIII auctoritate regis institutus, ed. Caley, J., 6 vols, London, Record Commission, 1810–24.

The Victoria History of the Counties of England:
    Dorset, vol ii, ed. Page, W., London, 1908.
    Gloucestershire, ed. Page, W., Elrington, C. R., and Herbert, N. M., vols ii, vi, viii, x, London, 1907–72.
    Hampshire, ed. Page, W., 5 vols, London, 1900–14.
    Hertfordshire, ed. Page, W., 5 vols, London, 1902–23.
    Lincoln, vol ii, ed. Page, W., London, 1906.
    Northampton, vol ii, ed. Serjeantson, R. M., and Adkins, W. R. D., London, 1906.
    Oxford, vol iii, ed. Salter, H. E., and Lobel, Mary D., London, 1954.
    Somerset, vols i–ii, ed. Page, W., London, 1906–11.
    Suffolk, vol ii, ed. Page, W., London, 1907.
    Wiltshire, ed. Pugh, R. B., and Crittall, Elizabeth, vols i–ix, London, 1955–73.

Visitation Articles and Injunctions of the Period of the Reformation, 1536–75, ed. Frere, W. H., and Kennedy, W. M., 3 vols, Alcuin Club Collections, xiv–xvi, 1910.

Wallis, P. J. *Histories of Old Schools: a revised list for England and Wales,* Department of Education, University of Newcastle-upon-Tyne, 1966.

Watkin, Dom A. Last Glimpses of Glastonbury, *Downside Review,* 1948–9, pp 76–9.

Weaver, F. W. Foundation Deed of Bruton School, *Somerset and Dorset Notes and Queries,* iii, 1892–3, pp 241–8.

Weekes, Ethel Lega. *Some Studies in the Topography of the Cathedral Close at Exeter,* Exeter, 1915.

Wells City Charters, ed. Shilton, Dorothy O., and Holworthy, R., Somerset Record Society, xlvi, 1932.

Wilkins, David. *Concilia Magnae Britanniae et Hiberniae, 446–1717,* 4 vols, London, 1737.

Williams, T. W. Gloucestershire Medieval Libraries, *Transactions of the Bristol and Gloucs. Archaeological Society,* xxxi, 1908, pp 78–189.

Williams, T. W. *Somerset Medieval Libraries . . . prior to the dissolution of the monasteries,* Bristol, Somerset Archaeological and Natural History Society, 1897.

Wordsworth, C., and Robertson, Dora H. Salisbury Choristers: their Endowments, Boy-Bishops, Music Teachers, and Headmasters, with the History of the Organ, *Wiltshire Archaeological and Natural History Magazine,* xlviii, 1937–9, pp 201–31.

Index

Abbot, Thomas, student, 183 n7
Absolon, William, schoolmaster, 85, 89–90
Alcock, Philip, choirmaster, 98
altarists—see Salisbury and Wells, cathedrals of,
Amesbury, Wilts., priory and education at, 201
Andrew, John, schoolmaster, 179
Andrew, William, schoolmaster, 56–7
Angel, Thomas, schoolmaster, 190
archdeacons and education, 13, 43–55, 59, 74
archischola, office of, 65–6, 82
Arscote, John, schoolmaster, 168
arts, study of, 2–4, 15, 68–9, 86, 96
Arundel, Thomas, archbishop of Canterbury, 206
Ashburton, Devon, schools at, 111–12; mentioned, 11, 16, 30
Ashby, Adam of, chancellor, 67
Augmentations, court of, 28, 122–3, 189–90, 201, 203–6, 210, 212
Austell, John, canon, 85
Austen, Richard, pupil, 69 n5
Awre, Gloucs., school at, 93; mentioned, 4
Awre, John of, 93

Balfront, Robert, schoolmaster, 146–7
Bannek, John, schoolmaster, 149
Barber, Nicholas, schoolmaster, 183
Barber, Walter, schoolmaster, 99
Barclay, Alexander, poet and schoolmaster, 85, 87–90, 166–7
Barnstaple, Devon, school at, 112–13; mentioned, 12, 30
Barre, Lady Joan—see Greyndour
Barre, Sir John, knight, 156–7
Bartholomew, bishop of Exeter, 45
Bartlet, John, chorister, 111 n3
Barton, Thomas, canon, 50
Bath, Som., abbey and teaching at, 201; mentioned, 25, 28
  school at 93–4; mentioned, 4, 6, 31–2

Bath, Adelard of, scholar, 35
Baynham family, 156, 158–9, 163
Beauchamp, Richard, bishop of Salisbury, 99
Beaufort, Lady Margaret, school foundress, 18, 184–5
Beckington, Som., 11, 182–3
Beckington, Thomas, bishop of Bath & Wells, 7, 11 n3, 12, 40, 79–81, 84, 203
Bedford, Thomas, Austin canon, 209
Beenlye, John, pupil, 194
Belde, John, pupil, 51
Bell, Alexander, choirmaster, 77
Bell, Edward, school founder, 165
Bellamy, John, rector and tutor, 100
Benest, Vincent, friar, 202
Bennet, Thomas, schoolmaster, 46, 100
Berdon, William, of Exeter, 51 n3
Berkeley family, 14, 190–9
Berkeley, Lady Katherine, school foundress, 16, 18, 190–6
Béthune, Evrard of, *Grecismus* of, 22, 63
Beynon, Philip—see Eynon, ap
Bingham, Robert, bishop of Salisbury, 67
Bird, John, schoolmaster, 132
bishops and education,
  as administrators and visitors, 7, 14, 26, 40, 58–62, 64, 97–9, 101, 117–19, 160, 166–7, 193, 203–4, 206, 208–9, 212–13
  as founders and benefactors, 14, 18, 47–9, 52–3, 57–8, 65, 67, 79–84, 94, 97, 105, 128–9, 139, 165, 167, 182, 204
Bishopston, Henry, canon, 23, 67
Blandford, Dorset, alleged school at, 113; mentioned, 30
Blount, John, schoolmaster, 183
Bodington, Laurence, schoolmaster, 56
Bodmin, Cornwall, priory at, 176
  school at, 113–14; mentioned, 16, 30
Bolter, John, schoolmaster, 163–4
Bonaventure family, 173
Bonaventure, Thomasine—see Percival

229

Bond, James, student, 183 n7
Bond, Nicholas, possible schoolmaster, 105 n1
Borington, John, schoolmaster, 19, 50, 51 & n4, 56
Bourchier family, 126–7
Bowen, Walter, schoolmaster, 112
Bowyer, Thomas, pupil, 69
boy bishops, 62, 106
Bradford-on-Avon, Wilts., school at, 114–17; mentioned, 16, 28, 30–1, 75, 122
Brampeston, Richard, possibly Austin canon, 203
Bramston, Richard, choirmaster, 91
Branscombe, Walter, bishop of Exeter, 167
Brantingham, Thomas, bishop of Exeter, 166, 212
Braunton, Devon, school at, 94; mentioned, 6, 12
Brayleigh, Richard, dean, 14, 18, 47–8
Breter, William, schoolmaster, 64
Brian, Sir Guy, chantry founder, 211
Bridgwater, Som., 31
    Franciscan friars and education, 201
    St John's hospital and education, 15, 94–5, 201
    school at, 94–5; mentioned, 4, 6, 8, 15
Bridport, Dorset, school at, 95–6; mentioned, 4, 22
Bridport, Giles of, bishop of Salisbury, 15, 68
Bristol, Gloucs., 35, 182
    All Saints church, 10, 38
    Augustinian friars and education, 202
    Cathedral school, 28, 32, 42, 184
    corporation of, 14, 41
    Dominican friars and education, 24, 202
    Franciscan friars and education, 24, 202
    Grammar school, 41–2, 184 n1
    Kalendars' guild, 23, 36
    St Augustine's abbey and teaching at, 202–3; mentioned, 8, 25, 28, 194, 197
    St Mark's hospital and education, 15, 37, 192 n3, 203
    St Mary Redcliffe church, 10, 38
    St Nicholas church, 10, 37–8
    schools at, 35–42; mentioned, 2, 4, 13–15, 197
Bristol, Simon, chancellor, 83
Brode, Richard, schoolmaster, 183
Broke, George, schoolmaster, 189–90
Browne, John, Austin canon, 209
Browning, Walter, pupil, 96
Broxmouth, John, friar, 202
Bruton, Som., abbey and teaching at, 203; mentioned, 25, 28, 120–2

Bruton, Som.—*continued*
    school at, 117–23; mentioned, 3, 15 n2, 16, 28–9, 116–17, 152
Buckland, Devon, abbey and teaching at, 203; mentioned, 8
Bulkeley, ———, schoolmaster, 41
Burdox, John, vicar choral, 77
Burnard, William, pupil, 213
Burnell, Robert, bishop of Bath & Wells, 94
Burnell, Walter, chaplain, 193
Bury St Edmunds, Suffolk, school at, 2, 36 n2
Byconill, Sir John, benefactor, 205

Caccherowe, John, choirmaster, 77
Calwoodleigh, John, schoolmaster, 56–7
canon law, study of, 2, 23–4, 40, 52–3, 67, 83, 162, 196
Cantelowe, William, merchant, 134–6
Carew, Sir Peter, as pupil, 50
Carne, Edward, chancellor, 74
Carpenter, John, bishop of Worcester, school founder, 18, 23–4, 182–3
Carpenter, Robert, chaplain, 76 n7
Carter, Peter, of Exeter, 51 n3
Cater, Robert, choirmaster, 80, 91
cathedrals and education, 2–6, 14–15, 23–4, 28, 42–57, 65–91
Chalurys, John, schoolmaster, 19, 96
Champernown, William, schoolmaster, 85–6
chantries and education, 16–18, 29–31, 111–99 *passim*
    survey and certificates of (1546–8), 29–30; mentioned, 105, 111–14, 117, 123–4, 127, 130–3, 147–52, 164, 168–9, 171–2, 180–1, 186, 197
Chedworth, John, bishop of Lincoln, school founder, 18, 128–9, 142
Cheke, Sir John, 186
Cheltenham, Gloucs., 31
    school at, 123–4; mentioned, 16, 30
Chester, William, merchant, 170
Chicheley, Henry, archbishop of Canterbury, 143
Chilcote, John, schoolmaster, 196, 199
Chippenham, Wilts., possible school at, 96; mentioned, 40
Chipping Campden, Gloucs., school at, 124–8; mentioned, 16, 21, 30–1
choirmasters, of cathedrals, 43, 45–6, 71–2, 77–8, 79–81, 86, 91

choirmasters—*continued*
   of collegiate churches, 10, 98, 166–7
   of monasteries, 8, 28, 150, 202–4, 206–7, 210, 212, 214
   of parish churches, 11, 38, 111, 130
   salaries of, 72, 80, 98, 130, 203–4, 206–7, 210, 212
Cholwell, William, schoolmaster, 149–50, 179–81
choristers, of cathedrals, 10, 14–15, 43–6, 54–5, 66, 69–72, 78–82
   of collegiate churches, 10, 97–8, 165–8, 182, 204, 211, 213–14
   of monasteries, 8–10, 28, 189, 202–3, 206–7, 210, 212–15
   of parish churches, 10–11, 38, 111, 130, 150, 171
   wages of, 44, 71, 80–1, 97–8, 166–7, 207, 210, 213
Chubbe, John, schoolmaster, 167
Churchdown, Gloucs., jurisdiction of, 59
Chyke, William, pupil, 120
Cirencester, Gloucs., 31
   abbey and teaching at, 203–4; mentioned, 8, 28, 130
   schools at, 96–7, 128–31; mentioned, 4, 11, 14, 16, 28, 30, 32
Cirencester, Elias of, choirmaster, 43
Clawsey, John, choirmaster, 91
Cleche, Edward, schoolmaster, 60
Cleeve, Som., abbey and teaching at, 204
clergy, parish, and education,
   education by, 7, 25, 46, 95, 98, 100, 102, 106–9, 132–3, 150–1, 182 & n7, 202
   education of, 23–4, 53, 67–8, 95, 100–1
Clerke, John, bishop of Bath & Wells, 206
clerks, of cathedrals, 10, 44–5, 46 n1, 55, 69–70, 78–9
   of collegiate churches, 10, 97–8, 165–8, 204, 211, 213
   of monasteries, 206, 214
   of parish churches, 11–12, 14, 38, 150, 198
   wages of, 45, 49, 79, 97–8, 165–8, 204, 213
Clifford, John, schoolmaster, 160–1
Clifton, William, schoolmaster, 198–9
Coburley, William, schoolmaster, 161
cockfighting, 62
Coldwell, Robert, schoolmaster, 20, 197–9
Colerne, Wilts., 11
Colet, John, dean of St Paul's, 119, 122
collegiate churches and education, 10, 13, 16, 29, 68–9, 97–9, 165–8, 182–6, 204, 211, 213–14

Combe, John, school founder, 18, 131–2
Common Pleas, court of, 62–3
Cook, John and Joan, school founders, 18, 64–5, 137–41
Cook, John, vicar choral, 77
Cooper, Hugh, monk, 215
Copeland, Thomas, schoolmaster, 103
Cornworthy, Devon, priory and teaching at, 204
Cosyn, Richard, schoolmaster, 89
Cotel, Walter, schoolmaster, 98
Cotes, George, lecturer, 208
Cothe, Robert, chaplain, 69 n5
Counser, Thomas, schoolmaster, 212
country-dwellers, education of, 12, 42–3, 45, 93, 96, 108–9, 112, 198
Courtenay, William, archbishop of Canterbury, 60–1
Cowley, William, chaplain, 170 n4
Cox, William, schoolmaster, 185 & n3
Cranfort, Gilbert, friar, 202
Crantock, Cornwall, collegiate church and education at, 204; mentioned, 10
Crediton, Devon, collegiate church and school at, 97–9, 204; mentioned, 4, 10, 13, 16, 29
Crewkerne, Som., school at, 130–1; mentioned, 16, 21, 30–1
Cromwell, Ralph, Lord, 143
Cromwell, Thomas, minister, 25, 116, 122, 139, 147, 179, 189, 207–9, 214–15
crown and education, 61–3, 66, 80, 128–9, 143, 206–7
   see also Reformation and education; chantries, survey of

Dakyns, John, schoolmaster, 89–90
Dale, John, schoolmaster, 199
Darcy, Richard, schoolmaster, 62–3
Dartmouth, Devon, school at, 99
David, Thomas, schoolmaster, 56–7
Davy, Richard, schoolmaster, 64
de la Pole, William, earl of Suffolk, 143
Dene, Richard, schoolmaster, 76
Dering, Richard, schoolmaster, 161
Derkeham, Robert, choirmaster, 203
Devizes, Wilts., 11
   school at, 99
Dick, Humphrey, schoolmaster, 190
Dinham family of Lifton, 176–81
Dodwell, James, schoolmaster, 127–8

Dorchester, Dorset, 6, 11
  Franciscan friars and education, 24, 205
Downton, Wilts., 11
Drake, Ralph, choirmaster, 210
Draper, John, schoolmaster, 86, 89–90
Driffield, Robert, vicar choral, 77
Droxford, John, bishop of Bath & Wells, 7
Duellard, Richard, pupil, 51
Duke, Thomas, prior, 60–1
Dunster, Som., school at, 99–100; mentioned, 4

Edmunds, Henry, choirmaster, 203
Edmunds, John, school founder, 18, 120
Edon, Richard, schoolmaster, 85, 87–90
Edward, duke of York (d. 1415), 63
Edward, John, 133, 135–6
Eleanor, daughter of Edward I, pupil, 201
Elyott, John, choirmaster, 212
Enford, Wilts., school at, 132–3; mentioned, 3, 6, 30
Etampes, Guy of, scholar, 66
Eton, Bucks., St Mary college at, 3, 11, 49, 86, 120, 129, 185–6
Everton, Michael, schoolmaster, 186
Every, William, schoolmaster, 56–7
Ewelme, Oxon., school at, 3, 143
Ewyn, John, clerk, 211 n6
Exbourne, Walter, schoolmaster, 48, 56
Exchequer, court of, 123, 150
Exeter, Devon, 42
  archdeacon of, 13, 43–55
  bishop's chapel, boys of, 15 n1
  cathedral, chancellor of, 23, 43–55
    choristers, 14–15, 21, 43–55
    clerk of the Lady chapel, 43, 46 & n1
    dean, 45, 49, 55
    precentor, 43, 49
    secondaries, 14–15, 21, 43–57, 79
    succentor, 43
  Dominican friars and education, 205
  Franciscan friars and education, 24, 205
  St John's Hospital and education, 15, 48–9, 51 n3, 54, 205
  schools at, 42–57
    Butcher Row, 46
    Exeter (Free) school, 55
    Godshouse, 7, 46
    high (grammar) school, 46–55; mentioned, 2, 4, 6, 13, 14–15, 21, 43–4
    song, 2, 44–6

Exeter, Devon—*continued*
  schools—*continued*
    theology and canon law, 23, 52–5
Eynon, Philip ap, schoolmaster, 162–3

Fabell, Roger, schoolmaster, 182–3
Fabri, John, friar, 209
Fadyr, Peter, vicar choral, 77
Farell, John, schoolmaster, 112
Farewell, Richard, pupil, 51
Farle, John, vicar choral, 77
Faukeys, John, schoolmaster, 40
Ferriby, John and Margery, school founders, 18, 124–7, 133
Fitzharding, Robert, of Bristol, 36
FitzJames, Sir John, school founder, 18, 116, 119–22
FitzJames, Richard, bishop of London, school founder, 18, 117–19, 120
Flanders, Nicholas of, pupil, 52
Flaxley, Gloucs., abbey of, 158, 162
Fletcher, Richard, schoolmaster of Gloucester, 138
Fletcher, Richard, schoolmaster of St Briavels, 168
Ford, Roger, schoolmaster, 164
Forde, Devon, abbey and teaching at, 205; mentioned, 8, 25, 28
Forncett, William, theologian, 74
Fosse, Richard, schoolmaster, 172
Fosse, Thomas, schoolmaster, 41
Fox, Edward, bishop of Hereford, 11 n3
Fox, Richard, bishop of Winchester, 14, 105, 185, 187
Foxe, Thomas, choirmaster, 212
France, pupil from, 107
French, study of, 107, 209
friars and education, 8, 24–5, 74, 201–2, 205–7, 209, 211, 213
Frocester, Walter, schoolmaster, 196, 199
Fryer, John, vicar choral, 77
Fryer, Philip, schoolmaster, 56–7
Frysmark, Walter, schoolmaster, 86, 89
Furbner, William, schoolmaster, 20, 115–16
Furlong, Andrew, schoolmaster, 169
Furse, Edward, pupil, 106

Gaveston, Joan, pupil, 201
Gaylard, John, choirmaster, 91
Genoa, John of, *Catholicon* of, 22, 85

Ghent, Simon of, bishop of Salisbury, 70–1, 73–4
Gibson, William, schoolmaster, 186
Giffard, Godfrey, bishop of Worcester, 59–60
Gilbert, William, abbot, 121–2
Giles, William, vicar, possible schoolmaster, 106–7
Glanfield, Christopher, schoolmaster, 189
Glasney, collegiate church—see Penryn
Glassman, Robert, schoolmaster, 128
Glastonbury, Som., abbey and teaching at, 206; mentioned, 8, 25, 28
Gloucester, 57
    corporation of, 138–41
    Crypt school, 137–41; mentioned, 16, 64–5
    Franciscan friars and education, 24, 206–7
    King's school, 28, 32, 141
    Lanthony priory—see Lanthony
    St Nicholas school, 133–7; mentioned, 16
    St Oswald's free chapel, later priory, and education, 57–64, 207; mentioned, 13
    St Peter's abbey and teaching at, 207; mentioned, 8, 25, 28, 58
    schools (medieval) at, 57–65; mentioned, 4, 7, 13–14, 21
Gloucester, Thomas, school founder, 18, 133–7
Godard, John, vicar choral, possible schoolmaster, 87, 89–90
Gold, John, schoolmaster, 183
Good, William, schoolmaster, 88, 89–90
Goode, John, schoolmaster, 64
Gorfen, Walter, royal clerk, 135–6
Gourge, Stephen, schoolmaster, 149–50, 182
Gournay, Robert de, hospital founder, 37
grammar, study and teaching of, 2–4, 21–2, 25–6, 39–40, 51–2, 63, 69 n5, 85, 93–4, 95–6, 107, 121, 129, 165, 185–6
    university degrees in, 40, 56 n 9, 57 n16, 73, 138 n3, 164 n7, 177, 182
Grandisson, John, bishop of Exeter, school founder, 18, 48–9, 53, 97, 100, 165–7, 204
Great Torrington, Devon, school at, 100
Greek, study of, 54
Greenhalgh, James, schoolmaster, 85, 89–90
Greenwood, Thomas, lecturer, 207
Greyndour family, 153–9
Greyndour, later Barre, Joan, school foundress, 18, 154–63
Greyndour, Robert, esquire, 153–4, 156, 159
Griffith, John, vicar, schoolmaster, 202
Grove, Edward, schoolmaster, 124
guilds (religious) and education, 36, 111–13, 170
Guterius, Andreas, grammarian, 85 n2
Gye, John, choirmaster, 91

Hailes, Gloucs., abbey and teaching at, 207–8; mentioned, 25, 187–8
Hamelin, John, schoolmaster, 61–3
Hamo, schoolmaster of Gloucester, 207
Hanley, John, schoolmaster, 56
Hanney, Thomas of, *Memoriale Juniorum* of, 96
Harding, Thomas, pupil, 112
Harris, Thomas, possible schoolmaster, 151
Hart, Walter, schoolmaster, 56–7
Hartland, Devon, abbey and teaching at, 176, 208
Hartwell, Nicholas, schoolmaster, 108
Hawkbrook, John, schoolmaster, 73, 76
Haynes, Robert, schoolmaster, 196, 199
Hazleton, William, schoolmaster, 196, 198–9
Heanton Punchardon, Devon, teaching at, 100; mentioned, 8, 12
Hebrew, study of, 54
Helcombe, John, choirmaster, 86, 91
Henry II, king, education of, 35
Henry III, king, benefaction by, 206–7
Henry VI, king, educational circle of, 80, 128–9, 143
Hereford, school at, 61
Heynes, Simon, dean, 53–5
Heytesbury, Wilts., school at, 141–8; mentioned, 3, 16
Hide, Robert, schoolmaster, 190
Higham Ferrers, Northants., school at, 143
Hill, Robert, schoolmaster, 87, 89–90
Hill, Roger, benefactor, 18, 105
Hinton, Som., priory at, 28, 115–17, 208
Hodgkins, Richard, schoolmaster, 185
Hody, John, pupil, 7, 108–9
Hogges, John, choirmaster, 210
Hogyn, William, schoolmaster, 196, 199
Hooker, John, pupil and historian, 8, 46 n4, 102
Horsley, John, monk, 150
Horton, Humphrey, schoolmaster, 130–1
Horton, James, pupil, 114
Horton, Thomas, school founder, 18, 114–17
hospitals and education, 37, 48–9, 94–5, 102, 141–8
Huddleston, Sir John and Lady Joan, benefactors, 186–8
Huel, John, friar, 202
Hugh, schoolmaster of Bristol, 37

Hughes, Thomas, pupil, 198
Hugutio, *Derivationes* of, 22, 96, 107
Hungerford family of Heytesbury, 141–8
Hungerford, Margaret, Lady, school foundress, 18, 143–6
Hungerford, Robert, Lord, pupil, 142–4
Hungerford, Walter, Lord (d. 1449), school founder, 18, 128, 134, 141–3
Hungerford, Walter, Lord (d. 1540), 147
Hyet, Isabel, benefactress, 163
Hygons, Richard, choirmaster, 91

Ilchester, Som., Dominican friars and education at, 209; mentioned, 24
Ilchester, John, friar, 209
Ilminster, Som., school at, 100; mentioned, 15 n2
Ing, Hugh, archbishop of Dublin, 11 n3
Ireland, Gilbert of, pupil, 52
Ivychurch, Wilts., priory and teaching at, 209; mentioned, 8, 9.

James, schoolmaster of Plymouth, 103
James, John, schoolmaster, 196, 198–9
Jane, Thomas, bishop of Norwich, 11 n3
Janyns, Edward, schoolmaster, 162
Jewel, John, pupil, later bishop of Salisbury, 8, 12, 94, 100, 104, 112
John, theologian of Exeter, 23, 52
Jon or Jonys, John, of Exeter, 51 n3
Joye, Thomas, schoolmaster, 196, 199

Kegewyn, John, choirmaster, 72, 77
Kellway, Robert, chantry commissioner, 29–30
Kent, son of John, pupil, 105
Keynsham, Som., abbey and teaching at, 209; mentioned, 13, 36
Kidderminster, Richard, abbot, 25, 64, 188, 214–15
Kingscote, John, bishop of Carlisle, 11 n3
Kingston, Alice, of Warnford, 134–5
Kington, Roger, archdeacon, 74
Knight, Elizabeth and Jane, pupils, 204
Knight, Robert, schoolmaster, 197
Knight, Thomas, choirmaster, 72, 77
Knight, William, bishop of Bath & Wells, 11 n3 87

Laborne, Edward, schoolmaster, 185–6
Lacock, Wilts., abbey and education at, 209–10
Lacy, Edmund, bishop of Exeter, 97–8, 167
Lane, John, schoolmaster, 73, 76
Lanthony near Gloucester, priory and teaching at, 58–65, 210; mentioned, 8, 14, 28, 126, 138, 160
Latimer, Hugh, bishop of Worcester, 139, 148 & n1, 208
Latimer, William, rector, 128
Latin—see grammar
latinitates, school exercises, 51–2
Launceston, Cornwall, priory at, 100–1, 210; mentioned, 15, 149
  school at, 100–1, 148–50; mentioned, 3–4, 15–16, 30, 181–2
Lavington, Robert, vicar choral, 77
Lawrence, Robert, pupil, 100
Leach, A.F., historian, 2, 31, 59 n4, 170, 190 n4
Ledbury, Herefs., school at, 178
Leddride, Gilbert, friar, 202
Leke, Henry, pupil, 69 n5
Leland, John, antiquary, 36, 113, 132
Leland, John, grammarian, 39 & n2, 51
Lentall, William, Austin canon, 203
Lewis, Thomas, student, 183 n7
Liber Gutrumni, grammatical work, 85
licences to teach, 40, 55, 98–9
Liskeard, Cornwall, 31
Littleskill, John, schoolmaster, 19, 87, 89–90
Loder, John, school founder, 18, 151–2
logic, study of, 3, 96
Lombard, Peter, *Sentences* of, 25, 214
Londe, Robert, schoolmaster, 20, 38–40, 96
London, St Paul's school at, 117, 121
Low, Richard, schoolmaster, 50, 56–7
Lucas, John, schoolmaster of Exeter, 56
Lucas, John, schoolmaster of Heytesbury, 146
Luttrell family and education, 12 n1, 99–100
Lybbe, John, schoolmaster, 148
Lyde, William, schoolmaster, 89–90
Lyme Regis, Dorset, education at, 150; mentioned, 11

Macclesfield, Cheshire, school at, 175–6
Maister, Richard, schoolmaster, 56
Major, John, schoolmaster, 56
Malmesbury, Wilts., schools at, 101, 150; mentioned, 4, 30
Malton, William, vicar choral, 77

INDEX

Man, Laurence, vicar choral, 77
Manchester, Lancs., school at, 3
Marlborough, Wilts., 11, 31
    school at, 101–2; mentioned, 4
Marlborough, Thomas of, canon lawyer, 52
Marldon, Devon, alleged school at, 151; mentioned, 30
Martin, Sir William, alderman, 170
Martival, Roger, bishop of Salisbury, 70–2
Maslyn, Richard, probable schoolmaster, 73, 76
Matthew, tutor in Bristol, 35
Mayne, Stephen, chorister, 111 n3
Medford, Walter, dean, 84
Mells, Som., school at, 102; mentioned, 6
Menheniot, Cornwall, teaching at, 102; mentioned, 8
Meriet, Walter, chancellor, 53
Middleton, John, chancellor, 83
Middleton, William, abbot, 151–2
Mildmay, Sir Walter, chantry commissioner, 29–30
Mills, William, pupil, 100
Milton Abbas, Dorset, abbey at, 18, 210
    school at, 151–2; mentioned, 16, 18
Mitchelden, Gloucs., alleged school at, 102
Moffat, Thomas, schoolmaster, 19–20, 41
Molland, Simon, schoolmaster, 129
monasteries and education, 8–10, 13–15, 18, 25–6, 28–9, 201–15; mentioned, 36, 57–65, 101, 104, 116–17, 120–2, 129–31, 176, 183, 188–9, 194
More, John, pupil, 198
More, John, schoolmaster, 183
More, Thomas, schoolmaster, 61–3
Moreman, John, rector and tutor, 102
Morkyn, Walter, pupil, 194
Moul, John le, pupil, 93
Mounslow, Richard, abbot, 189
Muchelney, Som., abbey and teaching at, 210; mentioned, 8
Mulder, William, Austin canon, 202–3
music—see organs; song
Mynever, Rowland, schoolmaster, 88–90

Nelme, John, schoolmaster, 60
Netherbury, Dorset, school at, 152; mentioned, 6, 16, 30–1
Newent, Gloucs., 31
Newland, Gloucs., school at, 153–65; mentioned, 3, 6, 15–16, 21, 30, 32, 197

Newton, Henry, chancellor, 53
Newton, John, friar, 74
nobility and gentry, education of, 35, 39, 50, 105–6, 109, 142, 178, 201, 204, 209
Northallerton, Yorks., school at, 2
North Curry, Som., 11
Northcurry, Richard, schoolmaster, 85, 89
Norton, Richard, schoolmaster, 163
Nugges, Henry, schoolmaster, 73, 76
nunneries and education, 201, 204, 209
Nyweton, ———, clerk of Exeter, 47

Oakwith, Henry, schoolmaster, 56–7
Oldham, Hugh, bishop of Exeter, 98, 185, 213
Oldsworth, Nicholas, rector, 207 n7
Oldsworth, Robert, lecturer, 207
Ordericus Vitalis, education of, 7
organ playing and organists, 8, 72, 104, 152, 166, 203–4, 206, 210, 212
Orum, John, chancellor, 53, 83
Osmund, bishop of Salisbury, 65–6
Osney, Berks., abbey and teaching at, 183
Ottery St Mary, Devon, collegiate church and school at, 165–7, 211; mentioned, 4, 7, 10, 16, 29
Ottery, Roger, chancellor, 53
Oxford University,
    Canterbury College, 212
    chancellor and masters of, 129, 142
    Corpus Christi College, 88, 90, 105–6, 187–8
    Exeter College, 48–9, 131
    grammar schools at, 11, 39, 73, 76 n10
    Magdalen College, 128, 146 n3, 172, 208
    Magdalen College school, 46 n1, 57 n13 & 16, 77 n4, 117, 121
    Merton College, 118, 120, 128–9, 142, 214
    New College, 49, 86, 108, 114, 179
    Oriel College, 183
    University College, 142

Packer, John, schoolmaster, 196, 199
Paradise, John, schoolmaster, 20, 196, 199
parish churches and education, 7–8 & n1, 10–11, 38, 109, 111, 130, 150, 171
parish clergy—see clergy, parish
parish clerks—see clerks in parish churches

Parker, Thomas, Austin canon, 209
patrons of schools, 13–14, 17, *et passim*
Peers, Thomas, pupil, 41
Pendock, William, chaplain, 193
Penryn, Cornwall, 31
    Glasney collegiate church and school at, 167–8, 211; mentioned, 3, 10, 16, 30
Percival, Sir John, school founder, 174–6
Percival, Lady Thomasine, school founder, 18, 173–9
Peter, schoolmaster of Sherborne, 103
Pevesey, ———, vicar choral, 77
Philip, John, clerk, 211 n6
Phillips, William, schoolmaster, 162
Piere, Richard, schoolmaster, 73, 76
Pitt, John, monk and schoolmaster, 201
plague, 121, 188
Plecyz, Bartholomew, pupil, 101
Plymouth, Devon, friaries of, 25
    school at, 103
Plympton, Devon, school at, 103; mentioned, 4, 13
Pole, Reginald, cardinal, 148, 185
Pollard, Walter, of Exeter, 51 n3
Polton, Thomas, bishop of Worcester, 97
Pontesbury, Nicholas, benefactor, 107
Poseris, John, friar, 202
Pounde, John, schoolmaster, 168
Power, Richard, vicar choral, 77
Poynt, John, would-be schoolmaster, 179
Price, Walter, schoolmaster, 89–90
Pullen, Robert, scholar, 23, 52
pupils, ages of, 20, 51, 72–3, 84, 96, 105, 107, 109, 161, 168, 194, 204, 206
    boarding, 15 & n2, 43–5, 50–1, 68–9, 70–1, 80–1, 94, 100, 107, 123, 161, 165–7, 178, 201–15
    corporal punishment of, 41, 81, 97, 121
    exhibitions for—see scholarships
    names and careers of, 7, 8, 11, 20–1; individual names occur throughout the index
    origins of—see country-dwellers; nobility and gentry; town-dwellers; women

Quinel, Peter, bishop of Exeter, 52–3

Raven, William, schoolmaster, 146
Rawlins, John, Austin canon, 202
Raymund, schoolmaster of Exeter, 45
reading, teaching of, 2–4, 7–8, 38, 46, 98, 121, 133, 146, 149–50, 160, 168, 173
Reformation and education,
    under Henry VIII, 26–9, 54, 116, 122–3, 131, 147, 167, 169, 183–4, 189–90, 208
    under Edward VI, 29–32, 54–5, 75, 87–8, 98–9, 123, 147–8, 181, 186; see also chantries, survey of
religious orders and education, 1, 8–10, 24–6, 201–15
Renynger, James, choirmaster, 206
Retford, Thomas, chancellor, 83
Reviers, Baldwin de, earl of Devon (d. 1263), 13, 103
Richard, schoolmaster of Malmesbury, 101
Richard, schoolmaster of Salisbury, 76
Richards, Robert, benefactor, 130
Rivere, Sir John, chantry founder, 213
Robbins, John, benefactor, 102
Robert, earl of Gloucester, 35–6
Robert, schoolmaster of Bristol, 37
Robert, schoolmaster of Salisbury, 76
Rode, Som., 11
Roger, canon of Chewton, 14, 18, 83–4
Roger, precentor of Salisbury, 23, 67
Roger, schoolmaster of Gloucester, 59
Rolleston, Staffs., school at, 3
Romeyn, John, archbishop of York, 59–60
Ross-on-Wye, Herefs., projected school at, 47 n4
Rous, John, antiquary, 24
Row, Thomas, schoolmaster, 179
Rowe, John, pupil, 49 n2
Russell, David, friar, 205
Russell, John, schoolmaster, 73, 76
Russell, Thomas, pupil, 107
Ruthall, Thomas, bishop of Durham, 129–30
Rydeler, John, schoolmaster, 89
Rynd, Thomas, chapel clerk and schoolmaster, 214

St Albans, Elias of, chancellor, 74
St Briavels, Gloucs., school at, 168–9; mentioned, 3, 30
Salisbury, Wilts., 11, 31, 65–7
    cathedral, altarists, 14, 69–70, 72–3, 79
        boys of the hall of the vicars choral, 15, 69 n5
        chancellor, 13, 23, 65–9, 72–4, 146, 148
        choristers, 14, 21, 69–73
        instructor of the choristers, 71–2, 77–8

Salisbury, Wilts.—*continued*
  cathedral—*continued*
    precentor, 65–7, 71
    sub-dean, 68–9
    sub-master of the choristers, 71, 77
    succentor, 66
    treasurer, 65, 70
    vicars choral, 69, 71–3
  De Vaux college, 15, 68–9
  Dominican friars and education, 211; mentioned, 24
  St Edmund's college, 68
  St Thomas church, 8
  schools at, 65–78; mentioned, 7, 117, 172
    arts, 15, 67–9
    grammar, 64–5, 72–5; mentioned, 2, 4, 6–7, 13, 15
    song, 2, 64–5, 71–2
    theology and canon law, 15, 67–8, 73–4
  'university' of, 67–9
Salisbury, John of, scholar, 7, 20
Saltash, Cornwall, school at, 169; mentioned, 30
Samson, bishop of Worcester, 57–8
Saunders, Anthony, lecturer, 189, 208, 214
Savage, Thomas, archbishop of York, 175–6
scholarships and exhibitions, 14–15, 37, 43–5, 48–9, 69–72, 78–82, 94–5, 101, 104, 161, 163, 183, 189, 193, 197, 202–15
schoolboys—see pupils
schoolmasters—see also choirmasters, 2, 18–20
  clerical and lay, 19, 50, 55–6, 73, 85, *et passim*
  examining ordinands, 50
  graduate and non-graduate, 19, 50, 73, 85, 177, 183, *et passim*
  liturgical duties, 72, 82, 84, 86–7, 140, 144, 160–1, 166, 176–7, 185, 193, 198
  married, 41, 46 & n4, 104, 140
  in monasteries, 25, 183, 189, 201–15
  names of—noted throughout the index
  papal judges-delegate, 85–6, 96, 101, 103, 108
  qualifications of, 19–20, 50, 73, 76–8, 85, 89–91, *et passim*
  salaries of, 20, 25; examples of, 54, 82, 87, 112–13, 117, 121, 124, 127, 129, 131–2, 135, 140, 144, 152, 160, 164, 166–9, 172, 180–2, 184–5, 189, 197, 201–2, 205–7, 212
  status of, 20
schools, almonry, 8–10, 201–15
  benefactions to, 12–18, *et passim*
  boarding—see pupils, boarding

schools—*continued*
  books used in, 21–2, 39–40, 51–2, 63, 85, 95–6, 107, 161
  buildings of, 14, 36–7, 44, 47–8, 59, 61, 64, 71–4, 79, 80, 83–4, 99, 100–2, 104–5, 109, 112, 121–2, 130, 132, 138, 160, 166, 170, 173, 177, 185–6, 207
  chantry, 16–18, 29–31, 102, 111–99
  choir—see choirmasters, choristers
  continuity of, 4–12
  curricula of—see arts; canon law; grammar; reading; song; theology
  definition of, 1–4
  distribution of, 4–12, 178
  endowments of, 12–18, *et passim*
  fees in, 47, 63, 122, 160–1, 164, 204
  grammar, 2–4, *et passim*
  holidays and recreations in, 21, 44, 62, 81, 106, 121–2, 161, 177, 188–9, 194
  monopolies claimed by, 13, 47, 58–64
  patrons of—see patrons
  private, 1, 7–11, 12 n1, 37–8, 46, 95, 100, 102, 201–15
  reading—see reading
  religious activities in, 2, 22, 52, 81, 83, 85, 107, 121, 161, 176–7
  size of, 10–11, 15, 21, 84, 105, 127, 132, 198, 206
  song—see song, study of
  statutes of, 80–1, 120–2, 144–5, 159–62, 176–7, 188–9, 193–4
Scolemaister (various spellings), 97 n2
  John, of Dunster, 99–100
  John, of Stow-on-the-Wold, 104
  John, of Tiverton, 106
  Laurence, of Dunster, 99
  Richard, of Dunster, 99
  Simon, of Launceston, 101
  Stephen, of Cirencester, 97
secondaries—see Exeter, cathedral of; Ottery St Mary
Seman, John, schoolmaster, 198
Sevenaysshe, John, schoolmaster, 56
Shaftesbury, Dorset, 11
  school at, 103; mentioned, 4, 6
Sharington, Sir William, school spoliator, 147–8
Shepham, Richard, school founder, 171
Sherborne, Dorset, abbey at, 15, 104, 211
  school at, 103–4; mentioned, 15, 31–2, 211
Sherborne, William, friar, 209
Sherwood, Hugh, schoolmaster, 122–3

Short, Thomas, of Bristol, 39
Shrewsbury, Salop, tuition at, 7
Shrewsbury, Ralph, bishop of Bath & Wells, 79, 83
Sigrith, Walter, schoolmaster, 60
Simon, Anthony, schoolmaster, 104
Simpson, Michael, schoolmaster, 131
Siward, priest of Shrewsbury, 7
Slapton, Devon, collegiate church and education at, 211; mentioned, 10
Smith, David, schoolmaster of Newland, 164
Smith, David, schoolmaster of Week, 179
Smith, John, choirmaster, 91
Smith, John, pupil, 49 n2, 51 n3
Smith, John, schoolmaster, 86, 89–90
Smith, Martin, schoolmaster, 152
Smith, Simon, schoolmaster, 186
song and song schools, 2–4, 8–11, 14–15; examples of, 37–8, 43–6, 71–2, 78–82, 95, 97–8, 106–7, 111, 130, 150, 160, 166–7, 173, 202–4, 206–7, 210–15
South Molton, Devon, school at, 104; mentioned, 12
Spenser, John, schoolmaster, 56
Sprye, George, manciple, 180–1
Stafford, John, bishop of Bath & Wells, 79
Stanbridge, John, grammarian, 39
Stanley, Wilts., abbey and teaching at, 212; mentioned, 25, 28
Stapledon, Walter, bishop of Exeter, 7, 12, 15, 18, 47–9, 53, 111–12, 208
Stephen, king, benefaction by, 66
Stephens, Robert, schoolmaster, 146
Stewe, Thomas, pupil, 138
Stirche, Robert, chorister, 211 n6
Stokes, Thomas, schoolmaster, 163
Stone, John, schoolmaster, 194, 198–9
Stot, Thomas, schoolmaster, 94
Stow-on-the-Wold, Gloucs., possible schools at, 104, 170–1
Stratton, Cornwall, school at, 104–5
Sudbury, Simon, archbishop of Canterbury, 74
Sussex, Richard, vicar choral, 77
Sutton, Sir Richard, college founder, 175–6
Sutton, William, schoolmaster, 86, 89
Sway, ———, vicar choral, 77

Taprell, Nicholas, schoolmaster, 113–14
Tattershall, Lincs., school at, 143

Taunton, Som., 11, 31
priory and teaching at, 212; mentioned, 8, 28
school at, 105–6; mentioned, 4, 6, 14, 21
Taverner, Paul, pupil, 109
Tavistock, Devon, abbey and teaching at, 106, 212; mentioned, 8, 25, 28
Terumber, James, clothier, 171
Tewkesbury, Gloucs., 31
abbey and teaching at, 213; mentioned, 8, 25
theology, study of, 2, 23–6, 52–5, 67–8, 73–4, 83, 87, 119, 203, 205–7, 214
Thorne, John, schoolmaster, 89
Thorne, Robert, school founder, 41
Thorne, William, Austin canon, 202
Tiverton, Devon, school at, 106
Toker, Nicholas, choirmaster, 46 n1
Toll, Elizabeth, benefactress, 14, 130
Tolre, Walter de, schoolmaster, 105
Toppe, John, chorister, 211 n6
Tormarton, Gloucs., collegiate church and education at, 213
Torrington—see Great Torrington
Totford, John, monk and schoolmaster, 206
Totnes, Devon, school at, 106–7
Tour, Hugh de la, pupil, 105
Towen, John, schoolmaster, 199
town-dwellers, education of, 41, 102, 107
Tredenecke, Henry, pupil, 213–14
Tredwyn, William, pupil, 95
Trowbridge, Wilts., schools at, 171–2; mentioned, 11, 30–1, 75
Truro, Cornwall, Dominican friars and education at, 213; mentioned, 24
school at, 172–3; mentioned, 3, 30
Truro, Thomas, friar, 213
Tucke, John, choirmaster, 207
Turpin, Richard, chorister, 111 n3
Tybbat, William, Austin canon, 209
Tyler, William, schoolmaster, 205
Tyndale, William, reformer and tutor, 12n1
Tywardreath, Cornwall, priory and teaching at, 213–14; mentioned, 10, 25

Urswick, Christopher, archdeacon, 187–8
ushers, school, 21, 47 & n4, 54, 62, 73, 76 n13, 85, 88, 89–90, 122, 149, 179–81, 185 & n3

Verney, John, monk and schoolmaster, 206
Veysey, John, bishop of Exeter, 53–4

INDEX

Villa Dei, Alexander de, *Doctrinale* of, 22, 63
Vimont, Nicolas, pupil, 107
Vincent, schoolmaster of Bridport, 95
vulgaria, school exercises, 39–40

Wakefield, Henry, bishop of Worcester, 60, 213
Walby, William, benefactor, 106
Wales, Gerald of, scholar, 207
Walsh, Sir John, knight, 12 n1
Walweyn, Christopher, student, 159
Warminster, Wilts., 31
Warwick, school at, 2
Watson, Thomas, student, 183 n7
Weaver, John, choirmaster, 77
Week St Mary, Cornwall, school at, 173–82; mentioned, 6, 15 n2, 16, 19, 21, 30, 32, 105, 149–50
Wellington, Som., school at, 107–8; mentioned, 4, 22, 96
Wells, Som., 11, 78
    cathedral of, altarists, 14, 79
        chancellor, 13–14, 23, 82–3
        choristers, 14, 21, 78–82
        dean, 79, 82
        instructor of the choristers, 80, 91
        precentor, 78–80
        tabellars, 79
    schools of, 78–91; mentioned, 94
        grammar and liberal arts, 82–8; mentioned, 2–4, 6, 13, 14–15, 21–2
        song, 80–2; mentioned, 2, 4, 14–15
        theology and canon law, 83
Weryng, Walter, schoolmaster, 73 n7, 76
Westbury-on-Trym, collegiate church and school at, 182–4, 214; mentioned, 10, 16, 29, 32, 172 n1
West, Richard, schoolmaster, 199
Westerly, William, schoolmaster, 86, 89
Weymon, John, schoolmaster, 166
Wheeler, John, chaplain and tutor, 95
Wheteacre, Robert, schoolmaster, 171–2
White, Richard, chantry priest, 8 n1
Whittock, Richard, vicar choral, 77

Wile, Thomas de la, schoolmaster, 73 n7, 76
Willcher, ——, schoolmaster, 186
William, earl of Gloucester, 36
William, pupil at Cirencester, 97
William, schoolmaster of Gloucester, 65
Wilson, William, choirmaster, 130
Wilton, Wilts., school at, 108; mentioned, 4
Wilton, Hugh of, archdeacon, 52
Wimbolle, John, schoolmaster, 150
Wimborne Minster, Dorset, collegiate church and school at, 184–6, 214; mentioned, 16, 21, 30–1
Winchcombe, Gloucs., abbey and teaching at, 214–15; mentioned, 8, 18, 25, 28, 129–31, 188–9
    school at, 186–90; mentioned, 16, 18, 28, 32, 152
Winchcombe, Tideman, bishop of Worcester, 61
Winchester, Hants., high school at, 73, 76 n9
    college of St Mary at, 49, 185–6
        headmasters of, 16, 63–4, 76 n8
        scholars of, 3, 11, 86, 108, 112, 114, 122, 179
        ushers of, 73, 76 n13, 122, 179, 185 n3
Winchester, Peter of, chancellor, 82
Winter, Roger, schoolmaster, 164
Winwood, Roger, schoolmaster, 85, 89–90
women, education of, 201, 204, 209
Woolavington, Som., school at, 108–9; mentioned, 4–6, 7
Worcester, Carnary library at, 23
Worcester, William, antiquary, 39–40
Wotton-under-Edge, Gloucs., school at, 109, 190–9; mentioned, 4, 13–16, 18, 21, 30–1, 40, 96
Wrington, Som., school at, 109
Wykeham, William, bishop of Winchester, 49
Wynard, William, benefactor, 46
Wynn, Thomas, schoolmaster, 76

Yarnscombe, Devon, 48–9
York, archbishops of, 59–60
York, Ralph of, chancellor, 73
Young, Thomas, schoolmaster, 140

Orme
(S) Education. History.

370.9423

LIBRARY